LOGISTICS CLUSTERS

LOGISTICS CLUSTERS

Delivering Value and Driving Growth

Yossi Sheffi

The MIT Press
Cambridge, Massachusetts
London, England

MIT Press books may be purchased at special quantity discounts for business or sales promotional use. For information, please email special_sales@mitpress.mit.edu or write to Special Sales Department, The MIT Press, 55 Hayward Street, Cambridge, MA 02142.

This book was set in Sabon and Helvetica condensed by the MIT Press. Printed and bound in the United States of America.

Library of Congress Cataloging-in-Publication Data

Sheffi, Yosef, 1948-
Logistics clusters : delivering value and driving growth / Yossi Sheffi.
p. cm.
Includes bibliographical references and index.
ISBN 978-0-262-01845-6 (hardcover : alk. paper) 1. Business logistics. 2. Business logistics—Management. I. Title.
HD38.5.S546 2012
658.5—dc23
2012015464

10 9 8 7 6 5 4 3 2 1

CONTENTS

PROLOGUE

In early 2002, I was invited to give a keynote address at a logistics conference in Zaragoza, Spain. The invitation came from Emilio Larodé, a professor at the University of Zaragoza, who got in touch with me as a result of the recommendation of my MIT colleague, Ralph Gakenheimer, the well-known urban planning guru. Before I could respond, however, I first had to locate Zaragoza on a map. I had never been there nor had I heard of this modest city in the middle of Spain.

During my visit, I learned about the government's plan to develop a large logistics park next to the city, as well as about the quality of the local food and wine ("típico típico" as my hosts would declare with pride about every new dish and bottle). Zaragoza is not a port, not a large city, and not a major airport—yet I felt that the project had a good chance to succeed. The city is roughly equidistant from Spain's four largest cities (Madrid, Barcelona, Valencia, and Bilbao), as well as from the Atlantic and the Mediterranean. Furthermore, the airport has the capacity for large cargo airplanes. Just as important, the government's plans included an intermodal yard, which would be key to a "dry port." At the same time, the central government was planning for a high-speed train connecting Madrid and Barcelona through Zaragoza. The third section of chapter 1 tells the full story of how the Zaragoza logistics park came to be.

My discussions with the Aragónese government focused on how to distinguish the planned park from others in Spain and elsewhere in Europe. I suggested the development of an international academic center for research and graduate education in logistics and supply chain management. Because logistics is, by its nature, an international profession, I long thought that the MIT Center for Transportation and Logistics should have "outposts" around the world, working with local industry. Instead of placing the new center on the campus of the University of Zaragoza, we could "build the university into the laboratory" by placing the new Zaragoza Logistics Center within the logistics park. Such a location would foster close cooperation among companies, students, and researchers.

While the Aragónese Government pushed ahead with the development of the logistics park, known as PLAZA (Plataforma Logística de Zaragoza), I heard nothing for a few months about the academic center idea. In late 2002, however, Alan Cuenca and Manuel Lopez, representing Aragón's finance ministry and education ministry, respectively, came to visit me in Cambridge, England, where I was spending a sabbatical year. During an afternoon discussion, on the 6th floor of the Judge Business School in the old Addenbrooke's Hospital building, they excitedly brought the message that the Aragón Government was ready to move ahead.

The story of the Zaragoza Logistics Center (ZLC) is laid out in more detail in chapter 8, including its academic success. This meeting in Cambridge, however, marked the beginning of a fruitful collaboration, now entering its second decade among MIT, the Aragónese Government, two local banks, PLAZA, and the University of Zaragoza. It was also the start of my personal involvement with the PLAZA project and the community of Zaragoza, and of strong friendships made in the process. I came to appreciate the foresight, vision, and execution capabilities of the government of the autonomous Spanish community of Aragón. More cities, regions, and states should be this fortunate. Learning from the success of the ZLC, MIT has opened similar logistics research and education centers in Bogota and Kuala Lumpur, combining these centers in the Supply Chain and Logistics Excellence (SCALE) global network.

It was the economic success of PLAZA, however, that motivated the research that ultimately led to this book. I wanted to understand why PLAZA, as a greenfield development, in small city with a limited industrial base, was so successful. My curiosity led me to investigate logistics clusters worldwide, a subject that has received scant attention in the economic literature. I spent several years visiting logistics clusters in Rotterdam, Panama, Singapore, Saõ Paulo, Los Angeles, Chicago, Memphis, Louisville, Dallas, and many other regions. These visits were spent observing activities, collecting data, and interviewing executives, government officials, consultants, and academics.

THE BOOK

When I began to look into logistics clusters, I intended simply to tell their stories and shed light on their development. These clusters exhibit certain characteristics and offer certain advantages that are not common to the more frequently discussed industrial agglomerations, such as the geographical concentration of biotechnology firms in Cambridge, Massachusetts or of financial services companies in Manhattan, New York. Chapter 2 offers a new twist on the general industrial clusters literature by comparing the concentration of artists and art shops in Renaissance Florence to Silicon Valley's array of information technology companies and entrepreneurs. Chapter 3 delves into four logistics clusters—the Netherlands, Singapore, Panama, and Memphis—outlining some of their history and characteristics and sharpening the definition of the term. In addition to the mechanisms that feed the development of any type of industrial cluster, chapter 4 shows how the economics of transportation add to the positive feedback loop that makes logistics clusters grow. Logistics clusters also generate other industrial activities, and chapter 5 outlines many of the value-added activities that are economical to perform on products "while they are there."

Chapter 6 describes the infrastructure components that are the building blocks of every logistics cluster, and chapter 7 highlights the role of governments in developing and nurturing them. This role includes not only the financing of long-lived investments but also regulatory regime and trade policy. While logistics is sometimes thought of as a profession of "moving boxes," modern supply chain management involves sophisticated processes, complex machinery, and advanced information and communications technology. Thus, chapter 8 describes various levels of educational institutions, which are an integral part of many logistics clusters.

As my research continued, I realized that logistics clusters offer important economic opportunities in today's environment. Chapter 9 brings together many of their specific advantages: (i) most logistics jobs are not "offshorable"—distribution must be performed locally as a result of the economics of transportation; (ii) late-stage product customizations are best performed locally, because postponement allows for timely response to demand, leading to further economic activity in logistics clusters; (iii) logistics clusters attract other industries, such as manufacturing, which values the low transportation costs and high levels of service found in such clusters; (iv) while high-technology clusters offer employment opportunities to engineers and scientists, logistics clusters offer opportunities to many unskilled and less-educated workers; (v) logistics companies value front-line experience and tend to "promote from within," enabling low-skill, entry-level workers to achieve middle-class and even executive wages; and (vi) logistics services feed multiple industries, making the region less vulnerable to specific industry downturns.

Chapter 10 describes the global role of logistics clusters and their efforts to become more environmentally sustainable. It also examines various elements that make logistic clusters successful or unsuccessful.

SPECIAL THANKS

This book was based, in large part, on primary research, including interviews all over the world. As a result I owe deep thanks to almost two hundred people who gave their time generously, provided data, and pointed me in new directions. Without them this book would not have been possible.

The list of individuals who helped with this research effort is given at the end of the book. At this juncture, however, I would like to thank a few people who helped directly with the research and the writing. First and foremost these include the talented and friendly Andrea and Dana Meyer of Working Knowledge, who were instrumental in helping develop the concepts, as well contributing to the research and ensuring that the results were presented in readable English; Jonathan Hayes, who helped with the initial interviews in Spain; Liliana Rivera, my PhD student at MIT who helped me (with limited success) think like an economist; Dan Dolgin, who edited and made numerous suggestions, enhancing the manuscript; and Jonathan Sheffi, my able son, who kept insisting on clear writing.

I also would like to thank my colleagues at the MIT Center for Transportation and Logistics: Chris Caplice, Jim Rice, Edgar Blanco, Jarrod Goentzel, Mahender Singh, Bruce Arntzen, and Roberto Perez-Franco for their support and comradeship. A finer group of supply chain management professionals is difficult to find.

Finally, I would like to thank my wife of over 43 years, Anat. I cannot imagine a better mate to go through life with. This book is dedicated to her.

1

OF FISH AND BLOUSES AND THE FUTURE OF REGIONAL ECONOMIES

A Japanese school girl snatches the last sheer black blouse off the rack at a Zara store in downtown Tokyo. She had popped into Zara for some casual browsing, recognized the blouse from a recent music video, loved it, noticed it was the last one in the store, and feared it might not be there the next time she went shopping. On the other side of the world, a Madrid housewife carefully selects two large fresh fillets of Namibian hake at a Mercadona grocery store. From her experience, she knows that the fish—caught, cut, and packed by Caladero—will be fresh from the sea.

These two very different products in very different locations share a common connection: the products spent a brief stint, perhaps only a few hours, in Zaragoza, Spain, only a short time before they were bought by the two consumers. Zaragoza is no giant metropolis and is known neither for manufacturing clothing nor for catching fish. In fact, with fewer than 800,000 people, the modest Zaragoza metropolitan area has one-sixth the population of greater Madrid or Barcelona. Nor is Zaragoza a big fishing port; it sits 250 kilometers northwest of the Mediterranean and 250 kilometers southeast of the Atlantic Ocean. Some might say that Zaragoza sits in the middle of nowhere.

So why isn't Zara's fashion business handled in the clothing capitals of Europe, like Paris or Milan, or in the low-cost textile manufacturing regions of China? Why would the fish-processing company Caladero send 200,000 metric tons of fish a year to an arid, land-locked warehouse 250 kilometers from the sea? The answer lies in the economics of how and where goods move from a myriad of global sources to a multitude of global consumer outlets.

These two companies, and many others, chose this particular small city in Spain because of the agglomeration of economic activities, known as a *logistics cluster*, that is centered there.

THE STORY OF ZARA

Although one might think that making a blouse starts with a bolt of cloth, it really begins with a bolt of inspiration. Zara's young designers and store managers constantly scan the fashion world, celebrity trendsetters, and Zara's own sales data for ideas and insights into customers' desires. Like young people everywhere, Zara's designers go to concerts, party in nightclubs, people-watch, and talk with everyone they know. In the fast-paced world of fashion, speed wins. At Zara, speed means spotting trends quickly, crafting designs quickly, making clothes quickly, and getting them into stores quickly.

For example, when Madonna wore a certain blouse at the beginning of her 2005 concert tour, one of Zara's 300 designers realized that his customers would love the singer's look. And with an average of 50,000 screaming fans per concert location, the designer knew that Zara could sell a lot of clothing if it could get the blouse into stores before the concert tour's buzz wore off.

Most clothing retailers could never have hoped to tap into Madonna's new look without extensive preparations, market research, and the approval of senior managers—a process spanning many months. These slow and careful processes mean that most clothing retailers stick to just two to four carefully planned major seasons per year (e.g., their spring/summer, fall/winter collections).

But Zara isn't like most retailers. When Zara designers see a hot new look, they have the authority to do what it takes to bring the idea to market. Zara's designers don't need endless committee meetings to launch a new line or tinker with an existing one. They are empowered to tap inventories, redesign garments, authorize manufacturing (by trusted local seamstresses who can quickly sew the pattern), and then ship the new clothing off to stores. In this particular case, Zara designed a Madonna concert–inspired blouse and got it into stores in only three weeks, before Madonna finished her tour.[1]

Zara's speedy response to the Madonna concert wasn't a one-off fluke or the result of a special effort. To go from idea to sales, Zara needs just five to six weeks for totally new designs and only two weeks for a modified design. Thus, as the *Economist* reported, "When Spain's Crown Prince Felipe and Letizia Ortiz Rocasolano announced their engagement in 2003, the bride-to-be wore a stylish white trouser suit—which raised some eyebrows among those concerned with royal protocol. But within a few weeks, hundreds of European women were wearing similar outfits"—designed, made, distributed and sold by Zara.

Zara's fast design-to-display operation may seem risky, but Zara makes only small batches of new styles. If the new style fails to sell well in the first week, Zara cancels it. If a new design does sell well in the first week, Zara might make more until some other new design supplants the old one. Few clothes stay in the warehouse for long. In an average two-month period, the stock turnover will be around 70 percent. Zara's speed has earned it a sterling supply chain reputation; the stores get all the replenishment products they demand in less than two days.

With so many new styles every week in Zara stores, customers know they will always find something fresh and exciting when they shop. They also know that they need to buy fast, because Zara replaces styles very quickly. As Luis Blanc, a director for Zara's parent company Inditex, explains, "most important, we want our customers to understand that if they like something, they must buy it now, because it won't be in the shops the following week. It is all about creating a climate of scarcity and opportunity."[2] The result: the average Zara customer visits a Zara store an average of seventeen times per year, compared to an average of three visits per year for customers of other clothiers.

Local Labor: A Small Price to Pay for Faster Response

Haute couture, perhaps, but Zara can't be expensive. To keep costs low, Zara optimizes and automates its logistics operations. Leading-edge robots take instructions from state-of-the-art algorithms to handle most of the tasks in Zara's massive distribution center, which is located in the middle of the immense Zaragoza logistics park.

Although Zara automates many manufacturing and logistics activities, sewing still requires deft human hands. For fast fashion items, like the Madonna-inspired blouse, Zara relies on a network of hundreds of local sewing cooperatives in northwestern Spain and northern Portugal. Although these small shops are among the least expensive in Europe, their labor costs are six to sixteen times higher than those of their Chinese counterparts used by most other clothiers.

But Southern European workers offer something that China can't: affordable speed. Ocean freight from China to Europe adds three to seven weeks to the design-to-display process and to the replenishment cycle time. Fast airfreight from China to Europe costs many times more per kilogram than ground transportation within Europe (and has a heavy carbon footprint). Using nearby producers means fast turnaround—an order of magnitude faster than competitors—obviating the need to forecast what customers will want many months in advance. As a result, Zara stocks lots of fresh merchandise on the shelf when consumers want it and avoids having too much stale merchandise that can be moved only by lowering the price. Fast revenues and very little discounting lead to superior financial results. "If you produce what the street is already wearing, you minimize fashion risk," notes José Luis Nueno, a marketing professor at IESE Business School in Barcelona.[3] To get from hundreds of factories to hundreds of stores—each with the right assortment, colors, and sizes—Zara uses the Zaragoza distribution center.

Zara Comes to Zaragoza

Despite the similarity of names, Zara didn't start in Zaragoza but in the town of Arteixo in the extreme northwestern corner of Spain, just off the Atlantic's Bay of Biscay. Zara grew rapidly with its savvy eye for fashion and quick design-produce-distribute retailing model. As the company expanded, it started thinking about a location for a new state-of-the-art distribution center to handle the shipments to retail outlets in the seventy-seven countries where it does business.[4] "We needed a location closer to Europe than the existing facility in northwest Spain," said Raúl Estradera, Zara's director of communications and industrial relations. "It needed to have a good transport infrastructure and qualified human resources."[5]

While Zara's parent company, Inditex, was inking a deal with the Spanish community of Catalonia to build a large new distribution center in Barcelona, the neighboring state of Aragón and the city of Zaragoza were crafting a bold plan to build the largest logistics park in all of Europe, called PLAZA (Plataforma Logística de Zaragoza). Zaragoza and Aragón envisioned a literal "green field" development that would convert farmland into a bustling 1,200 hectare (3,000 acre) logistics park with excellent highway, rail, and airfreight connections. Hearing of Inditex's intention to build in Barcelona, the Aragónese creators of PLAZA rushed to woo the retailer to PLAZA. PLAZA's organizers knew that Inditex's reputation for logistics expertise would make Inditex a key first customer that would validate the PLAZA project. If Inditex said "yes," then others would come to PLAZA, too. And if Aragón could get PLAZA off the ground, the large size of the park and the resulting economies of scale would deter others in southeastern Europe from building competing facilities.

Inditex agreed to abandon the Barcelona deal and come to Zaragoza, but only if PLAZA accelerated its development plans to meet Inditex's schedule for opening the distribution center. Inditex insisted on stiff multimillion euro penalties for any delays, and PLAZA's government developers—with obvious trepidation—agreed. In 2002, Inditex sent a team led by Jorge Méndez, Lorena Alba, and Juan Villacampa, who make up the core of the firm's logistics department, to Zaragoza to oversee the development of what was at the time the first fully automated warehouse facility at Inditex. By 2003, Inditex had inaugurated the gargantuan distribution center, covering a whopping 120,000 square meters (1.3 million square feet)—about the size of twenty-three American football fields—under one roof. The structure is 20.8 meters high, about seven stories.

Orderly Ordering: A Choreography of Clothing

Zara's distribution center typifies the kind of activities that take place in modern distribution facilities. Twice a week, Zara replenishes its stores to keep the latest fashions in stock and to deliver new designs to its retail outlets. Store managers review the list of available items provided by headquarters and submit their orders by 7 o'clock every Monday morning, after the busy weekend selling period. Zara's commercial department then allocates inventory to stores, a process that includes the challenge of allocating high-demand clothing for which store orders exceed the available supply. Next, Zara's Warehouse Management System converts the clothing allocations into millions of commands to robots that pull the allocated articles of clothing out of storage, place them onto conveyors, and send them to the automated sorting equipment that routes each garment to the right packing area. Once packed, each box of garments is loaded and shipped to one of more than 1,500 Zara stores worldwide.[6]

Zara's systems automation manager, Jorge Savirón, is a man with a mission. "The job we have here at the distribution center is to serve the stores with the products they need, on demand and on time," he told me as we walked through the mammoth building. To keep equipment utilization high, this automated warehouse splits each of the two weekly picking-and-packing operations into four half-day batches: one on the Monday/Tuesday and the other on the Thursday/Friday work cycle. On each day, sorting ends by 5 p.m. to meet the loading deadline for the outbound trucks and airfreight shipments at the nearby Zaragoza airport.

Although 800 people work inside the Zara distribution center in Zaragoza, the vast scale of the facility, the extensive automation, and the multiple work shifts make the building seem eerily empty. A few people appear here and there, standing out amid the shine of state-of-the-art mechanical equipment housed in the enormous complex. Robots replace manual-labor workers, conveyors replace forklift drivers, barcodes and scanners replace human eyes, and computers replace paper files and clipboards. Workers oversee the machines, monitor the progress of each picking, packing, and loading cycle, and make sure the right clothes go to the right store on the right truck. Ubiquitous computer terminals and hand-held scanners make it possible for a small crew to handle millions of items a week under tight deadlines with high accuracy.

Trucks Outbound, Inbound, and All Around

On one side of the distribution center, workers load clothes into dozens of trailers for delivery to Zara stores around Europe. Because no one Zara store needs a full truckload of clothing twice a week, Zara consolidates multiple store orders on each trailer. Workers load each trailer in reverse order of deliveries: the last box in the trailer will be the first one out at the first delivery stop. In some cases, a truck from Zaragoza drops its load at a small distribution center in the destination country or city, and smaller trucks perform capillary distribution to the individual stores. Clothes bound for overseas outlets go by air.

When the workers load the last item in a trailer, a big silver Mercedes tractor backs up to that trailer, hitches to it, and pulls the trailer onto Spain's wide-open highways for the delivery run.[7] On the other side of the warehouse, similar silver Mercedes trucks back their trailers into the distribution center's loading bays to replenish the warehouse. As of 2011, Zara could deliver product ready for sale to all European stores within 24 hours and all stores worldwide within 48 hours.

Wanted: More Space and More Speed

As Zara grew from a single store opened in 1975 on a downtown street in A Coruña, Spain, to more than 1,500 stores worldwide in 2011,[8] it grew its Zaragoza distribution center as well. Only a few years after the Zaragoza facility opened, Zara enlarged it by 50 percent to a total of 180,000 square meters (nearly two million square feet). Adding physical floor space was just one of Zara's solutions to growth. Innovation, in the form of new processes and upgraded software, doubled the capacity of key pieces of equipment. While the size of the Zara distribution center increased by 50 percent, its productive capacity increased by more than 100 percent. Zara anticipates more growth in the years ahead. By 2014, it expects to sort a million garments per day and have automated storage systems holding some thirty-four million articles of clothing. Inditex has invested more than 220 million euros in Zara's Zaragoza distribution center, generating 800 direct jobs and an estimated 1,600 to 2,000 indirect jobs.

FLYING FISH

Forty-five nautical miles off the coast of Namibia, the *Nora* hauls in the final catch of the day. Like other fishing boats plying these waters, the *Nora* comes here to take advantage of a rare natural occurrence. Off the southwest coast of Africa, dark cold waters well up from deep in the Atlantic, bringing nutrients and an ecosystem of plankton and other sea creatures that produce a rich bounty of fish. Spaniards' favorite white-meat hake and flavorful horse mackerel thrive in these waters. Only a few places in the world produce these marine multitudes; one location is here, making Namibia's sparsely populated 1,500-kilometer-long coast a fertile fishing ground.

To bring this bounty to market, boats like the *Nora* set out from Walvis Bay, Namibia, and other African ports. Using either nets or long lines of hooks, the fleets of fishermen cast their luck to Neptune and hope for a full hold of fish for Caladero, the largest processor and distributor of fresh fish in Spain. Catching the fish is the first of a long chain of events that brings the fish from Namibia to places like one of Madrid's supermarkets.

Below deck, the crew of the *Nora* quickly stores the catch in high-performance refrigerated storage facilities. The *Nora*'s hold keeps the fish in ideal conditions: very cold but never frozen. The moment the *Nora* pulls the fish from the ocean, Caladero's freshness clock begins its inexorable countdown. Because the Spanish are the second-largest consumers of fish per capita, behind only the Japanese, Caladero knows it must please a very discerning clientele. Even with the best of refrigeration technology, Caladero must get the fish into consumers' kitchens within a few days to ensure the freshest "taste of the sea" flavor.

What's the Catch of the Day?

Like all fishing boats, the *Nora*'s catch varies from day to day. That poses a real challenge for Caladero, because getting top dollar for fish means selling the fish fresh—not frozen—and that means selling everything the boat catches rather than what each food retailer might have ordered. Caladero doesn't want any surprises in terms of unsold fish or unhappy customers.

Fortunately, information travels faster than fish. As the boat turns for home, the *Nora*'s captain calls Caladero on a satellite telephone. Caladero asks only one question of the captain: "What is the catch?" Today, the captain has good news. The *Nora* snagged large numbers of hake and a smattering of orange roughy, a fish sometimes referred to as "the diamond of the sea." Caladero records the data about the catch from the *Nora* as well as other boats around the world—from the waters of Nova Scotia to Peru, Scandinavia, India, and Japan—and immediately starts contacting grocery store chains and retail fish markets to negotiate orders and to craft retail promotions if the day's catch was larger than expected. Caladero wants to find a home for every fish the *Nora* caught before those fish ever arrive in Spain.

The Route of a Trout

After reaching the port, Namibian officials inspect the catch to ensure the Nora pays her taxes and doesn't exceed her quota. Next, the fish goes to Caladero's processing plant for sorting and packing for the journey to Spain. Stacks of Styrofoam trays hold heavy mixes of fish and ice. As the crow flies, 7,260 kilometers lie between Walvis Bay, Namibia, and Madrid, Spain. In theory, direct operations could fly fresh African fish straight to the Madrid airport in only eight hours. Add a few hours on either end for loading, unloading, retail distribution, and packing, and fish could go from the fisher's boat to the shopper's basket in one day.

But that's not what happens, for two important reasons. First, Walvis Bay provides only a relatively small fraction of Caladero's fish supplies from Africa. Furthermore, this amount fluctuates from one day to the next. The catch at Walvis Bay wouldn't consistently fill even a small freighter plane. Second, Walvis Bay has only 80,000 people, which means very little airfreight traffic comes to it. For direct airfreight operations, Caladero would need to pay the full cost of an empty plane to come to Walvis Bay and then pay for the flight to Spain, even if the flight to Spain was half empty. To make the fish affordable, Caladero consolidates all of its African fish supplies at the nearest big airport, which is Johannesburg's international airport in South Africa. Such consolidation achieves two important goals: First, it justifies the use of a very large cargo plane to take the fish coming from several African ports to Spain—thereby lowering the cost per pound flown. Second, the combination of loads from many boats in multiple African ports tends to arrest the daily fluctuations of each boat's catch. Highs and lows from different boats and ports tend to cancel each other out, allowing Caladero to plan its transportation needs with confidence.

Thus, instead of a fast flight to Spain, Caladero's fish cross 1,200 kilometers of forbidding Kalahari Desert to reach Johannesburg. With as much as 500 kilometers between gas stations in the desert, Caladero trusts its perishable cargo only to special trucks with additional fuel tanks, advanced refrigeration units, and seasoned drivers. Two border crossings (Botswana and South Africa) and animals on the highway add to the challenges of getting the fish to Johannesburg on time. Sensors constantly monitor the temperature of the truck's precious cargo, ensuring that the Kalahari's worst doesn't spoil Caladero's best.

Into the Belly of the Beast

As the catch of the day trundles its way across the hot, dusty stretches of Namibia, Botswana, and South Africa, a Boeing 747 freighter flies to meet it. The 747 is one of the fastest, largest commercial cargo planes in existence. Four engines with a total of nearly a quarter of a million pounds of thrust push the 875,000-pound loaded plane to a cruising speed 85 percent the speed of sound. On this southbound journey, the plane that will carry Caladero's fish does not come to South Africa empty. Rather, it carries fashionable clothing, high-tech equipment, medicine, and other items that are either of high value, perishable, or in need of timely delivery.

On the ground, the sleek leviathan reveals a big secret. The nose of the plane flips high into the air to expose a gaping maw 8 feet high and 10 feet wide that opens onto a cavernous deck over 170 feet long. A second 10-foot high door behind the wing and smaller fore and aft lower deck cargo doors provide full access to all the cargo areas. Special powered rollers built into the deck enable workers to quickly load up to thirty 8-foot by 10-foot pallets of freight on the main deck and another thirty-two standard airfreight containers on the lower deck.

As the freshness clock ticks, the airfreight operations at Johannesburg do what they can to speed the turnaround-time of the plane. Caladero already has its pallets of fish sitting in a refrigerated warehouse near the plane and ready to go as soon as the carrier unloads it. The ground crew quickly loads the cargo, secures it, and completes the paperwork for the flight.

The Economics of Maximum Capacity

This whale of a plane can swallow almost a quarter of a million pounds of fish for the journey to Spain. For both Caladero and the airfreight company, filling the plane to maximum capacity makes economic sense because it minimizes the cost per unit of cargo. But this issue reveals a crucial fact about the economics of logistics. Planes, trucks, rail cars, ships, and other logistics conveyances have two definitions of capacity: weight and volume. A Boeing 747-8F freighter can carry a maximum of 308,000 pounds (140 metric tons) of cargo, or it can carry a maximum of 30,000 cubic feet (858 cubic meters) of cargo. In freight transportation lingo, if a conveyance carries very dense cargo, such as fish, engine blocks, or liquids, then it is said to "weigh-out" when it reaches its weight limit before its volume limit. For example, 308,000 pounds of liquid (e.g., water) fills less than 5,000 cubic feet or 1/6 the volume capacity of the plane. On the other hand, if a conveyance carries very light cargo, such as fluffy fabrics or fragile goods surrounded by packing peanuts, then it is said to "cube-out" when it reaches its volume limit before its weight limit.

For Caladero and the airfreight company to really get the highest-utilization, least-cost shipping—or greatest profit from a plane, truck, or other conveyance—the freight planners try to combine dense and light cargo to reach capacity nirvana: filling every cubic foot while tipping the scales right to the weight limit. Like a real-life game of Tetris, these planners optimize the shape, size, and weight of consolidated freight as much as possible. In the case of Caladero's chartered 747, the company talked with Inditex (the parent of

Zara) about filling the unused volume of the 747. Caladero and Zara are located next to each other in the Zaragoza logistics park, PLAZA. Also, Zara has a need to import wool. South Africa is the world's largest producer of mohair and fifth largest producer of wool. Fluffy fabrics or yarns make the perfect lightweight cargo to counterbalance the dense pallets of fish. By combining the two cargos with just the right mix of weight and volume, Caladero and Inditex can both enjoy lower shipping costs.

Destination: Less-Known

Occasionally, on its way to Europe, the plane will dip down for a quick stop in Uganda to pick up a load of fresh Nile perch, and that evening the fish will arrive in Spain. But the 747 does not fly to Madrid, the largest city and largest airport in Spain. The reason is that as big as Madrid is, the city doesn't consume enough of Caladero's fish to justify chartering such a large plane flight just for that city. So, instead of going direct to Madrid or any of the other large Spanish cities, Caladero's fish goes from Johannesburg, South Africa, to Zaragoza, Spain.

Zaragoza's airport has less than 1 percent the passenger volume of Madrid (435,000 vs. 48 million passengers a year). In 2010, Zaragoza airport handled only about 35 daily civilian aircraft operations, as opposed to 1,200 aircraft movements a day in Madrid. Thus, planes can take off and land in Zaragoza almost anytime they like. Despite its small population size, however, Zaragoza doesn't have just a small commuter airport with puny runways. In the 1950s, US Air Force engineers helped enlarge the airport to handle the heaviest military aircraft for the Cold War, such as bomb-laden B-52 strategic bombers. Even today, the Spanish Air Force still uses the facility; and the airport provided a backup landing site for the US Space Shuttle. As a result, the extra-long, heavily reinforced runways provide a perfect landing and take-off spot for loaded air freighters like the one carrying Caladero's catch of the day. In this way, Zaragoza enjoys a peace dividend in the form of high-capacity infrastructure now being shared with civilian freight applications.

From Net to Slam-Dunk in Sales

As the loads of fish sail into Walvis Bay, truck across the Kalahari, and fly toward Zaragoza, Caladero works feverishly to find buyers for the inbound catch. This task of matching inbound supply to outbound demand falls on the athletic shoulders of Alfredo Fabón García, the commercial director at Caladero. The former professional basketball player[9] uses his two meters (6'7") commanding presence to lead a fast-paced team. As information about fish supply and supermarket orders floods in, he speaks with the urgency of a team coach facing seconds left on the clock during a big game, because the freshness clock never stops.

While the chartered 747 flies to Zaragoza, Alfredo worries about more than just that one African fish shipment. African fish comprise a small part of Caladero's global network of over two dozen seafood sources. Caladero owns over eighty fishing vessels deployed around the world. Other planes bring fish from such places as Chile, Argentina, Canada, Vietnam, Japan, and the Indian Ocean to converge on Zaragoza. Moreover, Caladero hauls in more than just fresh wild-caught fish; it also buys farmed fish such as salmon, bass, bream, and turbot, as well as frozen shellfish such as shrimp, prawns, cuttlefish, and squid. In total, the company handles over a million pounds of fish and seafood every single day, of which about 75 percent is wild. Just as Johannesburg consolidated several African fish sources in one location, so, too, Zaragoza consolidates the global inbound flow of fish for Caladero, to be distributed throughout Spain.

Caladero can't control the weather or the fortunes of fishermen, but it can work with the grocery stores and other wholesalers to find a place for every fish caught. Alfredo Fabón García represents a new breed of managers in the fisheries industry. When I visited the facility in 2010, he said that until recently "the bulk of the fisheries industry was very traditional and did not always operate in accordance with modern standards of efficiency. Often it was not very professional." In contrast, high efficiency and flexibility let Caladero counterbalance the stormy variations in the daily catch. For instance, if one of the fishing areas fails to catch much fish, Caladero might increase purchases from independent fishermen and from other parts of the world. And if the chartered 747 in Johannesburg isn't full of fish (and wool), they'll offset the cost of the flight by taking on other cargo such as fruit or wine for export to Europe. If, on the other hand, Caladero's fleet catches too much fish, then they can codesign a promotion with supermarkets on the fly to encourage more purchases. For example, while I visited the company, Caladero's regular group of fishermen caught a massive supply of bluefish—three times more fish than customers had ordered. The company crafted a special radio and Internet advertising plan in conjunction with Mercadona, its largest supermarket partner, sold all the fish to retailers within 12 hours, and had the fish in stores within 24 hours.

Efficiency and speed means utilizing all of Caladero's assets to ensure timely delivery of product at the lowest possible prices. Centralizing operations at a single location is the only way Caladero can balance worldwide supply and demand in real time.

Boundary-less Inbound/Outbound Operations

The need for efficiency in a fast-paced operation with unpredictable supply patterns pushed Caladero to develop a somewhat unusual organizational structure. "When I started out here a few years ago," Alfredo told me, "the commercial team was divided in two different departments: purchasing and sales." This traditional back-office/front-office split between purchasing and sales is quite common among many companies, but the operational results suffered because the left hand that was selling the fish didn't know what the right hand that was catching the fish was doing: the sales department would sell fish that Caladero didn't catch or would fail to sell surges in the catch. The result was disappointed customers, unsold fish, and errors in orders.

Caladero realized that because nobody knows the available inbound fish situation better than the buyers, it made sense to merge the purchasing and sales departments to create a "war room" for more effective fast-paced information processing. A third function, logistics, also needed to be in the new war room. Logistics knew the in-transit status of all the inbound and outbound fish and was responsible for acquiring transportation assets and negotiating with transportation carriers. They knew when the shipments of fish would reach key locations and could adjust operations to get the right fish processed and moved as quickly as possible. The merged team does buying, selling, and coordinates the logistics that route the fish from supply to the market. By colocating all these functions in a single place, where the fish were processed, Caladero shortened the communication times, increased efficiency, and reduced errors.

Adding Value Means Adding Volume

When the fish finally land in Zaragoza, workers quickly roll the chilly pallets into Caladero's sprawling 59,000 square meter (633,000 square foot) facility. The giant building sits so close to the runway that the company had to sink it 20 meters (66 feet) into the ground to prevent aircraft from clipping the roof as they touched down on the runway. When the facility runs at full capacity, 600 workers in fluorescent-yellow safety vests operate 33 automated production lines, three automated warehouses, and two container supply stores. Flexibility means the plant can handle 60 different types of fish, from tiny anchovies to massive tuna. Both optical and x-ray scanners examine the fish for quality and freshness. Caladero designed and operates every aspect of the facility to preserve the freshness and taste of the fish.

Any place where goods congregate becomes a natural location for doing more—adding value to those goods as they pass through the hub. For that reason, Caladero became more than just a wholesale fish distributor. In the past, supermarkets bought whole fish from Caladero, and supermarket personnel filleted and prepared the fish for sale at the market's fish counter. Then, Caladero started offering to perform this service in their automated centralized plant, which could be far more efficient than the supermarket's own fish department.

Supermarkets liked buying display-ready fish because it cut down on their labor costs, reduced the smell of handling the raw fish themselves, and improved food safety because the fish spent less time in the open air of the retail store. Caladero then expanded its offerings from plain fish fillets to include various preprepared seafood products such as the Spanish favorite of hake stuffed in green peppers, ready-to-grill fish brochettes on skewers, premade shrimp cocktail, and a seafood medley for paella. As of 2010, Caladero was preparing over 500,000 trays a day. Fast, efficient logistics and value-added services contributed to Caladero's 20 percent annual revenue growth from 2005 through 2010.

Along with the services brought by Caladero come opportunities for suppliers. This includes attracting other companies to the PLAZA logistics park in Zaragoza, companies that would not be there if it weren't for Caladero. For example, Caladero encouraged Sealed Air Corporation to build a specialized packaging plant in PLAZA that offers a high-tech solution to the fresh-fish shelf-life challenge. Simply put, oxygen is the enemy of fresh fish: air oxidizes the fish, encourages bacterial growth, and creates strong odors and stale flavor. Sealed Air Corporation developed a special Styrofoam tray, named Cryovac, which keeps freshness in and oxygen out. Innovative active coatings on the tray even absorb any residual oxygen inside the package to add days to the shelf life of the fish. Highly specialized manufacturing equipment in the Caladero plant packs the fish in an oxygen-free environment. As an added bonus, the Cryovac prevents fishy odors—even those from the most aromatic anchovies—from leaking into the grocer's store or the consumer's refrigerator. A second supplier, Logifruit, which makes recycled plastic containers for the fish, also moved to Zaragoza to better serve Caladero.

Caladero's high performance and new services mean new investments and more jobs. Caladero alone invested some 110 million euros in its PLAZA distribution center/factory and generated 600 jobs in Zaragoza. Caladero's new facility was so important to Mercadona, its main supermarket partner, that in 2009 the retailer invested 24 million euros (in exchange for which it got a 16.5 percent minority stake in the fish processor) to help finance the project. The investment and tighter partnership gave Caladero the money it needed to complete the factory and ensured Mercadona a steady supply of high-quality seafood.[10]

Deconsolidation: The Fish Stream Out in All Directions

Finally, the fish leave Caladero's Zaragoza plant through one of thirty-four truck docking doors. Sealed trays of fish, in either display-ready consumer-friendly packaging or in wholesale trays, go from the refrigerated building into a refrigerated truck for the final leg of the journey. From here the fish will disperse across Spain. Caladero distributes fish to over 1,300 stores in the Spanish Mercadona grocery distribution system—the Walmart of grocery stores in Spain with 30 percent of the market—as well as to many other supermarkets and fish markets. In essence, a single massive river of processed fish splits into many streams as Caladero's delivery trucks fan out from Zaragoza to deliver their still-fresh catch to supermarkets and city wholesale markets around the country.

Zaragoza's location at the literal crossroads of two major highways lets Caladero distribute fish across Spain with a minimum of delay. Zaragoza is Spain's fifth largest city and sits equidistant from the first four: Madrid, Barcelona, Valencia, and Bilbao. Thus, it is within only a little more than three hours' drive from the major Spanish population centers. This location enables Caladero to bring the freshest possible fish to the greatest possible number of people. With efficient and timely logistics, consumers know that when they finally put the Caladero-provided fish in the pan or on the grill, they'll enjoy that fresh "taste of the sea."

CREATION OF A LOGISTICS CLUSTER

Neither Zara, Caladero, nor other similar companies would be in Zaragoza were it not for the investment and support of the regional government of Aragón and the municipal government of Zaragoza. That government support arose from the personal experiences of Juan Antonio Ros, a native of Aragón and a stalwart civil servant, who relayed the story over lunch at the modern restaurant at the Hotel Rey Fernando II de Aragón in PLAZA. He and his brothers and sisters could not find worthwhile jobs in the Aragón area. That inspired Ros to try to create regional economic development opportunities. In 1993, Ros went to Aragón's then-president Emilio Eiroa and said, "Mr. President, Aragón needs to look for something new because we are highly focused on just one the industry: automotive. We have to look for something else. We cannot rely on the GM factory forever."

The president's initial response was not encouraging because, at the time, GM's local Opel plant was still growing and hiring. Yet Ros was given permission to submit proposals to the president's ministers. This initial, noncommittal response would be the first of many non-encouraging, yet nondiscouraging responses for Ros. Allowed to continue and develop his plans, Ros embarked on a multiyear effort to create and refine a vision for new economic opportunities for the Aragón region. His efforts would span five presidential administrations and involve both municipal and national governments before finally leading to the PLAZA logistics park.

Initially, Ros focused on the Zaragoza airport as a key resource for his economic development proposals. The years 1992 to 1994 marked the phase-out of US Air Force control of the Zaragoza Air Base and the turnover of the facility to the Spanish government. The new-found availability of the facility for civilian use made potential commercial opportunities possible. Ros initially proposed aviation-related economic development projects tied to the Eurofighter aircraft manufacturing program and the potential for an aircraft repair and maintenance hub at Zaragoza. These ideas failed to gain interest. "I was preaching in the desert," Ros told me. "It was almost impossible to find anyone in the Government at the time who fathomed the implications. So I said, 'we'll have to think of new ideas.'" Those new ideas took Ros in the direction of logistics.

A Well-Connected Region

Ros started thinking more broadly about the geographic and infrastructure resources of the region. He considered the potential value of the region's central location. In addition to its place at the crossroads of well-developed highway and railway connections between Madrid, Barcelona, Valencia, and Bilbao, Zaragoza sits equidistant from both coasts of Spain (Atlantic and Mediterranean) with ready access to four of the five largest Spanish seaports: Barcelona, Tarragona, Valencia, and Bilbao. Further links extend west across Spain to Portugal, east to France (especially the Toulouse area with its industrial concentration) and the rest of continental Europe. "We are in the middle of an area of influence, a nexus between major cities in Western Europe," Ros mused, "how can we profit from that?"

The answer was logistics. As the saying in real estate circles goes, "the three most important factors in determining value are location, location, and location." Central crossroads such as Zaragoza offer consolidation and efficient distribution opportunities from and to multiple places. Zaragoza's location optimized access to a dispersed network of suppliers and customers on the Iberian Peninsula. According to Zara's Savirón, "Zaragoza is a good distribution location for us because here at PLAZA we are right next to the airport and have fast access—with no traffic—to major European highways. Barcelona and Madrid are a mere three hours away, and even Paris is relatively close." For Zara's distribution into Europe, the Zaragoza location reduces the distance traveled by many goods by some 800 kilometers (500 miles) compared to the original location in northwest Spain. Over twenty million people representing about 60 percent of Spain's GDP live within a 300 kilometer radius. A daylong truck journey of 1,000 kilometers (600 miles) delivers goods across the entire Iberian Peninsula, to all of France, Switzerland, and into parts of Belgium, Germany, and Northern Africa.

Even being inland, with no port access, became an advantage rather than a hindrance. The Zaragoza logistics cluster has become an inland port for multiple Mediterranean and Atlantic ports. And connectivity was Zaragoza's other main advantage beyond location. Zaragoza's multiple modes of transportation give new and growing companies more opportunities to optimize the size, frequency, cost, and shipping time of inbound and outbound shipments.

Choosing the Right Plot of Land

Picking the right plot of land around Zaragoza meant finding a spot with plenty of open space and uncongested access to Zaragoza's road, rail, and air infrastructure. To be economically viable, the development needed to find inexpensive land and lots of it. Ros literally bicycled the perimeter of Zaragoza looking for promising land. Fortunately, a large swath of unpopulated farmland sat nestled in a broad curve of both the main Madrid–Barcelona highway and the railway between Madrid and Barcelona. This area sat at the end of the runway of the Zaragoza Airport. Ros researched the landowners to minimize the chance of opposition.

Ros labored for nearly six years trying to further his proposed logistics project. Although he won unanimous support from the usually antidevelopment Zaragoza city council and got some seed funding from Aragón, he couldn't convince the central government in Madrid to fund the project. He also encountered numerous bureaucratic roadblocks related to the airport, railways, and a nearby eighteenth-century canal. Burned out from the hard work and slow progress, Ros quit his job in 1999.

Only six months later, a new Aragón administration asked Ros to return to his post. New laws, new political support, and new leaders in key ministerial positions convinced Ros to return. "The new man in charge of my department was Carlos Esco, who was Aragón's President Iglesias' right-hand man. The new administration had made several good decisions, the first of which was to pass a new zoning law. So I thought it was worth giving it another try," Ros said.

The new minister of public works, Javier Velasco Rodríguez, who looks like a distinguished Spanish warrior from an El Greco painting, picked his words carefully when we sat in his office at the magnificent Pignatelli building (originally built at the end of the eighteenth century and now the seat of the Aragón Government) in Zaragoza. "Entering the Government of Aragón in 1999," he recounted, "we performed a careful analysis of the region's situation. We determined that Aragón was excessively dependent on the automobile industry." Velasco continued telling the tale, leaning forward, palms out before him. "A lot revolved around the automobile sector. We were conscious that much more had to be done. As the newly inaugurated President of Aragón, Marcelino Iglesias became a strong advocate for diversification. We needed to broaden the industrial base of our economy."

The new administration crafted a new type of zoning law, used for the first time in Aragón. The zoning law became known simply as the Logistics Center Law. It enabled land to be reclassified as an "area of strategic economic interest" that enabled expropriation and protected that land from other types of development. The new law also created the legal notion of "supramunicipal" status for projects that would help avoid any disagreements between the regional government of Aragón and the municipal authorities of Zaragoza and surrounding towns. In essence, the law let Aragón take the lead on regional economic development projects, of which PLAZA would be the first. The government also developed special "execution procedures" that were far more flexible than those stipulated under the Autonomous Planning Legislation, allowing fast-tracking of many issues. A public corporation "PLAZA, Sociedad Anónima" oversaw the project. Shareholders in PLAZA included the government of Aragón, the city of Zaragoza, and two large local banks, Ibercaja and Caja de Ahorros de la Inmaculada (CAI).

Velasco led the battle to create a new nexus of economic activity in Aragón. A shrewd and consummate deal maker, Velasco played a major role in negotiating all the public-sector and private-landowner dealings, getting the required approvals, avoiding obstacles, and obtaining the land needed for PLAZA.

Creating the 1,200-hectare development meant purchasing 1,000 hectares of land from private landowners. Although the government considered involuntary expropriation of the land on the basis of a clear public need, that tactic carried significant financial risks. With expropriation, aggrieved former landowners could readily wage a multiyear legal battle, and a judge might easily declare a land price two to three times higher than what the government expected, which would ruin the economics of PLAZA. Fortunately, Velasco convinced 99 percent of the landowners to commit to a joint negotiation in which all landowners got the same consensus price. After extensive haggling, the government reached a deal with all but one landowner and voluntarily bought 999.5 of the needed 1,000 hectares. Only one landowner refused to sell and the government expropriated that last 0.5 hectare. "That half-hectare of land is still giving us headaches," sighed Velasco.

Build It and Make Them Come

Next, the government had to convert pastoral farmland into a modern business park. That meant investments in infrastructure. They built a crosscutting network of wide roads to enable large trucks to move freely within the park and to connect PLAZA to the highway network. They installed all the required utilities, such as electricity, telecommunications, gas, water, and sewage. They also constructed green-spaces and jogging trails to create a more human atmosphere. Whereas the land cost some €85 million, adding basic utilities and services cost on the order of €300 million. Another €228 million was earmarked for rail infrastructure, but then clever coordination with the central government rolled that spending into the national railway budget.

Just building PLAZA would not be sufficient, so the developers marketed the park throughout the process. Even as they worked to plan PLAZA, the developers "presented the idea at the Logistics Trade Fair in Paris and then at SIL, the Barcelona logistics fair, accompanied by prominent Aragón businesses to showcase our new vision," Velasco said. At the same time, Inditex, the parent company of Zara, was negotiating to build a new distribution center near Barcelona. Once Velasco and Esco learned of Inditex plans, attracting Inditex as the "anchor tenant" of PLAZA became the government's number-one priority. EU regulation limited the kinds of subsidies that Aragón and Zaragoza could offer, but they did what they could to make PLAZA attractive to Inditex. In fact, Inditex signed the contract to buy into the project before the government even owned the land. PLAZA also marketed itself outside Spain, to China and Latin American countries such as Brazil, Mexico, and Colombia.

Other Logistics Activities in Aragón

The PLAZA logistics park is but one part of the larger, regional Aragón logistics cluster. The Aragón Government developed other, specialized logistics parks in the vicinity of PLAZA, including the following:

- *Plataforma Logística de Teruel (PLATEA)* Connects the Atlantic and the Mediterranean via a railway corridor,

"Cantábrico–Mediterráneo." The first phase of the park— 862,000 m²—was finished in 2007, and the plans call for tripling its size.

- *Plataforma Logística de Huesca (PLHUS)* Includes 700,000 m² dedicated to logistics activities. It is a new park, based on highway connections: the A23 highway (Somport-Sagunto) and the A22 road (Lérida-Huesca-Pamplona). As of 2010, five companies were operating in the park.

- *Plataforma Logística de Fraga (PLFraga)* Sits at the midpoint between Zaragoza and Barcelona, where it serves mostly as a transport relay point for motor carriers serving Northeast Spain.

- *Mercados Centrales de Abastecimiento de Zaragoza (Mercazaragoza)* This agri-food logistics park specializes in distribution and wholesale of fresh fruits and vegetables, as well as meats (with a slaughterhouse) for the Ebro valley.

- *Parque Tecnológico de Reciclado López Soriano (PTR)* Specializes in recycling and the search for new industrial opportunities for optimizing the lifecycle of materials as well as energy regeneration.

- *Centro de Transportes de Zaragoza (CTZ)* One of the oldest logistics parks in Spain, over 25 years old. The twenty companies operating there are all transport and logistics enterprises.

- *Terminal Marítima de Zaragoza (TMZ)* An inland port for Barcelona, founded in 2001 and located inside the Mercazaragoza. It has a direct rail connection to the Barcelona Port. From TMZ, freight forwarders have access to the same type of services as if they were located in the port of Barcelona, with the same costs and level of service commitments. In 2010, the number of TEUs processed in TMZ increased by 72 percent compared to 2009.

While PLAZA is by far the biggest of these parks, together the parks constitute the Aragón logistics cluster.

The Competitive Advantages of Being Big

One of the boldest development decisions made by the Aragón Government was how big they made PLAZA right from the start. PLAZA is the largest logistics park in Europe. With a total area of 12,826,898 square meters, it is six times bigger than the next largest logistics park in Spain (Guadalajara, north of Madrid, at 2,100,099 square meters, followed by CILSA in Barcelona at 2,000,000 square meters). Why did Aragón commit to such a large park? Why didn't the government think to develop the park in stages, thus minimizing the risk?

The answer lies in two factors. First, the bigger a logistics park is, the more efficient it is. A larger park has lower and more stable transportation costs into and out of the park. More important, larger parks offer higher levels of transportation service in terms of frequency, equipment availability, and range of transportation options.

The other factor supporting Aragón's decision to commit to a mammoth park right from the beginning was the competitive positioning of the park within Spain. By building such a large park, Aragón deterred other regions from developing similar logistics hubs. Indeed, economists call this strategy "entry deterrence." Spence argued in 1977[11] that an incumbent firm would sometimes hold "excess capacity" in order to deter entry. Later, other economists referred to this phenomenon as a leader/follower "Stackelberg Game[12]" in which a leader firm obtains an advantage by committing to produce a large quantity of some homogeneous good. The follower, upon observing the leader's choice, then optimally decides to produce less of the good and the leader thereby gains market share and profit at the expense of its rival. While I found no direct evidence that the Aragónese government used game theory in their analysis, entry deterrence was clearly their intention. To this end, much of the publicity and marketing campaign prior to PLAZA's opening may have been aimed at potential competitor regional governments within Spain.

Economic Impacts

For the community of Aragón, Zaragoza was a build-it-and-they-will-come story. On my first visit to the area, the PLAZA site looked pretty barren: a couple of small construction management buildings on a wide expanse of weedy, dusty dirt with many large earth moving bulldozers working about and raising dust. Given Inditex's tight schedule, the Zara distribution center was among the first major buildings to go up. Next, other companies such as Imaginarium (toy retailer), Memory Set (IT equipment wholesaler) and DHL (express packages) moved into PLAZA. Then others came, including ARC International (tableware supplier), Pikolín (Spanish bed and mattress company), Bosch-Siemens (German home appliance maker), Caladero, and Decathlon (French sporting goods giant). As additional logistics and distribution operations moved into PLAZA, supporting supplier companies moved to the area, too. Trucking companies and airfreight carriers came, followed by maintenance shops that serve those companies. Other service businesses moved in, too. As of 2010, PLAZA had three hotels, several restaurants, and a shopping mall. According to Isabel Velasco, PLAZA's sales manager, in May 2010 the park had more than 250 companies under contract, with 160 companies already operating there. With the companies under contract, PLAZA reached 80 percent capacity in terms of sale and leases of land.

Before PLAZA opened in 2000, Zaragoza's airport ranked eighteenth in Spain in freight volume with a paltry 0.6 percent of the air freight in Spain, which was much less than the volume expected given that Zaragoza represents 1.8 percent of Spain's population. By 2009, Zaragoza's airport ranked third in Spain in freight volume with 6.5 percent of all airfreight in Spain. In essence, Zaragoza went from having much less than its fair share of airfreight to having many more times its fair share.

Unfortunately, at the time of this writing, Spain, like many other European economies, is mired in a torrent of asset declines, excess debt, declining GDP, growing trade deficits, and rising unemployment. This dark economic climate obscures the shining example that PLAZA represents, and from which hope should emerge for re-energizing developed economies. Aragón developed the PLAZA project with fastidious, long-range economic planning, extensive private agreements, government regulatory changes, broad public involvement including opposition parties' endorsements, and holistic infrastructure coordination. In addition to this commercial success, the result was over 10,000 direct jobs in the logistics park, leading to educational and research activities and an international reputation for excellence.

2

THE ART AND TECHNOLOGY OF ECONOMIC CLUSTERING

Consider Silicon Valley technology, Florentine Renaissance art, Hollywood movies, Burgundy wine, Detroit automobiles, Paris fashion, Swiss watches, or Madison Avenue advertising. Throughout history and into the modern era, certain regions rise to become world-renowned centers for a particular industry or skill. These regional economic booms attract workers, entrepreneurs, investment, companies, political interest, and intellectual capital. Economists, historians, and business school academics give these special regions names such as economic clusters, industrial clusters, agglomerations, and industrial districts. More pointedly, Perroux[1] referred to them as "growth poles," while Hirschman[2] called them "growth centers." Politicians, regional boosters, and business executives eagerly seek the economic and financial benefits of clusters.

Silicon Valley may be the "poster child" of clusters, but many regions have grown and prospered by becoming clusters of various industries. Why do these clusters form and how can governments encourage their formation to bring economic prosperity? To help understand the answers, this chapter examines one very old and one new cluster—one brought beauty and also technology into being; and the other brought technology and also beauty.

FLORENCE: THE SILICON VALLEY OF THE RENAISSANCE

In the annals of art, the names Michelangelo, Leonardo da Vinci, Donatello, Botticelli, Giotto, and della Robbia rank high. These artists, and dozens of others, share a common thread. All came from or worked in Florence during the fourteenth through sixteenth centuries, when that wealthy Tuscan city became a cluster for artistic endeavors of all kinds. Similarly, in the annals of technology, the names Intel, Hewlett-Packard, Oracle, Google, Apple, Cisco, and Facebook rank high. These companies also share a common thread: they arose in Silicon Valley during the late twentieth and early twenty-first centuries when this northern California region became a cluster of high-technology endeavors of all kinds. The experience of Florence, like the experience of Silicon Valley half a millennium later, shows how a concentration of resources, knowledge, innovation, and culture can create a positive feedback loop leading to long-lived economic booms in industries as diverse as art and technology.

Riding the Economic Boom

Wealth drove the rise of the Florentine art scene. Major works of art required both time and manpower. Some projects, such as Ghiberti's twenty-eight gilded-bronze panels on the north doors of Battistero di San Giovanni in the Piazza del Duomo, took the artist and his workers some twenty-one years to complete. Artists' workshops supported not only the master and his family but also upward of dozens of apprentices, journeymen, and itinerant artists. Artists also required a range of high-cost materials such as multiton blocks of marble and large castings of bronze, as well as rare imported ingredients such as vivid dyes, mineral pigments, and specialized oils. For example, the exquisitely blue ultramarine pigment created from lapis lazuli imported from Afghanistan was as expensive as gold.[3] Florentine painters actually belonged to the same guild as doctors and pharmacists because these artists bought so many of their compounds from apothecaries.

Florence's initial wealth came from international trade in the city's exquisite textiles.[4] Growing international trade called for logistics expertise and for capital to cover the high costs of raw materials, labor of craftsmen, shipping, and protection of goods. Florentine firms became multinational organizations with branch operations in key cities across Europe and the Mediterranean.

The city's wealth led to growing interest in, and increasing ability to pay for, art in religious, public, and private lives. Florence became a Mecca for artists creating frescos, oil paintings, ceramics, marbles, and bronzes—and Florence became an arts cluster.

Like Florence, Silicon Valley arose in a time of growing prosperity and expanding knowledge. The Valley became a cluster for electronics and computing in the post–World War II decades of the Baby Boom. New electronics technologies from WWII and successive waves of inventions such as the transistor, the silicon integrated circuit, digital computers, Internet networking, the World Wide Web, and social media drove successive waves of entrepreneurship in Silicon Valley.

As with the varied artistic media of Florence, the stars of Silicon Valley worked their arts in multiple technological media, too. Silicon Valley companies pioneered key areas such as electronics and computer hardware (HP, Fairchild, Intel, Apple), storage (Seagate, Quantum, Maxtor), networking (Cisco, Juniper Networks), database systems (Oracle, Sybase), Internet applications (eBay, Google, Yahoo), and social media and entertainment (YouTube, Pixar, Electronic Arts, Facebook). A groundswell of computerization started in military applications and business, spread to the rising middle class of developed countries, and then became deeply embedded in even the most mundane consumer appliances. The world went from a time in which urban legend has it that Thomas Watson, head of IBM, said in 1943: "I think there is a world market for maybe five computers"[5] to a time when there are more than five computers per living person.

INNOVATIONS

Silicon Valley is dedicated to and almost synonymous with technological innovation. The innovations in the valley include new ideas in the realms of mathematics, materials, and advances tied to the human world. Mathematical innovations came in the form of new computer languages (such as SQL and Java) and innumerable mathematical constructs related to digital logic circuits and computer algorithms. Of course, Silicon Valley derives its name from the material used to make semiconductors, which replaced germanium. In 1961, Fairchild Semiconductor Inc. built a circuit with four transistors on a single silicon wafer, thus creating the first silicon integrated circuit.[6] By September 2009, Intel CEO Paul Otellini introduced the twenty-two-nanometer 3D Tri-Gate chip family, with three billion transistors packed into an area the size of a fingernail.[7]

The entire history of chip making is a story of companies learning how to paint ever smaller and faster circuits onto a silicon canvas. On average, Silicon Valley found a succession of innovations to double the number of transistors on a chip about every 1½ to 2 years for the last five decades. Valley companies accomplished this pace of improvement through advanced materials, new manufacturing technologies, and new software-based chip design methods.

Florentine Art Innovations

Florentine artists introduced many new innovations in materials and forms that fueled the explosion of artistic output. These include the introduction of perspective, anatomy, new materials, and combinations of these innovations:

Linear Perspective

Florentines pioneered the development of linear perspective in art, starting with Ghiberti, Brunelleschi, and Masaccio in the early 1400s.[8] Prior to these developments, many paintings had a flat quality, with figures sized by importance; pre-Renaissance artists rendered a foreground crowd of adoring worshippers as small figures with an over-sized Madonna and Jesus in the background. The artistic innovation of perspective brought the science of optics to art. Ghiberti developed and wrote about his notions of perspective and applied these ideas to the rendering of objects in drawings, paintings, and bronzes like his famous Baptistery doors.[9]

The introduction of linear perspective led to significant changes in methods and results, with Masaccio producing some of the first major art works rendered in proper perspective. Artists learned mathematical and geometrical methods for properly creating the vanishing points and foreshortened shapes in a perspective view. They also crafted images with the proper proportioning and positioning of figures in the foreground and background. The advent and acceptance of these new techniques would make Florence a leading region of art education as artists flocked to the city to learn the techniques.[10]

Natural Figures: Anatomy

Renaissance Florence also brought a new interest in more lifelike compositions and representations of people. The artists worked at understanding the articulation of the joints and the delineation of muscles and tendons to convey effort and strain. This pursuit of knowledge includes Leonardo da Vinci's controversial studies of human anatomy, with his explorations of internal organs by dissecting corpses.[11] Florentine artists helped popularize portraits, landscapes, and nudes as art shifted from strictly religious themes to more secular images. The result was a change from static, standing figures to more dynamic compositions with the figures caught off-balance in mid-motion. Overall, Florentine artists innovated by representing what the eye saw in real life rather than presenting an idealized or stylized image.

Materials

Florentine artists also innovated with the materials they used. For example, sometime before 1445, Luca della Robbia refined a formula for opaque-white tin-oxide glaze and firing methods that converted dull, fracture-prone terracotta sculpture into especially lustrous, durable, marble-white works of art.[12] Adding other metal oxides (cobalt for blue, antimony for yellow, manganese for purplish-brown) enabled della Robbia to create vivid colors that made his pieces much favored by the Medicis and others.[13] Florentine merchants exported della Robbia's works across Europe and his workshop grew to include an extended family and a large volume of production of polychrome terracotta pieces of all shapes and sizes. As a result of his success, in 1471, della Robbia was elected president of the Florentine Guild of Sculptors.[14]

Financial Innovations

Talented painters, sculptors, and other artists needed one crucial ingredient for success—money; the same ingredient that budding hardware and software entrepreneurs required 500 years later to fuel the high-technology boom of the late twentieth century. And the rise of both Renaissance Florence and Silicon Valley involved financial innovations that fueled the respective arts and IT waves.

Florentine Finance

At least two Florentine financial innovations enabled the accumulation of wealth in Florence. The first was the use of double-entry accounting among Florentine merchants and banks, starting sometime just before 1300.[15] The new method let the Florentines track the interplay of revenues, costs, assets, and debts in a way that reduced errors. Proper accounting let them track the profits from individual ventures, which aided management of the inherently complex transactions of international trading firms. The success of Giovanni di Bicci de' Medici, founder of the Medici bank in the late 1300s, spawned a dynasty that would effectively dominate Florentine politics from 1415 through 1737.

For the second financial innovation, Florence broke with Christian prohibitions on usury to semilegalize interest-bearing loans in 1403. On one hand, the move prompted outrage in parts of Europe. Leaders in some key trading locations, most notably Martin "the Humane"—King of Aragón, Valencia and Sardinia—expelled the free-wheeling Florentine bankers.[16] Yet the expulsions didn't change the financial need for money in global trade, or the desires of investors to find a return on their capital. Florence enjoyed a significant influx of money; even the pope put his money in the Medici bank.

By the mid-fifteenth century, Florence was a leading European financial center. And it wasn't just the Medicis who made Florence so wealthy. Some eighty banks arose in Florence, making the city a major source of capital during the Renaissance,[17] much like Silicon Valley venture firms did in California 500 years later. The Medicis and other Florentine bankers had outposts in important cities throughout Europe such as London, Bruges, Lyon, and Geneva, as well as branches in large Italian cities such as Rome, Venice, Pisa, and Milan.[18] So powerful was Florence as a financial and merchant trading center that its currency, the *florin*, became an international standard.[19] The florin lived on as a name given to various coins minted in a dozen lands ranging from Britain to the Netherlands, Hungary, and New Zealand.

Venture Capital in Silicon Valley

Silicon Valley also rode a wave of financial innovation: the rise of the venture capital firms as a new type of financial institution that aggregates the money of private investors and invests in highly speculative new ventures such as high-technology startups. The venture capitalists of Silicon Valley are the patrons of modern times. While entrepreneurs supply the inspirational ideas, the venture capitalists supply the money as well as some guidance to bring those ideas to life. In this way, one might say that the top VC firms are the Medicis of Silicon Valley. Entrepreneurs aggressively court these top-flight investors because attention and investment from one of these major firms all but guarantees a steady supply of funding and support for a new startup.

The waves of technological inventions starting in the second half of the twentieth century earned prodigious profits for technology companies and their venture capitalist investors. Sand Hill Road, connecting El Camino Real and Interstate 280, became a minicluster of venture capitalists, including leading firms such as Kleiner, Perkins, Caufield & Byers (KPCB), Sequoia Capital, Battery Ventures, Draper Fisher Jurvetson (DFJ), and scores of others. These companies provided the money, advice and support to entrepreneurs, leading to several eye-popping returns for their investors. For example, KPCB paid $4 million in 1994 for about 25 percent of Netscape and probably made close to a $1 billion from Netscape's IPO and its subsequent $4 billion acquisition by America Online. An investment of $8 million in Cerent returned around $2 billion when the optical equipment maker was sold to Cisco Systems for $6.9 billion in August 1999. The same year, KPCB teamed with Sequoia Capital to invest $25 million for 20 percent of Google; as of October 2010 Google's market capitalization was about $200 billion. Other successful investments of KPCB include Amazon.com, AOL, Compaq, Electronic Arts, Flextronics, Genentech, Intuit, Lotus Development, Sun Microsystems, and many others. As of 2011, over 150 of the 475 KPCB-backed companies had gone public since 1972.

New companies lived on venture capital, and existing companies accumulated deep pools of cash from sales of their highly profitable high-tech products. During the dot-com boom, venture-backed start-ups went public to raise billions of dollars in additional capital that repaid the early investors. As a result of the widespread and deep use of stock options to attract talented, risk-taking employees, Silicon Valley created instant millionaires among the employees who were attracted to and then helped build the firms that went public. This created the seeds for the next generation of entrepreneurs and venture capitalists and excited the imagination of budding entrepreneurs the world over, many of whom immigrated to the valley to start new companies.

The Role of Patrons

The Medicis may have been patrons extraordinaire and strong political leaders for much of the Renaissance, but they were really only the most famous tip of the patronage iceberg in Florence. Development of Florence's art cluster both predated the Medici's rise and survived the volatile political fates of that most famous arts-loving family. Other wealthy Florentine families, such as Strozzi, Ricci, Macchiavelli, Brancacci, Canigiani, Frescobaldi, and Pucci, commissioned artistic works such as frescos and altarpieces for family chapels, sculptures for gardens and villas, polychrome terra-cotta reliefs for interiors and exteriors of buildings, and family portraits.[20] Wealthy patrons and guilds competed to upstage each other in the latest and greatest works of art, fueling increasing commissions that attracted even more artists in a mechanism similar to the technology boom of 1995–2001 and another beginning in 2009 in Silicon Valley. The density of wealthy patrons attracted a density of artistic ideas and the density of new ideas in art, in turn, attracted the interests of wealthy patrons, fueling the positive feedback that resulted in the timeless works of art that characterized the place and the period.

Just as leading venture capital firms took an active role in managing the start-up companies they funded, Florentine patrons actively directed work of artists, rather than passively financing art production. Patrons made specific demands, which suggest an awareness of artists' materials, an interest in artistic design, and a desire for personal promotion through art. For example, when Florentine banker Giovanni Tornabuoni commissioned Domenico Ghirlandaio (Michelangelo's teacher) for new frescos in the chancel of Santa Maria Novella in 1485, the banker specified in the contract the saints, scenes, the amount of gold to be used, and the quality level of the blue pigment.[21]

LABOR, EDUCATION, AND THE FLOW OF KNOWLEDGE

Without various formal and informal methods for education and knowledge transfer, artistic innovations would have remained the idiosyncrasies of individual Florence artists. Likewise, without Silicon Valley's free flow of ideas and tacit knowledge transfer among software engineers and chip designers, many of today's household technology companies would not have succeeded.

Florentine Guilds and Improvement Processes
Florence illustrates how the organization of labor and training encouraged economic cluster development through both knowledge sharing and productivity improvement. Three facets of Florentine society—the workshop system, trade guilds, and access to art—drove the city's economic rise as an art cluster and the aggregation there of artistic endeavors.

Artists have long practiced imitation as means of developing new skills and new methods. More than just a form of flattery, the intentional studying, sketching, and copying of other artists' works enabled an artist to learn new skills. Art historians can readily trace the sharing of artistic knowledge in the works of the artists. Compositions, techniques of line, shading, coloring, and the execution of particular details (e.g., the folds of drapery) provide a code to the influences on a given artist over time. Surviving letters and records attest to the times when artists met, befriended, and studied other artists. Given a timeline of an artist's oeuvre, historians can even detect when artists gained particular ideas from particular colleagues.

Florentine artists' workshops were rarely the quiet havens of inspiration for solitary artists. Instead, they were bustling factories (and schools) for art production. Florentine artists used a workshop system in which boys or young men started as apprentices in the workshops of established master artists.[22]

The workshop system of training enshrined copying as a key skill, which aided the subsequent flow of knowledge. Artists-in-training copied their master's style because they were expected to augment the productivity of their master. Only after the young artists achieved mastery could they leave the workshop, seek their own commissions, and develop their own style. Nor did artists stop learning from each other when they reached mastery. Learning was sometimes mutual between two masters, not just unidirectional from master to apprentice. In the early 1500s, for example, Raphael befriended Fra Bartolomeo.[23] Raphael helped the older Bartolomeo learn perspective, and Bartolomeo helped Raphael in coloring and handling of drapery—a joint venture by any other name.

Artistic knowledge also moved across fields when artists started life as apprentices in one field and then moved to another. For example, della Robbia started as a jeweler's apprentice but then moved into sculpting marble and glazed terracotta reliefs. Brunelleschi, Botticelli, Ghiberti, Ghirlandaio, and Verrocchio all started as apprentice goldsmiths.[24] Many of the more famous Renaissance artists (e.g., Michelangelo and Verrocchio) produced both paintings and sculptures. This spillover between forms enhanced all the artistic disciplines. Five hundred years later another genius—in Silicon Valley—led the development of the personal computer, the graphic user interface, the mobile music industry, advanced wireless communications devices, and computerized animated movies.

Knowledge also moved across the artists' workshops owing to an additional formal structure: the guild system. Florentine guilds were formed by groups of independent craftsmen, merchants, or business owners in a given industry, creating centers of knowledge-sharing among guild members. For some periods of the Renaissance, painters belonged to the guild of doctors and apothecaries, while sculptors were affiliated with the guild of sculptors and architects, which was part of the stone-working guild.[25] Many of the more famous and multitalented artists often aligned with the prestigious goldsmiths guild, which was, at times, part of the silk guild.

Silicon Valley Culture

Burning Man is an annual event held in the Black Rock Desert in northern Nevada. It is a free-for-all week-long unstructured "happening" celebrating self-expression and community participation based on self-reliance without commercial interventions. In many ways, it symbolizes the culture of Silicon Valley, especially during its early technology boom days.

This culture can be characterized by openness and networking, leading to efficient deal making. One can find a lot of information on the Web sites and blogs of Silicon Valley entrepreneurs. They understand that great ideas require a dedicated team that shares their vision, and that such openness will attract top engineers as well as smart and helpful investors. In a book comparing Silicon Valley to Boston's Route 128, AnnaLee Saxenian[26] argues that networking—the "face-to-face shop talk and gossip of workers in bars and restaurants, at trade association meetings and in more formal business-sharing arrangements"—allows people to quickly recognize and adjust to the fast-changing high-technology environment. Both the openness and the networking lead to fast deal making and a stream of new companies.

Students, Defectors, and Job Hoppers

Whereas Renaissance artists had little formal education, the workers and entrepreneurs of Silicon Valley come from a tradition of intensive formal education, usually in engineering or the sciences, and often involving advanced degrees. Stanford, San Jose State, UC Berkeley, and more than a dozen other universities produce highly skilled workers for the valley. And in attracting top technology talent from around the world, Silicon Valley also harvests the cream of the crop of national and international name-brand schools. But education in Silicon Valley doesn't stop with a formal degree.

As with the Florentine workshop system, Silicon Valley workers continue their education while on the job.

Silicon Valley also has some unusual dynamics in workers' relationships with companies. From the very beginning of Silicon Valley, innovation spilled out of companies as employees quit one company to found their own companies, in a mechanism similar to apprentice artists leaving their master's shop to open their own in Florence. For example, William Shockley literally brought silicon to Silicon Valley when he left Bell Labs in New Jersey in 1953 to form the Shockley Semiconductor Laboratory in Mountain View, California, to develop silicon-based transistors. He picked the southern end of San Francisco Bay because of its pleasant climate and the proximity of Stanford University as well as his aging mother. In a pattern that would repeat itself many times in the valley, eight young engineers, who would become known as "the traitorous eight," defected from Shockley's company in 1957 to form Fairchild Semiconductor. In 1968, two of the "traitorous eight"—Robert Noyce and Gordon Moore—would leave Fairchild to found Intel and still other Fairchild employees would leave to form National Semiconductor and AMD.

In addition to this pattern of defectors founding new companies, Silicon Valley workers job-hop much more frequently than do high-level employees in other industries. These hops occur as engineers look for more exciting opportunities in other companies or when companies stagnate or fail. In the roiling entrepreneurial environment of Silicon Valley, people can learn by failing and have no stigma attached to them. These entrepreneurs and engineers carry all the knowledge gained from the failure to their next venture or employer.

Competitive Geeks

If Florentines celebrated art and artists, Silicon Valley celebrated technology and geeks. Silicon Valley bred a culture tied to engineers' joy of problem solving and an intrinsic love of new technology. By and large, it was engineers and technologists, not business and marketing people, who started firms in Silicon Valley. Stories such as Bill Hewlett and Dave Packard's founding of HP in a garage in Palo Alto epitomized the area's engineering-focused, build-a-prototype, start-up culture. This culture attracted engineers and geeks who loved cool technology and all it that could do. These geeks wanted to be the next HP, Intel, Apple, or Google by creating the next great thing.

This focus on technological performance meant that Silicon Valley has always had rivalries in the same way that Florentine artists' shops competed for great new commissions and patronage. And these rivalries spurred innovation, attracting more talent and more money in a positive feedback loop that contributed to the growth of the cluster.

Fresh Ideas Bring Fresh Talent

Renaissance Florence was filled with exciting small- and medium-sized businesses that defined the core of the economy. The Ponte Vecchio Bridge, alone, hosted forty-four goldsmiths' shops. Each artist's workshop was, in fact, a small business. The growth of the Florentine economy and the success of many of these workshops fueled the creation of new businesses.

An Influx of Artists

Some of the growth in new workshop business came from an influx of outsiders. Florence attracted artists from around Italy, including Raphael, Pietro Perugino, and Piero della Francesca, as well as artists from around Europe such as the Flemish-born Giovanni Stradano (Jan Van der Straat). For example, Raphael (Raffaello Sanzio da Urbino) was born in Urbino and apprenticed in Urbino and Perugia throughout his teens. He moved to Florence in 1504 and spent four years studying Florentine methods, which significantly influenced all his subsequent works. [27]

Commercial opportunities and money also attracted talent. For example, Pietro Perugino (from Perugia, Umbria), seems to have been attracted to Florence by the availability of commissioned work. He opened a workshop in Florence and appears to have spent more than a dozen years (1486–1499) working on commissions for Florentines. [28]

A Silicon Gold-Rush

As with Florence, and similar to the 1849 California Gold Rush, the opportunities of Silicon Valley attracted people, money, and attention from outside the region. More than half of the companies founded in Silicon Valley in recent decades included a foreign-born founder. Prominent companies with foreign-born founders or cofounders include Google, Yahoo, Sun Microsystems, YouTube, eBay, and PayPal. And just as Florence attracted non-Florentine artists to set up second workshops in Florence, Silicon Valley also attracted existing non–Silicon Valley companies to form divisions or research centers to tap into the valley's deep pools of knowledge and innovation. Thus, beginning in the 1950s, New York–based IBM created a research center and disk drive manufacturing operation in Silicon Valley that developed the first disk drives and the SQL database language. And Rochester, NY–based Xerox created its famed Palo Alto Research Center in 1970.

THE COMMONALITIES OF CLUSTERS

Although separated by 500 years and representing seemingly opposite ends of the arts and sciences spectrum of human accomplishments, the Florence and Silicon Valley clusters share many common characteristics. It has long been observed that industries tend to be geographically "clustered." Some well-known clusters were mentioned in the introduction to this chapter, including the concentration of information technology firms in Silicon Valley, California, and their counterparts along Route 128 outside Boston, Massachusetts. Other well-known examples include casinos in Las Vegas, Nevada; film production in Hollywood, California; life science companies in Medicon Valley (extending from Eastern Denmark to Western Sweden); cork products in Portugal; household furniture in High Point, North Carolina; finance and investment banking in and around Manhattan; and computer chips in Taiwan.

In addition, certain corporate functions tend to be clustered. Examples include biotechnology research and development centers in Cambridge, Massachusetts; garment and shoe design in Northern

Italy; corporate innovation centers in Silicon Valley; and corporate planning and marketing in Zurich and Geneva.

This agglomeration of firms, or corporate functions, that draw economic advantages from their geographic proximity to others in the same industry or stage of value addition is a phenomenon that was originally observed and explained by the British economist Alfred Marshall in his classic 1920 work, *Principles of Economics.*[29] Marshall hypothesized that the development of industrial complexes implies the existence of positive externalities of colocation. He attributed such externalities to three main forces: (i) knowledge sharing and spillover among the colocated firms; (ii) development of a specialized and efficient supplier base, and (iii) development of local labor pools with specialized skills.[30]

In the 1950s and 1960s, Walter Isard developed some of the most compelling models of industrial agglomeration, laying the foundation for and leading the (new at the time) discipline of regional science. He suggested several ways to analyze "industrial complexes," or clusters, arguing that such methods can contribute to the understanding of regional growth and development.[31,32]

Michael Porter expanded on Marshal's hypothesis and Isard's work in a landmark 1998 paper,[33] providing a detailed framework for cluster analysis, as well as many more examples of clusters in various industries. His paper focuses on the competitive advantages and the increased innovation offered by clusters. He suggests that clusters affect competition by (i) increasing the productivity of the co-located companies, (ii) increasing the pace of innovation, and (iii) stimulating the formation of new businesses.

Type of Relationships among Cluster Members

The two major types of interfirm relationships that contribute to the success of clusters can be defined as "vertical" and "horizontal."

Vertical Relationships

Vertical relationships are links between trading partners. Trading partner relationships are important because the lion's share of value most nonservice businesses offer to their customers is obtained through procurement of parts and services from suppliers. On the procurement side, commercial enterprises interact with a network of material and parts suppliers and an array of service providers. On the sales side, they interact with distributors, customers, and other service providers. Managing these relationships is of prime importance, especially as firms move away from vertical integration and increasingly outsource many functions and stages of production. The ultimate examples of vertical clusters are those created by a single "channel master," such as "Toyota City" in the Aichi prefecture, or the cluster of aviation suppliers servicing Boeing in Everett, Washington. As an example of the wide economic effect of such a channel master, consider the impact of the BMW plant in Greer, South Carolina. It employs 5,000 workers directly and supports over 23,000 jobs in the state, because many BMW suppliers decided to colocate around Greer.[34]

An example of a cluster driven mainly by the availability of a specialized labor pool is the Dalian, China, high-technology cluster, which primarily serves Japanese companies. Because of Japan's colonization of Manchuria from 1931 to 1945, the area, including Dalian, has a large pool of Japanese-speaking workers. This led Japanese companies to set up operations in Dalian, hiring local engineers at less than one-third of the cost of Japanese engineers.[35] Dalian, for its part, started teaching Japanese as a second language in schools, thereby accelerating the trend.

Horizontal Relationships

Horizontal relationships are between firms at the same stage of production, such as automobile manufacturing plants in Detroit, Michigan, or film studios in Hollywood, California. These firms both compete and cooperate with each other along dimensions that benefit them. Horizontal relationships also exist between functions in firms of the same or different industries. Thus, human resources, legal, procurement, finance, and supply chain management functions may collaborate across companies and industries.

The presence of many qualified customers is both the effect and the cause of urban concentrations of businesses offering goods and services similar to each other. When hairdressers in Boston talk about working on "The Street," they do not mean Wall Street, but rather Newbury Street in the Back Bay of Boston, which is home to dozens of women's beauty salons along the eight blocks between Arlington Steet and Massachusetts Avenue. Similarly, there are hundreds of jewelry shops right next to each other in the four blocks of Liberato Street in Buenos Aires between Avenue Corrientes and Avenue de Mayo. And there are hundreds of merchants of knock-off goods in the Museum Market and the Yu Garden market in Shanghai.[36] Such agglomerations are clearly not driven by supply side considerations but by demand; customers understand that such clustering means competitive prices, high quality, and availability—and the foot traffic leads more businesses of that type to settle in the cluster.

Naturally, most clusters include both vertical and horizontal types of relationships. Thus, Detroit and its vicinity is composed not only of many automotive plants but also a legion of suppliers and subsuppliers' plants, as well as educational institutions and a large employee pool. Similarly, Hollywood includes major studios but also a myriad of technical and artistic suppliers, as well as the professional human resources necessary to bring films to life.

Clusters grow as a result of "positive feedback" or "reciprocal reinforcement" forces. As more companies of a certain type (or certain corporate functions) move in, more suppliers and customers move in, making the cluster even more attractive. Furthermore, as the cluster grows, its influence with government grows, affecting further infrastructure investments as well as advantageous regulations, attracting—again—even more companies.

WHY CLUSTER?

In many ways, the existence of clusters today is surprising. In the past, such agglomerations enabled communications. Consequently, one can understand the success of clusters like the Incense Route along the Horn of Africa; carpet-weaving in North-West Persia; glass-blowing in Phoenicia; and the obsidian industry of Teotihuacán, Mexico—all of which were important to perfecting the local state of the art and therefore key to economic growth. What is not intuitive is why such agglomerations still persist today, when we already have efficient supply chain management processes and advanced global communication technologies.

In many ways, Tom Friedman's bestseller *The World Is Flat*[37] popularized the idea that globalization means *The End of Geography*[38] and *The Death of Distance*,[39] as earlier authors argued. Yet—even in today's world of efficient global supply chains, instant communication, electronic worldwide financial industry, free flowing knowledge, and enhanced human mobility—over half the world's population now lives in urban areas,[40] and that portion is increasing. Commensurate with this trend, the economic leadership of megacities has become more pronounced.[41]

Urban areas are obvious clusters of human activity, leading to superior economic performance. The agglomeration of people and businesses means that it is economical to develop the many levels of infrastructure needed for enhanced economic performance, including the physical layer (roads and bridges, water and sewage systems, etc.); the energy system (power generation and transmission); and the myriad of services, basic and advanced, that urban areas provide (emergency, health, mobility, entertainment, cultural, educational, etc.).

Cluster Advantages

Industrial clusters form because they yield certain advantages, as noted by many economists. Some of these advantages include trust between cluster inhabitants, tacit knowledge exchange, a collaborative environment, the support for research and educational institutions, and the availability of a supply base.

Trust

By their geographical colocation, cluster inhabitants are subject to the same cultural environment, language, customs, and legal regime. Common experiences make it easier to develop trust among organizations and people, leading to lower transaction costs between firms, whether they are trading partners or horizontal collaborators/competitors. In most cases, this trust is based on relationships forged outside the work environment. Thus, Hollywood, Wall Street, and Silicon Valley are famous for their deal-making ability, based on deal participants' reputations and familiarity, giving them a competitive advantage over outsiders.

Tacit Knowledge Exchange

As systems and services become more complex, much of the knowledge associated with their development and operations cannot be codified in something as simple as an email attachment sent to a supplier. Tacit knowledge exchange requires discussions over specifications with a supplier; exchanging benchmarking information with a competitor; or supporting a customer—all made easier, faster, less expensive, and more effective when conducted within a cluster, particularly using face-to-face and chance meetings. This holds for both vertical and horizontal corporate relationships. A related phenomenon is *knowledge spillover*. As Rodríguez-Posea and Crescenzi argue: "the process of knowledge accumulation gives rise to spillovers that could benefit a whole set of potential (intended or unintended) beneficiaries."[42] Much of this knowledge exchange takes place informally, between programmers, traders, technicians, and growers, depending on the type of cluster involved. Knowledge spillover is characterized by chance interactions among individual contributors, unlike deal making or formal benchmarking.

Collaboration

The concentration of firms in the same industry, with their similar needs and concerns, gives natural rise to joint activities. These activities include lobbying for the provision of infrastructure, regulatory relief, incentives, and other government largess; development of and participation in organizations dedicated to cluster development, such as chambers of commerce; establishment of cluster-focused procurement strategies, leading to lower costs and higher quality for all members; engagement in cluster-specific marketing and branding activities; and so on. Such collaborative activities are conducted based on both horizontal and vertical relationships between firms in the cluster. Porter referred to the organizations through which such activities take place as *institutions for collaboration* (IFCs)[43], which can be either formal or informal.

Research and Education

The strength of engineering and computer science at Stanford University and biotechnology and engineering at MIT mean that companies located in Silicon Valley and "Bio-Cambridge" have access to state-of-the-art research and have a steady supply of educated employees. In addition, faculty and students can work in their laboratories on real problems using actual data. Such symbiotic relationships between universities and industry clusters are not limited to the information technology or biotechnology industries. For example, Sonoma Valley sports the Wine Business Institute in Sonoma State University, and the nearby University of California-Davis offers, arguably, the leading program in the United States for viticulture and enology. The relationship between universities teaching special skills and the neighboring commercial communities engaged in those skills is not dissimilar to the role of Florence's apprentice system that trained generations of Renaissance artists.

Many clusters support vocational education and training both to increase the supply of employees and to upgrade capabilities. While online training and education is an option, it is still not as effective as a classroom where students can learn as much from each other as from the instructors, and where they can interact with executives from various cluster firms, sharing their wisdom and interacting with students in a way that no webinar can yet match.

Supply Base

As mentioned by Marshall in 1920, clusters attract suppliers who see advantages in locating next to their customers. Even in today's environment, the opportunities for unstructured and chance interaction with customers, the opportunities to learn where their business is heading. and the opportunities to forge strong, trusting and collaborative relationships with customers are very important when firms make location decisions. From the customers' point of view, a strong supplier base with multiple suppliers bodes well for competitive pricing and supplier innovation, which are crucial for competitiveness.

One of the most important consequences of these advantages is that clusters can be very productive and efficient in spawning various new activities. The most significant of those activities may be innovation and the formation of new companies that can use the cluster resources to go to market, grow, and scale. But the existence of cluster expertise, knowhow, money and relationships does not only manifest itself in new companies. The entire movie industry is based on numerous experts—individuals and companies—coming together for a project, namely making a movie. These individuals include writers, producers, animators, cinematographers, editors, musicians, wardrobe designers, makeup artists, actors, sound engineers, special effect producers, and many others. Having all the required ingredients in Hollywood makes it easier to put together the required ensemble for a movie production. Similarly, it is easier to launch a new mutual fund in Boston or a sophisticated financial product on Wall Street. The presence of expertise and support functions enables and supports the innovation process, whether performed within a company or by forming new ones.

Making Clusters Work

Despite what some economists and academics argue,[44] governments do have a role in cluster formation and development. Even Silicon Valley, the high point of entrepreneurship, was helped by defense spending on technology around the Bay Area during and after WWII, and government grants were instrumental in funding research and development in the higher education institutions in the area. The influence of the public sector can be direct or oblique.

"State-Sponsored" Clusters

Some clusters have a strong "state-sponsored" heritage or origin, usually from military spending or government research laboratories.[45] For example, the telemarketing cluster in Omaha, Nebraska, owes much to the decision by the United States Air Force to locate the Strategic Air Command (SAC) there. Charged with a key role in the country's nuclear deterrence strategy, SAC had the first fiber optic telecommunications installation in the United States because fiber-optics are immune to the electromagnetic pulse generated by nuclear explosions. This government work gave the Omaha-based contractor, Kiewit Corporation, much experience in the new technology. The contractor went on to build private fiber networks, starting in Omaha and expanding to include the first nationwide fiber-optic network. With growing local experience in telecommunications and the ultralow cost, per call, of carrying calls on fiber, Omaha became a cluster for call centers. As of 2011, six fiber optic networks converged in the city; twenty-three corporate call centers there answer twenty million calls per day.

Cluster-Enabling Infrastructure

Governments provide a range of infrastructure and services that enable any economic system, and in particular free enterprise, to exist in the first place. Thus, physical infrastructure, regulatory frameworks, patent laws and law enforcement institutions, trade agreements, as well as an array of social, medical, educational, and other services are the cornerstone of any economic system. Naturally, governments can do more or less to help businesses succeed. To this end, global analyses such as the World Economic Forum's *Global Competitiveness Report*[46] or the World Bank's *Ease of Doing Business Index*[47] provide rankings of countries along business-relevant dimensions related to the ease of doing business in the countries studied.

Education and Research

Education and research, invariably with government backing, aid cluster development by enhancing a skilled workforce, developing new knowledge, and creating a source of entrepreneurs.

Advanced education in a cluster encourages entrepreneurship. More than 80 percent of the scientists from California research institutions who started their own biotechnology firms did so in California.[48] Similarly, a Kauffman Foundation study credited MIT-spawned companies with employing more than a million workers in Massachusetts alone.[49] Thus, education creates a positive feedback loop in which graduates of a given university stay in that locality, either joining local firms or starting new businesses in the university's strongest fields of study. These entrepreneurial alumni then support their alma maters, fund research, and support employee education.

Culture

Local culture shapes economic behaviors such as risk-taking, cooperation, and information sharing, all of which are also important to clustering. As mentioned on page 37, cultural differences between Boston's Route 128 and Silicon Valley's high-technology clusters—especially differences in openness and tolerance of failure—have been cited to explain the greater success of the California cluster.[50] Similarly, Baltimore hasn't developed a strong biotechnology cluster (despite Johns Hopkins's prominent position among the nation's leading medical research institutions) because, some suggest, of a persistent culture unwelcoming of entrepreneurship.[51]

I had an experience that may explain one facet of the effects of "culture." During 2002 and 2003, I was on faculty sabbatical at Cambridge University in the UK as part of the Cambridge-MIT Institute (CMI). CMI was funded by the UK government with the express goal of increasing entrepreneurship output of UK university research. MIT, with its long tradition in this area—MIT has spawned over 25,800 active companies employing more than 3.3 million people and generating worldwide annual revenues of $2 trillion[52]—seemed to be the perfect partner.

While conducting my own research (unrelated to the subject of entrepreneurship), I had discussions with dozens of government, academic, and business leaders in the UK on the subject of entrepreneurial culture. As a five-time entrepreneur myself, I had first-hand knowledge and experience in this area. It became clear to me that, at the time, one of the impediments to a higher rate of business formation in the UK could not be cured by work done at Cambridge University, nor at any other British university. In many ways, it was the attitude toward failed entrepreneurs that was the barrier. Among US venture capitalists, executives, and academics, a failed enterprise tends to be seen as evidence the entrepreneur is a person seasoned by hard experience. In the UK, by contrast, it seemed to be damning. A failed entrepreneur found it more difficult in the UK than it would be for him or her in the United States to raise funds, put together a team, and get the first few sales. In short, despite the learning experience, it was difficult for a failed UK entrepreneur to get another new business off the ground.

Why Not "Go all the Way"?

Given all the advantages that clusters bring, one can ask, why don't firms in a cluster end up acquiring each other to form larger enterprises, if closeness is so advantageous? Transaction cost economics[53] suggests that being part of a single organization can have many benefits, as incentives are more aligned, the need for formal contracting is eliminated, and decision-making can be faster. The answer, most likely, is that membership in a cluster provides what engineers and economists call "real options"—cluster membership gives member companies the right (or opportunity) but not the obligation to do business with any other cluster member.

In many ways, a cluster may be an optimal balance between the complexity, bureaucracy, lock-in with internal suppliers, unionization, and slow decision making that hamper innovation in large enterprises, and the lack of scale and reach that holds back smaller firms. In a dynamic environment, when innovation and fast market response are keys to competitive advantage, the tacit communication and trust building between smaller firms (and between their employees, who share culture and extensive personal contact) allows for joint learning and adoption of best practices. Yet the separate and independent decision making of the firms in the cluster may decrease "groupthink," allowing the cluster to adopt new technologies and process innovations, thus renewing itself and remaining competitive. Consequently, a cluster may be an advantageous organizational structure, balancing flexibility and fast decision making on the one hand with reach and resource availability on the other. In Porter's words, "A cluster allows each member to benefit *as if* it had greater scale or *as if* it had joined with others formally—without requiring it to sacrifice its flexibility."[54]

THE ONGOING QUEST FOR ECONOMIC ELIXIRS

In large part because of the influence of Porter's work (as well as others), many governments have chosen the cluster development path to foster economic development. The reason may have a lot to do with the phenomenal success of the well-known clusters of Silicon Valley, Hollywood, and Wall Street. As some economists have argued, it also gives policymakers a strategy and rationale for economic interventions and the implementation of industrial policy. In addition, the cluster model is intoxicating in that many governments believed that they only have to start the "flywheel" and the positive feedback loop of early companies getting economic advantages that draw in more and more companies will grow the cluster "automatically." This seems like a panacea—just put in some of the initial ingredients and the cluster will grow on its own.

Many economists, however, have pointed out several negative effects of clusters and risks associated with pursuing cluster-based development strategies. They argue that some of the very ingredients that make clusters successful can be their Achilles' heels.

Downside of Clusters

Unlike diamonds, clusters are not forever. Most clusters have life cycles, starting with a nascent period generated by innovation or internal investments; growth, when imitators and competitors move in and entrepreneurs spin off new companies; maturity, when competition is based on costs and more outsiders move in; and decay, when products or services become replaceable by lower cost and/or better substitutes elsewhere.[55]

For example, in the 1940s, St. Louis, Missouri, was dominated by the shoe industry. As the saying went then, "St. Louis was first in shoes, first in booze, and last in the American League [in Major League Baseball]." Yet, a few decades later, the shoe industry was basically gone. Similar fate was experienced by the British cotton industry in Lancashire;[56] the copper smelting industry in Swansa, Wales;[57] and the tire industry in Akron, Ohio. In a detailed analysis, Donald Sull chronicled how the tire industry, which was among the most innovative in the United States between 1900 and 1935, faltered between 1970 and 1980 in the face of the radial tire technology introduced by the French company, Michelin. In the span of eighteen months, three of the four Akron tire manufacturers ceased to exist as independent corporations.[58]

One of the explanations for cluster decline and failure is that their very advantage—the flow of information and knowledge—can create a kind of groupthink that hampers the ability of cluster firms to respond to external changes. Such a phenomenon is likely to take place in mature clusters, which have settled on a dominant design and "best" set of processes. The benefits of all forms of knowledge exchange decline as the cluster matures, while the risks of inertia rise. Existing processes and common wisdom are taken for granted, regardless of changes in the competitive environment.[59] Furthermore, bureaucratic processes set in and the resistance to change grows.[60] In his 2012 book about the near-death and resurrection of the Ford Motor Company, Bruce Hoffman describes this phenomenon at length within Ford and at the two other Detroit auto giants, leading to government bailouts of GM and Chrysler, the bankruptcy of GM and the takeover of Chrysler by Fiat.[61]

Risks of Cluster-Based Development Strategy

As national and local governments pursue cluster strategies, they should be aware of several risks associated with such a course of action. First, such economic development strategy calls for "picking winners." In other words, the government has to decide which industry it intends to support for cluster development. Governments, however, may not be adept at this and may not be able to bring together all the ingredients of successful clusters. Thus, projects like Tsukuba, Japan's "Science City," and Egypt's "Silicon Pyramid" have not developed into the engines of economic growth that their backers hoped.

A 2011 story in the *Wall Street Journal* chronicled the failed effort to start a chip-making industry in Orlando, Florida. A public-private coalition spent more than a billion dollars to build advanced microchip labs. They also offered further grants and tax breaks to other semiconductor companies, and funded job-training programs at local universities. The industry, however, shifted to Asia and the advanced labs were physically demolished in 2010. The article outlines several other failures of cluster building efforts.[62]

Making matters worse, the essence of cluster strategy is to promote only certain industries, thus "putting many eggs in a single basket." In other words, such a strategy may accentuate the risk of a regional recession when the cluster fails, as happened in Akron when the tire industry there failed. In fact, the main impetus for the development of the logistics cluster in Zaragoza, Spain (see the third section of chapter 1) was the drive to diversify the local economy, which was strongly dependent on the local automotive cluster around the local GM Opel plant.

In many cases, cluster strategies are aimed at supporting existing local industries. The main analytical tool used to identify such industries is the so-called "Location Quotient" (LQ), which is the ratio of the percent of people employed locally in a given industry to the percentage of employment in that industry nationally. A ratio greater than 1 indicates the prevalence of a particular industry in a location, possible existing export activities, and that this high-ratio industry qualifies as a target for public investment. More advanced approaches augment the LQ by adding other factors. For example, the method developed by the Regional Economic Development Research Laboratory at Clemson University[63] identifies local industrial clusters by adding other screens to the LQ, including the number of establishments of a particular industry in the region and an identification of the industry's value chains' tie to companies in the cluster under study.

The basic criticism of such approaches is that despite recent advances, they can identify only past and present strengths and therefore may lead to investments in past industries—"chasing smokestacks." And since, as every investment advisor tells her clients: "past performance is no guarantee of future results," the effects on investments in current industrial strengths are not clear. It is unlikely that emerging or nascent industries will be identified as investment candidates by any method looking at past and present numerical data. Such shortcomings may also take place, in part, because existing industries in a region have the money and political connections to press for public investments benefiting them.

Logistics Clusters

This book focuses on a specific type of cluster—logistics clusters. These clusters include firms providing logistics services, such as third party logistics service providers (3PLs), transportation carriers, warehousing companies and forwarders; the logistics operations of industrial firms, such as the distribution operations of retailers, manufacturers (for both new products and after-market parts) and distributors; and the operations of companies for whom logistics is a large part of their costs.

As outlined in the following chapters, successful logistics clusters require certain geographical attributes, such as a central location and significant government investments in physical infrastructure. These are in addition to an appropriate labor pool, information and communications technology infrastructure, availability of a strong financial services industry, and a competitive regulatory regime.

Many locales are looking to develop logistics clusters for four main reasons:

First, in developed economies, the logistics industry can replace lost manufacturing jobs, as happened in southern California in the last part of the twentieth century and the first decade of the twenty-first.

Second, the logistics industry is less susceptible to "off-shoring" because of the technology and economics of transportation and distribution. The first and second factors mean that logistics clusters can ease unemployment pressures, especially for low-end jobs, while also adopting, relying on, and developing leading-edge information and communication technologies.

Third, a logistics cluster can serve as "infrastructure" to other industries that require specific logistics capabilities. This phenomenon seems to be the case in China, where a significant number of large logistics clusters have been developing at the beginning of the twenty-first century and new ones are under development in support of the manufacturing base and the burgeoning internal markets of China.

Finally, the logistics industry does not depend on a single industrial vertical; logistics clusters serve multiple industries and thus are less vulnerable to the vagaries of any particular industry.

These themes are revisited, in more detail, in later parts of this book.

3

GEOGRAPHY OF LOGISTICS CLUSTERS

Basic logistics services—transportation and storage—enable trade. By the seventeenth and eighteenth centuries, the prevailing strategy of trade-based economic growth was mercantilism, which called for maximizing exports through subsidies while minimizing imports through tariffs. Adam Smith, the father of modern economics, realized that mercantilism could not create economic growth for all nations at the same time because one nation's export is another nation's import. In 1776, he published the concept of *absolute advantage*, using labor productivity to explain that all nations can simultaneously get rich if they focus on their absolute advantages and practice free trade.[1] To follow his argument, assume that the United States can produce more wheat per worker-hour than can the United Kingdom and that the UK can produce more yards of cloth per worker-hour. If the labor wages are the same in both countries, then the US should produce wheat, the UK cloth, and they should trade them freely, causing both nations to be better off compared to each producing everything. Of course, export-import trade grows naturally when there are no local substitutes. Japan buys oil from Saudi Arabia, and China buys Chilean copper because Japan does not have local sources of oil and China doesn't have enough local copper ore to meet local demand. Ditto aluminum, steel, gold, wheat, fruit, and so on.

This, however, is only half the story of trade, because some nations may have no absolute advantage in anything. The notion of *comparative advantage* explains how trade across geographies can create value for both trading parties, even if one party can produce all goods with fewer resources than can the other. Comparative advantage means that one party can manufacture a product with the highest efficiency relative to all other products that it could manufacture. The notion of comparative advantage is attributed to the English political economist David Ricardo, who used England and Portugal as representative examples in his 1817 book.[2] Ricardo supposed that Portugal could produce both wine and cloth cheaper than could England, but the relative costs of production are different in the two countries. In Ricardo's example, the English could produce cloth at moderate cost and wine only at a very high cost. In contrast, the Portuguese could make both wine and cloth very inexpensively. With these relative production cost structures, Portugal would benefit from producing more wine for export to England, even if it meant sacrificing local cloth production in favor of importing the more expensive English cloth. That is, the Portuguese economy would do better to convert fields of flax and cotton and sheep farms to highly profitable export-oriented vineyards. Therefore, while it is cheaper to produce cloth in Portugal than England, it is cheaper still for Portugal to produce excess wine and trade that for English cloth. England will also benefit, because while its costs of producing cloth have not changed, it can now get wine at a lower price, closer to the cost of cloth. Thus, each country gains by specializing in the goods in which it has comparative advantage and trading that batch of goods for the other. A succinct numerical example of the same argument was recently outlined by Krugman in his *New York Times* column.[3]

Interestingly, neither Smith nor Ricardo included logistics costs in their analysis. Trade requires two basic logistics functions: transportation and storage, the costs of which must be carried by the price of the goods. First, goods must be moved from the place of production to the place of consumption. Second, goods may need to be stored for reasons that include: (i) differences between the rates of production and consumption; (ii) the use of large, discrete shipments favored by the technology and economics of transportation; (iii) uncertainties of supply and demand; and (iv) opportunities to take advantage of temporal and spatial price fluctuations. Obviously, if the costs of transportation (and the warehousing associated with it) are high relative to the price of the goods, there will be no trade.[4]

The technology and economics of transportation often favor movements through central consolidation facilities rather than directly between origin and destination (see chapter 4). These transportation consolidation hubs have naturally been associated with important transportation infrastructure facilities, such as ports and crossroads. Given the flow of goods through the hubs, many other logistics-related services, including warehousing and distribution, naturally migrated to these hubs, causing them to develop, in many cases, into full-fledged logistics clusters. As the need for logistics activities grew over the centuries and accelerated with rising globalization at the end of the twentieth century, these logistics clusters grew in size, importance, and economic impact. The growth in globalization is, in significant part, the result of the efficiency of the global logistics system. Thus, logistics clusters have contributed to the efficiency of the global systems of shipping and storage and therefore to outsourcing, international trade, and globalization, which in turn caused more global trade flows, leading to larger and more efficient logistics clusters.

This chapter introduces four key logistics clusters (The Netherlands, Singapore, Panama, and Memphis) to illustrate the interplay of logistics principles, geographic features, and historical events leading to the co-development of high-performance logistics and regional economies.

THE NETHERLANDS: NATURAL ROUTES, PORTS, AND TRADERS

Two thousand years ago, Julius Caesar recognized Holland's importance for logistics when he brought his legions down the Maas River and across the Rhine River to extend the reign of the Roman empire into northern Europe in the 50s BCE. The pattern of Roman activities illustrates how geography influences the development of logistics hubs. River ports, such as those along the Rhine, and seaports, such as those along Europe's northern shores, made for natural nodes in a supply chain in both ancient and modern times.

Minimizing the Cost of Pax Romana

In order to control and impose their will on an empire stretching from today's England, most of Europe, northern Africa, and the Middle East, the Romans stationed troops throughout their vast empire. Keeping large armies in remote hinterlands required significant logistics prowess; a single Roman legion spanned a force of 4,000 to 5,000 men with associated war horses and draft animals that, in turn, required tons of food, water, and animal forage every day. Inducing Roman soldiers and their leaders to spend years in cold northern European postings also meant supplying some familiar southern European creature comforts such as olive oil, wine, and garum (a Roman condiment made from fermented fish).

The unit costs of transportation—typically measured as the cost of moving one unit of weight across a unit of distance, such as dollars per ton-mile—varied across transportation modes in Roman times, as they do in modern times. Seaborne freight was the least expensive; river barges cost about five times more than ocean freight, and land-based freight was probably twenty to sixty times as expensive as ocean freight.[5] But the unit cost of each mode does not tell the whole story, because the constraints of geography mean that different modes require different distances to move between any two given points. Although ocean freight might be the least expensive unit cost, the long ocean distances from Rome around the Iberian peninsula and into the rough Atlantic made the sea no panacea, especially for supplying inland locations like Colonia Claudia Ara Agrippinensium (now Cologne, Germany), which was the Roman provincial capital of Germania.

The 1,232-kilometer-long Rhine River, with its north/northeasterly flow, made a natural choice for moving the Roman supplies around the northern limits of the empire. The Romans' string of dozens of forts, camps, and river ports testifies to the empire's use of the Rhine and affiliated rivers as natural arteries for moving the Roman legions and supplies from south-central Europe into the Gallic and Germanic parts of Europe. As an illustration of the scale of the Roman logistics operations, consider that a single tax collection expedition in 16 CE involved constructing and sending 1,000 vessels of various types down the Rhine.[6]

Changing Modes Leads to Logistics Nodes

During Roman times, the main flow of the Rhine entered the North Sea at the Roman naval base of Lugdunum (now Katwijk, the Netherlands).[7] This settlement at the boundary between river and sea exemplifies a common type of transportation network node: a terminal facility dedicated to the interface between two modes of transportation. In many cases, because of the different characteristics of the modes involved, timing issues, and other considerations, such transportation nodes were also used for warehousing and distribution activities, making them important logistics hubs.

The Romans also used the mouth of the Rhine River for crossings to Britain in the first century CE, according to the contemporaneous historian Strabo.[8] At Lugdunum, the Romans would off-load supplies from the small flat-bottomed river barges coming down the Rhine and then reload them onto larger, deeper-bellied ocean-going vessels for the channel crossing to Britain, feeding the Roman legions conducting campaigns there. Lugdunum was also used for inbound shipments—ocean freight, such as wine from Gaul (now France), came to Lugdunum, where it would be transferred from ocean freighter to river barge and distributed to the Roman facilities along the Rhine. Because of the mismatch of schedules and capacities of the various vessels and the need for holding supplies that might be distributed to various garrisons up the Rhine or other local rivers, Lugdunum would have held stockpiles of many goods, as evidenced by the large granaries in Roman ruins near Katwijk. Although Rome would fall, this region at the end of the Rhine would continue as a node in the global logistics network, handling the flow of goods between inland Europe and global trade by sea.

Dutch East India Company

The rise of modern-day Holland as a logistics cluster came with growing global trade in the fifteenth and sixteenth centuries, especially with new opportunities for trade in luxury goods such as South Asian spices (pepper, cloves, cinnamon, cardamom, nutmeg, etc.), Chinese crafts (porcelain and silks), Indian textiles, and Japanese lacquerware. The promised riches of the spice trade encouraged a frenzy of investment and new expeditions in the late 1500s by seafaring European countries, including the Dutch. The Dutch government saw, as early as 1598, the undesirability of intra-Dutch competition for Asian trade and nudged the major players to pool their capital and fleets to form a single trading company. In return, the government promised to give the combined entity a twenty-one-year monopoly on the spice trade and trade relations with Asia.[9] In 1602, traders and investment pools from six Dutch cities merged to form the governing board of the Dutch East India Company—*Vereenigde Oost-Indische Compagnie* (VOC) (literally meaning *United East India Company*).[10] Of these six cities, Middelburg, Rotterdam, and Amsterdam grew to be major logistics nodes in the global commerce of the era.

The Dutch East India Company was the first major multinational company, with immense, even quasi-governmental powers. It had its own armed forces, conquered lands, established colonies, negotiated treaties, coined money, and imprisoned and executed convicts. During the sixteenth and seventeenth centuries, it employed, in total, almost 5,000 ships in Asia-Europe and inter-Asia trade.[11]

In One Pier and Out the Other: Transshipment Nodes

Logistic terminals are geographic locations—nodes in the logistics network—where the shipments that flow through the network from multiple origins to multiple destinations transfer from one conveyance to another. The purposes of such transfer include consolidation (and deconsolidation), changing modes of transportation, or forwarding from one carrier to another. In airports, for instance, shipments move from airplanes to trucks or to other airplanes, or from trucks to airplanes; in seaports, shipments move between ships or between ships and railroad or trucks; in rail intermodal yards, shipments move from rail to trucks or trucks to rail, and so forth. Many terminal operations also store shipments as they wait for the next leg of their journey.

One measure of the importance—as well as of the performance—of a transportation hub is the fraction of transshipments—goods transiting the terminal (e.g., imported and then immediately

exported) rather than remaining in the local area. High transshipment volumes reflect a terminal's importance and efficiency because they represent goods coming to a place for no other reason
other than to perform logistical functions there. Given the significant costs of route deviation, stopping, unloading, storing, and reloading goods, transshipment through a hub would not occur unless that hub could offer significantly reduced transportation costs,
improved transportation service, or the availability of other services. For example, Dubai has developed into a logistics hub; while
it imports $17 billion annually, it is a gateway to an estimated (in
2009) $150 billion export/import market every year.[12] In contrast,
ports such as Shanghai and Tianjin in China or Los Angeles/Long
Beach (LA/LB) are important for a different reason: they serve as
departure or entry points for cargo leaving/entering China and
cargo entering/leaving the United States, respectively. These ports,
however, also serve important transshipment functions since the
goods are not originated from or destined to the local area (such as
the LA basin or the city of Shanghai) but rather used to ship goods
from/to the entire United States and China, respectively.

Major logistics nodes in the global supply and distribution
network tend to have high percentages of transshipment. Such
transshipment-dominated nodes are known as entrepôt (from the
French for "warehouse"). The advantages of transshipments are
the reason for the structure of many transportation systems as hub-
and-spoke networks, with a transshipment node at the network's
hub. Even as early as 1567, more than 30 percent of Dutch port
operations were re-exports. This percentage grew to 50 percent in
1650 and nearly 70 percent in 1770. Today, transit and re-export
shipments constitute over 50 percent of the Dutch ports' freight
volume.

Rotterdam: Rise of a Modern Port

The culture, geography, and expertise developed during centuries
of trade enabled the Netherlands to continue to be a trading center
even after the demise of the Dutch East India Company in 1796.
The Dutch invested continuously in transportation infrastructure
to remain competitive in logistics operations. To this end, they built

more and larger canals; Amsterdam, for example, built large new canals in 1825, 1876, and 1952. Some canals created new routes or shortcuts, such as the Amsterdam canals to the Rhine River and North Sea. Other canals, such as those around Rotterdam, replaced or enhanced pre-existing natural water courses that had silted up over the years. Through the centuries, other modes of transportation (rail, truck, and air) arose and the Dutch adopted them, too. The country became crisscrossed by a network of freeways and rail lines connecting to major European networks. A network of 1,500 kilometers of pipelines buried underground throughout Holland, Belgium, and Germany handles the petrochemical products refined at Rotterdam. Amsterdam's Schiphol airport handled over 1.5 million (metric) tons of cargo in 2010, making it the fourth largest airport in Europe in terms of freight movement.[13]

For nearly forty years, the largest port in Holland—in fact, the largest port in the Western hemisphere—has been Rotterdam.[14] What began in the 1200s as a small fishing village a few dozen kilometers up the Maas River from the sea expanded to cover both banks of the Maas and extend all the way out into the sea. The Dutch use the comforting term of "haven" as their word for a ship's harbor, and Rotterdam has dozens of these havens nestled along both banks of the Maas. Starting from the sea, a tour of the 40-kilometer-long massive port complex finds all manner of named havens from the quixotic Tennesseehaven, the aspirational Europahaven, the honorary Princess Beatrixrhaven, and the depressingly functional Petroleumhavens 1E through 8E. Each one of these "havens" includes one or more terminals, where maritime logistics operations—unloading, storing, sorting, and loading—between ships, river barges, rail cars, and trucks take place. As one travels up the Maas River, the large ocean-going ships thin out and narrow river barges take their place. At any given time, more than 300 vessels might be in Rotterdam and, over the course of a year, some 34,000 seagoing vessels and 133,000 inland vessels call at Rotterdam.[15]

What happens off the water matters even more because of all the logistics activities that occur on land. These include storage, customs processing, distribution, and value-added activities. Next to Rotterdam's havens stand warehouses, factories, petrochemical tanks, refineries, power plants, and container yards. For example, the energy and petrochemical industry sector of the Rotterdam port comprises over 100 sites and attracts new investments of over one billion euros per year. Throughout the port, roadways and railways ramify like capillaries to both nourish and draw nourishment from the hundreds of port facilities lining the route to the sea. Modern trains shuttle freight on dedicated cargo rail lines between the port of Rotterdam and the German industrial regions. In total, the port employs about 86,000 people directly. Another 200,000 workers depend on the port's activities for their jobs.[16]

Rotterdam's rise came from a long-running series of infrastructure projects that cemented the city's role as a logistics hub. For example, in the mid 1300s, a canal connected Rotterdam to the larger industrial towns of the north, including Delft. This spurred Rotterdam's rise as a transshipment port for three directions of trade: North Holland via the canal, Germany via the Rhine, and the rest of the world via the sea. Vessel-to-vessel transshipments still account for more than 35 percent of Rotterdam's traffic. Of the rest, about 50 percent is transit volume that moves through the port to the rest of Europe, including 60 percent of containers.[17] Today, the port covers 105 square kilometers (40.5 square miles) and extends into land reclaimed from the sea. What began in medieval Europe now finds itself in a logistical geographic center of Europe, with 150 million consumers within a 500-kilometer radius.

Cosmopolitan Community

Daniel Defoe, the English writer best known for his novel *Robinson Crusoe*, commented on the Dutch character in 1728: "The Dutch must be understood as they really are, the Carryers of the World, the middle Persons in Trade, the Factors and Brokers of Europe: . . . They buy to sell again, take in to send out: and the greatest part of their vast commerce consists in being supply'd from all parts of the world that they may supply all the world again."[18] The Dutch propensity for world trade comes, in part, from a high degree of cultural tolerance that enables trade. By definition, global trade means dealing with outsiders. This implies both a citizenry that tolerates foreigners and immigration policies that enable foreign traders (e.g., ex-pats) to live and work in a trading country. Whether a cultural predilection for tolerance led the Dutch to be traders or whether being traders led the Dutch toward greater tolerance isn't clear.

Regardless of the original cause, centuries of Dutch history include examples of immigrants fleeing religious persecution or seeking better livelihoods in the Netherlands. Anne Frank's experience in Amsterdam in World War II as a Jew hidden from the German police wasn't the first example of the Dutch penchant for accepting and sheltering refugees from persecution. During the Inquisition, on the Iberian Peninsula in the fifteenth and sixteenth centuries, Jews fled to the Netherlands; during the Protestant Reformation in the sixteenth century and leading up to the English Civil War in the seventeenth century, English Protestants came to the Netherlands. Similarly, Protestant Huguenots fled Catholic persecution in France and came to the Netherlands in the sixteenth and seventeenth centuries. Even the American Pilgrims, who founded Plymouth Colony in Massachusetts in the United States, first spent about a decade living in Holland on their long journey to escape English religious persecution.

Nor was the influx of foreigners without tangible economic benefits. Iberian Jews not prohibited by creed from lending or borrowing money helped establish Amsterdam as a major financial center. Flemish printers, fleeing Catholic restrictions on publishing, made Holland a major center for knowledge and book printing. As a result of centuries of immigration, the Netherlands has an extremely cosmopolitan demographic. Ethnic Dutch are almost a minority in Rotterdam, and this inclusiveness continues—in 2009, Ahmed Aboutaleb, a Moroccan-born son of an Islamic preacher, became the mayor of the city.

SINGAPORE: A TRADING HUB

On the southern tip of the Malaysian peninsula sits the island of Singapore. Less than one-quarter the size of Rhode Island, Singapore is home to five million people and an economy that provides a standard of living higher than that of the United States. Yet Singapore has almost no natural resources. Its wealth derives from its location and its people. Like Rotterdam, Singapore thrives on transshipment; it transships a full fifth of the world's maritime containers.[19] In fact, Singapore is the world's busiest transshipment port; about 85 percent of the containers that come to the port of Singapore never officially enter the country and over half of the remaining 15 percent eventually leave Singapore as re-export.[20] A significant part of the nation's economy comes from the logistics activities built around its port and airport, through which more than $500 billion in goods flow every year. Goods don't "go to Singapore" as much as they "flow through Singapore." Singapore became a major node in global trading networks for four reasons: geography, weather, culture, and continuous investments by the government.

Geography: Meet You at the Corner of East and West

First, the Malacca strait between the Malaysian peninsula and the large island of Sumatra represents a natural meeting place between the East Asian economies on the Pacific Ocean (China, Japan, Korea, Taiwan, and Vietnam) and the South Asian and Western nations (e.g., India, the Middle East, and Europe via the Suez Canal). Sea-borne goods between the two regions traverse the Strait and turn the corner at Singapore. In historical times, Chinese junks (boats) were laden with silks, damasks, porcelain, pottery, and iron. Indian and Arab ships brought cotton textiles, Venetian glass, incense, and metal. Finally, the Malaysian peninsula provided its own products for trade, such as pepper, gambier (a dye for silk and leather), and tin. Written records of Singapore, then known as Temasek, date back to 1349, although sketchier records suggest trade in the area going back to the second century CE. In 1819, when Sir Thomas Stamford Raffles chose Singapore as a British base for trade, he picked it for crucial logistic qualities including location, the depth of the port, ample fresh water, and abundant timber for repairing ships.

Weather: Enabling Reliable Trade

Second, Singapore's equatorial location brings another advantage to reliable transportation—almost no extreme weather. Large cyclonic storms such as typhoons and hurricanes arise from the interaction of tropical low-pressure systems and the Coriolis effects of the Earth's rotation. These rotation effects mean that storms in the Northern hemisphere spin counterclockwise, those in the Southern hemisphere spin clockwise, and storms on the equator don't spin at all. This lack of spin in equatorial storms means they never organize and grow into the destructive behemoths found in higher and lower latitudes. Singapore's climate can best be described as monotonous, with lows around 75°F (24°C) and highs near 90°F (32°C) all year round. In the past hundred years, Singapore has not seen temperatures colder than 67°F (19°C) or hotter than 97°F (36°C).

What does vary are Singapore's prevailing winds, and they played a crucial role in the early history of the region as a trading node in the global transportation network. From June to September, the prevailing winds enabled Arab and Indian traders to sail to Singapore. From December to March, the prevailing winds enabled Chinese traders to sail to Singapore. The winds that brought the Chinese junks also enabled the Indian and Arab ships to sail home and vice versa. Each group sold its products at the trading center and bought back wares brought by the other traders. Thus, Indian and Arab goods moved to the Malacca straits and then to China and other East Asian markets while Chinese and East Asian goods flowed in the opposite direction. This pattern of trade also made Singapore a multicultural society.

Culture: A True Nation of Traders

Third, Singapore is even more cosmopolitan than Rotterdam. From the beginning, the city's only reason for existence was international trade, which brought a massive influx of Chinese, Indian, Arab, British, Dutch, and Indonesian traders to the island. Although culturally diverse, the immigrants to Singapore shared a culture of trade and an understanding of the associated economic gain. Ethnic Malays may be the nominal natives of Singapore, yet they, too are mostly immigrants from other areas and comprise a scant 13 percent of Singaporeans. Raffles' original city plan for Singapore divided the city into ethnic quarters. Although these divisions survive as quaint ethnic tourist areas, the descendants have moved into largely integrated, modern high-rise apartment buildings. To this day, Singapore remains multiethnic with four official languages: English, Malay, Chinese, and Tamil.

Investment: The Literal Growth of an Island

Finally, like Rotterdam, Singapore isn't satisfied with its natural geography. While the Singapore River and surrounding waters provided a natural harbor for servicing nineteenth-century sailing vessels, growing trade and growing vessel sizes soon stretched the limits of the natural harbor. The advent of bigger ships changed the definition of "deep water" for harbors. In 1849, Singapore identified Keppel Harbor (then known as New Harbor) for expansion, which led to the development of thousands of feet of new piers and wharves. As trade expanded, Singapore undertook various infrastructure projects, such as filling in beachfront space to create a main road between various port facilities. Singaporeans also built breakwaters, replaced wooden piers with earth and concrete quays, dredged deep channels and ports for larger ships, and filled in the sea between small outlying islands to create larger, more functional land. To do this, Singaporeans leveled local mountains and imported sand from neighboring countries. Since the 1960s, the island's land mass has grown 21 percent (581.5 km^2 in the 1960s to 712 km^2 in mid-2010).[21]

Ultimately, the very geography of the Malacca Strait may limit Singapore's growth as a maritime hub and therefore the future of its logistics cluster. The 25m depth of the strait at its shallowest places an upper limit on the size of ships (called Malaccamax) that can take that route. Already, some of the largest crude oil carriers exceed this specification and must take other routes between Middle East oil sources and Asian oil customers. As a result, Singapore and surrounding nations might dredge deeper channels in the strait to permit the passage of ever-larger vessels.

PANAMA CANAL: A MAN-MADE SHORTCUT

The North and South American continents stretch over 8,700 miles from the often-frozen Arctic north to the ever-stormy Cape Horn in the south, separating the Pacific Ocean from the Atlantic Ocean. In the early days of American civilization, crossing from the east coast to the west coast of the Americas required either a long, arduous overland journey or an even longer, arduous sea voyage. The quest for the fabled Northwest Passage, the Louis and Clark expedition, and the lives of many explorers testify to the extreme interest in finding a path between the seas. Fortunately, halfway between the top and the tail of the Americas sits the conveniently narrow Isthmus of Panama, which in its natural form is but a swampy stretch of tropical forest.

Developing this isthmus into the Panama Canal and establishing a logistics cluster around the canal illustrates a somewhat different type of cluster than either Rotterdam or Singapore. Rotterdam represents a mode-changing node where most goods move from ocean-going vessels to and from smaller ships, barges, rail cars, trucks, and pipelines, for distribution to Germany and the rest of Europe's hinterland. Because cargo must be unloaded, sorted, stored, and loaded, its handling involves many logistics-related operations and an opportunity for even more value-added activities. Singapore represents a central consolidation/deconsolidation hub focused on transshipments between ocean going vessels.

In contrast to Rotterdam and Singapore, the Panama Canal was conceived as a link—a connector—in the international maritime trade network; it was developed neither as a consolidation node nor as a mode-change terminal node. It is an artificial conduit of maritime traffic (think of it as a toll road) between the Pacific and Atlantic Oceans. To make sure that it leverages the canal's traffic, and especially the increased traffic expected to follow the latest expansion, Panama focused its 2010–2014 strategic plan in large measure on logistics, with a vision to become "hub of the Americas" and specifically on "leveraging the [canal's] traffic to generate incomes by providing services with added value to the products which go through Panama."[22] In other words, Panama is investing in the conditions for logistics clusters development around its canal. Panama's goal is to provide more value to the passing traffic than just a shortcut, becoming a hub of distribution and logistics operations between East and West.

The history of Panama is the history of three increasingly costly investments in transportation infrastructure—a road, a railroad, and a canal. These investments in this geographically propitious location created a new route, and new midpoint in many East–West journeys, and thus led to the development of a logistics cluster in Panama.

The First Path between the Seas

The first significant man-made path between the seas was the Camino Real—literally, the King's Road. In 1519, 4,000 native slaves built a 50-mile-long isthmus-spanning wagon road that was wide enough for two carts. Slaves and mule trains carried cargo on multiday treks between the Atlantic and Pacific sides of Panama. Incan gold and silver from Peru crossed from the Pacific side to the Atlantic seaport of Portobello to await pickup by an annual arrival of a small fleet of ships from Spain. European goods, brought annually by the Spanish fleet, traveled from the Atlantic to the Pacific side to support Spanish aristocrats, merchants, and clergy operating on the western coasts of both North and South America.

Later, the Spanish developed a second crossing—Camino de las Cruces—that cut the overland part of the trek in half, using the Chagres River for the Atlantic-side half of the journey across the isthmus.[23] Most merchandise followed this combined river and land route, but the Spanish avoided using that route for precious metals because the short coastal leg from the mouth of the Chagres to the Caribbean seaport of Portobelo was too exposed to pirate attacks.[24] These land and river crossings would suffice for more than three centuries until the collapse of Spain's New World ambitions reduced the volume of trade flowing through Panama in the early 1800s. Trade declined so much that the jungle had reclaimed all the wagon roads across the isthmus by the 1940s.[25]

The Second Path between the Seas

The second path between the seas came in the mid-1800s. Although Spain's New World Empire had collapsed, new developments in the Western Hemisphere brought new trade flows. With the steady development of the western frontier of the United States, people and goods began to go west to places such as California and the Oregon territories. In the mid-1800s, westbound settlers traveling from, say, New York to San Francisco had only three ways to reach the Pacific side of the United States: a 3,000 mile trip, much of it by horse and wagon across 1,700 miles of wilderness and high mountains inhabited by sometimes-hostile Indians; by a long 13,000 mile sea journey around Cape Horn; or by a two-legged 5,000 mile sea journey that included a trek across Central America in Panama, Nicaragua, or Mexico.

Although crossing Panama by foot or cart took only a few days under good conditions, the journey was beset by profiteers, bandits, pestilence, and mud. In 1847, one year before gold was discovered in California, a group of New York financiers founded the Panama Railroad Company. They planned to build a railroad following the now unused Camino de las Cruces route. Construction of just 47 miles of railroad (and 300 bridges) cost the investors $7.5 million (over $200 million in 2012 dollars) and cost 12,000 workers their lives as a result of poor sanitation, malaria, yellow fever, and Chagres fever.[26] Per mile, this was the most expensive railroad in the world to use—a one-way ticket for the three-hour journey cost $25 in gold (about $650 in 2012 dollars).[27]

Despite the cost, the Panama Railroad offered a major improvement in transcontinental transportation. Rail could move more goods, heavier loads, and at higher speeds than could mules. Rail also had higher immunity to weather and the sticky blue-black mud of the Panamanian jungles. Completed in January 1855, the railroad earned back its lavish costs by 1862 as traffic surged during the California gold rush. At one point, Panama Railroad shares became the highest-priced stock on the New York Stock Exchange.[28]

Sometimes even a great shortcut, like the Panama Railroad, can be trumped by an even better route. In 1869, the Panama Railroad lost traffic when the Union Pacific Railroad completed its transcontinental line directly from Omaha, Nebraska, to Sacramento, California. The new railroad meant that US transcontinental traffic could take the train 3,000 miles directly between the coasts and totally avoid the 5,000 miles of sea journey involved in the Panama route.

The Third Path between the Seas[29]

The third path between the seas would be the most ambitious and most expensive. A canal would enable large ships to pass directly between the Atlantic and Pacific with no unloading, land-based transport, and reloading of goods. The US Government had, since 1804, been interested in a canal across Central America, in part because it would allow the US Navy to move warships more quickly between the Atlantic and Pacific sides of the Western Hemisphere. To this end, President Ulysses S. Grant sent seven expeditions to Central America between 1870 and 1875.

Meanwhile, after Ferdinand De Lesseps and the French successfully completed the 105-mile Suez Canal in 1869, De Lesseps turned his attention to Panama. Backed by as many as half a million French citizen-investors, he planned to copy his Suez design by creating a sea-level canal at a projected cost of $120 million (about $2.4 billion in 2012 dollars) over a three-year period. The French started their efforts by purchasing the Panama Railroad Company for $20 million. They would use this existing transportation mode to support construction of the new mode. The canal would parallel the railroad and the railroad would move supplies to the canal construction site and carry millions of tons of earth away from the canal diggings.

De Lesseps's efforts were doomed by disease, corruption, ineptitude, and the magnitude of the project. The terrain of Panama was unlike that of the flat Suez region, and De Lesseps's sea-level canal plan called for moving mountains, literally. After five years of work, the company went bankrupt in 1889. A new French company attempted to restart the work, but it failed, too. In total, the French spent some $287 million (in 1893 dollars, equaling over $7.5 billion in 2012 dollars) on the failed effort,[30] which was more than three times what they spent on the Suez Canal. In addition, some twenty to twenty-two thousand men lost their lives in the French effort. The scandal of the misadventure led to the trials and convictions of Ferdinand De Lesseps, Charles De Lesseps (his son), Gustave Eiffel (creator of the eponymous tower), and a number of others involved in the project.

In 1902, the US Congress agreed, conditionally, to buy the assets of the failed French canal efforts for $40 million. Following complex negotiations with Colombia, Panama, and France—and after helping the Panamanian independence movement secede from Colombia—the US government completed the transaction in 1904. The United States agreed to pay the French, pay Panama, and pay for the completion of the canal but only under the condition that the United States retain control of the canal, and had certain rights (and obligations) to the newly formed government of Panama. Most important, the United States was given control of a 10-mile swath through Panama on both sides of the canal, an arrangement cemented in the Hay–Bunau–Varilla Treaty in 1903.

The American attempt to complete a canal would use some of De Lesseps's channels but not the original sea-level crossing. Instead, the new design would raise and lower ships by 85 feet to accommodate the terrain through a system of locks. The Americans also widened the canal at the request the US Navy, which wanted ample width for the largest future American battleships.[31] Each lock chamber would be 110 feet wide and 1,000 feet long. The system consists of twelve lock chambers (three double-chambered locks on each end of the canal) and 92 swinging lock gate doors weighing an average of 650 tons each.

Finally, in August 1914, the Panama Canal opened the third, and largest, path between the seas. In total, some $352 million (in 1914 dollars, equaling more than $8.5 billion in 2012 dollars) were spent, and as many as 5,600 additional lives were lost during the American completion.[32]

The canal opened in the same month that fighting in World War I began in Europe. In World War II, the canal proved its military value when the United States quickly moved warships from the Atlantic Ocean in order to restore the decimated Pacific Fleet after the Pearl Harbor attack. Owing to the original US Navy requirements, the United States could move its Essex Class carriers back and forth through the canal, as well as the largest battle ships, such as the Missouri, which transited the canal in October 1945 after hosting the Japanese surrender ceremony on Tokyo Bay.

Following rising tensions between the United States and Panama, President Carter signed the Torrijos–Carter Treaty, transferring the canal back to Panama at the end of 1999. Commercially, the canal thrived under Panamanian rule. Led by its capable chief executive Alberto Aleman Zubieta, the Panama Canal Authority (Autoridad del Canal de Panamá or ACP) improved service and installed a sophisticated pricing system based on reservations, auctions and yield management, increasing from 230 million Panama Canal tons in fiscal year 2000 to 322 million Panama Canal tons in fiscal year 2011.

Since its transfer to Panama on December 31, 1999, the Panama Canal Authority has contributed to the National Treasury B/.6,577 million in direct contributions, compared to B/.1,877 million delivered during 86 years of U.S. administration, mainly attributed to the strategically designed business model to ensure increased and sustainable financial results.

Building a Logistics Cluster

For many years, shipbuilders limited the size of most military and commercial vessels to fit the canal's dimensions—designated as *Panamax vessels*. Larger vessels built later were designated as *Post Panamax*. As the numbers of Post Panamax vessels grew, taking a large portion of international trade, Panama became concerned about the future relevance of the canal. In 2006, Panamanian voters approved an expansion project to add a new set of larger locks and double the capacity of the canal. It is scheduled for completion in 2014, 100 years after the inauguration of the original canal.[33]

Aleman and the Panamanian government understood that just charging tolls would shortchange the potential impact of the expansion, as reflected in the Panamanian 2010–2014 strategic plan. He outlined his vision to me during two conversations: the first in his ACP office in the canal administration building, an imposing 1914 structure with a breathtaking rotunda, and the other in Kuala Lumpur while keynoting an MIT conference there. In both cases, Aleman stressed that while Colón, at the Atlantic end of the canal, is already a significant transshipment port, Panama has to maximize the canal's potential by providing more services, becoming a center of logistics and related maritime value-added activities. In fact, Panama aims at nothing less than becoming the logistics hub of the continent. It is therefore investing in the development of new logistics parks as well as new terminal facilities along the canal—in particular at its Pacific and Atlantic mouths.

The Panamanian government also enacted several laws to enhance the attractiveness of Panama to companies moving their logistics operations (as well as administrative and headquarters functions) to Panama. In her Spartan office in Panama Pacifico, the developing logistics park on the canal's Pacific side, Angelica Bertoli, the lead counsel for the park's master developer, London & Regional, outlined for me several elements of the government's regulatory efforts.

For example, a 2007 law exempts foreign companies from the cap on the number of expats employed; eliminates income tax on provision of service to affiliates abroad (Panama has no tax anyway on operations outside Panama); and facilitates work permits for workers coming into Panama. Earlier, a 2004 law[34] gave companies operating in certain "special economic areas" benefits such as streamlined coordination of all government functions and licenses; no indirect taxes and waiver of most direct taxes; and longer-term work visas, including family visas. Most important, the 2004 law eased labor rules, letting companies choose their own weekly day of rest for employees, capping overtime charges, and easing the termination of labor contracts. Most logistics parks in Panama have been classified as special economic areas, including Panama Pacifico and the port of Colón, on the canal's Atlantic side.

Such efforts have borne fruit. By 2009, several multinational companies had anchored their Latin America logistics and related operations in Panama Pacifico. These companies include the 3M Company, Panamericana S.A. (the largest logistics company in Venezuela), BASF SE, Caterpillar Inc., and Dell Inc.

MEMPHIS: A CLUSTER IN THE HEARTLAND

As with the Rhine River, the Mississippi River offers both logistical opportunities and perils. The fourth longest river in the world, the

Mississippi provides access to a vast swath of the central United States. The tributaries of the Mississippi river system underlie a water transportation network that spans from Nebraska in the west to Pennsylvania in the east to northern cities such as Minneapolis and Chicago (via portage or canal). The river provides a natural channel for bulky commodities such as petroleum, corn, wheat, soybeans, cotton, wood, coal, and iron carried to and from the port of New Orleans on the Gulf of Mexico. In 1819, John Overton, James Winchester, and Andrew Jackson (who later became president of the US) founded the city of Memphis on flood-resistant bluffs above a bend in the river.[35] The founders named the city Memphis, after the ancient Egyptian capital and overseer of the mighty Nile.

A Slave to Cotton

As a result of its flood-resistant central location on the Mississippi river, Memphis became a center for cotton trading in the 1800s. Because the cotton economy of the antebellum South depended on the forced labor of large numbers of African-American slaves, Memphis also became the largest slave market in the mid-south.[36] As the town grew, so did its connections. A steamship line connected Memphis to New Orleans in 1834 and a railroad line linked Memphis to the Atlantic Ocean at Charleston, South Carolina, in 1857. In the 1850s, the city's population quintupled to 33,000 people. After the Civil War and the end of slavery, Memphis continued to trade in cotton and cotton byproducts as well as hardwood lumber and hardwood byproducts. In 1892, Memphis got its first bridge across the Mississippi, the southernmost bridge at the time. A total of eleven trunk railroad lines connected the city in all directions.[37]

Memphis's role as a barge and rail logistic hub continues to this day. It is the second largest inland port on the Mississippi and handles nineteen million tons of cargo annually. Five Class I US railroads[38] connect Memphis to 60 percent of the US population by overnight rail.[39] When trucking grew as a mode for freight transportation, Memphis became home to 400 trucking terminals. But the biggest change was the rise of a new mode of transportation: time-definite airfreight, which attracted a new breed of logistics operations to Memphis.

Fred Smith's Crazy Idea[40]

In 1965, a dashing young southern heir to a regional bus company wrote a college term paper at Yale on a new idea for a reliable nationwide airfreight package delivery service. Fred Smith proposed that the company would use a hub-and-spoke system by flying all the parcels to one location in the evening, sorting them quickly, and sending them on to their destinations in the wee hours of the morning. Smith's professor was not impressed by the paper's idea, and legend has it that he commented that "in order to have a better than a C grade, the idea has to be feasible."

In the summer of 1969, after two years with the Marine Corps in Vietnam, the 25-year-old Captain Fred Smith returned home to a hero's welcome, a new baby daughter on the way, and the tatters of his stepfather's failing aviation services business in Little Rock, Arkansas. Smith took over management of the company and looked for new opportunities, such as executive jet spare part sales and brokerage of the small executive jets that were then coming into fashion. Smith also began to think about his old term paper in response to his own experiences with horribly unreliable airfreight shipments. A shipment of airplane parts sent by the "fastest" airfreight service might arrive days or even a week late. That experience and market research showed Smith that existing airfreight companies weren't satisfying customers' needs.

Smith realized that consolidation of freight at a central hub was the way to create needed economies of scale. Any added delays in flying packages to a central hub and back were irrelevant as long as FedEx Corporation (or Federal Express, as it was known then) could meet the delivery deadline (e.g., next day 10 a.m. delivery or afternoon delivery). During an evening at the Memphis zoo, while hosting a group of supply chain management executives in April 2010, Smith mentioned that the idea of central consolidation was based on the process of check clearing by banks through a central clearing house.

In 1971, Smith started purchasing a fleet of more than two dozen Dassault Falcon business jets; working to change federal air-taxi regulations to permit the use of the Falcon; modifying Falcon jets for freight use; and seeking financing for his venture. Although

Smith started Federal Express in Little Rock, Arkansas, he soon moved the young company to Memphis in 1973 when, as legend has it, the Little Rock airport authorities refused to expand the airport because they thought neither Smith nor airfreight had any future. Memphis was also geographically better for FedEx because it was 500 miles closer to the population centers of the East Coast and would thus save fuel and time.

After several near-bankruptcy experiences, which Smith overcame by leveraging his name, his family's trust, and his shares in the company, FedEx earned a profit in July 1975. In 1978, the company went public, the stock doubled in price in four months, and the company grew. As of 2011, the Memphis FedEx super-hub spanned 500 acres of the Memphis airport, used 300 miles of internal conveyers, had 15,000 employees in the hub alone, and handled 1.5 million packages per day.[41]

Getting in the (Time) Zone

Memphis was a good choice for two key geographical reasons. First, Memphis's east-central location optimizes the distances and flight schedules from and to the East and West coasts. FedEx choreographs the flight patterns to match both the needs of customers (e.g., end-of-day pick-up and beginning-of-day delivery) and the limits of conveyances and infrastructure (e.g., speed of aircraft and airspace congestion). Airfreight from the East Coast leaves in the evening and arrives in Memphis in the early part of the night, Memphis time. In contrast, West Coast airfreight leaves in their evening and arrives much later at night. Staggered arrivals avoid congestion around the Memphis airport. The time between the last inbound arrival from the West Coast and the first outbound departures gives FedEx just enough time to sort all the packages without clogging the sorting hub.

The time zones of the United States mean that the population centers of the East Coast start their business day one hour earlier than does Memphis, while the West Coast rises two hours later. Yet Memphis is closer to the East Coast. Thus, a flight from Memphis to Washington, DC, may leave Memphis at 3:00 a.m. and get to Washington, DC, at 6:00 a.m. local time following a two-hour flight. A San Francisco-bound flight can leave Memphis also at 3:00 a.m. and arrive at 6:00 a.m. local time following a five-hour flight, because of the time zone difference. The fact that FedEx flies mostly at night means it uses the underutilized capacity of the airport during off-hours, when few passenger airliners fly.

Weather Permitting

Second, Memphis's south-central location optimizes the various threats from weather. For FedEx to live up to the company's old slogan of "When It Absolutely, Positively Has to Be There Overnight," it needs a location that rarely has severe weather. Memphis is far enough south to avoid severe winter weather, far enough north from the Gulf coast to avoid the brunt of hurricanes, and far enough east to avoid the tornado alley of the US plains. "It's one of the most weatherproof areas in the United States, untroubled by hurricanes, blizzards, or prolonged periods of icy weather," explained Tom Schmitt, chief executive officer of FedEx Global Supply Chain Services in his office on Hacks Cross Road at FedEx's headquarters in Memphis.[42]

WHAT'S IN A NAME: CLUSTERS, PARKS, AND HUBS

So far, we've examined five logistics clusters: Zaragoza, the Netherlands, Panama, Singapore, and Memphis. These clusters exemplify a broader phenomenon appearing in the economies of a wider range of communities. Later chapters explore these five clusters in greater depth and include insights gleaned from other logistics clusters such as Duisburg in Germany, Saõ Paulo in Brazil, Chongqing in China, and Chicago, Louisville, Dallas/Fort Worth, New York/New Jersey, Miami, Kansas City, and Los Angeles in the United States. Other logistics clusters not described in this book but whose lessons are used include Busan in Korea; Tianjin, Shanghai and Shenzhen in China; Dubai in the UAE; Frankfurt in Germany; and several other locations throughout the world.

Note that in some cases logistics clusters are inexorably tied to clusters of heavy industry. Thus, Detroit is an automotive cluster, but it also includes a significant number of logistics service operations, making it a logistics cluster as well. Logistics service companies locate operations in an industrial cluster in order to serve manufacturers, but in the process they make the region more attractive to other manufacturers, being part of a positive feedback loop that feeds regional growth. In other cases, the logistics cluster comes first and attracts value-added activities and manufacturing sites, as described in chapter 5.

A Fuzzy Definition

So what, exactly, is a logistics cluster? Clearly, the massive logistics complexes in Rotterdam, Singapore, and Shanghai are clusters by sheer force of their high rankings in freight traffic figures as well as the number and density of distribution centers, warehouses, logistics companies, and the logistics-related operations of manufacturers and retailers. Economists and regional scientists have long discussed the definition of what distinguishes and delineates a cluster. Different authors use different terms—such as clusters, hubs, or centers—to describe regions characterized by intensive logistics activities. Terms used by businesses around the world may be adding to the confusion. They include *logistics parks* in the United States and China, *transport centers* in Denmark, *logistics platforms* in Spain, *freight villages* in Germany ("GVZ," or Güterverkehrszentren in German), *distriparks* in India, and *logistics centers* in other places. For example, the term "Aerotropolis"[43] refers to an economic region comprising aviation-intensive businesses clustered around a major airport. Such Aerotropolis regions can be found around the Memphis Airport, Schiphol in Amsterdam, Hong Kong International Airport, Frankfurt am Main Airport, Shanghai Pudong Airport, Inchon International in Seoul, Jaipur Airport in India, Indianapolis International Airport, Louisville Airport in Kentucky, and many others.[44]

Logistics per Capita or per GDP

This book defines a cluster as a region with a very high concentration of logistics activities relative to the local population or economy. For example, Memphis, Tennessee, with only 1.3 million people, handles an astounding 3.69 million tons of airfreight per year (nearly 3 tons of airfreight per person per year). In population terms, the Memphis MSA (metropolitan statistical area) ranks around 43rd in the United States. In logistics terms, Memphis ranks number 1 in airfreight, number 3 in rail shipment, and number 4 in inland barge freight,[45] making this smallish city on the Mississippi a significant logistics cluster. Economists use more technical measures of the concentration of logistics activities. For example, de Langen[46] used a modified logistics quotient (LQ—see p. 53 in chapter 2) to map out logistics "hot spots" in Brabant in the Netherlands, based on a register of local companies. In my own work with Rivera,[47] aimed at identifying the important logistics clusters in the United States and their development path, we used a two factor criterion based first on a modified LQ criterion, known as Horizontal Cluster Logistics Quotient (HCLQ),[48] and second on an index capturing the number of logistics establishments in the region under study. This type of work identifies the locations of logistics clusters in the area of interest—be it a Dutch county or the entire United States—allowing for various analyses and insights.

Logistics clusters vary markedly in size. In some cases, a logistics cluster might be fairly compact, such the Aragón cluster with its flagship PLAZA in Zaragoza. In other cases, a logistics cluster might span a much larger, more diffuse, region. For example, logistics activities in Panama span the width of the country, extending along the canal and including ports on both the Pacific and Atlantic Oceans. Or consider the "Dutch Logistics Corridor," which stretches 150 kilometers from Rotterdam to the German border. This corridor includes, naturally, the port of Rotterdam with its terminals and concentration of logistics service providers; Brabant with its focus on sustainable logistics; Breda, along the main highways connecting the hinterlands of Amsterdam, Rotterdam, and Antwerp; and Fresh Park Venlo on the German border, which sports around 130 companies providing trading, transport, warehousing, and value-added services dealing with fresh products. A similar massive logistics cluster in southern California stretches from the Los Angeles/Long Beach Ports and the surrounding logistics infrastructure; to southeast Los Angeles in the north; Orange County and John Wayne Airport to the south; and Anaheim, and the Inland Empire to the east, including Riverside, Ontario (with its airport), and San Bernardino.

Logistics Campuses, Parks, and Clusters

To help sharpen the definition of logistics agglomerations, this book distinguishes between *logistics clusters*, *logistics parks*, and *logistics campuses*. Whereas a cluster is an amorphous agglomeration of companies and facilities with logistics-intensive operations with fuzzy borders and no central management, logistics parks are clearly defined by their ownership and geographic property boundaries. A logistics park is developed by an agency which can be a real estate investment trust (REIT), such as publicly traded ProLogis, Cache Logistics, and DCT Industrial; or by private companies such as CenterPoint Properties, Hillwood, and Watson Land Company; it can be a port/airport authority, such as the Panama Canal Authority (ACP) or the Schiphol Area Development Company (SADC); or it can be a government agency, such as Dubai Holding.

A logistics campus is a special type of a logistics park with even more tightly coordinated operations, where not only the land and the buildings are operated by a single entity, but this same entity handles all the logistics and distribution activity in the park. An example is the logistics campus of United Parcel Service Inc. (UPS) in Louisville, Kentucky, housing many customers for whom the UPS Supply Chain Solutions division manages transportation, distribution, inventory, forwarding, customs brokerage, and multiple value-added activities. Some large, multidivision enterprises may create their own campus. Steve Carter, director of transportation planning and strategy at the Target Corporation mentioned that Target sometimes colocates its own food distribution center, regional DC (for general merchandise), dot-com DC, and an import warehouse next to each other to get some campus advantages.

Thus, logistics clusters, as extended regions, often contain more than one park as well as a range of other logistics-related facilities. A cluster might have multiple logistics parks. For example, Singapore's Air Logistics Park (ALPS) next to Changi airport and Singapore's large Pasir-Panjang seaport operated by PSA International are both logistics parks within the logistics cluster of Singapore.

Similarly, while PLAZA in Zaragoza is a logistics park, the broader logistics cluster in the state of Aragón includes logistics parks in the nearby towns of Teruel, Huesca, and Fraga, as well as private logistics facilities elsewhere in the region (see p. 22 in chapter 1).

What matters to managers more than neat lines on a map are the relative costs and performance levels of logistics in, near, or far from a notional cluster of logistics facilities and infrastructure. Inside a logistics park, companies enjoy easy access to freight capacity, a choice of modes, and a range of special services. Companies sited near the park in the broader environs of the cluster also enjoy many of these advantages and probably pay less for the land, but they may experience more delays and may pay more for drayage (drayage is the short-distance movement of freight from a storage area to a long-distance conveyance). For example, inside CenterPoint Intermodal Center south of Chicago, Walmart pays on the order of $25 for draying a 40-foot container from the co-located BNSF Railway Company's intermodal yard to its warehouse. In contrast, draying that container to locations outside the park might cost $150. Parks might also offer special amenities within their boundaries, such as roads that can handle over-weight cargo (see also the discussion of terminal infrastructure on p. 148 in chapter 6), and various shared services (e.g., employee training).

Clusters can also transcend political or jurisdictional boundaries. For example, Memphis's Logistics Council oversees a region of some sixteen counties spanning three states in its planning efforts. This multicounty, multistate agglomeration defines the Memphis cluster in terms of critical infrastructure, the span of logistics companies, and the regional labor force that works in logistics. Thus, the boundaries of most clusters remain fuzzy.

NATURAL ADVANTAGES

The histories of these logistics clusters illustrate the strong contribution of natural geographic and climatic factors to the development of logistics. Such factors have led, over the years, to a culture and expertise in trading and logistics. Four natural geographic factors contribute to logistics cluster formation.

The Middle Ground

Places such as Memphis, Singapore, Chicago, and Zaragoza sit in the geographic middle between major regions of supply and major regions of demand and become, in turn, major centers for logistics activity. When a high volume of goods transships through a certain region, that region becomes a natural location for warehouses, consolidation/deconsolidation terminals, and transportation carrier operations. Naturally, the geography of population centers, placement of natural resources, and geography-influenced routing of transportation all affect what constitutes the middle.

Geographic Cost Cuts and Shortcuts

Managers in manufacturing, retail, and distribution typically consider logistics costs as a necessary evil. While all corporate functions are subject to cost pressures, functions such as engineering and manufacturing contribute to a product's form and function; marketing and sales contribute to branding and revenue; and finance helps with raising funds and managing money. While logistics management contributes directly to customer service and sales, its importance has not traditionally been recognized, and many senior executives see transportation and logistics as a cost to be minimized. Some geographic locations, such as the port of Rotterdam and navigable rivers like the Rhine and the Mississippi, offer transportation cost advantages. Chicago sits at the edge of the Great Lakes, which allows water transportation to the East Coast and Europe from America's hinterland. Natural or artificial geographic shortcuts, like the Malacca Straits or the Panama Canal, respectively, attract a high volume of shipments. Places situated along the shortest route, such as Singapore or Panama City, represent natural locations to consolidate shipments, change between regional carriers, locate warehouses, or have refueling and repair depots.

Natural Geographic Boundaries between Modes

Trucks and rail can carry goods only so far. Long-distance global trade requires crossing the oceans by ship or aircraft. Seaports such as Singapore, Rotterdam, and Los Angeles/Long Beach create a natural nexus where continent-crossing transportation (such as truck and rail) terminates and ocean-crossing transportation begins. The modal exchange at airports is typically from airplanes to trucks and vice versa. While some airports serve as transshipment hubs, the first and last leg of any air shipment requires a truck to haul the cargo between the plant or warehouse and the airport. Similarly, intermodal yards are terminals where truck and rail transportation systems interchange loads. One of the roles of distribution centers and freight yards at terminals is to match load sizes across different conveyances. In addition, many of these terminals involve export/import and therefore include government agencies to handle the formalities of international trade, including export controls, import inspections, customs payments, and free trade zones.

Weather Advantages = Reliability Advantages

Modern-day logistics depends on the absence of adverse weather conditions, especially extreme weather. Locations such as Memphis, Los Angeles, and Singapore derive some advantage by being out of reach of most major types of dangerous weather like hurricanes, tornados, and snowstorms. Weather delays aren't acceptable in a world that depends on just-in-time deliveries for manufacturers, retailers, and distributors. Thus, logistics hubs located in good weather locations offer one of the performance elements shippers need most—reliability. (The shippers in a cluster include both beneficial freight owners [BFOs] such as manufacturers, distributors, and retailers running their own logistics operations, as well as third party logistics providers, who manage logistics on behalf of their customers, who are BFOs.)

Nature vs. Nurture

Geography plays a significant role in cluster formation, but the histories of these clusters show that natural factors alone can't explain everything. Many of the clusters discussed in this book have geographic advantages that apply to a broad region, rather than to a specific town or unique point on the map. Rotterdam wasn't the only Dutch city between the Rhine and the North Sea. Memphis wasn't the only town on the Mississippi that's beyond the normal reach of snowstorms and hurricanes. Similarly, Singapore might easily have lost to other Malaysian trading centers in the Malacca Straits, such as Melaka or Penang.[49] The Panama Canal might have been the Nicaragua Canal. Although a region's natural attributes (land forms, waterways, and climate) might make an area attractive for logistics operations, the specific town, county, or country that takes the lead in logistics is not preordained. Visionary investments in ports, canals, terminals, roads, and new businesses can turn a particular locale in a logistically favorable region into a thriving cluster. For example, FedEx's move to Memphis and UPS's establishment of its hub in Louisville, Kentucky, helped these locales grow as clusters of logistics activity.

Nor do geographic advantages ensure a logistic cluster's success in perpetuity. To this day, a Nicaraguan canal remains under serious consideration. Such a canal would reduce the distance between Los Angeles and New York City by about 500 miles, or one day of vessel travel. Similarly, Thailand might build a canal across the Kra Isthmus, attracting much of the ship traffic that now goes to Singapore. And the expansion of the Panama Canal, mentioned above, threatens US West Coast ports as the enlarged canal would enable more containers to travel on larger, more efficient ocean freighters directly to the East Coast. Such changes may create new logistics clusters on the East Coast and partially reduce the logistics intensity of activities in the western US ports and on the railroads carrying containers from the West Coast to the large clusters in Chicago, Kansas City, Memphis, and Dallas/Ft. Worth.

Natural geographic features might explain why some areas have more logistics activities than others, and why they may be initially attractive for transportation and logistics developments. But someone must still make investments in infrastructure, train the workers, lobby for favorable regulations, and attract companies to the area to support cluster formation. In a conference call organized by Bill Marrin, managing director of the World 50 Organization, several senior logistics executives responded to my questions regarding joint lobbying efforts. Randy Eck, director of global transportation and logistics outsourcing at Intel Corporation, gave an example, "We're spending a significant amount of time [with the government] on how to get products in and out of Vietnam as quickly and at as low cost as possible." Eck added, "[We collaborate] with anybody in the area that we can get to come out. I mean we'll pull in all our suppliers and work with them as much as we possibly can because there's strength in numbers." His comments were echoed by Howard Smith, senior vice president of global supply chain operations of the Ralph Lauren Corporation and Les Woch, director of global logistics at Mars Chocolate, who added more examples of joint lobbying of regional and national governments throughout the world.

4

OPERATIONAL ADVANTAGES

I asked logistics and supply chain management executives around the world why their companies picked a particular region for their operations—"why Singapore?" or "why Memphis?" Many of the answers mentioned computerized network analysis. Using a database of supply and demand locations, integer-programming-based computer models fed with expected product flows and costs, as well as real estate rents, tax regimes, and other data, would spit out "optimal" regions for locations of distribution activities. Such models, though, are typically incapable of finding real business-optimal solutions because of both their mathematical shortcomings and the inherent forecasting challenges.[1] Other answers noted a location's natural geographic advantages, such as a central location, river accessibility, or port proximity, some of which would be identified by the network models while others would be "obvious."[2] Yet those weren't the only reasons or the most interesting ones. Much of the rest of the book delves into the deeper reasons; they explain why logistics clusters can thrive and grow and therefore why certain locations are more attractive than others.

Just like industrial clusters, logistics clusters enjoy certain advantages deriving from the concentration of similar activities. In addition, however, these clusters enjoy unique operational advantages. Many of these advantages are rooted in the interchangeability of transportation and logistics assets. Unlike suppliers of most manufactured products, suppliers of transportation services offer nearly interchangeable services. The content of the packages going through the UPS Worldport, or loaded into a maritime container in a manufacturing plant in Shenzhen, are varied and not interchangeable. In contrast, the services performed on the package—such as the picking, sorting, loading, transporting, unloading, and delivery operations—are identical, regardless of what the package contains. Consequently, transportation and logistics assets can handle packages containing a large variety of goods in a standard manner. Furthermore, rail cars, containers, trailers, barges, and airplanes all come in standardized sizes and capacities, dictated by regulations, international standards, or prevailing conveyance designs. Thus capacities, reach, and velocities are similar regardless of the company logo on the tractor's door, ocean shipping container side, or airplane tail.

There are two categories of operational advantages that logistics clusters can offer their tenants over logistics facilities not located within a cluster. First, when transportation carriers move freight between areas that generate or absorb large amounts of freight—read logistics clusters—the technology and cost structure of transportation movements can create lower costs and better service. Carriers can then offer these lower costs and better service to the shippers in the cluster, attracting even more shippers, causing the cluster to grow and making the carriers even more efficient. Second, when distribution operations are in close proximity to each other, as they are in logistics clusters, they can enhance each other's performance as a result of the sharing of resources and the larger range of available warehouse space. These performance enhancements grow with the size of the cluster. Both of these factors create a positive feedback loop: a reciprocal reinforcing dynamic that makes the cluster more attractive as it grows, leading to further growth.

TRANSPORTATION ECONOMICS

Some of the most important drivers of cluster growth arise from the economics of transportation. Transportation services can be classified into *direct operations* (DO) and *consolidated operations* (CO). In direct operations, a carrier takes a shipment directly from the pick-up location to the delivery location with one conveyance carrying only that one shipment between the two locations. In consolidated operations, a carrier picks up multiple shipments in a local region, consolidates them to share a larger conveyance for the trip toward the destination, and then makes multiple deliveries in the destination region. On the way, each consolidated shipment may be unloaded and loaded to different conveyances several times. With DO, the shipment travels the shortest possible distance between origin and destination with no intermediate stops; with CO the shipment takes a more circuitous route with intermediate stops and handling. With DO, the shipment bears the full cost of the conveyance mobement for that journey; with CO, the shipment shares the costs of the conveyances involved in the trip with other shipments.

A similar dichotomy exists with passenger transportation. A taxi cab is a DO carrier; it takes a "load" directly from origin to destination, and the passenger pays the full cost of the trip. In contrast, passengers of a mass transit system share the space in the bus, trolley, or subway car with each paying a small portion of the costs—the per passenger fare. Transit passengers may take multiple buses or trains with different groups of passengers as they transfer in hub stations one or more times on their journey from origin to destination. Note that transit passengers, like CO shipments, undergo two types of consolidation: in-vehicle, while sharing a conveyance with others, and geographical consolidation, changing conveyances in a terminal.

Most flyers are painfully familiar with the hub-and-spoke system by which airlines consolidate and deconsolidate people, giving rise to the saying about the busiest airport in the world: "When I die, I don't know if I'll go to heaven or hell, but I know I'll change planes in Atlanta."[3]

Both DO and CO operations in and out of logistics clusters are more efficient as the cluster grows, because of the economics of transportation.

Utilization: Empty Costs as Much as Full

Transportation assets cost almost the same to operate empty as they do to operate fully loaded. Carriers must cover a long list of costs that vary little with the amount of freight carried by the conveyance. Load-independent cost factors such as driver wages, equipment depreciation, financing, administration, compliance and insurance amount to 70 percent of the cost of driving a truck (fuel being most of the other 30 percent).[4] Research on the energy efficiency of trucks shows that even the fuel costs don't change much between empty and full trucks, as a result of cargo-independent factors such as aerodynamic drag, engine losses, and the mass of the empty truck. An empty truck trip still consumes about three-fourths of the fuel of a fully loaded one.[5] Interestingly, tire wear—another important cost factor—is worse when a truck is driven empty.

Even toll payments are independent of load—and not only on highways. When crossing the Panama Canal, for example, vessels pay based on their container *capacity*, with ballast paying only 20 percent less than full containers and passenger vessels paying similarly 80 percent of the rate for an empty berth compared to an occupied one. Furthermore, on-deck containers on "other" vessels (not dedicated container vessels), pay the same toll per container whether empty or full. The minimal cost difference between partial and fully loaded conveyances motivates carriers to fill conveyances and prompts shippers to design operations that generate efficient full loads (or wait at origin points until they have a full load).

The Larger the Vessel, the Lower the Freight Cost

Regardless of the type of service, the cost of operating a transportation conveyance grows less than proportionally with the size of the vehicle. In other words, larger full vehicles have a lower cost per ton-mile hauled than do smaller full vehicles. For this reason, carriers have steadily shifted to larger conveyances over the years. For example, fifty years ago, truck trailers in the United States were 32 feet long. But over the ensuing decades, they grew to 35, 40, 42, 48, and, eventually, 53 feet long. At the same time, trucking companies developed "road trains" with one tractor towing two, three, or even as many as six trailers in some specialized road trains in Australia.[6] These changes enable one driver and one tractor to pull ever-increasing amounts of freight for lower cost per ton-mile.

Similarly, the growing size of conveyances is evident in the history of rail cars, locomotives, and length of trains. The BNSF, for example, sends trains that are almost two miles long from the

Los Angeles area (mostly originating at the Los Angeles and Long Beach ports) to Chicago's logistics parks.

Airfreight exhibits the same pattern. FedEx made its first deliveries using the Dassault Falcon 20, an executive jet carrying a meager 6,500 pounds of airfreight—that's the equivalent of about 1/7th of a standard full truckload. In 1977, FedEx made the jump to the much larger and more efficient Boeing 727s (carrying 42,000 pounds). Today, FedEx flies planes as large as the Boeing 777F lifting loads of up to 226,000 pounds. Similarly, UPS Airlines now owns nothing smaller than a Boeing 757 (holding up to 87,700 pounds) and also flies Boeing 747 freighters, carrying up to 270,000 pounds. At the Louisville airport, UPS's air freighters tower over the small Embraer regional jets and Boeing 737s that bring people to and from the small city of Louisville.

In ocean shipping, the very first makeshift container ship in 1956 held only 58 containers. Size grew quickly with the first purpose-built container ship carrying 610 containers in 1960. Sizes further increased to about 1,500 containers in 1969, 3,000 containers in 1972[7] and 4,000 containers in 1981. Size growth slowed for a decade—container ships didn't break the 4,500 containers barrier until 1988 as a result of the size limits of the Panama Canal.[8] Ultimately, the volume of freight between pairs of major ports with no Panama Canal transits, such as Singapore to Rotterdam, or Shanghai to Los Angeles/Long Beach, justified building massive ships. A trans-Pacific journey on a fully loaded post-Panamax ship with capacity of 8,000 twenty-foot equivalent units ("TEUs") containers costs about $200 a container less than it does on a 4,000-TEU, loaded canal-compatible Panamax vessel.[9] In 2006, Denmark's Maersk Line, the largest container shipping carrier in the world, put in service the Emma Maersk with a capacity of about 14,000 TEUs; as of 2010, almost 20 percent of the container fleet was post-Panamax size and 5 percent was larger than 8,000 TEU.[10] In 2011, Maersk ordered new 18,000 TEU container ships,[11] offering the lowest cost per container moved (see also p. 282 in chapter 10).

Container ships aren't the only vessels creating economies of scale by growing to gargantuan proportions. The MS *Vale Brasil*, which is part of a fleet of the largest bulk carriers in the world, is

362 meters long and 65 meters wide, rides 14.5 meters deep, and can carry enough iron ore to make three Eiffel Towers.[12] The ship is so large that, when fully loaded, it can dock at only a few ports in the world and then only during high tide.[13] About ten times a year, the *Vale Brasil* picks up a massive load of iron ore at Ponta da Madeira in Brazil for delivery to Rotterdam. In Rotterdam, the ore is transshipped on barges to Germany's Ruhr-region steel mills.

These cost-scaling factors hold across modes, too. High-capacity modes such as rail, barges, and ocean shipping cost progressively less per ton-mile than do small-capacity modes such as trucking. A gallon of fuel moves one ton of cargo about 60 miles by truck, 202 miles by rail, and 514 miles by barge.[14] Larger capacity modes also offer labor cost advantages in terms of how much cargo a single driver, locomotive engineer, or ship's crew can handle. But taking advantage of these cost savings requires filling much larger conveyances. A full truck can carry as much as 48,000 pounds in one trailer, a single rail car can carry 200,000 pounds, a single barge can hold 3.5 million pounds, and the largest ocean-going bulk freighters, the *Vale Brasil* and its sister ships (*Vale China*, *Vale Italia*, *Vale Rio de Janeiro*, and *Vale Beijing*) can carry nearly 800 million pounds each.

The cost advantages of larger conveyances motivate shippers to consolidate their activities in order to create shipping scale. Likewise, operators of these large conveyances gravitate to locations where they can find adequate volumes of freight to fill their behemoth conveyances. Both of these trends feed the growth of logistics clusters. Moreover, as discussed in chapter 6, such clusters can justify the investment in the development of the high-capacity infrastructure and handling equipment needed to service large conveyances.

Direct vs. Consolidated Transportation Operations

If a shipper has enough freight from a particular origin to a particular destination on a particular day to fill a conveyance, say a trailer, then the shipper will contract with a carrier to haul that full trailer directly from the origin to the destination in a DO operation using a single vehicle. Carriers that predominantly offer DO services include: truckload motor carriage, unit trains, and charter operations (in all modes of transportation). The shipper pays, in this case, the full cost for the movement of the conveyances regardless of how much the shipment weighs or what fraction of the conveyance is full.

If the shipper does not have enough freight going to a particular destination to fill the conveyance, does not wish to pay the full price for direct operations with a partially filled conveyance, and/or cannot wait for more orders to the same destination to materialize because of time commitments to the customer, then the shipper will use a CO carrier who consolidates other small shipments into full-conveyance loads. Examples of CO carriers include: less-than-truckload (LTL) motor carriers, parcel delivery carriers, postal services, freight airlines, ocean carriers, barge operators, and railroads.

In a typical LTL motor carrier operation (known as "groupage" operations in Europe), the carrier dispatches a truck from a local city terminal to collect shipments from shippers' docks and bring them back to the local terminal. There, the carrier sorts the shipments by destination and consolidates multiple shipments bound for destinations in the same general direction. The carrier then hauls the consolidated shipments in full trucks through a system of main terminals ("hubs" or "break bulk terminals") to the destination local terminal. At each hub, the carrier deconsolidates inbound loads and reconsolidates them into outbound loads. Finally, at the local destination terminal, the carrier sorts the incoming shipments and loads them onto local trucks for delivery to the various customers using routes that group together nearby customers.

In a typical freight train service, the railroad consolidates and deconsolidates rail cars into complete trains. Shippers load rail cars staged on sidings, and railroad locomotives then pull the cars to a local classification yard where the railroad groups cars heading in the same general direction to build a long train. Locomotives pull the train to the next classification yard on the way, where the railroad separates the individual cars and regroups them into subsequent trains. The operation repeats until the rail car reaches the local yard closest to the destination, where a locomotive will drop the car at the consignee's yard. In contrast, the DO version of rail is the unit train, in which an entire train of cars moves from a single origin to a destination without any midway car classification operation.

Maritime carriers use a similar process of moving containers to ports on rail, truck, or barge and then loading them onto a container ship that will take them toward the destination. In many ports, short sea shipping and inland waterways bring containers to larger ports and take collections to smaller ports as part of consolidated operations. At the final destination port, carriers move containers by truck, rail, or barge to inland destinations. Maritime carriers also offer break bulk services for non-containerized freight; such movements are generally (but not always) conducted in DO mode due to the inefficiency involved in unloading and reloading non-containerized cargo.

Barges are also designed to operate in a CO mode. Along the Mississippi or the Ohio River one often sees 1,000-foot-long assemblies of 15 to 50 tightly lashed barges heaped with coal, gravel, and other bulk commodities trundling up and down the river. At the back of this block of barges, a 4,500 horsepower, triple-screw towboat churns the waters, pushing the consolidated shipment. The flotilla stops along river ports, drops some barges, and adds others to the flotilla as it travels up and down the river.

CO operations involve circuitous routing—going through the break bulk terminals—and the added cost of unloading the inbound conveyance, sorting shipments, and loading the outbound conveyance at these terminals. Yet, for small shipments, CO costs less than DO because the conveyance costs are shared across the shipments. Furthermore, typical CO services operate on a fixed schedule (mostly daily for LTL), offering frequent pickup and delivery options.

ADVANTAGES OF CLUSTERS FOR CONSOLIDATED OPERATIONS

CO carrier hubs offer natural locations for logistics clusters to develop. Such hubs may be anchored around the operations of specific carriers, such as the air hubs of FedEx in Memphis, UPS in Louisville, DHL in Leipzig/Halle, or TNT in Liège.[15] They can also be anchored around large ports—such as Singapore, Hong Kong,

Rotterdam, Antwerp, Hamburg, Dubai, New York/New Jersey, and Los Angeles/Long Beach—and around significant railroad hubs, such as Chicago and Kansas City in the United States, Duisburg in Germany, Saõ Paulo in Brazil, and Birmingham in the United Kingdom. Naturally, many central locations with good highway accessibility have large LTL break bulk terminals.

Tenants in logistics clusters located where no carrier has a hub operation or not at a major port or airport will also see benefits when using CO carriers. These benefits are rooted in frequency, the carrier's load plan, and the pickup and delivery portions of the service.

Frequency Advantages for Shippers: The Sooner the Better

While DO services take place "on demand" (recall the taxi analogy), CO are, for the most part, scheduled (recall the city bus or passenger airline analogy). CO activities typically follow a schedule because the system depends on coordination between freight coming into a terminal and freight moving out. A familiar analogy here is the "bank" of inbound and outbound flights that passenger airlines operate at their hubs, ensuring that outbound flights leave shortly after inbound flights come in.

More freight originating from and destined to a location means higher frequency of transportation service. Such higher frequency implies higher levels of service, because shipments do not have to wait long for the next scheduled departure or arrival. Higher frequencies of transportation services are particularly evident around transportation hubs. While many origin-destination pairs may not have enough volume between them for frequent direct transportation service, a hub-and-spoke system consolidates many different point-to-point pairs to provide a high frequency through the hub. Consequently, many shippers are drawn to transportation carriers' hub locations, contributing to the development of a logistics clusters there.

Advantages of Bypassing Intermediate Terminals

Shipping to and from large clusters by CO carriers can be more efficient than shipping between areas that do not have a lot of traffic.

This is due to more direct routing of loads by the carrier. For example, instead of sending LTL shipments from the local terminal to the next main terminal in the network (and from there through the network of intermediate terminals to the destination—unloading, sorting and reloading at every terminal), large outbound volumes from a cluster allow greater aggregation and increased use of direct routes to more distant terminals in the system. In fact, if the volumes are large enough, shipments can be sent directly from the originating local terminal to the destination local terminal, bypassing several break bulk operations on the way.

This effect is not unique to LTL trucking but rather is applicable to all CO carriers. Unlike the usual train service, which requires moving the trains through classification yards for the car disassembly/assembly operation, movements between large logistics clusters such as the western ports in Los Angeles/Long Beach or Seattle/Tacoma, and the large logistics clusters in Chicago, Kansas City, Dallas, or Memphis can employ long trains assembled in a western port and traveling to the Midwest cluster without stopping for car classification at any intermediate railroad yard.

The same effect takes place with barges that can travel in large, unimpeded trips from origin to destination, when going from and to a logistics cluster. Places like Rotterdam and Memphis have sufficient scale not only to support local barge and tow operators, but to make direct barge flotillas to distant destinations.

Reducing the numbers of intermediate consolidation/deconsolidation steps for LTL, rail, and barge operations lowers the transportation cost. Moreover, it improves the service by: (i) shrinking the total time in transit from origin to destination (each break bulk operation in a main LTL terminal can add a day to the service time), and (ii) reducing the damage and sorting/routing errors associated with freight handling at terminals.

Density Advantages of Pickup/Delivery for Carriers

LTL carriers operate a system of local terminals that are responsible for picking up and delivering freight from and to shippers' docks. From the local terminals, the freight enters the system of break bulk terminals that route and move each shipment to its destination. The pick-up and delivery operations are typically performed by small trucks running "milk runs"—tours through several shippers' docks—starting and ending at the local terminals. In many ways, this "last mile" operation is the most expensive part of the service offered by CO carriers (per ton-mile).

Logistics clusters and parks contain many shippers and consignees in close proximity to each other. Consequently, distances between stops are shorter than they would be if shippers' docks were spread out over a large nonclustered area, increasing the efficiency of pick-up and delivery tours.

This phenomenon is particularly evident in trucking operations, but it affects all modes because regardless of the "trunk" mode of CO services, the pick-up from and delivery to a shipper's dock is typically made by a motor carrier.

ADVANTAGES OF CLUSTERS FOR DIRECT OPERATIONS

DO transportation is typically preferred by shippers because it offers shorter travel times, less chance of misrouting, and a lower chance of handling damage to the shipment. The challenge for shippers is to accumulate enough freight to fill a conveyance to make direct operations economical. It should be noted that because of the circuitous routing and extra handling involved in CO services, a conveyance does not need to be full in order to be cost effective in comparison to a CO service. For example, even shipments as small as 12,000 or 15,000 pounds sent in a truck that can hold 40,000 pounds may be less expensive to send using a truckload carrier, compared to using LTL. Such underutilization creates opportunities for collaboration between shippers in a cluster, sharing conveyances to reduce costs.

The Conveyance Cycle

Freight flows are not balanced, in the sense that some regions generate more outgoing flows by certain modes of transportation (e.g., mines and factories) while others absorb more incoming flows (e.g., major consumer population centers). Similarly, the trade imbalance between China and the United States means that cargo vessels laden with full containers move from Chinese ports to US ports while little freight moves from the United States to China. However, carriers must somehow get both vessels and containers back in order to reload them. The same phenomenon exists in every mode of transportation. For example, while there is freight that moves on trucks from the US Midwest into Florida, very little moves back on trucks, creating a flow imbalance. Yet the trucks have to get back to regions where they can be loaded again—thus after dropping one load, they travel empty to pick up the next load. As a result, trucks, rail cars, ships, airplanes, and containers keep moving in an endless sequence of loaded-empty-loaded-empty trips, as conveyances are repositioned for the next loaded move following each delivery.

Carriers naturally try to minimize the empty movements because those movements do not earn any revenue. Rather than move empty conveyances back to the point of origin, DO carriers look for the next load at a point close to the last delivery place in order to minimize the length of the empty move. While all carriers are affected by flow imbalance, this is less of an issue for CO carriers since they operate a fix network in which the vehicles are scheduled according to a predetermined plan.

In fact, the empty miles percentage is one of the metrics by which truckload companies are measured. For example, the empty miles percentage of Werner Enterprises, the fourth largest truckload carrier in the United States, ranged from 11.4 percent to 13.5 percent over the five-year period of 2006 to 2010, with the lowest figure for 2010 as the economy in the United States was coming out of the recession.[16] The largest truckload carrier, Swift Transportation, reported 13.24 percent in 2009 and 12.1 percent in 2010, as the economy improved.[17] Private fleets—those owned by shippers and typically dedicated to that shipper's operations—report empty-miles figures that are typically twice those of common carriers such as Werner and Swift because private fleets only transport that single shipper's loads and thus have fewer reloading opportunities.[18]

Empty miles for motor carriers in Europe are significantly higher. An estimated 25 percent of all freight vehicles in Europe run empty and over 50 percent run with only partial loads.[19] Some of this is the result of structural flow imbalances, while the rest may be attributed to inefficient operations. The high percentage of empty miles in Europe is becoming a focus of green efforts to reduce the carbon footprint of trucking operations.

Of course, instead of moving empty, a conveyance can wait after delivery until another load materializes in the destination area. An idle conveyance, however, also costs money—a 747 freighter sitting on the ground can consume $1,500–$2,000 per hour in finance charges alone,[20] and that doesn't include the cost of a parking space at an airport or the various maintenance and inspection activities required to keep the aircraft in air-worthy condition. Idle trucks, trains, and ships also accumulate costs and represent lost opportunity for revenues.

To maximize the fraction of revenue (loaded) movements, carriers need to minimize the conveyances' idle time and empty movements. Such objectives create an impetus for DO carriers to gravitate to logistics clusters. Delivering freight into a logistics cluster means that there is a high likelihood that there will be a follow-on load going out of the cluster. This is due both to the large number of logistics operators in such a cluster and to the interchangeable nature of freight flows described in the introduction to this chapter.

In addition, DO carriers, like truckload motor carriers, also need terminals, but unlike LTL carriers, these are not consolidation terminals but operational bases for maintenance and driver domiciles. Locating such bases in a logistics cluster, which is served frequently by the carrier's vehicles, makes economic sense. Doing so, however, means that trucks have to be routed to the cluster location every so often, increasing the availability of trucks in the cluster and, in some cases, lowering inbound and outbound rates.

Horizontal Collaboration to Share a Conveyance

SC Johnson & Son Inc. is a manufacturer of home cleaning, pest control, air care, home storage, and auto care products, with annual sales of $9 billion. The Energizer Battery Company is the largest manufacturer of batteries in the United States, with more than $4 billion in sales. Michael Murphy, director of customer supply chain for SC Johnson, described during a 2011 conference in Atlanta, how colocation helps the two companies collaborate in more efficient distribution.

Both companies have distribution centers in Fairburn, Georgia, which is part of the Atlanta logistics cluster. Both companies sell to some of the same retail chain customers. One such shared customer is CVS Caremark Corporation, the giant health, beauty and household goods retailer. CVS has a distribution center in Vero Beach, Florida, a little over 500 miles from Fairburn. Both SC Johnson and Energizer approached CVS about trying to optimize their distribution operations through collaboration and coordination between the two of them and CVS. CVS, in turn, agreed to an experiment in the Vero Beach distribution center.

The essence of the collaborative effort was to consolidate loads for more efficient transportation using DO trucking. Prior to the project, SC Johnson shipped one trailer-load per week from its Fairburn distribution center to the Vero Beach CVS DC, averaging 20,000 pounds of freight per shipment with a truckload carrier. Energizer shipped an average of 9,000 pounds each week to the Vero Beach distribution center using an LTL carrier. Because both shipments could easily fit in one 40,000 lb-capacity trailer, the companies sought to consolidate their loads and share the costs of a single truckload shipment a week, keeping the same service frequency from Fairburn to Vero Beach.

CVS agreed to modify its order system so both SC Johnson and Energizer would get the order for shipping on the same day and have a single delivery appointment at the Vero Beach DC. Once CVS releases the order, a truckload carrier picks up at the SC Johnson facility, goes to the Energizer facility next door to pick up its shipment and drives the 500 miles to deliver the combined load to the CVS facility. Naturally, the proximity of SC Johnson and Energizer in the same location in Fairburn enabled the smooth planning and execution of the new process.

The results of this collaboration created multiple improvements. Both shippers reduced their transportation costs and improved their carbon footprint. Energizer improved its on-time delivery and reduced shortages and damage by avoiding break bulk LTL operations. SC Johnson reduced its transportation costs without affecting its customer service. CVS also enjoyed positive impacts including more predictable lead time and increased inbound dock efficiency resulting from the reduced number of inbound trucks.

The pilot program was so successful that SC Johnson then expanded the program to collaborate with other manufacturers located near its distribution centers in Georgia and Pennsylvania for deliveries to CVS distribution centers in the Southeast and Northeast of the United States. It was also expected to launch collaborative efforts with more manufacturers and more retailers.

Other companies in other clusters have similar initiatives. Over lunch in a garden restaurant in Rotterdam, Patrick Haex and Rene Buck of Buck Consultants International (BCI) shared with me the example of three Scandinavian companies in the forest and paper products business. StoraEnso, Norske Skog, and UPM consolidated their inbound flows on a single, dedicated, short sea-lane vessel. The vessel picks up inbound material in Sweden and Finland for delivery on a biweekly schedule into the Antwerp port and logistics cluster, where the three companies have distribution centers. By collaborating, the companies reduced their transportation and handling costs, and improved service through more frequent and reliable replenishments of the Antwerp distribution centers.

In another European example described by BCI, two tire manufacturers, Bridgestone and Continental, decided to comanage their outbound distribution in order to better compete with Michelin, the market leader. To this end, the companies built an "H-shaped" joint regional distribution center outside Orleans, France, with each company occupying one side of the H. They used the middle bar of the H to stage and handle the combined outbound shipments.[21] The collaborative DC operation resulted in lower costs and more frequent service to the dealers than would have been possible with each company operating independently.

A small Belgian company called Tri-Vizor bills itself as "the world's first orchestrator of horizontal collaboration." Its value proposition is to facilitate such "car pools for cargo." Its first project was to coordinate the shipments of two healthcare manufacturers: Baxter International and UCB Healthcare. In a fashion similar to the collaboration between SC Johnson and Energizer, the two pharmaceutical companies combined their TL and LTL shipments from Belgium to Romania into a single shipment to the Genk rail yard and from there onto a train to Oradea, Romania, from which the shipments were distributed to various Romanian cities.

The bigger a logistics cluster gets, with more shippers sending and receiving shipments to and from more places, the higher the likelihood and greater the ease of shipper-shipper ("horizontal") collaborations.

Shipment Properties: Intermingling Heavy and Light

Look inside a shipping container, an air freighter, or a fully loaded truck operating in a DO mode, and you might be surprised to see that it's half empty. As mentioned in chapter 1 (see p. 11), dense freight causes the conveyance to "weigh-out," while light objects typically cause the conveyance to "cube-out."

This dual definition of capacity creates another type of conveyance-sharing opportunity in a logistics cluster based on intermingling diverse types of cargo—some from distributors of dense goods and other cargo from distributors of light goods. Naturally, this can be economical only when the two types of freight share proximity of origins and proximity of destination, as is likely to happen in a movement from, to, and between logistics clusters.

This type of opportunity is more than theoretical. Patrick Haex and Rene Buck recounted several case studies concerning pairs of Dutch shippers that consolidate heavy bottles of canned goods with lightweight paper products. Specifically they mentioned Hero Netherland B.V.,[22] a beverages and packaged food company, collaborating with SCA Packaging in joint transport. Hero has dense and heavy shipments, while SCA's shipments are light and loose. Together, the combined shipments can simultaneously meet the weight and volume capacity of the conveyances for maximum efficiency.

The example in chapter 1 of Caladero mixing heavy pallets of fish with fluffy mohair yarn also falls into this category. As the diversity of customers increases in a cluster, the variety of cargos increases, too, leading to more opportunities like this.

THE ADVANTAGE OF MULTIPLE CARRIERS

One of the advantages of any industrial cluster is that it induces suppliers to locate close to their customers. The availability of large volumes of freight in logistics clusters leads transportation carriers to serve the cluster and even locate operations centers and terminals there. The presence of 400 trucking companies in Memphis attests to carriers' desire to locate operations where they can find freight. In Aragón, the number of commercial trucks registered increased from 7,529 in 2002 to 19,557 in 2007, as the PLAZA logistics park and the other, smaller parks developed and shippers moved into the Aragón cluster, attracting motor carriers to the area.

The presence of many transportation carriers in a cluster leads to a wide range of services, as well as to competitive and stable pricing. Both of these factors improve with the size of a cluster.

Increased Reach and Scope

As more shippers move into a cluster, more carriers join them to offer a variety of transportation services. In order to create some differentiation and serve their customers better, these transportation companies frequently offer new services as they come in, be it service to new destinations that were not served from the cluster before, nonstop service to destinations that formerly required going through a consolidation hub, or new types of services, such as temperature-controlled transportation and hazardous material transportation.

Every new service offered by logistics providers in a cluster immediately increases the range of services available to all existing shippers and logistics service providers in that cluster. Shippers can then leverage the new logistics services to offer new or improved service to their customers. A growing range of logistics services enables a growing range of shipper services and performance levels.

Competitive Transportation Offerings

Having a large number of transportation carriers serving a cluster increases competition among them, leading to lower prices to and from the cluster. Competition among transportation carriers in logistics clusters is stronger compared to competition among suppliers in other types of economic clusters, because of the minimal differentiation between transportation service providers.

But the competition is not limited to services offered between carriers of the same mode and similar types of services and equipment. It also takes place between modes of transportation. While walking me through his hot and noisy steel plant, its floors covered with fine steel dust, Thad Solomon, general manager of NUCOR's plant in Memphis, explained the cost advantages of the Memphis cluster. These cost advantages arose, he said, because "we have options, we have competition, and it allows us to reach farther out there." Both the multiple modes (barge, rail, and truck) and the very large number of carriers create a basis for cost-competitive transportation. "So that component of access to transportation and access to competitive logistics was absolutely key to our decision to come here," Solomon said.

Similarly, Cargill's international business development manager, Jon Thompson, and its commercial operations manager, Jeffrey Rott, explained the value of a multimodal location when they said that Cargill's plant in Memphis was built there because of access to both rail and river transportation. Cargill brings in corn to its Memphis plant, about half by rail and half by barge, while shipping sweetener and other corn byproducts two-thirds by rail and one-third by truck, with a small amount sent on specially designed barges. These amounts fluctuate so that Cargill can achieve the best combination of cost and service under all conditions. "Sometimes the river is cheaper and sometimes the rail is cheaper. This plant cannot survive on 100 percent of either one," Thompson told me.

A related argument comes into play with facilities and conveyances that are specialized in a certain type of operation but can also be used for another. Consider, for example "cold chains." Whereas most freight tolerates a wide range of temperatures, some freight requires more careful handling. Caladero's fish shipments that were described in chapter 1 exemplify *cold chain operations*: supply chain operations at low, carefully controlled temperatures. Specialized transportation and storage services can provide anything from controlled room temperatures (not-too-hot and not-too-cold), refrigerated (i.e., 2–8°C), frozen (–20 °C) to deep frozen (e.g., –80°C). Such cold chains are used for fresh foods, temperature-sensitive pharmaceuticals, flowers, deep-frozen foods, and even deep-frozen lab-grown human tissue. In the Netherlands, Venlo Fresh Park has 130 companies specializing in handling fruit, vegetables, and ornamental plants with nearby cold chain connections to highways, rail, airports, and the Rotterdam seaport.[23] Both Singapore's Air Logistics Park (ALPS) and UPS Supply Chain Solutions Inc. healthcare facilities in Louisville offer five temperature zones of handling.

The flexibility associated with cold chain logistics comes from being able to use some of the same assets and handling equipment found on the noncold chain side of logistics. For example, the same truckload carrier that brings in a refrigerated load of frozen food can leave with a load of computers, with the trailer's refrigeration unit turned off. For the carrier, this is better than having to drive empty or wait for another frozen food load that may take a long time to materialize. From the shippers' point of view, this increases the competition among carriers serving a logistics cluster even beyond the commonality of their equipment and technology to include related assets and operations.

Flexibility through Multimodal Operations

Logistics operations use more than a single mode of transportation, depending on service requirements, to optimize costs—and sometimes more than just costs. Consider, for example, Medtronic's distribution operation in Memphis, outlined to me by Rob Varner, senior director of Medtronic's North America distribution operations.

When a surgical team in Boston prepares for a prescheduled spine operation on Thursday, the hospital orders a spinal kit from Medtronic on Tuesday. Although CAT scans help the surgeon plan the surgery, the surgeon wants to be ready for whatever he or she finds during the operation. To get all the parts and tools needed, the surgeon needs a full kit filled with all manner of plates, rods, odd-shaped brackets, and screws in a range of sizes of parts. Because of the advanced materials and manufacturing technologies used to make these surgical supplies, each kit costs upward of $120,000, and most hospitals do not keep them on hand.

Instead, the hospital orders a kit and Medtronic puts it on a FedEx plane on Tuesday night. The kit arrives at the hospital on Wednesday morning, gets inspected, and is sent to the operating theater. Once the operation is over, the hospital repackages the kit and airfreights it back to Memphis the same day or the next day. Medtronic inspects the kit, cleans it, replenishes the used parts and sterilizes the kit for the next use. Furthermore, in the event of an emergency surgery, Medtronic sends the kit using next-flight-out (NFO) service, mostly via Delta Airlines, which has a passenger hub in Memphis. With NFO service, a courier delivers the kit to the airline counter in Memphis, and the airline then takes the kit onto the next flight to the destination city, where the courier delivers it directly to the hospital. Depending on flight schedules, such shipments can take only a few hours from order to delivery.

Thus the availability of both FedEx and Delta Airlines hub operations in Memphis allows Medtronic to offer both standard and emergency service from its Memphis distribution center. The significant presence of competing carriers in Memphis, such as UPS and other passenger airlines, means that the dominant transportation service providers have to keep their rates and services competitive.

As a cluster grows, it attracts carriers from different modes of transportation and different service levels. Each mode and service offers a different combination of cost, hauling capacity, travel time, service reliability, and reach. Having several modes of transportation increases the flexibility of shippers in the logistics cluster to adjust to various requirements and economic conditions. It also allows them to serve customers efficiently with different service requirements and different price sensitivities. Time-sensitive goods (such as critical repair parts, emergency medical supplies, documents, and high-value goods) often go by air while less time-sensitive shipments may go by truck or even rail—depending on the distance and shipment size involved.

All logistics parks as well as regional and national economic development agencies have brochures that promote the benefits of multimodal operations by citing distances to major highways, rail terminals, ports, and airports. Clusters offering three colocated modes (air, truck, and rail) include Zaragoza in Spain and AllianceTexas. Memphis prides itself on being quadramodal (air, truck, rail, and barge). Rotterdam offers five modes (ocean, barge, rail, truck, and pipelines) and a sixth mode of air if you count the large air cargo hub in Amsterdam's Schiphol only 20 miles to the north. A cluster might be renowned for one mode (e.g., air express in Memphis or Louisville), but the presence of other modes provides added options and economies for shippers.

At their Memphis headquarters, I interviewed Neely Mallory, president of Mallory Alexander International Logistics, and fourth generation of the Mallory family heading the company. He told me, "My theory on it is they come here because of FedEx, because they can go anywhere absolutely positively overnight. Once they get here, everything doesn't need to be there overnight so they may use [LTL motor carrier] American Freightways, they may use [parcel carrier] UPS Ground, or they may use [TL carrier] Swift."

Liquidity Leads to Price Stability
During a group discussion in the futuristic Accenture office in Singapore, Eelco Hoekstra, president of Royal Vopak, described a cluster's ability to smooth volatility in terms of liquidity in the local logistics market. Liquidity in this context is defined by the ready availability of conveyances for shippers and the ready availability of freight for carriers. As with any market, liquidity helps bring price stability. "With this liquidity, which is important, you get price-setting, because the more volume you bring into a market, the better supply and demand work, the more stable the price," explained Hoekstra. Noncluster locations and small hubs will have higher volatility in freight volumes and conveyance availability, which leads to prices volatility. In contrast, a large hub with many diverse flows of freight and many competing carriers will, in general, offer more stable prices as a result of the so-called "risk pooling" effect—while some shippers' requirements maybe high on a particular day, others' may be lower, with the highs and the lows canceling each other.

Naturally, liquidity is driven, in part, from the commodities traded. "Singapore has developed as a price center for oil product," Hoekstra added, and he then summed it up: "I think that's why Singapore works—you see that once it has liquidity, it attracts more because of price setting." The same holds true for oil in Rotterdam and Houston as well as other commodities in certain locations around the world—the price setting attracts flow, bringing in both demand and supply for transportation.

While certain commodity flow leads to liquidity both in the underlying commodity price and the resulting transportation demand/supply balance, large clusters enjoy transportation liquidity even without a serving as a hub for specific commodity trading. The ubiquitous nature of transportation means that the size of the transportation activity alone is likely to lead to liquidity in the demand for and supply of transportation services, and therefore to price stability. Such stability allows both shippers and carriers to plan their activities with more certainty.

TIMELINESS: BIGGER AND FASTER

In their influential book, *Competing against Time*,[24] Stalk and Hout outline the strategic value of speed. While their book focused on time to market and strategic responsiveness, operations managers also understand the advantages of fast and timely transportation service.

In addition, a particular set of logistics activities geared to time-sensitive shipments has developed around major overnight shipping hubs, such as Memphis (FedEx), Louisville (UPS), Liège (TNT), and Leipzig (DHL). The advantages of Memphis for Medtronic in responding to hospitals' needs all over the United States were described earlier in this chapter. The focus in that section was on the availability of multiple modes. This section focuses on the timing of airfreight movements in such hubs, which create unique opportunities for time-sensitive services that make such hubs attractive to logistics cluster development.

Inventory Considerations Drive Centralization

Shippers use safety stocks to buffer between unpredictable changes in demand and preplanned production schedules that are difficult to change "on the fly." Yet keeping inventory incurs various costs, including the cost of capital tied up in inventory; the cost of obsolescence; and the cost required to store, secure, insure, and service the inventory. To keep enough safety stock and yet minimize the amount of inventory held, companies hold large stocks in centralized locations. The reason is the same "risk pooling" phenomenon mentioned earlier with regard to truck availability and liquidity. While requirements of some customers may be high at some point, the requirements of others may be low and thus the highs and the lows tend to cancel each other. The result is that the total amount of inventory required to provide timely service to customers grows less than linearly with the number of customers served.

Thus, inventory tends to be centralized, and distribution centers tend to hold large amounts of inventory, which, maybe paradoxically, tends to minimize the total inventory required in the supply chain. Consequently, such distribution centers require both large shipments of inbound freight—which is best served by large conveyances—and frequent outbound services, because customers keep low inventories. Logistics clusters offer advantages on both fronts.

Timing Advantages: Shipping Late-Orders

The flipside of higher frequency is tighter timing. Cluster locations offer timing advantages for certain activities. During any evening in any location in the United States, you can decide to send flowers to a loved one or a sick friend. Even if you decide late in the evening, you can call 1-800-Flowers or go online and choose from an array of bouquets that will be delivered the next morning by FedEx.

The 1-800-Flowers.com fulfillment center in Memphis is operated by Mallory Alexander International Logistics. When I asked Neely Mallory how they do next-day delivery so late at night, he explained, "We take orders over the internet on these flowers until midnight Eastern Time, and then we still need to build the bouquets." 1-800-Flowers.com manages to ship flowers long after the normal express-delivery pick-up times by locating their fulfillment centers next to the FedEx airfreight hub in Memphis. The key is Mallory's ability to dovetail into FedEx's flight schedule. Recall the nightly cycle for next-day air delivery operations described in chapter 3: from around the nation, the express carrier's planes come in late at night laden with packages, the hub sorts the packages after midnight, and then, in the wee hours of the morning, the planes depart back to their nationwide locations for delivery later than morning. Mallory can bring shipments of flowers to the hub after midnight while the express carrier's planes are landing and unloading, putting Mallory's shipments into the stream of packages being sorted and loaded into outbound planes. "We have to be there by 2 a.m. during peak season shipping schedules," said Mallory.

Similar opportunities are available to shippers located in and around Louisville. If your Christmas shopping includes shoes from Zappos.com, you can place your order by December 23rd and, as long as the order was placed before 4:00 p.m. Eastern time, it will arrive on December 24th anywhere in the United States. In that case, the gift will arrive by UPS because Zappos has its fulfillment centers in Shepherdsville, Kentucky, near the UPS Worldport in Louisville.

In both Memphis and Louisville, many companies use a similar late shipping cutoff model as 1-800-Flowers.com and Zappos. The Web site of Future Electronics, the giant Canadian distributor, states: "Thanks to the location of our Global Distribution Center in Memphis, Future Electronics is able to extend the cut-off times for next day delivery all the way to midnight Eastern Standard Time." Many large technology retailers and distributors with distribution centers in Louisville make similar claims. Other companies use the same model to ship emergency repair parts to field technicians or to restock retail stores with fast-moving high-tech products. Jason Vaughn of UPS Supply Chain Solutions explained that "in order to serve their customers, a company like Silicon Graphics had to strategically locate their [critical parts distribution] centers near their customers. So if there was a 24 [hour] service requirement, they would put those things at the 'end of the runway' in a location such as Louisville or Memphis." Such critical parts distribution centers allow customers of Dell, GE, or Siemens to order a part until the cutoff time, which would be late in the evening, and get the part at 8:30 the next morning, avoiding long down time of expensive machinery.

Duration-Advantages: Working Two Days per Day

The timing advantages of clusters located around air transportation hubs also provide added time for fast-turnaround activities such as emergency repairs. When an executive's laptop breaks, time and speed matter. And if time and speed matter, then the location of the repair depot matters. Toshiba contracted with UPS Supply Chain Solutions Inc. (SCS) to create a repair center in Louisville near the UPS Worldport air hub. By locating in Louisville, the repair center receives the laptops sooner and can work on them longer before they ship out than if the repair center were not situated at an express carrier hub. Rather than the usual 10 a.m. delivery, the laptops arrive in the early hours of the morning and repair technicians can start to work on them immediately. Toshiba also has a parts distribution center in Louisville, so technicians can quickly get replacement parts during the day. The technicians have all day and late into the night to find the problem, fix the computer, test the repaired machine, and take it back to the UPS air hub so it can make the plane's 2 a.m. departure that will deliver the laptop in the early morning to its user.

In essence, with early inbound receiving and late outbound shipping, the repair technicians have time for two days of labor (up to 20 hours in two 10-hour shifts) crammed into one calendar day. A Toshiba customer can ship her laptop on Monday night for a repair and get it back by Wednesday morning. Similar operations take place in Memphis and Singapore. For example, Denise Jack of Flextronics Global Services in Memphis told me, "users send their laptops to our facility, we repair them same day and ship them out same day, that night, through FedEx."

RESOURCE SHARING

Most of this chapter discussed how transportation services into and out of a cluster exhibit lower cost and improved service as the cluster grows, leading to the relocation of more logistics activities to the cluster and even lower costs and better service. Logistics clusters, however, offer even more benefits, beyond those tied to transportation. For all the fierce competition between logistics service providers, these companies cooperate on many dimensions to ensure that their customers experience a high level of service. And these cooperative instances are especially easy when the service providers reside in close proximity to each other.

The unspecialized, interchangeable nature of many facets of logistics operations is a double-edged sword. On one hand, interchangeable assets and freight handling capabilities create a crucible of cost competition that limits the profit margins of transportation and logistics service providers. On the other hand, interchangeability also means that transportation and logistics providers can share resources in a way that improves their respective operational performances.

Sharing Physical Resources

When UPS fills its daily flight out of Singapore to its Asia-Pacific hub in Shenzhen, the carrier does not turn away any overflow packages, ask the customers to wait 24 hours for the next flight, or charter another aircraft for those few extra packages. Instead, UPS sometimes utilizes common carrier airlift capacity (typically belly freight in passenger airliners) from Singapore to move a few overflow shipments—sometimes directly to their final destination. Having multiple carriers located within the Airport Logistics Park of Singapore (ALPS) makes it easy to arrange for such cross-carrier shipments.

Sharing of physical resources takes place on a larger scale as well, in response to the ebb and flow of freight volumes for different industries at different times. The last time I visited the UPS Worldport, in Louisville, it handled about one million packages, which was normal for a chilly Monday night at the end of January.

But just a month earlier the facility handled 2.5 million packages per night for the holiday rush.

What's helping cluster operations is that many shippers have different peaks and lulls. For online retailers, the days before Christmas create the biggest surge, while the distribution centers of brick-and-mortar retailers experience the surge weeks earlier as they replenish the stores in preparation for the holiday rush. For 1-800-Flowers.com, the peak is Mother's Day, and for the Vermont Teddy Bear Company it is Valentine's Day that brings big volume. Companies of all stripes experience end-of-month or end-of-quarter surges when salespeople try to make their quotas. In addition to these patterns, which can be forecasted and planned for, many shippers face unexpected surges—when launching a new product, when a competitor falters, or when handling a product recall.

To accommodate the flow variability, warehouse operators in a cluster can shift excess flow to other nearby warehouses when one warehouse temporarily runs out of space and another has space to lease. They also share equipment such as forklifts when a sudden surge requires it.

When a single entity (which may be a real estate company, a port authority, a government agency, etc.) manages a logistics park, the park manager may facilitate such arrangements. Furthermore, in many logistics parks, a single logistics service provider may serve multiple customers in a logistics campus environment, such as in the UPS Supply Chain Solutions in Louisville or Exel in Alliance-Texas (see below). In these cases, the logistics service provider can share management, administration, forklifts, and processes across its local customer base. This can be particularly important when an unplanned surge takes place.

Sharing Human Resources

The AllianceTexas Logistics Park north of Fort Worth supports a different kind of sharing—human resource sharing. Exel, a leading contract logistics services provider,[25] operates eight distribution centers in and around AllianceTexas on behalf of major consumer packaged goods (CPG) and technology companies. As its customers' needs fluctuate, Exel shifts its trained warehouse workers from one facility to the next. Because all of the workers have well-defined skill sets and know Exel's systems for operating distribution centers, these workers can be shifted between the customers' operations and go right to work. I discussed this aspect of their operation with Gregory Kadesch, Exel's senior director of operations, contract logistics—Americas. "When you walk into one operation versus another, they all look the same. And the expectations are very similar, so that's yet another advantage of having everything very close," he told me. "A worker might be picking toys one day and mobile phones the next day," he added.

Exel shares labor so often that it devised an online software tool to automate the process and make it easy. Kadesch explained how a general manager in one warehouse can request extra labor, and general managers in other Exel-run warehouses with spare labor can lend out workers to keep workers on the payroll. Specifically, general managers can use the software tool to determine how many people are needed elsewhere, what skill sets they need, and for which shifts they are needed. Any general manager can reassign his or her spare workers, and the requesting manager receives a list of who's coming in to help. The tool even tracks labor hours shared across the Exel network and, coupled with the networked payroll system, ensures that each customer pays only for the labor it used.

Other logistics firms have similar practices. ATC Logistics and Electronics, in the same AllianceTexas Park, uses local temporary staffing agencies to move workers not only between its own facilities and customers, but, in fact, sharing the pool of trained workers with other logistics service providers in the park and even outside the AllianceTexas Park—with the many logistics companies that comprise the Dallas/Fort Worth logistics cluster. UPS Supply Chain Solutions in Louisville can shift skilled workers from customer to customer as needed, even down to the level of moving people in the middle of a shift. If UPS's warehouse workers finish packing the orders for one customer early in their shift, they can go help another.

Get Set ... Ready ... Recall: Unexpected Reverse Surges

Changing peak shipping periods across clients in a logistics cluster or a logistics park can be handled with certain advance preparation through resource swapping, as mentioned in the last section. Distribution operations in a logistics campus environment offer the ability to tackle unexpected requirements as well, thereby providing a significant value-added level of service.

Product recalls are the sort of events that keep upper management awake at night. A recall can be voluntary—when the company recognizes a defect in the product, or involuntary, when a regulatory agency orders a recall. In 2010, the Consumer Product Safety Commission in the United States issued 433 recall orders, while recently the Federal Drug Administration has been pulling more than 250 drugs off the market every year. The number of recalls reached 229 in the United Kingdom in 2010. And the number of recalls in the United States and Europe is expected to grow as regulation and enforcement are tightened.

Steffen Frankenberg, vice president DHL Solutions & Innovations said that "When it happens, the first thought is about brand protection and liability. The last thing being considered is the logistics capability in handling a product recall."[26]

The stakes are, of course, substantial. In 2009, Maclaren recalled a million strollers after twelve children suffered fingertip amputations.[27] Not being fully prepared led to chaos, the company's CEO admitted: "We immediately realized we would need more of everything." A well-handled recall can limit the damage to the brand and occasionally can actually enhance it. A 2010 study suggested that "87 percent of the 1,000 respondents agreed they are more willing to purchase from, and remain loyal to, a company that handles its product recall in an honest and responsible way."[28]

Communications are of the utmost importance in recall situations, but the next most important thing is speed—replacing or repairing the defective product quickly. Getting ready ahead of time and having a plan for the logistics of handling the surge of reverse product flow can make the difference between a successful recall and a problem. To this end, large logistics service providers, such as UPS Supply Chain Solutions and DHL Solutions, can offer instant "ramp up" capabilities by reassigning warehouse belts, reallocating equipment, and shifting workers to a temporary short-term operation. Such flexibility exists only in the largest logistics campuses and parks. Another case of a logistics campus handling an unplanned surge caused by a regulatory edict is described on p. 130 in chapter 5.

Emergency Response

The resources available in a logistics park allow for many kinds of emergency responses, not only a product recall. Advanced Bio-Healing Inc. (ABH) is a San Diego–based manufacturer of Dermagraft, a bioengineered skin substitute made of living tissue. Once the complex manufacturing process is complete, the product is cryopreserved at minus 75°C (minus 103°F). In 2011, ABH contracted with UPS SCS for warehousing and distribution of Dermagraft. The decision proved to be prescient.[29]

On the evening of September 8, 2011, a major power outage knocked out electricity for up to five million people in Southern California, Arizona and Mexico. Two nuclear reactors were offline after losing electricity, and San Diego was brought to a standstill; all outgoing flights from San Diego's Lindbergh Field were grounded.[30] Mike Whitmore, ABH's logistics manager, said, "We knew that with traffic congestion caused by the blackout and the airport's inactivity, we had to rely on UPS to ship that day's supply." The looming problem resulted from the fact that ABH's shipments are often synchronized with an appointment for a patient awaiting treatment. Patients—who may have mobility issues or other health problems—see their doctors for treatment on the same day that the Dermagraft arrives. But during the power outage, ABH could not ship anything out of the San Diego airport.

It was late in Louisville already, and UPS's ABH operations team had left for the day. However, UPS was able to call them back and bring other qualified workers to the temperature-controlled warehouse. "There are a lot of requirements concerning how Dermagraft is handled, and all of those have to be followed or the product is no longer viable," said Whitmore.[31] For example, while UPS's pharmaceutical-grade freezers in Louisville are maintained at the proper temperature, Rich Shaver, division manager at UPS Global Logistics and Distribution, Health Care added that "the freezer doors can be opened for just two minutes at a time when removing product and then they have to be kept closed for at least two hours before reopening them." Yet, the UPS team was able to fulfill 100 percent of the day's orders.

Sharing Knowledge When Contracts Change

The same interchangeability of assets that gives logistics providers flexibility brings with it a difficulty in keeping customers long term. If the trucks, ships, and aircraft of different carriers are all much the same, then customers can readily switch between competing service providers to gain the lowest cost and best service. Such customers routinely use bidding processes to find the current best cost/service combination, resulting in relatively frequent shifts of logistics contracts from one provider to another. When this is done by a multinational company operating a global logistics network, the logistics providers' outposts throughout the world have to move the business to the other provider. Such a change affects the way the customers' shipments are collected, routed, delivered, tracked, and paid for, throughout the world.

I witnessed one of these transfers while visiting the Air Logistics Park Singapore (ALPS), next to Changi Airport, where several logistics companies' representatives talked candidly about these gyrations—one carrier's loss was another's gain. While I was there, DHL and UPS were in the middle of transferring a contract from DHL to UPS to handle regional freight for Phillips Health Care. When I interviewed Sing Kiew, solutions manager at Asia Pacific UPS Supply Chain Solutions, I was struck by the professionalism and customer orientation of both companies during the contract transfer process. "Our team and the DHL team, plus the customer—we were all involved in the meetings and talking about how to scale the transfer, with no baggage, no emotional hiccups, no rivalry," said Kiew. These comments were echoed by Mary Yeo, UPS vice president supply chain operations South Asia Pacific, while describing the cluster operations in Singapore.

The uninitiated may be surprised that the "losing" company would support the change and cooperate fully with the "winner." The reason for such magnanimous behavior is that everyone knows that the winner in this round of bidding might be the loser in the next round. Although the two carriers might be bitter rivals on the business front, the workers behind the scenes know that traffic ebbs and flows. The best strategy for everyone is to help ease the transfer for the benefit of the customer. "The customer is ultimately who we are going to support, or who we are going to serve, so that's important for us and for our competitors as well," added UPS's Lai Sing Kiew. The same "customer-first" attitude was also evident when I visited the DHL offices in Singapore, discussing the issue with Stephan Muench, head of DHL In-house Consulting, Asia Pacific.

Clusters aid this transfer process. When a manufacturer or distributor changes logistics providers, the new provider needs to quickly learn the shipper's processes, facilities, hours of operation, personnel, and various special requirements. When the logistics providers reside in the same location, it's easy for them to coordinate the handover and provide the customer with a smooth transition.

Room for Growth

In addition to changes in demand caused by seasonal variations and economic conditions in various markets, the flows in a company's logistics network might see large shifts as a result of new product launches, mergers, acquisitions, spin-offs, and strategic re-alignments. Such shifts may require the acquisition of new assets or divesting existing distribution center space.

Large logistics clusters include many companies operating in different industries and subject to different economic forces. The constant changes in business volume mean some growing companies need to lease more distribution space, and others may be downsizing by moving to smaller spaces or subleasing portions of their space. Unlike industrial infrastructure, such as manufacturing plants, warehouses can share equipment (e.g., floor space, shelves, conveyors, and forklifts) across industries, thus allowing the movements into and out of adjacent distribution space with relative ease.

Chicago, for example, has more than 1.1 billion square feet of developed warehouse and industrial space. With typical vacancy rates of about 6 to 9 percent, Chicago has 70 to 100 million square feet of space available at any given moment (and, unfortunately, 140 million square feet vacant during the 2009 downturn).[32] Companies seeking spaces or selecting locations with an eye for future expansion will gravitate toward locations that have plenty of possible sites in a wide range of sizes.

When LEGO Systems Inc. needed to expand its distribution center in AllianceTexas by about 50 percent, Hillwood Development Company, the park developer and operator, was able to move LEGO from its 402,500 square foot facility to a 596,000 square foot facility down the street. The deal demonstrated the park operator's ability to accommodate a customer's growth.[33]

Such flexibility obviates the immediate need to move to a new geographical location, which may be costly because of the need to alter the logistics network. A new location may also require new procurement of transportation services and renegotiation of transportation service contracts, as well as potentially changing service commitments to customers and renegotiating supplier service agreements. In addition, it may require a new labor force, labor agreements, and potentially using a new logistics service provider. In clusters, the availability of larger and smaller nearby spaces enables the shipper or distributor to maintain a stable network even as volume grows or shrinks.

COST AND SERVICE

Shippers and logistics service providers impose multiple requirements on their transportation carriers regardless of the product shipped. These include low and predictable price; short and consistent travel times; high departure and arrival frequency; high equipment availability; accurate and damage-free delivery; and ease of doing business with the carriers.

No single carrier can usually achieve all of these performance dimensions simultaneously for all types of cargo and all destinations, so shippers may have to trade off, say, low cost against fast service. For example, overnight air service is fast yet expensive, while truck service may take longer but costs less. This is clear to anybody who orders online from Amazon.com or other online retailers who offer a portfolio of shipping options: generally, the faster the delivery the more expensive the shipping.

Clusters bring improvements on each of these dimensions. A large concentration of logistics operations means large flows of goods. Carriers can lower their costs (and, in turn, their prices) by using larger conveyances, getting high utilization, using efficient pickup and delivery tours, and getting follow-on loads. Shippers' costs can also be lowered by the ability of companies in a cluster to adjust the mode of transportation based on changing business conditions. Service is improved as a cluster grows because large clusters enjoy higher frequency service and more direct connections to more destinations.

The size of the cluster smoothes out freight flow fluctuations, creating predictable costs for carriers and predictable prices for shippers. Many of these advantages are rooted in the attraction of logistics clusters to multiple carriers, which creates a competitive environment. In addition, the large number of diverse products handled in a logistics cluster means that one company's peak can be another company's slack, allowing for shared distribution assets. It also offers long-term adjustment opportunities as the business environment changes.

All these factors contribute to companies' location decisions and their ability to take advantage of collaboration opportunities. As Les Woch of Mars Incorporated commented in a telephone interview discussing companies' location decisions (see p. 86 in chapter 3), "the collaboration point is absolutely something that we're looking to optimize or maximize."

The positive feedback loops discussed in this chapter are important mechanisms that help explain the growth of logistics clusters. These, however, are only partial explanations. Other factors contribute to both the launch and the growth of logistics clusters. Later chapters examine the role of infrastructure and government in enabling and nurturing logistics clusters. The next chapter shows the significant degree to which logistics service companies add value to the goods they handle and do more for themselves and their customers than just logistics, with clusters being the natural location for such activities.

5

ADDING VALUE

Alert readers may have noticed that chapter 4 strayed from logistics a bit. Basic logistical activities don't include repairing laptops or arranging flower bouquets. Yet these are the sorts of value-added activities found in logistics clusters in addition to the more plebeian tasks of moving and storing goods. Over time, a logistics cluster becomes more than just a location for warehousing and transportation activities. Logistics providers and shippers' logistics operations within a cluster add value to the goods they handle in the cluster. Also, the availability of low-cost, high-performance logistics services found in logistics clusters attracts manufacturers, distributors, and other shippers that depend on efficient logistics.

A logistics cluster offers two main advantages for performing certain value-added activities: it allows for postponement of product-differentiation closer to the time the product is sold, and it typically offers a cost-effective opportunity for performing operations beyond logistics. Along any supply chain, various companies touch the product as they transport it, store it, or change it in some way. Each of these "touches" costs money as a result of the labor associated with finding the item, removing it from the shelf, doing something, recording the action, and sending it somewhere or putting it somewhere. The incremental cost of "doing something more" while the product is in a warehouse or distribution center is lower than moving it to a special facility because the product has been "touched" at this point anyway.

Robust logistics services serve as infrastructure for other economic activities, such as manufacturing. In fact, as chapters 6 and 10 will show, this is one of the important contributions of logistics clusters to economic development. The logistics infrastructure available in a cluster attracts manufacturers and suppliers who create their own "miniclusters" or "subclusters" that add to the region's economic strength.

All these types of value-added operations in a logistics cluster mean that the jobs performed there go well beyond moving and storage. Many of these jobs require special skills and command high salaries.

ADDING VALUE LATE IN THE SUPPLY CHAIN

Supply chain operations have become more volatile and less predictable over the last two decades for numerous reasons. First, the growing variety of goods available in every segment of the market means that each brand and product variant sells in a small quantity, which creates higher inherent demand variability.[1] Second, increased customer expectations for product availability, coupled with decreasing "product loyalty," means that if a product is not on the shelf (or "in stock" at an Internet retailer warehouse), then customers may switch rather than wait. Third, shorter product life cycles, particularly in fashion and high technology, offer little historical data on trends and seasonality, reducing forecast accuracy. Fourth, globalization creates long supply lead times during which demand can change. Fifth, globalization also entails more complex supply chains with dozens of actors, resulting in high susceptibility to disruptions, delays, quality problems, political upheavals, and natural disasters. One can add to this list the increased frequency of extreme weather phenomena and other factors.

One strategy for coping with supply chain volatility is to wait as long as possible before customizing or differentiating products. In the best of circumstances, a company may try to wait until it has a specific order in hand. At that point, however, the company must fulfill the order very quickly. Thus, companies may stock undifferentiated "vanilla" or "base" products that can quickly be customized with last-minute changes or additions, such as packaging, colors, decals, tags, or other features that do not require lengthy manufacturing processes and therefore can be performed just prior to shipping an order. Such coping strategies are known as *postponement, delayed differentiation,* or *mass customization.* Logistics clusters play a major role in these strategies because a distribution or fulfillment center offers the shipper one last chance to modify, customize, or augment the product while it is handled and before it is shipped to the customer. Furthermore, the superior transportation service associated with logistics clusters helps get the product to the customer quickly, after it has been customized.

Postponement allows manufacturers to reduce inventory carrying costs while keeping a high level of service—keeping inventories of undifferentiated products in a distribution center amounts to demand *risk pooling* (see the inventory discussion on p. 109 in chapter 4). The total inventory required to maintain a certain level of service is lower when stocking undifferentiated products in the distribution center as compared with stocking products in final, differentiated form. Ergo, risk pooling creates lower inventory carrying costs and satisfied customers.

The examples below highlight this aspect of the benefits of conducting such postponed customization in a distribution center.

Preparing for Retail Sales

Distribution centers often support retail operations by receiving goods in bulk from manufacturers, many of whom are located in Southeast Asia, and then distributing smaller quantities to a network of retail outlets. Most retail outlets have limited space and cannot handle large deliveries or large inventories. Consequently, distribution centers must send mixed shipments of various items to stores on a regular basis. As mentioned above, however, it is advantageous to perform value-added operations at the distribution center because its location offers an opportunity to perform late customization.

Kitting

At the simplest end of the value-added spectrum are logistics operations that kit, bundle, label, or otherwise prepare a product for retail sale. For example, UPS Supply Chain Solutions in Louisville handles all of Nikon's distribution of photographic equipment for the Americas. Much of UPS's activity for Nikon consists of "standard" high-performance full service logistics: managing air and ocean transport and the related customs brokerage, as well as providing digital visibility to Nikon for all its freight moving from Nikon's factories in Japan, Korea, and Indonesia to Louisville, Kentucky. UPS then ships the cameras, lenses, and other photographic equipment to Nikon dealers in North America, South America, and the Caribbean.

But what arrives in the Louisville warehouse on the UPS SCS campus isn't quite ready for store shelves. Before the cameras are shipped to stores, they are either being "kitted" with accessories such as batteries, chargers, and promotional material, or repackaged for in-store display in accordance with a retailer's requirements.[2] As a result, retailers can specify what they need right before the selling season, once they better know consumer preferences, rather than ordering months in advance and waiting for shipments from Asia.

Similarly, UPS SCS works with Deer Stags Inc., a manufacturer of premium footwear sold by US retailers. Deer Stags ships finished product in bulk from Asia and Brazil to a UPS SCS distribution center. When a retail chain (or a store) orders the product, UPS customizes the shoes for the store by adding bar code labels, price tags to the eyelet, and color coding to the cartons, all according to the retailer's requirements.

Another common task is building promotional bundles either for the product maker or for the retailer. "There are some operations that do bundling, where you put two selling units together and over-wrap them. There are other operations where we do coupon inserts," explained Greg Kadesch, Exel's director of operations. For example, a company might want to bundle a sample of its new product with an existing product, or offer a two-for-one promotion.

Custom Packaging for Promotional and Personalized Orders

In a phone interview, Jim O'Brien, director of operations for consumer products at BIC, said, "BIC is making a significant move towards postponement because it is a competitive advantage."[3] The BIC product line includes lighters, razors, and stationery. Companies use these products to create personalized items with company logos and event memorabilia. In addition, retail outlets use business products in promotional activities in various bundles as well as for seasonal packaging. BIC currently operates manufacturing plants all over the world but has two distribution centers in the United States in Cerritos, California, and Charlotte, North Carolina, where customized packaging operations take place. Since developing the packaging postponement, BIC has seen volumes grow 10 to 15 percent each year between 2000 and 2005. Based on its ability to customize quickly and efficiently, the company has become more of a customized product company, with over half of its products made for promotional and personalized orders. And this fraction was expected to grow significantly.

Numerous other examples of kitting and packaging services can be found in consumer electronics, apparel, and consumer packaged goods. For example, Stephan Muench, head of in-house consulting Asia Pacific for DHL described to me, in his Singapore office, how DHL's Global Forwarding unit in the Netherlands also helps prepare clothing for retailers by adding price tags, security tags, labels, and plastic hangers before distributing the garments to the retail outlets. In fact, Exel promotes, in several of its published case studies, the benefits of having packaging customization operations colocated within its distribution centers. Discussing one such operation for a consumer packaged goods manufacturer, Chad Herr, Exel's director of operations for the consumer industry, commented "we were able to demonstrate [to the CPG manufacturer] that ... the right choice to manage secondary packaging [is] in the distribution center."[4]

Retail Display Preparation

Logistics providers also prepare retail display pallets. The displays consist of temporary cardboard and plastic structures that hold quantities of a new product, holiday-themed promotion, or a special deal. When delivered, they'll sit in the retailer's space, often at the end of an aisle or on prominently located open floor space.

Preparing the displays is part of creating a promotion, so it makes sense for the distribution center, which is already fulfilling the retailer's promotional product order, to supply the matching displays as well. In addition, most displays include the product it-self. Because the distribution center carries the products that are scheduled for promotion, it can marry the structure of the display with the product samples to create the store displays.

Variations in store layout, merchandising, and retailer interest mean variations in the displays ordered by a retailer. While discussing Exel's value-added operations in AllianceTexas, Greg Kadesch of Exel gave an example: "For many CPG customers we're creating display pallets where you have multiple facings of different products on one pallet that will sit in the store aisle. Those facings are selectable by the buyer. Rather than the CPG manufacturer having a prescribed set of products on the display, the customer [a retailer] can pick and choose what products it wants and on which facings of the pallets it should be displayed. We build the displays and stock them to the customers' specifications."

Product Finishing

Value-added activities in logistics clusters can go beyond the relatively minor postponement operations such as the kitting, bundling, and labeling mentioned above. Sometimes, the last stages of the manufacturing process itself take place at a distribution center—an even more advanced type of late customization.

A Sporting Chance at Last-Stage Customization

Sports fans around the world show their support and pride in winning teams and players by buying and wearing team-logo apparel. Sales of fan apparel track the fluctuating on-field performance of the teams and players. Moreover, some sports leagues have management policies that influence the predictability of who wins and who loses, with direct implications for the supply chain management process for team merchandise.

The US National Football League (NFL) manages player recruitment differently than do other professional league sports around the world, such as soccer. In the NFL, teams draft players from colleges in a well-controlled process. To ensure a competitive league, every year the team with the worst record in the previous season picks first, the team with the second worst record picks second, and the Super Bowl champion in the previous season picks last. A weak team in one year can thus pick up strong new players for the following year. Add to this a cap on the total amount that each team can spend on players' salaries and one can understand why "On any given Sunday, any team in the NFL can beat any other."[5]

To understand the consequences of this set of rules and processes, consider the European soccer leagues. There, teams may sign any player they want and pay any amount they can afford. Good players create successful teams, and successful teams enjoy better ticket sales and higher merchandise sales. Growing revenues let successful teams pay even higher salaries, attracting even better players. The opposite mechanism works for poorer teams who cannot afford the best players. The result is that the UK Premier League is dominated by clubs such as Manchester United, Chelsea, Arsenal, and sometimes Manchester City, Tottenham, and Liverpool. Other teams are decidedly in second and third tiers and have little chance of having success against the leaders. This phenomenon is even more pronounced in the Spanish Primera Division, where FC Barcelona and Real Madrid dominate.

The difference between the American and European leagues has supply chain management implications. Whereas soccer merchandise suppliers can easily predict sales of team jerseys of UK or Spanish soccer teams, this is not the case for the NFL in the United States. The balanced strength throughout the NFL means no one knows which quarterback will lead his team to success or which running back will break records. Not only is it not clear before the season, but teams and players' fortunes can change dramatically during the season.

As a principal supplier for the NFL, Reebok[6] sells over 1.5 million jerseys to football fans each year with team colors and players' names. To control costs, Reebok cuts and sews the clothing in Central America, taking 6 to 24 weeks for the jerseys to reach the distribution center in Indianapolis.[7] But because Reebok cannot predict which team will be "hot" and which player's star will suddenly shine, Reebok also sends blank jerseys to the distribution center. Only when it is clear which player has signed late in the season with what team and which team exhibits early success are the jerseys printed and embroidered with the player's name. Furthermore, demand usually spikes a week or so after a team's big win or a player's outstanding performance. Fortunately, Indianapolis is a logistics cluster with 1,500 logistics-focused companies, a "crossroads" central location for trucking, and a large regional airfreight hub for FedEx.[8] Once a trend materializes, the Reebok distribution center in Indianapolis finishes the jerseys and supplies the retailers at breakneck speed. While it may be less expensive to finish the jerseys at the Central American source, the long lead time from there would invariably result in lost sales of some jerseys and extra, unwanted leftovers of others. At a retail price of $25 for a long-sleeve T shirt or $250 for an authentic jersey, the high cost of lost sales dwarfs the modest incremental cost to finish a jersey at the Indianapolis distribution center.[9]

Country Customization

Hewlett-Packard manufactures its popular Deskjet and Deskwriter printers in its Vancouver and Singapore plants and distributes them to the United States, Europe, and Asia. Selling printers in Europe means meeting each country's requirements for printer configurations: different decals, a country-specific power plug, and language-specific manuals. In the past, Hewlett-Packard forecast demand for each European country and then manufactured the appropriate numbers of printers for each country. Unfortunately, the vagaries of forecast errors meant that HP might have had, for example, not enough printers for Denmark yet too many printers for Slovenia, without any way to convert Slovenian printers into Danish ones. Six printer models and twenty-three different country configurations meant that HP had 138 versions of the finished printers. The result was frequent shortages and overstocks.

To increase product availability without increasing the retailers' inventory carrying costs, HP changed its processes in the early 1990s, switching to a pan-European forecast and shipping generic printers to its European distribution center in the Netherlands. HP chose Holland for the reasons mentioned throughout this book: frequent transportation connections to all European destinations, advantageous costs structure, and a trained workforce. As orders came in from specific retailers for specific countries, an easily accessible side panel in the shipping carton let HP's Dutch distribution center workers quickly configure printers according to the destination country. This postponed customization operation converted a box containing one of the six generic printer models into one of the twenty-three country-specific printers.

Of course, HP still had to forecast the pan-European demand for each printer model, but this aggregated forecast was more accurate than any one of the twenty-three country-level forecasts for each model because of risk pooling. The result was a lower level of printer inventory needed to achieve high service levels to the European customers.

Extending the same supply chain design worldwide, HP outfitted its five other regional distribution centers around the world for postponement. Using postponement, HP reduced inventories by 18 percent while maintaining service levels.[10] Overall, Hewlett-Packard cut printer supply costs by 25 percent.[11]

Building on its success, HP also extended the postponement concept to its packaging operation. HP began shipping printers in bulk to the distribution centers and packaging them for distribution to retailers only after it received the orders. Postponing both the configuration and the packaging afforded HP several additional advantages. First, shipping costs from the plants to the distribution centers dropped by millions of dollars. Because retail printer packaging includes a lot of cushioning, sending printers in bulk without that packaging increased the shipments' density. That meant that HP could ship 250 percent more printers in a container-load from its plants to its distribution centers. Second, storage of the bulk-packed printers required 60 percent less space in the distribution centers. Third, dealing with unpacked generic printers simplified the configuration work at the distribution centers. Fourth, HP was able to offer its customers language-specific packaging rather than multilanguage packages. In addition, the printer cartons were "fresh" when arriving at the customer location, with no soiling or scuffing from the extra handling on the long voyage across the Atlantic.

Coping with Regulatory Edicts

When drug regulators make last-minute changes during a new-product launch, manufacturers must implement those changes prior to the launch. Having the ability to deal with late changes in requirements can be the difference between being the first to the market with a generic drug ... or not.

Dr. Reddy's Laboratories Inc., one of the largest pharmaceutical companies in India, specializes in generic and over-the-counter drugs. In 2007, it contracted with UPS SCS to distribute both its generic and its over-the-counter drugs out of UPS's Healthcare Logistics Center in Louisville, Kentucky.[12] Generic drug makers live for the end of patent protection on popular medications. When a blockbuster drug goes off patent, generic drug makers swoop in to provide more affordable alternatives to the original medication. The goal is to be the first drug maker to bring a generic version to market. A delay of only a few weeks can mean the difference between being a market leader and ceding the market leadership to competitors. Consequently, UPS accumulates the necessary inventory to be ready for the approval of the generic drug, which can take place as late as the day of the patent expiration. "Our customers expect a fulfillment blitz the moment of launch approval," says Jeannie Dunk, UPS vice president for North American sales operations.[13]

One of generic drug makers' major challenges is the regulatory requirement to implement any last-minute labeling changes required by the FDA. These governmental mandates sometimes call for relabeling of already produced, labeled, and warehoused drugs before they can be shipped to market. When the FDA requires a change to the label, UPS now handles the relabeling task instead of shipping the drugs back to Dr. Reddy's for relabeling, which saves weeks. UPS workers pull the affected stock, strip the old labels, apply corrected labels, and restock the goods. Leveraging the large healthcare workforce of the UPS SCS Louisville campus enables the company to conduct the relabeling operation over a weekend with "all hands on deck" using qualified workers from throughout its healthcare logistics operations in Louisville.

Although relabeling the medications seems like a simple job, the FDA's stringent regulations on the handling of pharmaceuticals mean that UPS had to be licensed by the FDA as a repacker/relabeler. To this end, UPS trains its workers in the healthcare industry's current good manufacturing practice (CGMP)[14] and operates a 21 CFR Part 11 validated warehouse management system (WMS).[15]

A 10-Minute Window on Doors

The postponement activities described in this chapter include traditional manufacturing steps that are being outsourced to logistics companies—typically in logistics or manufacturing clusters. They all include customization of the finished product. A different type of value-added activity takes place upstream in the supply chain—again involving activities traditionally performed by manufacturers. These types of activities lead to the formation of industrial clusters—driven by logistics needs and including many logistics service providers—around large original equipment manufacturers (OEMs), such as automotive manufacturers. The OEMs attract their suppliers because they operate a lean manufacturing and supply chain discipline. The OEMs require the suppliers to deliver the parts or subassemblies right into the production line (as opposed to the stock room), *just-in-sequence* of the production schedule and *just-in-time*. To achieve this precision, many of these suppliers have located in proximity to the automotive plants they are feeding, creating a cluster in the process.

ARD Logistics delivers harnesses manufactured by Delphi Packard in Juarez, Mexico to the Mercedes auto manufacturing plant near Tuscaloosa, Alabama. There, Mercedes builds the M-Class sport utility vehicle, the R-Class crossover vehicle, and the GLK-Class luxury sport utility vehicle. The ARD warehouse, situated next to the Mercedes plant, receives the harnesses, each of which is built for a specific automobile. ARD temporarily stores the harnesses and then sequences them for delivery to the plant according to Mercedes' production schedule.[16] This allows the Mercedes plant to delay the decision regarding which harnesses should come to the plant when, until the exact sequence of building the cars is finalized.

An example of delayed manufacturing is DHL's support for the Audi Neckarsulm assembly plant in Germany. Exactly 300 minutes before an Audi A6 gets to the point on the production line where the four doors have to be attached to a vehicle, an order for that vehicle's door side panels is printed in DHL's Offenau facility, 5.8 kilometers away.[17] In less than five minutes, DHL assembles the correct set of door side panels, going through laminating, punching, welding, screwing and final inspection. DHL loads the panels into special containers and every 90 minutes a truck picks up twelve containers and dispatches them to Neckarsulm for the nine-minute drive. Each truck must hit a ten-minute time window to deliver its correctly sequenced products just in time. Note that each door side panel includes about 100 components, and there are 7,000 configurations possible for the door panels. In 2011, Audi Neckarsulm produced 700 vehicles a day, requiring 2,800 door side panels daily.

So, instead of just sending material to the Audi plant, DHL assembles the door panels from its warehouse inventory, sequences it according to the production schedule, and delivers it just in time to the plant. Such value-added activities allow Audi to specify the type of door panel it requires only five hours before the doors are attached to a specific automobile on the production line, helping Audi reduce inventory carrying costs and reduce the complexity it has to deal with at the plant.

UP THE INCOME CURVE

Over time, logistics clusters attract work that requires higher levels of skills than traditional logistics activities. The first-order effect of such activities is increasing employment of higher-skill workers with their higher salaries. The second-order effect, attracting new logistics-intensive manufacturers, is discussed in the last section of this chapter.

A Second Life for Second-Hand Products
Technology retailers face a significant problem with new product returns. Consumers return about 11 percent to 20 percent of purchases of consumer electronics such as cell phones, laptops, computers, media players, TVs, and the like. When Accenture studied

the reason for these returns, it found that very few of the returns were true product defects.[18] In 68 percent of cases, consumers returned items as the result of a mismatch of expectations—the device was too hard to set up or didn't work the way the consumer expected. Buyer's remorse struck another 27 percent of the consumers who brought goods back for no other reason than regret. Accenture found that only about 5 percent of return products had a true defect. Ninety-five percent of the returns could be resold.

Retailers or manufacturers can recover much of the value of new product returns by refurbishing the goods. This entails shipping the returned item to a convenient central location where technicians perform tasks such as removing any customer data or apps; resetting the software to factory condition; testing the device for any faults; repairing the device if needed; cleaning and polishing the case and display; replacing any scratched body components; repackaging and ensuring the box contains all the manuals, power bricks, and accessories; and adding the manufacturer's "refurbished" label. A logistics cluster provides a natural location for repair and refurbishment because it is centralized and it enjoys high-quality transportation services. Furthermore, the logistics company providing the service may already be engaged in the distribution of the new products. Accordingly, it already has relationships and processes in place for coordination with the manufacturer and the retailers and there is no need for a special set of processes for the refurbished products. Finally, the refurbished products can be distributed with the new ones, obviating again the need for a specialized distribution operation for refurbished products.

Dave Lyon, director of operations at ATC in AllianceTexas Logistics Park, walked me through ATC's cell phone repair operations in the park. One of the key tests for assessing a cell phone's functionality uses sophisticated electronics connected to an antenna built inside a special shielded box. The electronics and the box mimic a cell phone tower. A specially trained technician puts the phone inside the box and runs a test that attempts to communicate with the phone inside the box in order to test the multiple transmitters and receivers of the phone. The technician then interprets the results—testing whether the radio side of the phone is functioning normally or otherwise isolating the deficient part of the phone. "What we're trying to do is to very quickly determine, 'Is there really a problem with that phone?'" Lyon explained. Value-added activities like repair operations require specialized skills and equipment. Many of the electronics technicians doing repair and refurbishing services in these clusters have two-year associate degrees or other vocational training beyond high school.

Similarly, Flextronics' Memphis Logistics Center diagnoses and repairs 1,500–2,000 laptops for Lenovo and other manufacturers every night, according to Denise Jack, director of operations at Flextronics Global Services. Flextronics' operations in Memphis include "standard" distribution services for customers such as Kodak—taking product manufactured in Asia, holding it in the warehouse and then sending it, as required, to retailers' (such as Best Buy or Walmart) distribution centers. (In case of late arrivals, Flextronics may send the product directly to stores.) The diagnostics and repair services, however, rely on both FedEx and UPS services in Memphis to get the products to the facility and distribute them back to customers. Jack added: "The business that we currently do in Memphis started as a laptop repair depot for Apple laptops. The users send their laptops to our facility, we repair them same day and ship them out that night, through FedEx." Flextronics provides similar services to Kodak out of its Venray, Netherlands, distribution center for Kodak's Europe, Africa, and Middle East business.

Second-Hand Heavies

The same reasoning works for Neptune Lines, a Miami-based forwarder with operations in Panama's Colón Free Zone, albeit for much larger pieces of equipment than high-tech consumer gadgets. With proper maintenance, heavy construction equipment can last for decades. Caterpillar's second-hand equipment division buys used Caterpillar equipment, refurbishes it, and resells it. In the past, Caterpillar temporarily stored the used equipment in Panama, typically for several months. When Caterpillar got an order and knew exactly what the customer required, it would hire Neptune Lines to manage the shipment of the equipment to Miami for refurbishment and then ship the equipment to the customer.

Sitting in the Colón Free Zone office of Manzanillo International Terminal, on the Atlantic coast of Panama, overlooking stacks of containers and long queues of trucks entering the port, I discussed with Juan Carlos Croston, its vice president of marketing, several aspects of the Colón Free Zone operations. At one point in the conversation, he mentioned that Neptune Lines saw an opportunity to provide value-added services to Caterpillar, transforming itself in the process. Neptune told Caterpillar, "If you are sitting here for two months, taking this to Miami, why don't you do the refurbishing in Panama?" Caterpillar agreed. Instead of moving the heavy equipment from Panama to Miami and then from Miami to the buyer's location, Neptune Lines would refurbish the equipment in Panama and then make a single move directly from Panama to the customer's location.

Providing this value-added service required a significant investment by Neptune Lines in Colón. Training the mechanics, buying the tools needed to refurbish Caterpillar equipment, and getting certified by Caterpillar took ten months. But the investment paid off. Soon, the company was refurbishing hundreds of those big pieces of equipment annually.

"But," Croston added, "the story didn't end there." Caterpillar's competitor, Komatsu, noticed this and asked Neptune Lines to replicate the same service for them. As of 2011, Neptune handles 5,000 pieces of equipment per year on behalf of the two equipment makers. Komatsu shut down its operations in Miami and Chile and consolidated them in Panama. The arrangement works well for the equipment makers, the logistics service provider, and Panama. Neptune Lines makes more money by refurbishing the equipment and getting closer to its customers; the equipment makers pay less in transportation by skipping the move from storage to a refurbishment center; and the region—in this case Panama—gets more high-paying mechanical equipment repairs jobs requiring specialized skills.

Caterpillar, for its part, did not object to Neptune's relationship with its competitor. Daniel Stanton, a distribution research consultant with Caterpillar Logistics Inc., wrote in response to my email about the subject: "The answer probably is that we all benefit from the freedom in the relationship. The investments that our suppliers make in training and equipment to support our needs are more economical if they can be spread across other customers, too." He then added, "We share many common logistics providers with our competitors. For example, one of our heavy-haul carriers has a shipping yard across the street from my office, and it is quite common to see competitors' equipment there, side-by-side with Cat machines." The phenomenon of a supplier serving several competing customers is unique neither to the heavy equipment business nor to logistics services. It is common, for example, in the high-tech industry where large contract manufacturers build products for many competing brand owners.

Operations such as ATC's cell phone repairs in AllianceTexas, Flextronics's laptop repairs in Memphis, UPS Supply Chain Solutions for Toshiba computer repairs in Louisville (described in chapter 4), and Neptune Lines' heavy equipment repair in Panama, provide another important economic benefit to the local economy. The availability of a technically trained workforce in the area can attract other companies needing technical skill, leading to more high paying jobs and a positive feedback loop for the cluster.

Customer Service: Value-Added Becomes Visible

So far, this chapter discussed only "behind the scenes" value-added activities. In the preceding examples, the skilled workers in a value-added fulfillment center might handle the merchandise or returned items, but they don't interact directly with the customer. Some logistics providers, however, go well beyond these less visible services.

Customer-facing value-added services are a natural follow-on to warranty repair services offered by advanced logistics service providers (such as UPS and Exel) and contract manufacturers (such as Jabil and Flextronics). For example, UPS described how a laptop that is covered by the manufacturer's warranty might arrive at their repair facility in Louisville, but the repair technician might find unambiguous evidence of situations that would void the warranty. These include Starbucks latte residue inside the keyboard, customer modifications inside the case, or outright damage from being dropped.

The simplest option, in cases of abuse, is to refuse service and ship the damaged product back as "out of warranty." Although contractually defensible, it is certainly not the best option for anyone. Instead, UPS's client (the brand owner) authorizes UPS to call the consumer on its behalf, explain what the repair technician uncovered, and offer to fix the item for an appropriate fee. Often, the consumer understands why the repair isn't covered and pays for the repair. Offering such customer service adds value for everyone—consumers get their products repaired, the logistics provider earns repair revenues, and the brand owner gains a reputation for better service.

Taking on such value-added service, which is a natural extension of repair services, requires staffing by customer service representatives with technical know-how and problem-solving ability, as well as appropriate telephone etiquette.

Is There a Doctor in the (Ware)house?

One doesn't expect to find a doctor in the middle of a warehouse. But online retailing allows home delivery of prescription orders to be shipped directly from the warehouse instead of through retail pickup. UPS also fulfills prescriptions[19] directly to consumers. This service requires a pharmacy within the warehouse, staffed with professional pharmacists. Moreover, because the United States has a state-by-state approach to fulfilling prescriptions, any company that wants to dispense prescriptions through home delivery to all fifty states must have the licenses required in every one of the fifty states. Although some states have reciprocal relationships (e.g., a pharmacist licensed in Florida can readily get a license in Arizona[20]), enough states have their own idiosyncratic licensing requirements, tests, and application processes that no single pharmacist can cover the entire county. To this end, UPS SCS Healthcare Division employs more than twenty pharmacists in its Louisville campus to ensure that the company always has the required licensed professionals in its fulfillment centers to distribute prescription orders in all fifty states.

Becoming a pharmacist requires at least six years of college (to get a doctorate in pharmacy), multiple rotations of clinical experience, a professional examination, a state license, and continuing education. Pharmacists earn[21] on the order of three times the salary of hourly warehouse workers.[22]

NEW TYPES OF BUSINESSES MOVE IN

Logistics clusters attract other nonlogistics businesses in three ways. First, suppliers of companies conducting logistics operations are attracted to the cluster in order to be physically next to their customers. This phenomenon is not unique to logistics clusters and is evident in many other industrial clusters. The second way in which logistics clusters attract other businesses, particularly manufacturers, is by serving as "infrastructure" that can help these companies get raw material, receive inbound parts, and distribute the finished products to their customers. In both cases, the logistics cluster contributes, over time, to the creation of high-paying jobs in various industries. Third, logistics clusters are a fertile ground for forming new logistics-dependent businesses.

Suppliers to the Logistics Industry
Suppliers to logistics firms in a cluster include both "direct" suppliers, who service the transportation and warehousing industry, and "indirect" suppliers, who service value-added activities performed in the cluster.

Conveyance Repair and Maintenance
Although emergency repairs can happen anywhere, carriers can defer many types of conveyance repairs and maintenance tasks until the conveyance reaches a convenient location. Conveyances can have non-emergency repairs, such as when an auxiliary generator on a ship isn't working right, a hydraulic cylinder leaks a little oil, or one of the radios breaks down. These breakdowns don't prevent the conveyance from completing a delivery but motivate corrective actions when the conveyance arrives at a depot. Conveyances also have a wide range of periodic maintenance activities such as oil changes, belt replacement, bearing regreasing, engine refurbishment, repainting, or mandatory reinspections to maintain certification.

Much like a NASCAR pit stop, the carrier wants its conveyance to get in and get out in the shortest time possible. Ideally, carriers want to repair conveyances en route between revenue-generating jobs and to minimize the time that the carrier can't use the conveyance. If possible, carriers prefer to prearrange for minor repairs and maintenance to take place during loading and unloading operations when the vehicle is already at a port, an airport, or another terminal location. This means that the best sites for repairs will be cluster locations—places with a high density of conveyance activities that attract both scope and scale of repair service companies. For example, Singapore has some 100 companies offering a wide range of ship repair services that include gearbox repair, hydraulics, engine oil systems, desalination plants, HVAC, and rigging.[23]

When a logistics cluster location becomes a hub of minor maintenance and repair activities, it is a short step to providing full-service maintenance operations—those requiring pulling vehicles from service and, in the case of ocean-going ships, literally pulling them from the sea. Removing the ship from the water enables crucial services such as cleaning the entire hull, repainting, and repairing damage or wear of underwater parts of the vessel, such as hull panels, propellers, rudders, and bow thrusters. Dry docks also enable a thorough inspection of the ship by a surveyor from a classification society to certify the ongoing seaworthiness of the vessel. Singapore's largest dry dock at the Jurong Shipyard can handle ultra large crude carriers (ULCCs) of up to 500,000 dead weight tons.

As these repair and maintenance operations develop and increase in their scope of services, they employ high-level technical talent, including marine engineers, mechanical engineers, factory-authorized repair technicians, and a highly skilled workforce comprised of welders, mechanics, and electricians.

Adding Value-Added Suppliers

Visit any distribution hub and you'll find packaging suppliers—companies that provide pallets, crates, cardboard boxes, plastic wrap, cushioning materials, packing tape, and the like. With the rise of value-added activities comes a rising volume of business with suppliers who support those value-added activities.

For example, retail displays call for more than just plain cardboard. Retail displays require full-color graphics on high-quality glossy stock instead of brown corrugated cardboard. Moreover, retail displays need extensive engineering to design the intricate cuts and folds that make an attractive display and can hold hundreds of pounds of product. Such designs require significantly more skill and equipment than does assembling standard cardboard boxes. A logistics cluster with sufficient volume attracts new suppliers and induces local packaging suppliers to upgrade skills and equipment to meet the requirements of value-added distribution activities. The need for last-minute production of displays resulting from a production launch or a last-minute promotional surge means that shippers will prefer local production of the displays. A sampling of the dozens of display suppliers in the Chicago logistics cluster include: Joliet Pattern (retail signage, display graphics, merchandising kiosks), Rapid-Pac (packing supplies distributor), Rose Laboratories (contract packaging and assembly of creams and liquid products), and Advanced Packaging Concepts (custom-manufacturer of foam, cardboard, and wood packaging, boxing, and crating solutions).

Another example of this phenomenon is the move of Sealed Air Corporation to the PLAZA logistics park in Zaragoza (see p. 16 in chapter 1). Sealed Air developed the Cryovac system to help preserve Caladero's fish freshness during the distribution process from Zaragoza. Its plant is located right next to the Caladero facility, allowing for coordination and the development of new and improved systems to seal in freshness.

Specialized Labor for Specialized Tasks

Logistics clusters can attract some unexpected types of specialized workers, such as photographers and photo editors. Zappos.com, the online shoe and apparel retailer, located its fulfillment center in Shepherdsville, Kentucky, just down the road from the UPS hub—a fact made obvious by the large number of Zappos boxes noticeable every night to anybody touring the UPS sorting facility. Zappos sells a staggering 116,932 styles of shoes and other apparel across 1,265 brands.[24]

Before Zappos.com can sell a product, it needs a high-quality photo of the product for its Web site. The manufacturers' photos don't suffice because they aren't consistent across brands, and Zappos requires that the photos on the Web site exactly match the items in the store and can be easily compared across brands. This means that Zappos shoots its own photos and product description videos. The most efficient location for Zappos to produce high-quality product shots is in the Shepherdsville fulfillment center. When a new style of shoe arrives in the facility, Zappos pulls a sample and creates the images and video for the Web site. This is accomplished by two shifts of photographers, photographers' assistants, editors, and the like. Every day, the photo department gets a first crack at incoming new products. In November 2010, the company celebrated its 50,000th product description video.[25]

Industrial Subclusters within Logistics Clusters

One of the processes feeding the growth of all industrial clusters is the movement of suppliers into the cluster to better serve their customers. This is also the case with logistics clusters. Both the Dallas/Ft. Worth and the Chicago logistics clusters include distribution centers of consumer goods suppliers, such as LEGO, Clorox, and General Mills. The suppliers serve these clusters' large distribution centers of retailers, such as Walmart and United Grocers. The proximity affords these companies not only the general advantages of close supplier-customer relationships, but it also minimizes the cost of the physical products hand-offs between the manufacturer and the retailer. Describing the suppliers and retailers, Vann Cunningham, assistant vice president for economic development at the BNSF Railway Company said, "Colocating offers them some significant advantages, both in terms of cost sufficiency, and also control over their supply chain. It reduces the risk and reduces their cost."

But the colocation in logistics clusters has a further effect. If a logistics cluster becomes renowned for certain combinations of storage, transportation, and value-added services, then the cluster may attract a concentration of companies from within a particular industry who all benefit from that mix of services. Furthermore, those companies, in many cases, nucleate a local industrial cluster within the logistics cluster.

Rotterdam Car Distribution

Brittanniëhaven on the south-central part of the Rotterdam port region illustrates this cluster-in-cluster effect. Drive past Brittanniëhaven on the A15 highway near Rozemburg, and you might be excused for thinking that you've found the world's largest car dealer. Tens of thousands of brand-new cars are parked row-after-row in tight diagonal formations. Groups of gray luxury sedans, white minivans, multicolored hatchbacks, and numerous makes and models sit waiting for buyers. Yet car buyers never come to this lot because all of these cars are destined for shipment elsewhere.

Brittanniëhaven is the center of a subcluster called the Rotterdam Car Center, dedicated to handling new cars. Massive, specialized Pure Car/Truck Carrier (PCTC) ships bring the cars to Rotterdam from overseas car makers. The tall boxy ships are like floating twelve-level parking garages holding 4,000 to 7,000 cars each. Cars are driven onto the ship at the automakers' ports in Asia and driven off at Rotterdam. From Rotterdam, the cars may go to other European countries via a second, smaller PCTC ship, a short-sea freighter, a barge up the Rhine, a rail-car carrier, or be loaded onto a car transport semitrailer.

Of the some 300,000 cars that land in Rotterdam every year, 80 percent receive value-added treatments to prepare the cars for sale in specific countries. Value-added activities include technical modifications, predelivery inspection, damage inspection, waxing and dewaxing, installation of accessories, and preparation of demonstration models. The area also handles the refurbishment of 15,000 used cars (mostly from car-rental fleets) and 15,000 excavators per year.[26] The value of this subcluster can be evident in Mazda's contract with the Rotterdam Car Center. Every year, 50,000 Mazda cars destined for England actually sail past the UK coast to come to the wrong side of the North Sea for final processing before taking a second short trip back to sea and to the UK.

Rotterdam includes two other large subclusters dependent on the port's extensive logistics. First, Rotterdam has a massive petroleum and petrochemical cluster associated with the eight Petroleum-haven ports that line the southern bank of the Maas from the port's western entrance (see p. 62 in chapter 3). This subcluster goes far beyond the energy infrastructure required to support the carriers that call on Rotterdam. The area includes more than forty chemical and petrochemical companies and three industrial gas manufacturers, generating more than 600 chemical products derived from oil and other bulk materials brought to the port.[27] A second major subcluster is Merwehaven (Fruitport) on the northeastern end of the port, which handles fruit, vegetables, and juices. The Fruitport subcluster includes thirty million square feet of conventional storage, 600,000 air-conditioned pallet spaces, and 250,000 cold-storage pallet spaces.[28] Fruitport has some 200 importers and exporters that trade and distribute fruit, vegetables, and fruit juices. In total, Merwehaven handles about one million tons of produce annually.[29]

Shared Assets Cement Relations in a Subcluster

On the other side of the world, Singapore's cement industry illustrates how tightly shared logistical assets can form the basis for an industrial subcluster. Large bulk carriers filled with clinker—nodules of the furnace-treated mineral amalgam that is the key ingredient in cement—arrive in Singapore's Jurong Port and offload their cargo into a shared conveyor system that carries the clinker toward the storage silos of six of Singapore's eight cement companies. "They're all using a common user facility, comprised in silos, all linked up together with a common distribution system," Lek Yuan Leng, vice president corporate development of Jurong Port told me. "It's then centrally distributed and allocated to all the six different cement companies." In total, the system handles about 3.5 million tons a year, which represents about 80 percent to 90 percent of the country's cement supply.

This subcluster arose in the 1960s. Initially, Singapore's cement companies dotted the island. But given Singapore's limited land area, the Singaporean government's Economic Development Board wanted to intensify land use. Instead of each cement maker having its own bulk carrier berth, the government offered to build a single berth at Jurong Port as well as a covered conveyor belt system to distribute the incoming clinker to the silos. The individual cement companies built and own their own storage silos. "There is a lot of efficiency being derived by having a model like what we have, in the long run," said Robert Yap, chairman and CEO of the YCH Group, when we discussed the effects of logistics clusters in Singapore. The result is that "Jurong Port actually has one of the world's largest common-user cement terminals," Jurong's Leng added. "Ultimately, it's very clear that you get economies of scale, by clustering together, or by banding together, I think that's why they do this," concluded Yap.

A Logistics-Dependent Healthcare Cluster

As a cluster develops, it becomes known for particular types of logistics, be it air connections in Memphis and Louisville, rail hubs in Chicago and Kansas City, or international maritime in Rotterdam and Singapore. Because companies from the same industry tend to have similar logistics needs, they tend to be attracted to the same logistics clusters. The result is industrial subclusters within the logistics cluster. Dexter Muller, senior vice president of community development at the Memphis Chamber of Commerce, told me that Memphis is the second largest city in the country for manufacturing and distribution of orthopedic devices. The area provides a home for three of the leading OEMs of artificial joints: Medtronic's Spinal and Biologics division, Smith & Nephew's Orthopedics division, and Wright Medical. All three companies share a similar need for ultrafast airfreight (see also the discussion of flexibility on p. 105 in chapter 4). When I asked Rob Varner, senior director of US distribution operations at Medtronic, what he thought about having his competitors in his own backyard, he said he wasn't bothered. In fact, he saw it as a positive factor because the presence of the three big companies attracted more of Medtronic's suppliers to Memphis.

The logistical rationale for the location gets a much larger economic ball rolling. "More and more OEMs are setting up shop here because there's economy of scale and enough volume here for them to do that," Varner said. The Greater Memphis Chamber works with local medical device companies to attract other medical device companies and suppliers to come to Memphis. "They know the industry better than I do, so they can pinpoint companies that would make sense to have across the street from them versus across the country," said Leigh Anne Downes, director of life science business development at the Memphis Chamber.[30] While Memphis is a significant biomedical cluster, it's a biomedical cluster because it's a logistics cluster. Memphis's central location, FedEx air hub, and other logistics services create the critical delivery time performance advantage needed by this industry.

A similar phenomenon occurred in Indianapolis. The region features some 1,500 logistics and related services companies, including FedEx, UPS, and CNH Logistics, as well as distribution centers for Amazon.com, Hewlett-Packard, CVS Caremark, Brightpoint, and many others. With four intersecting interstate highways, a central location in the US Midwest, good rail connections, and a leading airport, Indianapolis became a natural logistics cluster. Taking advantage of this connectivity and the logistics services available in Indianapolis was one of the attractions for many life science companies to move to the area, including industry giants like Eli Lilly and Co., WellPoint Inc., Dow AgroSciences LLC, Cook Group, Pfizer, and Roche Diagnostics. The cluster grew to $69 billion in total annual revenue[31] and, just as important, attracted a $140 million venture capital initiative dedicated to Indiana's life science companies.

New Nonlogistics Businesses

In addition to spawning new logistics companies (see chapter 9), logistics clusters also support the development of new companies in industrial subclusters that form in the logistics cluster. A case in point is the entrepreneurial activity in the biomedical cluster of surgical orthopedic implants and instruments in Memphis.[32] These new companies extend the industrial subcluster within the logistics cluster in three directions: becoming new suppliers to the subcluster's OEMs; offering products that complement the subcluster's OEMs; and becoming new OEMs, too.

An example of a new supplier is Y&W Technologies LLC. Willis Yates was a twenty-seven-year veteran of Smith & Nephew Plc (a maker of hip and knee implants with a facility in Memphis), when he struck out on his own to form Y&W in 2000 in Memphis. Y&W specializes in plating medical instruments by applying an advanced chromium surface treatment that dramatically improves the performance and increases the longevity of surgical instruments. In addition, Y&W provides high-tech treatments such as electro-polishing, titanium anodizing, surface passivation, gold plating, and laser marking. In the decade since its founding, Y&W has expanded in scale and scope. Y&W works for all three of the big Memphis medical device makers: Medtronic Inc., Smith & Nephew Plc, and Wright Medical Group Inc.

Big River is another Memphis startup that supplies complementary instruments used to insert the OEM's medical implants and devices during surgery. "These companies [OEMs] make their money off of implants, and with every implant, there's a suite of instruments that facilitate the device," said Tom Roehm, CEO of Big River. "Those have to be replenished and that's what we do."[33] Like Y&W, Big River does business with all three major device companies in Memphis. The company had fifteen employees in 2010.

The presence of so many local suppliers enables the big three OEMs to shorten their supply chains. When Y&W's Yates noticed that Smith & Nephew was sending its manufactured products to "four or five different places" for additional fabrication services, he decided to offer a one-stop shop for these services. Ted Davis, senior vice president of business development for Wright Medical, commented on the symbiotic relationships between big companies and entrepreneurial start-ups in the Memphis medical cluster. He noted that the more small suppliers form in Memphis, the more attractive the area is for any medical device company looking to relocate. At the same time, the larger companies in the area can contribute to the early and sustained growth of these smaller companies.[34]

The combination of recruited companies and start-ups pleases Medtronic. "Now we're getting the benefit of having more local suppliers available to us which, if we were on our own, we wouldn't have quite as much of that as we do," Varner said.

6

INFRASTRUCTURE

Watching Platforma Logística de Zaragoza (PLAZA) in Spain transform from a quiet farmland to a bustling logistics park gave me an appreciation for all the different infrastructures required by logistics clusters. The large scale and sophistication of assets such as ports, airports, warehouses, roads, railroad tracks, and canals, implies the need for large investments, careful stewardship, and astute management.

Supply chain operations generally handle three types of flows: (i) the physical flow of products moving downstream from suppliers to manufacturers to retailers, as well as the reverse flow of unsold goods, returns, and reuse, (ii) information flow, including specifications and orders moving upstream and status messages flowing downstream, and (iii) the cash flow associated with supply chain transactions and operations. Consequently, logistics clusters rely on information and financial infrastructures in addition to the physical infrastructure. Because logistics clusters are typically also transportation hubs, they require a robust energy infrastructure, too, to power conveyances and cluster operations.

PHYSICAL INFRASTRUCTURE

Physical infrastructure dominates logistics investments, amounting to trillions of dollars' worth of capital assets worldwide for conveyances, buildings, land improvements, roads, ports, airports, and associated management and control infrastructure. Although logistics certainly leverages natural resources such as rivers, harbors, and oceans, even these natural capital assets require investment in development and improvements to handle high volumes of freight and massive conveyances.

To take just one example, UPS's balance sheet[1] includes $1 billion in land, $6 billion in buildings and improvements, $6.6 billion in plant equipment, and nearly $20 billion in the company's 225 aircraft and nearly 100,000 delivery vehicles.[2] Yet these assets represent a tiny fraction of the physical infrastructure used daily by UPS. UPS could not deliver freight at high speed and low cost without an expansive milieu of physical infrastructure including the roads traveled by its brown trucks, the hundreds of airports visited by its brown-tail airplanes, and the railroads that handle about 10 percent of UPS's ground volume as intermodal shipments.

Several authors have developed a variety of accessibility metrics to capture the attractiveness of certain regions in terms of egress and ingress.[3] Such metrics can be helpful for companies contemplating locations of distribution centers and regional authorities assessing either their competitive position vis-à-vis neighboring regions or the need for further network investment.

Terminal Infrastructure: Portrait of a Park

The AllianceTexas development[4] illustrates many of the infrastructural features of a modern-day logistics park. Alliance is a 17,000-acre master-planned development, created by Hillwood Development Company LLC, a Perot company, just north of the Dallas–Ft. Worth Metroplex. As of 2011, companies and developers had invested $7.3 billion, and the park was only 40 percent complete.[5] Much of the AllianceTexas development consists of a series of commercial parks anchored by the Alliance Global Logistics Hub, where distribution centers are operated by two types of shippers: (i) beneficial freight owners (BFOs), including manufacturers, distributors and retailers who are operating their own logistics facilities and (ii) logistics service providers who offer warehousing, distribution, transportation, and many value-added services to the their customers (who are BFOs). As of 2011, Alliance had 31.2 million square feet of commercial space in use by more than 260 companies.

To connect all the warehouses and distribution centers to both inbound and outbound product flows, Alliance offers multiple transportation modes for the park's residents. The first is roadways. Interstate 35 bisects Alliance, giving park members ready access to the freeway. Other major east–west highways (Interstates 20, 30, and 40) intersect nearby to give the park good access to the entire south-central United States. Approximately forty-eight million people live within one day's trucking from Alliance, and 111 million live within two days.[6]

Alliance's second mode is embodied in BNSF's Alliance Intermodal Facility, which covers several hundred acres with train tracks, an intermodal terminal, and acres upon acres of container storage yards. As described by Vann Cunningham of BNSF, the company's double-track main line passes through the facility and fans out into 40 parallel tracks of classification yard. The intermodal terminal consists of four widely spaced, one-mile-long tracks on the eastern side of the facility, where trains are staged and containers are lifted from and onto the trains. BNSF handles about 600,000 lifts per year at Alliance, but it has the capacity to handle two million.[7] A 1,600-acre section of Alliance, immediately west of the BNSF facility, is devoted to companies requiring direct access to rail via a rail spur.[8] The Union Pacific Railroad also provides direct access to Alliance, giving park tenants the opportunity for using a second Class I railroad.

Third, Alliance has an airport dedicated to cargo operations. The developers put the airport in a central location in the Alliance Park, with direct access to the interstate, which minimizes drayage distances and times. The airport's on-site cargo-handling building uses a cross-dock design that lets freight flow between aircraft— including the largest wide-body freighters—on one side and trucks on the other side. On-site US Customs clearance features a centralized examination station that minimizes delays for foreign air-cargo.[9] Currently, FedEx uses Alliance as a regional sorting hub. Lee Roberts, a FedEx senior manager of the FedEx Southwest Regional Hub Operations, told me that Alliance is also used by FedEx as an overflow hub facility, backing up both the Memphis and the Indianapolis hubs.

"Professional Driver on Closed Course"

A standard twenty-foot ocean shipping container has a maximum permitted weight of as much as 24,000 kg (52,900 pounds), and a forty-foot container, which is the most common container size used in international trade, can weigh 30,480 kilograms (67,200 pounds).[10] Ocean-going vessels and railroads can readily handle these maximum-weight containers, but trucking companies in most countries cannot, as a result of legal weight limits imposed in order to reduce road damage caused by heavy loads. To a first approximation, the maximum legal weight for a tractor trailer truck on US highways is 80,000 pounds, but that limit includes the tractor, chassis, and container shell, thus reducing the maximum permitted net cargo weight to about 39,000 to 44,000 pounds.[11]

These conflicting maximum limits for ocean and rail containers vs. trucking put shippers of heavy containers in a bind. A shipper can either subdivide the load across more shipping containers at the source, or it can transfer the load of a single container to two containers[12] ("transload") at the destination port or rail yard. Both options add costs in extra containers, handling, and drayage. They also introduce delays and possible damages. But there's a third option: using private roads with higher weight limits to haul heavy containers from the rail yard to a distribution center.

Logistics park operators, such as CenterPoint,[13] the largest industrial real estate developer in metropolitan Chicago, circumvent road weight restrictions to the benefit of the park's tenants. In CenterPoint Intermodal Center (CIC), south of Chicago, the company designed and built the private roads in the park to higher standards than the public roadways, so they can take the heavy loads and not be subject to cargo weight restrictions. Consequently, a heavy container can be put onto a vessel in China, shipped to a US port, transferred to rail car, and delivered to the BNSF rail terminal in CIC. There, it can be drayed by truck directly to the floor of the Walmart distribution center, despite the fact that it exceeds the US public road weight limit. By comparison, a distribution center just outside the park may have to transload the container in the port or in the destination rail yard. Other parks, such as AllianceTexas,[14] have similar goals yet somewhat different approaches. Alliance negotiated an agreement with the local government to maintain park-area public roadways used by heavy loads and repair any resulting damage.

Developers' Roles

Developers and park operators such as Hillwood, CenterPoint, Prologis, the Allen Group, and Watson play a crucial role in the development and operation of local infrastructure. In addition to the site selection, land acquisition, layout design, the initial government-permitting interface, and the extension of public utilities, some developers build warehouse or industrial space speculatively while others leave the land undeveloped until a customer (either a shipper or a logistics service provider) specifies a need. The developer operating the logistics park might have a quasi-governmental role in defining covenants within the park, managing an association of the park's occupants, and adjudicating minor disputes.

Park operators also change the parks' functionality to match changing demand. For example, when Watson Land Company began building industrial parks in the Los Angeles area in the 1960s, 75 percent of the park's tenants were manufacturers. By the early twenty-first century, however, 90 percent of the tenants were logistics service providers and shippers conducting logistics and distribution-related operations. Starting in 2005, Watson renovated buildings and park facilities to support the changing patterns of use. The company changed to logistics-friendly rectangular building layouts with long walls of truck dock doors and increased the turning radius of entryways to improve maneuvering space for large trucks.

Wet Infrastructure in Rotterdam

Rotterdam exemplifies the types of physical infrastructure needed by major seaport logistics clusters. Because water covers one-third of the 10,500 hectares of the port of Rotterdam, wet infrastructure comprises a large portion of the port.[15] Although the Rhine and Maas Rivers were deep enough for the early ocean-going vessels in the era of sail, these natural waterways could never handle the massive ships of today. The largest container ships ride 15 meters

(49 feet) deep in the water, and the largest supertankers and bulk freighters extend even further beneath the waves. To answer the challenge of increasing size and depth of vessels, the Dutch transformed a natural geography of shifting oxbowed river channels and ever-changing flooded landscapes into an artificial geographic infrastructure of straight deep channels, dry industrial parks, and flood-preventing dikes.

Some aspects of Rotterdam's physical infrastructure serve to tame the forces of nature and secure the expensive physical assets of the port against storms and flooding. The Maeslant Barrier, for example, protects the main channel into Rotterdam from storm-surge—North Sea waters pushed inland by extreme winds and currents. The Barrier consists of two 240-meter-long curved doors that float in trenches on either side of the 360-meter-wide entrance to the port. Each door swings on a steel trusswork that is almost as long as the Eiffel Tower is tall.[16] The 635 million euro Maeslant Barrier is just one of nine storm barriers and dams built by the Dutch over a thirty-year period to reduce the chance of flooding in key areas of the Rhine delta region.[17]

Nor does spending on wet infrastructure end with its construction. Restless ocean currents and river silt constantly threaten deep-water ports and channels such as Rotterdam's. Maintenance dredging of Rotterdam's approach channel and port totals some sixteen million cubic meters of Rhine river silt and shifting ocean sand per year.[18] This annual volume of dredging is equivalent to a cube of earth, with each side equal to two and a half football fields in length. Other deepwater ports and canals have similar needs. For example, the US Army Corps of Engineers spends $10 million to $15 million every year dredging as much as three million cubic yards of material from Charleston Harbor. Port fees or taxes cover the costs of maintaining this maritime infrastructure.

The massive earth-moving efforts needed to create and maintain port infrastructure at large ports such as Rotterdam don't stop at the sea. Whereas the seabed rises steadily to meet the sandy coast of the Netherlands, ultra-large ships need deep-water channels from the sea to reach the port. At Rotterdam, a 22-meter-deep artificial channel extends 31 nautical miles out into the ocean.

Midway along this channel is a deep dredged basin almost two miles across that lets ships turn around. Other deepwater ports around the world have similar artificial undersea channels. With the inexorable increase in ship size comes the inevitable need to enhance natural harbors and channels to handle wider, longer, and deeper-draft vessels.

Similarly, the Panama Canal expansion project reflects this inevitable need to invest in larger infrastructure to serve larger ships. To ensure the canal's continuing role in maritime commerce, the Panama Canal Authority is enlarging the waterway and building a new set of locks to enable ships larger than the 4,500 TEU capacity Panamax vessels to traverse the canal (see p. 73 in chapter 3). The expanded canal will be able to handle ships with capacity of up to about 12,000 TEUs. This expansion is crucial to the continuing central role of the Panama Canal because ship sizes have grown dramatically. (Dozens of container ships already in service and on order in 2012 are larger than this; yet the expansion will allow most of the world's container fleet to use the canal.)

Land-Side Infrastructure of Rotterdam

Port authorities are, in fact, logistics park operators. They develop the land-side infrastructure, typically in some form of partnership with local and national governments. They also manage the tenants of the port, the most important of which are the terminal operators who handle the vessel/port interface.

Port infrastructure consists of the quays and terminals where large ships dock to unload or load cargo. Over the centuries, the Dutch developed these quay walls to an engineering art form of interlocking plates, anchor pilings, lateral stabilizing anchors, and injected concrete grout. The result is vertical underwater walls as tall as seven-story buildings and able to withstand the slosh and wash from daily tidal currents as well as the gentle nudges of 350 meter (1,000 foot) long container ships and their 30-foot diameter, 50,000-horsepower propellers.

Rotterdam has over ninety privately operated terminals handling a wide range of cargo and ship types such as bulk liquids (35 terminals), general cargo (17 terminals), dry bulk (15 terminals), container ships (9 terminals), roll-on-roll-off ferries (7 terminals), and fruits and juices (5 terminals).[19] Each of these terminals has corresponding handling equipment for transferring cargo to and from ships. For example, the nine container terminals have a total of 114 cranes for quickly unloading and loading containers.

Commercial sites fill almost half the area of the port of Rotterdam. The 5,000 hectares of development includes numerous storage areas such as container yards, tank farms, and warehouses, each with a distinct purpose and appearance. On the western end of the port, where the largest ships dock, container yards cover more than 200 hectares with tidy stacks of multicolored shipping containers. In the dry-bulk terminals, kilometer-long storage areas look like a dirty painter's palette with the various colored piles of red iron ore, gray gravel, black coal, and other ores and raw materials.[20] Large quantities of crude oil come to Rotterdam, and the port includes a substantial petrochemicals industry. Hundreds of tanks store a total of 28.4 million cubic meters of liquids.[21] Several terminals offer specialized storage and handling, including forty-three warehouses with London Metals Exchange (LME) certification for the storage of metals and 750,000 square meters of cold storage for fruits and vegetables. The more than 200 privately owned and operated warehousing and storage areas create a critical inventory buffer between the multiple modes of transportation that serve the port.[22]

Finally, the port would not be complete without a land-based infrastructure of roadways, railways, and pipelines connecting it to the centers of the European economy. About 20 percent (2,000 hectares) of Rotterdam's port is dedicated to roads/railways, service corridors, and residual greenways. A fractal network of capillary roads extends across the port and links each building or terminal to land-based modes of transportation. Once cargo reaches land, it travels south to the main road and rail lines, then turns east along the southern edge of the port, and exits the port area for destinations in the Netherlands, Germany, and the rest of Europe.

Networks: Interconnections and Interactions in Infrastructure

Zaragoza wouldn't be the crossroads of Spain without high-capacity roads, an intermodal railroad yard, and a rail hub, as well as a cargo airport connecting it to the world's trade flows. Similarly, clusters such as Chicago, Memphis, and the Los Angeles basin wouldn't exist at their current scales without a branching network of multimodal connectivity. Roads, railroads, waterways, and air corridors form a crucial infrastructure network connecting logistics clusters to the diverse sources and destinations of goods.

In response to shippers' need for high frequency service (see p. 95 in chapter 4), transportation movements often involve consolidation operations in hubs. In many cases, such hubs serve as a nucleus for the development of logistics clusters, further feeding the hubs' growth, which, in turn, improves the transportation service into and out of the cluster. In particular, logistics clusters develop around the largest such hubs, involving major intermodal yards, ports, and airports, with large conveyance trips connecting these hubs/clusters (long trains, large vessels, and large planes).

Roads

The four million miles of roads and streets in the United States carry about 70 percent of all US inland freight (as measured by value of the freight transported) and just over 30 percent of the ton-miles hauled.[23] The road transport fraction in Europe is higher, standing at 76 percent of all ton-kilometer freight movements within the EU.[24]

Logistics parks developers design both the parks' roadways and their connections to outside infrastructure. For example, PLAZA's designers laid out a grid of four-lane roadways with wide turnings so that trucks could freely move into, around, and out of the park. PLAZA's designers also developed the connections to the local road network in addition to being instrumental in attracting an intermodal rail facility and upgrading the local airport.

Railroads

Overall, US railroads invest almost $20 billion per year in capital expenditures.[25] BNSF Railroad, which owns roughly one-fourth of US rail infrastructure, illustrates the scale of this investment. The railroad comprises 50,000 miles of track, 6,700 locomotives, 76,800 freight cars, and 7,700 chassis and containers.[26] The company has forty intermodal facilities, including yards in large logistics parks in Chicago, Kansas City, Memphis, and Dallas/Ft. Worth. These intermodal yards attract distribution facilities of large retailers involved in international imports, as well as many other cargo interests.[27]

The role of rail transportation in logistics is expected to grow in the future, mainly as a result of its low cost of transportation and its lower carbon footprint, compared to trucking. US railroads have been investing in increased capacity during the last part of the twentieth century and into the twenty-first, by boosting the use of double-stacked containers, building double track routes, and even triple and quadruple tracking, allowing not only for bidirectional traffic but also enabling fast trains to pass slow ones. Based on these investments, as well as improved control systems, railroads are introducing higher-speed services that offer overnight shipping between selected points at speeds of 500 miles per day, which makes rail competitive with single-driver long-haul trucking.

Much of the growth for railroads is in intermodal services, hauling containers. To this end, their role as anchors of logistics clusters and even as coinvestors in such clusters is expected to increase.

Inland Waterways

Infrastructure for inland waters includes all the canals, harbors, and navigational aids required to allow for inland waterway shipping. The EU has some 37,000 km of navigable inland waters spanning twenty of the region's twenty-seven nations.[28] In total, some 12,600 inland freight vessels carry dry goods and bulk liquids on EU waterways.

The Netherlands and Germany alone account for 54 percent of inland cargo vessels and 77 percent of the freight moved on EU waterways, a large portion of which moves on the Rhine River and associated canals. The Dutch-German border sees 170,000 ship crossings a year carrying 160 million tons of freight.[29] Both the Netherlands and Germany have infrastructure maintenance programs aimed at keeping the Rhine River, associated canals, and port estuaries in navigable condition.

Similarly, in the United States, 25,000 miles of waterways carry about 13 percent of US ton-miles.[30] The US Army Corp of Engineers spends more than half of its $4.6 billion annual budget enhancing and maintaining 12,000 miles of commercially navigable channels; 257 locks; and 926 coastal, Great Lakes, and inland harbors. This includes dredging 255 million cubic yards per year to maintain the navigability of inland waters and ports.

Airports and Highways in the Sky

Fully loaded, a Boeing 747-400 freighter tops out at 875,000 pounds. Add the 180 mph take-off speed, crosswind forces, braking forces, deicing chemicals, and the slam of the occasional hard landing; and the runway surface must withstand severe punishment without cracking, buckling, spalling, sagging, or rutting. Runways for airports that handle "heavies" feature layers of high-strength concrete up to two feet thick with under-layers of clay and aggregate that spread the forces from thousands of weekly take-offs and landings. In fact, one of the main advantages of the Zaragoza freight airport was that it was built to handle the heavy B-52 strategic bombers during the Cold War (see p. 12 in chapter 1). The result was a long runway with thick pavement, able to handle the largest fully-loaded cargo planes.

The demands of logistics—24×7 reliability and capacity—mean that major airfreight carriers require multiple long runways designed to allow all-weather operation (given wind from any direction). Fred Smith moved FedEx from Little Rock to Memphis in the early days of the company, in part because of Memphis's superior airport infrastructure. Memphis has four runways, each 9,000 to 11,000 feet long. Three runways are set in the North–South direction (36/18),[31] in accordance with the prevailing winds; an additional runway, set in the East–West direction (27/09), is used when wind directions do not allow North–South operation. Advanced instrument navigation systems at the airport enable all-weather operation. Similarly, Louisville has two main North–South runways (35/17) and an additional East–West (29/11) runway.

Airports include more than just runways. Taxiways and tarmac for aircraft parking and hangar space mean millions of square feet of additional concrete and asphalt. Airfreight main sorting hubs, such as Memphis or Louisville, include multimillion square foot sorting facilities. UPS, for example, has invested more than $2.2 billion in its Louisville Worldport alone.[32]

SUPPORTING INFRASTRUCTURE

As mentioned in the introduction to this chapter, supply chain management involves the movement of information and cash, in addition to physical goods. Consequently, logistics clusters are supported by sophisticated information technologies and financial services. In addition, these clusters need a robust energy infrastructure for refueling conveyances.

Financial Infrastructure: Cash for Cargo

Supply chain operations involve the need to move money across continents, hedge for currency fluctuations, protect against default risks, and ensure that the dozens of parties involved in a single shipment all get compensated fairly and quickly. Inexpensive movement of goods requires inexpensive movement of money, too. Every delivery of physical goods may involve multiple financial transactions, in addition to the payment for the goods and services to the many parties involved. The additional transactions include tax accounting and payments; customs payments, including accounting for duty drawback and payments of countervailing duty; deductions for incomplete or damaged goods; and more. Many of these financial dealings involve foreign exchange transactions, exercising financial options, complex accounting, and other nontrivial financial activities. All of these transactions start with on-site physical movement or inspection of the goods and cannot be tracked in the virtual world unless first captured in the real world.

Local financial infrastructure and acumen support this business function. Consequently, trading activities and financial activities have grown hand-in-hand. For example, Chicago became a financial hub for commodities' trading because it was a physical hub for commodities' logistics.

Panama's pools of capital and financial expertise came from its status as a tax haven. After WWII, the country enacted very strong banking secrecy laws that encouraged a multidecade influx of foreign investment. As described in chapter 7, pressure from the US government and the World Trade Organization caused Panama to weaken these laws in later years. Yet, the Panamanians retained their expertise in international financial transactions, which was an important factor in supporting the logistics activities in Panama.

The international dimension of global logistics adds a layer of financial complexity. Each trading transaction includes a multistage process by which, for example: a foreign supplier hands goods to a carrier at a foreign port; the carrier notifies the supplier's bank that the goods are in the carrier's hands (through the bill of lading); the supplier's bank notifies the customer's bank that shipment has occurred; the customer authorizes the payment through the banks to the supplier; and the carrier hands over the goods once they reach the customer's local port. Each of these five stages involves dozens of transactional, financial, and legal details and a web of other participants such as freight forwarders, warehouse operators, and customs agents. Problems, errors, deductions, rebates, and exceptions complicate the process further. When researchers at Stanford University and TradeBeam mapped the basic process in detail, they identified 109 steps.[33] Financial firms serving logistics clusters must be adept at handling these complexities. To this end, note that Singapore operates the world's fourth largest foreign exchange trading center after London, New York, and Tokyo.[34]

Today's information and communications technology contributed to the geographic decoupling of modern finance from the underlying physical business activities. Yet, many logistics clusters still include sophisticated financial services industry representation.

Information Infrastructure: Bits for Boxes

An information supply chain parallels each physical supply chain. Specifications, orders, required delivery dates, and various regulatory details move upstream in the supply chain—from retailers to distributors to manufacturers to suppliers and to the suppliers' suppliers. As the items are shipped from supplier to manufacturer, or manufacturer to distributor or retailers, information about what was shipped, when it will arrive, who is transporting it, and so forth, is sent downstream. Furthermore, the transportation companies feed frequent data about current locations, times, and conditions to both the shipper and the consignee at every leg of the journey. As the shipments progress, other information elements are exchanged with customs and security authorities. Even once a shipment is delivered, the information flow continues regarding the conditions of delivery, payments, insurance claims, and more.

Companies involved in logistics and supply chain management use sophisticated information and communications technologies to plan and control their internal operations. For example, UPS Worldport in Louisville, Kentucky, processes over 400,000 packages per hour using advanced sensors and automatic computer-controlled conveyor belts (150 miles of them) while scheduling aircraft and delivery trucks in a nightly dance.[35] And every FedEx package gets at least twelve scans en route from pick-up to delivery.[36]

To maintain its industrial strength and support its logistics cluster and its financial centers, as well as new industries such as digital media and biomedical sciences, Singapore has been undertaking major investment during the second decade of the 21st century. Its Next Generation National Infocomm Infrastructure (NGNII) plan calls for a nationwide ultra-high-speed fiber access infrastructure and a complementary pervasive wireless network creating anytime/anywhere connectivity.[37] The NGNII is expected to be instrumental in enabling grid computing and accelerating its adoption in the business and commercial sector of Singapore. It will be important for many industries but particularly for the logistics industry, with its immense data flows, speed, and mobile information access requirements.

Singapore, with its multiple information and communications technology applications for managing its port and other logistics activities, is possibly the most advanced example of what a cluster can do to improve the operations of all its tenants and users. Another forward-looking example is Dinalog—the Dutch Institute for Advanced Logistics—which is funding several projects as part of its cross-chain control centers initiative.[38] One demonstration project there merges the spare parts operations of multiple companies into a single coordinated activity.[39] Another project focuses on coordinating home deliveries across Internet e-commerce sites to reduce the inefficiencies of independent deliveries.[40] A third project seeks closed-loop coordination of forward and reverse logistics for better sustainability.[41] By merging multiple supply chains, the projects can find greater economies and efficiencies than individual companies (especially smaller ones) could achieve on their own.

Other Dinalog projects seek to address more general large-scale logistics coordination challenges in a geographic context. For example, one cross-chain control center project seeks to improve distribution into cities.[42] Another is looking at multimodal networks for efficiently connecting the main ports of Rotterdam and Amsterdam to the hinterlands.[43] Both of these projects seek reductions in congestion and emissions.

Each project includes the collaboration of several shippers, carriers, or third-party logistics companies and one or more universities. By working with companies whose logistics operations are located in the Netherlands—ranging from Fujifilm to Marel Stork Poultry Processing—and by demonstrating innovations in cross-chain control centers, the leaders of the projects hope to prove the viability of the ideas and encourage early adopters of these innovations.[44] Other aspects of Dinalog are described in chapter 8.

Energy Infrastructure: Fuel for Freight

Logistics activities consume prodigious amounts of energy, principally in the form of fossil fuels for transportation. In a 2011 white paper, the World Economic Forum reports that about fifty-one million barrels of oil are used every day to power "the world's cars, trucks, planes and other modes of transportation."[45] About a third of this oil is used for freight transportation.[46]

The largest Post-Panamax container ships burn on the order of one gallon of bunker fuel—the dark, viscous oil used to power ships—every second, or about two million gallons in a typical three-to-four week journey from Asia to Europe or America. Major ports, such as Singapore or Rotterdam, might refuel dozens of ships a day, which means delivering tens of millions of gallons of bunker fuel every day. Singapore, the biggest bunkering port in the world in terms of sales, sold an average of more than thirty-five million gallons of bunker fuel per day in 2010.[47] On the other end of the speed spectrum, FedEx consumes about 3.5 million gallons of jet fuel each day[48] to deliver some seven million packages.

Fill'er Up with Freight and Fuel

Efficient, large-scale energy infrastructures provide a competitive advantage for a logistics cluster. Carriers typically refuel at points where they stop to load/unload (and vice versa) because they can refuel while conducting terminal operations and avoid any added delays and costs of separate refueling stops. As a result, major logistics hubs sport significant energy infrastructure including pipelines, terminals for large crude carriers, and efficient refineries. In turn, the development of efficient fuel delivery at a hub makes that location attractive for logistics operations. For example, Anchorage and Dubai started as refueling points for airfreight but have since become logistics hubs in their own right.[49]

Crude Moves: The Logistics of Fuel

Pipelines provide the lowest cost per ton-mile shipped of all transportation modes and handle about one-third of the world's oil trade (both crude oils and refined products). For example, crude oil comes to Memphis via pipelines running across the southern United States from oil fields in Texas and Oklahoma. At a riverside refinery, Valero Energy Corporation refines the oil into jet fuel, diesel, gasoline, and other petroleum products. A five-mile pipeline delivers millions of gallons of fresh jet fuel directly to the Memphis airport every week.

Although Rotterdam receives crude oil from supertankers, it distributes refined petroleum products and related chemicals via 1,500 kilometers of pipelines in the port area. Rotterdam's massive petrochemical complex then supplies other major European pipeline systems, including the NATO-run 5,100-kilometer Central European Pipeline System (CEPS) that provides jet fuel to six international airports (Amsterdam, Liège, Brussels, Köln/Bonn, Frankfurt, and Luxembourg).

The port of Rotterdam operates an efficient network of pipelines to transport petrochemicals and gases among the companies in the port and the surrounding industrial area. One such network is operated as a joint venture between the port of Rotterdam and Vopak Chemicals EMEA B.V., called MultiCore. MultiCore operates a four-pipeline trunk system to which terminals and storage areas can connect and lease space for certain periods. By controlling various valves and pumps, MultiCore can move the material between facilities within Rotterdam. Once a shipment is complete, the origin and destination are disconnected from the main pipeline system; the used pipeline is cleaned and stands ready for the next shipment. [50]

All of these pipelines represent significant amounts of investment in infrastructure. For example, a new 120-kilometer pipeline for sending petroleum products from Rotterdam to Antwerp is expected to cost in excess of €100 million.[51] Private capital spending in Rotterdam by petrochemical companies averages one billion euros per year.[52]

As mentioned above, Singapore is the world's largest port for buying bunker fuel. Even during the 2008–2009 recession, sales at the port of Singapore rose, attesting to its role in the global sales of bunker oil. Ship owners have been increasingly buying bunker in Singapore not only because of its efficient and inexpensive bunkering operations but also because of its reputation for integrity in the bunkering process both in terms of quality and quantity supplied. It is the only country that regulates bunkering barge operators and suppliers.

As ships stop over in Singapore for their bunker needs, they use Singapore for crew change and ship provisioning, serviced by a strong and efficient network of chandlers. According to Simon Neo, chairman of the International Bunker Industry Association, Singapore's Maritime and Port Authority (MPA) encourages vessels to call on Singapore for refueling and ship services by minimizing and even eliminating port dues for such vessels.[53]

Kerosene with a Side of Ethylene

The energy infrastructure of a logistics cluster lends itself to the development of local energy-intensive and petrochemical industries.

The principal logistics fuels—like bunker oil for ships, "jet A" kerosene for aircraft, or diesel fuel for trucks and trains—represent just one fraction of the components of crude oil. Crude oil consists of a mixture that spans light and heavy molecules of oil and can most economically produce many types of petroleum products simultaneously. The heaviest-weight fractions provide asphalt, tars, waxes, and lubricating oils. Medium-weight fractions provide diesel and kerosene for trucks and aircraft. Lightweight liquid fractions provide solvents and gasoline for cars. Crude oil and natural gas also provide the feedstock for industrial gases, ethylene (for plastics), butadiene (for rubber), and the like. Any of these fractions can be burned for energy for chemical or industrial processes such as those used to make products in the Rotterdam's petrochemical cluster (see p. 143 in chapter 5).

Similarly, Singapore sports an Asian hub for oil and chemical products. In an ambitious land reclamation project completed in 2009, Singapore has connected seven of its islands to form Jurong Island as its petrochemicals hub. More than ninety-five companies invested more than SGD30 billion (about $24 billion) in Jurong, including heavyweights such as DuPont, Huntsman, BASF, Perstorp, Dainippon Ink & Chemicals (DIC), and Sumitomo Chemical.

The energy industry in Memphis supports the massive steel smelting furnaces at NUCOR and the boiling cauldrons of corn sweetener at Cargill, in addition to piping millions of gallons per week of jet fuel to the airport.

Higher-Order Infrastructure: Carriers as Infrastructure to Shippers

Memphis Light, Gas and Water Division provides necessary infrastructure for the Memphis airport. In turn, the Memphis airport provides necessary infrastructure for FedEx, UPS, Delta, and the other airlines there. The Merriam-Webster dictionary defines infrastructure as "the underlying foundation or basic framework" and "the resources ([such] as personnel, buildings or equipment) required for an activity." In that sense, FedEx, UPS, and the entire logistics industry in a Memphis serve as infrastructure for the area's manufacturers, retailers and distributors. Thus, for Medtronic in Memphis, logistics services such as FedEx, UPS, the airlines' NFO services, the hundreds of trucking companies around Memphis as well as the trained logistics workforce in the area are all "infrastructure." This infrastructure enables Medtronic in Memphis to send and receive products efficiently. The underlying complexities of getting its high-value, time-sensitive packages to any location in the country are invisible to Medtronic just like the complexities of electrical power generation are invisible to electricity users.

Carriers and third-party logistics service providers have progressively broadened their services to include more functions in their infrastructure-like service offerings. Global logistics service providers, such as UPS and DHL, leverage their vast worldwide IT and delivery infrastructures to create bundled services that combine offerings such as warehousing, transportation, forwarding, custom brokerage, factoring, and feet-on-the-street customer service. "We feel it's one of the areas [where] there's a significant opportunity to leverage the assets of UPS, including the small-package network, pickup capabilities and ability to manage supply-chain networks," said Phil Corwin, former director of marketing at UPS Supply Chain Solutions.[54] Third-party logistics service providers, or 3PLs—as central coordinators for logistics—become the front-ends of this extended infrastructure. 3PLs create a seamless service that insulates shippers from the complexities of logistics. Corwin added that the UPS SCS customers include "many smaller companies that don't want to—or can't—build and manage their own post-sales infrastructure."[55]

The presence of an extended logistics infrastructure enables the rise of companies that implicitly depend on high-performance logistics infrastructure. For example, inexpensive, high-reliability overnight package delivery services provide a higher-order infrastructure for dot-com retailers such as Amazon.com, Germany's Otto. de, or China's Taobao.com. Public warehouse operators provide a convenient and cost-effective turnkey distribution infrastructure for companies who don't want to invest in their own warehouse buildings, shelving, forklifts, and warehouse workforce. All these services are enhanced in logistics clusters because of the efficiency of logistics operations there, as explained in chapter 4.

INFRASTRUCTURE LIMITS: LAND AND CONGESTION

Although logistics clusters enjoy clear scale and scope advantages, they cannot grow indefinitely. Cluster growth finds a proximate volume limit in the capacity of its existing infrastructure and an ultimate limit in the land area available for more infrastructures. A cluster's economic success can also plant the seeds of its own suffocation when decades of urban development envelope the cluster. Faced with limited land, however, infrastructure operators can use a variety of productivity-enhancing strategies, such as leveraging information infrastructure or inland ports. As a last resort and a testament to the value of logistics, some ports like Singapore and Rotterdam are creating huge new additions by filing in the sea to make more land.

This section examines cluster size limits and congestion effects from the viewpoint of the logistics industry members, not the government or the broader society. (The societal impacts of congestion and other downsides of logistics clusters such as pollution are discussed chapter 7 in the context of regulations and mitigation activities as well as in chapter 10 in the context of sustainable clusters.)

Proximate Limits: Available Capacity

Every logistics asset has some upper limit on capacity: standard shipping containers can be stacked no more than nine-high; two trains can't occupy the same stretch of rail; a conveyer belt sorter can handle only so many packages per hour; a freight yard has only so many slots for containers, and so forth. Minimum distances between conveyances, maximum safe velocities, dwell times, and other operational details limit how much freight a given logistics asset can handle.

Infrastructure also has an upper-limit physical size for the passages of conveyances, such as the Panamax size limit, requiring the expansion of the canal. Similarly, the CSX Railroad had to enlarge a number of tunnels along its tracks to enable double-stacking of shipping containers. Another example is the Bayonne Bridge spanning the Kill Van Kull between Staten Island, New York, and Bayonne, New Jersey. While 12 percent of all US international containers pass under the bridge,[56] it blocks the largest container ships from coming into the port of Newark, where 83 percent of the port's container capacity resides. At high tide, the bridge provides only 151 feet of air draft clearance between the bridge and the water. When completed in 1931, it was the longest steel arch bridge in the world, with plenty of clearance for contemporary shipping. But now modern large container ships, such as the Emma Maersk, require over 200 feet of clearance—more if the ship is lightly loaded and riding high in the water. The Port Authority of New York and New Jersey is therefore planning to raise the bridge at an estimated cost of between $1 and $1.3 billion.[57]

A successful logistics cluster is a nexus for heavily utilized infrastructure. Whereas the volume of freight flowing on any given point-to-point lane might be modest, hub-and-spoke operations imply a significant concentration of activities. Large volumes of freight and conveyance activities in a small area lead to congestion. Frequent flyers know this well—some of the worst delays take place at hub airports.[58] The same problem can occur in major freight hubs.

Mutual Expansion for Matched Capacities across Clusters

Infrastructure improvements in one part of a logistics system typically invite increased utilization, which may create a bottleneck elsewhere. For example, although Zaragoza's PLAZA has spacious wide roads within the park, the park's exits and highway on-ramps often clog with the large numbers of trucks leaving the park at certain times of day. On a larger scale, the much-anticipated expansion of the Panama Canal might bring larger container ships and freight volumes to ports on the East Coast of the United States. South Carolina State Ports Authority chief executive Jim Newsome is excited about the expansion, describing it as "a game-changer" and "the biggest development since the advent of stuffing cargo into containers."[59] Bigger ships, however, mean deeper drafts and larger quayside berths, cranes, harbors, and shipping lanes. As of 2011, Norfolk, Virginia, is the only port in the eastern United States that can handle the larger ships that will be transiting the expanded Panama Canal.

Other ports are scrambling to upgrade their infrastructure to capture some of the hoped-for traffic. For example, Charleston is dredging its harbor from 45 feet to 50 feet (at a cost of $300 million). Similarly, port officials in Miami are in the process of dredging their port to a depth of 50 feet and at the same time plan to complete the Port of Miami Tunnel project by 2014, providing trucks (and passengers) direct interstate access between the port of Miami and the I-395 freeway. This will enable Miami to double its capacity for truck movements.[60] Port officials in Savannah, Georgia, want $588 million to deepen their harbor, and the port of New York/New Jersey is already spending $2.3 billion to dredge its harbor.[61]

In contrast, New York's nineteenth-century Barge Canal system (an enlarged successor to the Erie Canal and other canals in New York) faded because of insufficient logistics terminal infrastructure and inadequate investment in developing it (see also the discussion of cluster mortality on p. 285 in chapter 10). Examples such as the inadequate terminals on the Barge Canal, inadequate air draft clearance of the Bayonne Bridge, and ongoing plans to deepen East Coast ports illustrate how capacities of conveyances, terminals, and routes interact. Failure to meet increasing capacity demands may lead a port to dry up economically, affecting all the capillary economic elements around it. Larger conveyances demand larger-capacity terminals and routes. And larger capacity terminals and routes support the development of larger conveyances.

Ultimate Limits: Available Land

Expanding the capacity of logistics infrastructure requires vast expanses of land. A single Post-Panamax vessel covers more than four acres of harbor. Add channel clearance, cranes, container storage yards, and drayage access, and a single added berth might require a dozen acres. Similarly, building a 500,000 square foot distribution center requires more than eleven acres of land just for the building and requires double that amount after adding in the employee parking, a truck yard, rail spur, connecting roads, and greenways. Adding a 10,000-foot runway to an existing airport, with taxiway and safe all-weather separations from adjacent runways and airport fence lines consumes at least 900 acres. In addition to land for ports, terminals, and hubs, adding capacity to a logistics cluster means adding capacity to the connecting infrastructure. A single mile of US Interstate highway—constructed to the minimal standard of two-lanes each way—consumes nearly twelve acres.

These land-consuming additions may be quite feasible for young greenfield developments, such as PLAZA, but the multidecade, even multicentury life spans of logistics clusters such as Rotterdam mean that capacity additions occur in the context of a long-term built environment. With the initial creation of a major logistics facility comes ancillary development of adjacent commercial facilities. In addition, housing, consumer retail outlets, office buildings, and government facilities grow around centers of economic activity. All these activities fill the area around the original development until the land zoned for a logistics cluster has no room for expansion.

Ports, especially, become pinned between the sea and the urban and industrial development that grows up around a busy seaport. Many historic ports, like Rotterdam, New York, and Singapore, started life as trading centers that quickly became the city's original downtown business district. But as the city grew, these quaysides and docklands became too valuable for logistics use and were converted to retail arcades, high-rise ocean-view apartments, and skyscraper office buildings. Furthermore, as the city closed in, residents started resenting the truck, rail, and air traffic created by logistics operations.

Throughout Los Angeles, commuters compete with trucks hauling freight between the Los Angeles/Long Beach (LA/LB) ports and the myriad warehouses, rail yards, and other logistics facilities strewn throughout the Los Angeles basin. Similarly, commuters in the Chicago area have to share railway crossings with long freight railroads as well as numerous trucks distributing cargo in and out of Chicago's logistics parks. And a night flight ban in Frankfurt airport, enacted in 2011 following complaints from residents, is expected to impose tens of millions of euros of additional costs on airfreight operators such as Lufthansa Cargo, Night Express, and Condor.

Growing Capacity by Growing Productivity

Logistics operators have numerous strategies for increasing the productivity of assets, thereby increasing the effective capacity of those assets. For example, the adjacent ports of Los Angeles and Long Beach are the busiest port complex in the United States. Trucks carrying containers from the port to the US hinterland have to cross the city of Los Angeles, which has the most congested roads of any city in the United States. Because of the lack of land for expansion, the port focused its growth effort on increasing its hours of operations to include nights and weekends, coupled with increased fees for daytime operations to encourage off-peak operations.

Another congestion-reducing initiative at LA/LB is the Alameda corridor rail project aimed at shifting more freight from truck to rail. This twenty-mile "rail expressway" connects the LA/LB ports to the transcontinental rail network terminus east of downtown Los Angeles. Each train replaces 250 to 285 trucks[62] and takes less than half the time it took trucks to traverse LA.[63] The corridor carries about one-third of the ports' container volume.[64] The builders submerged a triple-track infrastructure below grade to eliminate or avoid 200 railroad crossings that could interfere with LA's traffic. Carrying freight by rail and reducing railroad crossings saves 15,000 hours per day in truck and vehicular traffic delays.[65]

Singapore's solution relies on information technology: developing systems that both regulate the flow and accelerate the passage of trucks. For example, rather than let dray trucks circulate at will, Singapore schedules each truck within a narrow window, ensuring that trucks flow through the port in a manageable stream. The Port Authority also created what it calls a flow-through gate. The port installed scanners at the port gates that quickly check the identity of the driver, weigh the truck, scan the container, and check the data against manifests. Within twenty-five seconds, the driver gets clearance and instructions on where to take the container. In his office on the thirty-sixth floor of the Port Authority of Singapore (PSA) building overlooking the vast expanse of the port of Singapore, Oh Bee Lock, head of operations of Singapore Terminals (part of SPA Corporation) told me, "We do this not because of technology; we do this for a pure practical reason—we don't have a lot of land for gates."

Not only does scheduling of trucks prevent wasted idling, but it also makes the entire port system more predictable. The PSA has confidence that it can unload and load a ship within a narrow scheduled time slot because it has confidence that the dray trucks will arrive as expected. And by having confidence in the completion of loading and departure of the ship, the port operator can tighten the scheduled arrival of the next ship. The result is high productivity of capacity-limited assets such as the quaysides, container yards, and port road infrastructure. As a result of these and other information technology applications, Singapore handles on the order of twice the number of containers per unit of port asset (e.g., per acre of port, per crane, and per foot of port quay) as most other major ports in the world.[66]

Other ports, logistics parks, and terminals have similar systems. The ports of Los Angeles and Long Beach use appointment systems to avoid long queuing times for dray trucks.[67] The advanced scheduling technology employed in the new (as of 2011) Union Pacific intermodal yard in Joliet Logistics Park coordinates all movement of rail cars, trucks, trailers, and containers throughout the facility. The system cut truck-processing time by an average of 75 percent.[68] Most of the benefits of such scheduling systems are rooted in mitigating congestion through better scheduling.

Inland Opportunities: Solving Congestion through Displacement

As logistics clusters, particularly around seaports, become enveloped by urban development and reach their productivity limits, they can still grow by displacing some logistics activities to new greenfield facilities outside the immediate cluster area. Instead of clearing customs, deconsolidating, transloading, warehousing, and distributing freight from the immediate vicinity of the port, containers are moved (typically via rail) directly from the ship to an "inland port," also known as a "dry port," located well away from the congested port area. Inland ports typically exhibit lower land costs and lower labor costs.

For example, the Virginia Inland Port, which lies 220 miles inland in Front Royal, handles cargo from the three state-owned port terminals (in Norfolk, Portsmouth, and Newport News) and supports efficient distribution to southern Pennsylvania, Maryland, and Virginia. Other US inland ports include AllianceTexas in Fort Worth, Texas; CIC in Joliet, south of Chicago; and Kansas City. In all three cases, railroads bring ocean shipping containers from West Coast ports, contributing to the development of these areas as logistics clusters. As another example, consider that it was the lack of expansion capacity around the ports of Barcelona and Valencia that contributed to the success and growth of the Aragón logistics cluster, serving as a dry port extension to the port of Barcelona.

Displacement can also be more extreme than shifting a part of the activity to a new location. Over time, the entire port or cluster can migrate to a new location. For example, the port of New York originally developed around the current Battery Park on the southern tip of Manhattan Island. But as New York became a city and Manhattan developed, the logistics industry moved across the Hudson and East Rivers to nearby locations such as Newark, Elizabeth, Red Hook, and South Brooklyn.

Airports, too, can become besieged by suburban development and congestion. Cities such as Chicago, Washington, DC, Denver, Houston, Paris, and Shanghai started with airports like Midway, National, Stapleton, Hobby, Orly, and Hongqiao, respectively, at the edge of each city. Then significant growth enveloped the airport and forced the cities to construct new, larger airports (O'Hare, Dulles, Denver International, Houston Intercontinental, Paris Charles de Gaulle, and Pudong International, respectively) much further from the city. These airports, in turn, became major air hubs.

Expanding Lands to Transcend the Limits

Whereas the port of Barcelona can displace activities to the inland dry port of Zaragoza, the island nation of Singapore has no place to go. Although Singapore's ongoing investments in improved processes and information technology do increase the country's ability to handle growing trade, the island simply needs more land. Thus, the Singapore Maritime Authority launched a S$2 billion land reclamation project in 2007 to increase the capacity of the Pasir Panjang Terminal by 40 percent.[69]

Nor is Singapore unique. The outer parts of the Rotterdam port are wholly artificial constructs. The current Maasvlakte complex is a 3,000-hectare industrial park and harbor complex built in the 1960s on reclaimed land. Maasvlakte 2, scheduled for completion by 2013, will add another 2,000 hectares to the port by bringing in 350 million cubic meters of sand dredged from the sea bottom. That's twice the volume of earth moved to build the Panama Canal. To prevent Rotterdam's new lands from slumping back into the ocean, the Dutch are importing almost 200,000 tons of basalt rock per month brought from a Norwegian quarry almost 1,000 kilometers away.[70] When I asked Hans Smits, CEO of the port of Rotterdam, how far the Rotterdam expansion will continue, he quipped that "Rotterdam won't stop expanding until we reach England."

These expansions and many others seem to indicate that even if urban development constrains a logistics cluster, it can find ways to expand and sustain the positive feedback loop that fuels its growth. Rotterdam's willingness to spend €3 billion on Maasvlakte 2 testifies to the huge economic opportunities embedded in logistics clusters. Rather than view congestion as a problem to be squashed by restricting activity, Rotterdam, Panama, and Singapore view congestion as evidence of the value of their locations, high demand for their services, and opportunities for growth. Instead of regulating economic activities to restrict use, they expand infrastructure and improve operating efficiencies to meet the challenge of growing demand. At a built cost of €1.5 million per hectare, the new land in Maasvlakte 2 is worth thirty-eight times the price of agricultural land in the Netherlands[71] yet is less than one-tenth the price of land in Rotterdam's city center.[72]

LARGE INVESTMENTS IN LONG-LIVED ASSETS

Large logistics clusters depend on extensive infrastructure comprising long-lived assets spread over large land areas. The Panama

Canal will celebrate its 100th anniversary in 2014. The first bridge across the lower portion of the Mississippi River—the 1892 Frisco Bridge at Memphis—is still in use for rail freight today.[73] The port of Singapore began its rise to prominence in the nineteenth century. Rotterdam has been a transshipment center for more than 650 years, since the completion of a shipping canal in 1350.

A logistics cluster requires several types of infrastructures to be able to offer sufficient capacity and interconnectivity without congestion. In discussing the nature of infrastructure development, Ricardo García-Becerril, PLAZA 's general manager, stressed to me "It's great to analyze how appropriate or not it is to develop a logistics park in a certain location, but beware, because the surrounding infrastructure is crucial. This applies to electricity supply, water, waste, and communications—not just Internet and telephone lines, but also intermodal connections to fast highways and rail."

The size of investment and the resulting long-lived assets required to launch and develop a logistics cluster mean not only that governments are likely to be involved, but that the planning process should be thorough. Indeed, the expansion of the Panama Canal was put to Panamanian voters in a 2006 referendum, following years of planning by the Panama Canal Authority. Similarly, the development of PLAZA in Zaragoza followed years of public debate and finally was supported by both the ruling party and the opposition in Aragón, as well as by the unions, the area's businesses, the city of Zaragoza, and other elements of the local civil society. Thus, logistics clusters become de facto or de jure public-private partnerships.

7

THE STRONG ROLE OF GOVERNMENT

Several observers note that many governments have aspired to create industry clusters, especially knowledge-based clusters of the "next Silicon Valley" type, without success. They see governments' efforts as discredited "industrial policy" and point to the failure of most governments to "pick winners" while attributing the success of clusters solely to entrepreneurial fervor and risk taking.[1] Examples of failed attempts include Tsukuba, Japan's science city; Akademgorodok, "City of Science" in Siberia; and Egypt's "Silicon Pyramid."[2]

Most economists, however, acknowledge the role of government in the investment and stewardship of a cluster. For example, Harvard's Michael Porter cites access to public goods and a wide array of institutions, including government agencies, as one of five factors contributing to superior productivity in clusters.[3] The stories of Zaragoza, Singapore, Panama, and other logistics clusters suggest that this type of cluster not only benefits from accommodating government policies in trade, taxation, and zoning but requires significant public investment in logistics infrastructure as well as regulatory support.

Unlike private investments, which are driven by economics, government investments involve many other goals, such as social equity, environmental stewardship, and other manifestations of public good.

GOVERNMENTS' ROLES IN CREATING LOGISTICS ASSETS

As mentioned in chapter 6, logistics requires a significant base of physical assets, many of which require both initial and on-going government funding and are subject to government regulations. First, logistics relies on government investment in transportation infrastructure such as public roads, ports, airports, and (in most countries) railroads. Second, governments also control the use of land. Urban planning, zoning regulations, and building permits directly influence the private creation of logistics assets such as logistics parks, intermodal terminals, and warehouses. Third, governments offer direct or indirect incentives to encourage new asset development and private investment to bring "good jobs" to specific areas. Fourth, governments provide "soft" public goods such as educational institutions and other incentives for workforce development. Last, governments control trade regulation, taxation policies, immigration rules, environmental policies, and other levers that can make a location more or less business-friendly to logistics operations. While showing me several logistics facilities in Memphis, Dexter Muller, senior vice president of community development of the city's Chamber of Commerce, summarized the role of government in logistics clusters' development: "Economic development is unavoidably tied in with government. Because they've got infrastructure. They have zoning. They issue permits. They have incentives."

Public Investment: Creating Large-Scale Shared Infrastructure

Governments fund, own, and maintain much of the physical infrastructure described in the previous chapter. Most of the government-funded logistics infrastructure is transportation-related and is shared with individuals, businesses, and the military. To fund the building and maintenance of these infrastructures, governments use a combination of general funds, fuel taxes, tolls, and other user fees.

Funding Roads

Heavily loaded trucks have an outsized impact on the lifespan of road surfaces—in fact, the process for pavement design calls only for estimating the expected number of heavy truck axle loads because cars and light truck traffic create almost inconsequential pavement damage by comparison. Heavy loads create compression and bending of pavements, leading to rutting and cracking.

For example, a 20,000-pound truck axle consumes over 1,000 times as much pavement life as a 2,000-pound automobile axle.[4] Consequently, heavy truck traffic requires continuous investment in maintenance and rehabilitation of highways around logistics clusters.

The shared use of roads by truckers and commuters can create public support for taxation and justify the use of general funds for transportation improvements. For example, some California counties, such as those of the Inland Empire east of Los Angeles, increased their sales taxes with provisions that the proceeds go directly to congestion-reducing transportation projects. Citizens voted for higher taxes to shorten their commutes and reduce frustrating traffic jams. Reducing congestion, however, helps both commuters and truckers around Inland Empire, which is one of the largest logistics clusters in the United States.

Most infrastructure development programs around the world are dwarfed by the pace of Chinese development in the first part of the twenty-first century.[5] The Chinese "7-9-18" plan calls for the development of a system of expressways modeled after the US Interstate system, with seven expressways radiating out of Beijing, nine north–south expressways and eighteen east–west expressways. The network will link all cities with populations over 500,000 and increase economic opportunities for the western provinces. The total length of the Chinese expressway system was 74,000 kilometers in 2010 (comparable to the length of the US Interstate system) and was expected to reach 108,000 kilometers by 2016. The total costs of the Chinese national expressway network have been estimated to be $240 billion. Almost all the roads in the system are toll roads built and operated by private companies and financed by loans from China Development Bank and from self-financing bonds.

Creating a Rail Network

In many countries, governments own and operate the national rail network as a result of historical factors. Whereas most US, UK, and German railroads are privately owned and operated, railroads are government owned in many other parts of continental Europe, as they are in most developing countries. In many of these cases, national priorities, favoring passenger service over freight, can lead to degradation of the reliability of rail freight services.

Some rail corridors in Europe, however, are specifically built for freight, especially around logistics clusters. For example, the Dutch spent nearly five billion euros on the 160-kilometer double-track Betuweroute for moving freight between Rotterdam and Germany.[6] Engineers tailored the line's design for freight trains. Extra-high-clearance overhead electrical lines and tall tunnels enable double-stack container traffic. High-voltage power lines support powerful locomotives pulling heavy freight loads and make the route incompatible with Dutch passenger trains. The corridor is a key part of the Trans European Freight Rail Network (TEFRN), which aims to allow freight trains free access across the entire EU without having to stop at borders or make way for passenger trains.

The US government has also supported freight rail, despite its private for-profit nature. For example, the CREATE (Chicago Region Environmental and Transportation Efficiency) project around Chicago includes seventy government-funded upgrades to rail infrastructure that will reduce congestion, increase train velocities, and increase capacity of the region's rail network. Congestion associated with heavy rail traffic adversely affects both commuters and local business activities. Each day some 500 freight trains pass through the Chicago region, with some of these trains almost two miles long—enough to block all at-grade rail crossing simultaneously in some Chicago-area communities.[7] Freight trains also vie with commuter rail in Chicago, where the conflicts create delays for both. A train that may take as little as forty-eight hours to travel the 2,200 miles from Los Angeles to Chicago spends an average of thirty hours traversing the Chicago region.[8] Traffic congestion creates long commutes, frustration, added fuel consumption, and a drag on the economy.

To alleviate this burden, project CREATE was launched in 2003 as a partnership between the US Department of Transportation, the state of Illinois, the city of Chicago, and both the commuter rail and the US freight railroads. By 2010, almost $3 billion was invested in dozens of transportation improvement projects in the area to alleviate the problems. Justification for the government's support includes increased employment, improved commuter rail operations, reduced road congestion, improved safety at rail crossings, and reduced pollution from slow-moving trains.[9] Los Angeles' Alameda corridor project, which involved a below-grade rail link from the port to the city's rail terminals, had similar objectives, as described on p. 170 in chapter 6.

As is the case with other infrastructure projects, the Chinese investment in rail—both high speed passenger routes and freight railroading—is massive. The Chinese rail system was 91,000 kilometers long at the end of 2010 but continued investment, driven in large part by increasing freight volumes, is expected to grow the system to 110,000 km by 2012. (This is still less than half the total mainline track in the United States.)

Maybe nothing is more symbolic than the new silk road inaugurated in July 2011—a freight rail line linking Chongqing, a Chinese logistics hub, to Duisburg, a German logistics hub,[10] running through the far western Xinjiang Uygur autonomous region, Kazakhstan, Russia, Belarus, and Poland, before finally reaching Germany. Even though the railway track existed for over a decade, it was not in use until China signed a strategic agreement with Russia and Kazakhstan to open the new freight route. The first train departed Chongqing in July 2011 carrying laptop computers and LCD screens.

The PLAZA That Aragón Built

PLAZA's development first got me interested in the subject of logistics clusters, and the Zaragoza project demonstrates how governments can successfully lead their development. In the case of PLAZA, the Aragón Government envisioned the project, designed the concept, developed a self-funding model, appropriated the land, built the infrastructure, and recruited key companies to locate to the park. In creating PLAZA, government officials used tools uniquely available to governments, such as creating new laws, expropriating one small patch of land from a recalcitrant landowner, and pushing essential approvals through the Spanish bureaucracy. The government also was able to take substantial financial risks by guaranteeing project completion dates for the first important tenant, Zara.

Military Infrastructure

Since the days of the Roman Empire, the military has depended on logistics and logistical infrastructure, which then also support civilian freight use. Roman Legions built the Netherlands' first canals to defend the Northern border of the Roman Empire. The United States funded the Panama Canal to aid naval defense of the Western Hemisphere. High-speed road networks, such as the German Autobahn and the US Interstate Highway system, provided mobility for military materiel. Yet these military infrastructure projects also supported civilian applications, including the movement of commercial goods.

With the end of the Cold War, logistics firms enjoyed a Peace Dividend. As mentioned in chapter 1, Zaragoza's airport—now the third largest in airfreight volume in Spain—was a former NATO airbase. Lessening of NATO defense concerns enabled expanded civilian use and the incorporation of the Zaragoza airport into the PLAZA concept. Similarly, the Joliet, Illinois, complex of logistics parks and intermodal facilities sits on a former US Army ammunition plant created in the run-up to WWII. These former military facilities often have large contiguous expanses of land, making them ideally suited for logistics parks. Moreover, the closure of a military facility creates a gap in the local economy that logistics operations can fill. Other military facilities redeveloped for civilian logistics include Subic Bay in the Philippines and Howard Air Force Base in Panama. Government investment in military logistics can thus aid contemporaneous or subsequent civilian logistics.

Education and Research

Besides investing in the physical assets that support a logistics cluster, governments invest in the human assets that work in the cluster, as well as in knowledge creation. In most countries, government funds training, education, and research in logistics, which drive both current performance and future competitiveness. The Zaragoza Logistics Center,[11] Dinalog (the Dutch Institute for Advanced Logistics[12]), the Logistics Institute Asia Pacific in Singapore,[13] and the Malaysia Institute of Supply Chain Innovation[14] exemplify the kinds of educational and research facilities that governments support. In a competitive environment, a quality work force, innovation, and technology define the difference between ineffective and efficient logistics. Chapter 8 delves into this crucial element of logistics clusters in greater depth.

Permitting Land Use and Regulations

"Sometimes the urban planning is very easily forgotten," said Ricardo García-Becerril, General Manager of PLAZA in Zaragoza. Whereas high-tech startups can sprout in any garage or urban loft, logistics facilities generally depend on vast tracts of cleared land. Moreover, roads, railroads, and canals have geographic constraints on straightness and slope, which limit their siting and may force governments to expropriate private lands. Governments' roles in permitting land use, assessing environmental impacts and issuing building and occupancy permits make them an indirect facilitator or inhibitor of private investment in logistics clusters.

Although not as injurious as heavy industry, logistics activities create heavy vehicle traffic, which degrades the environment with noise, pollution, and road congestion. Objections by residential and environmental groups can stymie development and hinder operations. For this reason, industrial real estate developer Watson Land Company in Los Angeles explicitly avoids developing land adjacent to residential areas or areas that might, in the future, become residential areas.

Land use in logistics can require far more than buildings and roads. The civil engineering needs of logistics often require large-scale modification of the land such as: leveling hills, cutting grades, dredging ports, and filling in parts of rivers and oceans. Thus, environmental laws in many parts of the world affect large-scale logistics projects such as port expansions. For example, the Pan American Highway remains incomplete near the Panama-Colombia border because of strong environmental concerns about the rain forests, tropical diseases, and indigenous peoples of the Darien Gap. In other cases, gaining approval for a major project may take years and include lengthy court battles.

Complex government permitting processes also affect the development of logistics clusters. Major projects at the port of Los

Angeles, for example, must gain the permission of the California Coastal Commission, the federal Environmental Protection Agency, as well as local authorities. To date, the port of LA has won the right to create new land and pursue large-scale land and sea modification projects by finding offsetting environmental remediation projects elsewhere in California. A "remediate-one-acre, build-one-acre" strategy can even create net environmental benefits because the new infrastructure is built to high sustainability standards.

Similarly, Rotterdam's Maasvlakte 2 project (see p. 173 in chapter 6) required a host of offsets in order to balance the environmental impacts. The port of Rotterdam agreed to build 750 hectares of nature habitat as well as new beach recreation areas, a seabed protection area, and a large landscape park around Rotterdam as part of the project. In addition, the Rotterdam Port Authority committed to constructing an electrical grid for barges moored at inland shipping docks, increasing the stowage rate of trucks, and decreasing pollution from lighting for the benefit of migratory birds.[15]

Governments can also accelerate development by streamlining regulatory and permitting processes. Panama, for example, reduced the burden on new companies coming to the country's new Panama Pacifico mixed-used development (including a logistics park), by creating a "one-stop shop" for permits and regulatory issues.[16] "There's one building here that deals with every single bureaucratic requirement that a company might have in terms of establishing [itself] in Panama. [Issues with the] Ministries of Works, social security, and migratory issues all get solved at a one-stop shop in one building," said Henry Kardonski, managing director of Panama Pacifico. This single point of contact for twelve different government ministries reduces the costs and complexities of relocating a company and its executives to Panama.

Attracting Private Investment: Incentives, Subsidies, and Taxes
In addition to providing a solid infrastructure base and accommodative regulations, most governments actively recruit companies through a wide range of incentives such as subsidized land, temporary tax abatement, loan guarantees, and preferential regulatory treatment. Whereas some aspects of a business-friendly climate

apply to all companies operating in the location, government incentives generally go only to specific companies that make new or additional investments. Incentives are but one factor in companies' site selection decision processes. Telephone interviews conducted by my colleague Bruce Arntzen with several big-box retailers in the United States about their location decisions for distribution centers elicited the opinions that other important factors are network economics and labor force quality. Commenting on the location decision process, David Rocco, director of logistics strategy for Staples Inc., stated that while Staples considers government incentives, they are but one of many factors influencing the location decisions for distribution centers. Similarly, Steve Carter, director of transportation planning and strategy at the Target Corporation, said that "The overall list of attributes offered by a site drives the ultimate decision, with price being one of several key factors." Specifically, Colby Chiles, director of online transportation at the Home Depot Company, said that once the general geography of a new distribution center has been chosen based on network optimization models, which account for total supply chain costs, the company will consider which jurisdiction can move faster to approve development and compare the incentive packages between these jurisdictions.

Government Recruiting of Land Developers

Governments sometimes take the lead in developing, or redeveloping, land for economic purposes. Aragón's role in PLAZA is one clear example. Another, Joliet, also illustrates the Peace Dividend effect. After the US Army decommissioned the Joliet Army Ammunition Plant in 1993, the government started working to clean up the heavily polluted land and convert it to civilian use.[17] Part of that project included transferring 3,000 acres to the state of Illinois. The state then created the Joliet Arsenal Development Authority (JADA) to spur economic development in the area.

JADA recognized that "the availability of a large parcel of land in the region, in proximity to major transportation infrastructure of rail and highway, made the JADA property a prime location for a major intermodal transportation facility."[18] Thus, JADA sought bidders for the land who would then develop it. In 1999, Center-Point bought 1,900 acres of the JADA parcel as well as 375 acres of private farmland to create the CenterPoint Intermodal Center (CIC). Today, the expanded CenterPoint Intermodal Complex located in the Joliet and Elwood areas spans 6,000 acres. The CIC-Elwood development attracted leading logistics tenants such as Walmart, DSC Logistics, Georgia Pacific, Potlatch, Sanyo Logistics, Partners Warehouse California Cartage, Maersk, and Bissel.[19] Other major JADA projects include the 776-acre ProLogis Park designed to accommodate regional and super-regional distribution centers. Local governments also helped through annexation, flexible zoning terms, and tax incentives. In turn, CenterPoint donated some land to the US Forest Service, to the city of Elwood, and for wetland conservation.

In another example, the Port Authority of New York/ New Jersey teamed with the New Jersey Economic Development Authority for its "Portsfield" initiative.[20] The redevelopment is converting seventeen brownfield sites within twenty-five miles of the ports into high-quality distribution space. Government aid includes financial support as well as administrative assistance with government bureaucracy and environmental regulations.[21]

Will Give Incentives for Work

To attract companies to a region, governments will offer direct incentives if the company promises to create jobs in the area. Jobs were the main reason that Aragón and Zaragoza pursued the PLA-ZA concept. The development has created an economic base and attracted numerous new businesses to the area, so much so that in 2009 Aragón reached a low unemployment rate of 11 percent and what the *Economist* referred to as "near full employment"[22] immediately following the 2008 World Expo hosted by Aragón.[23]

Similarly, economic development efforts by local governments in Illinois (Joliet), Panama, Singapore, Memphis, Rotterdam, and elsewhere focus on jobs. Memphis, for example, ties tax incentives to wages such that companies who promise to bring higher-paying jobs receive more incentives. Singapore and Panama offer lower corporate tax rates for companies who move regional or global headquarters to the country, because headquarters bring with them higher-paying white-collar and executive-level jobs.

Incentives and economic stimulus money can also forestall job losses during an economic downturn. Mary Yeo, UPS vice president of supply chain operations South Asia Pacific, explained that during the 2008 recession, the Singaporean government "gave us quite a bit of grants to help us tide over, but with the promise that we don't lay off our people." Similarly, the US government dispensed some $1.5 billion in Transportation Investment Generating Economic Recovery (TIGER) grants. Of these, the three largest projects gave money to private railroads to improve freight rail infrastructure, including in logistics cluster locations such as Memphis and Chicago.[24]

Build It and They Will Use It

Logistics companies may require new investments in infrastructure to support relocated or expanded operations. FedEx moved from Little Rock to Memphis because the former was unwilling to invest in more airport infrastructure. FedEx needed a second runway and buildings for a sorting hub to ensure reliable operations, but Little Rock refused to build it. In contrast, the Memphis airport offered hangers and ramp parking space. In addition, the chairman of the Memphis Airport, with the endorsement of the airlines serving Memphis at the time, led the efforts to float a $2.9 million bond to help FedEx establish its hub.[25]

In attracting developers to buy land in Joliet and invest, federal, state, and local governments secured $160 million in grants to create essential roadway components,[26] and new water and sewer systems, as well as other infrastructure.[27] These examples demonstrate that government's willingness to upgrade infrastructure can affect site selection decisions of logistics companies.

Logistics for No Money Down

Governments generally enjoy a lower cost of capital than do private companies, and that can help develop cluster infrastructure and other large-scale private logistics facilities. For example, during my visit to the Joliet logistics park, Neil Doyle, CenterPoint's executive vice president of infrastructure and transportation development, explained how O'Hare Airport in Chicago developed through a combination of publicly-raised capital invested in private development: "They were able to issue airport bonds for the construction of all the buildings, so government said, 'You know, we can get really cheap money doing this, but we're not putting the taxpayers of Chicago on the hook for you.' And the companies said, 'Fine, we'll back the bonds, but you issue them.'" The result is "everybody wins. We developed that whole park at 3.5 percent money. That's a big difference. We don't want to strain the taxpayers, but government has skill sets we don't have, tools we don't have," concluded Doyle.

Even Governments Get Regulated

Governments, too, face regulation from larger scale governments and the global community. In particular, the World Trade Organization (WTO) restricts countries from subsidizing local industries, which limits governments' abilities to offer blatant incentives to exporters. EU regulations echo this prohibition against government favoritism, with exceptions for economically disadvantaged areas. Aragón, for example, couldn't offer direct subsidies to potential occupants of PLAZA because Aragón was not considered economically disadvantaged at the time.

Global financial regulations also can limit what countries can do to attract capital and investment. In the past, Panama attracted investment and companies through very favorable constitutionally-guaranteed banking secrecy laws that made the country a tax haven. The system also helped to create a sophisticated financial sector that facilitated Panama's logistics companies' prowess in international trade. However, rising global concerns about tax evasion, money laundering, and terrorism have forced many countries, including Panama, to curtail or repeal their tax and financial haven laws. In 2000, the Financial Action Task Force (FATF) put Panama on its blacklist, which forced Panama to increase monitoring of banks and expand prosecution of money laundering.[28] In 2009, the Organization for Economic Co-operation and Development (OECD) put Panama on its gray list of countries that lack sufficient financial openness, which led some foreign banks to leave the country.[29] In 2010, Panama acceded to global regulatory demands for more openness by signing a Tax Information Exchange Agreement (TIEA) with the United States and curtailing some features of Panama's banking secrecy laws.[30] In addition, some of Panama's export incentives came under the watchful eye of the WTO, and Panama had to modify its laws accordingly. These larger-scale regulations can limit a government's ability to offer incentives or to create a preferential climate for recruiting companies to a cluster.

Governments' Impact on Logistics Operations

Governments affect the costs, speed, and reliability of logistics operations through taxes, regulations, energy policies, import/export procedures and other government-run processes. In turn, that affects both shippers and carriers' decisions to operate in, or to avoid, a given region. A 2010 study assessed the opportunity to turn the region of southeast Michigan, northwest Ohio, and southwest Ontario into a logistics cluster.[31] Most of the study's recommendations focused on government support in the provision of infrastructure, appropriate regulations and competitive taxation.

Logistics-Friendly Laws and Regulations

If "capital goes where it's appreciated," then logistics companies go where they can create the lowest operational cost structures to serve the highest possible freight volume. Government taxes, regulations, and policies affect logistics costs, which in turn affect a region's attractiveness as a transshipment and distribution hub. The most onerous taxes for logistics businesses include import taxes, property taxes, inventory taxes, vehicle taxes, and fuel taxes.

Non-Taxing Tax Structures

Singapore jump-started its status as a logistics cluster when Sir Thomas Stamford Raffles established the location as a free port in 1819. This free-port policy contrasted sharply with the stiff tariffs and duties charged by other neighboring ports in Malaysia and Indonesia. Instead of taxing ships and freight, the original colonial administrators of Singapore raised money through taxes on alcohol, gambling, and opium. News of the free port spread rapidly and within six weeks, 100 ships came to the new port; within five months, the new outpost had 5,000 inhabitants. In his farewell remarks, Raffles assured them that "Singapore will long and always remain a free port and no taxes on trade or industry will be established to check its future rise and prosperity."

Dubai Logistics City (DLC), the integrated development anchored on Jebel Ali port and Al Maktoum airport, was developed with an eye to optimize business logistics operations. To attract offshore company formation, DLC allows for 100 percent ownership with no taxation and 100 percent repatriation of capital and profits. These benefits are in addition to the tax and regulatory advantages of a free trade zone and low tariffs.

Logistics businesses located in the AllianceTexas Logistics Park enjoy "triple freeport inventory tax exemption." All three taxing entities—city, county, and school district—have enacted this exemption. The result is that at Alliance, companies pay no tax on inventories that are forwarded out of Texas within 175 days of the date the inventory was acquired or brought into the state. This is in addition to the Foreign Trade Zone designation of Alliance.

How governments collect the taxes matters, too. For example, VAT—Value-Added Taxes—have to be paid by distributors the moment they buy goods for inventory. In most countries, the distributor then applies for a refund when it sells the goods, and the customer pays the VAT. This refund can take months—as many as twelve months in some countries, like Italy. Under this refund-based collection process, the distributor's up-front VAT payment and delayed VAT refund becomes a de facto interest-free loan to the government and consumes the company's working capital. In contrast, the Netherlands has a distribution-friendly VAT collection method based on accounting principles. Companies track purchased and sold inventory and pay the net VAT accordingly. In the end, companies still pay the same total amount of VAT, but they avoid the hassles, costs, and working capital penalties of the refund process.

Government-related costs can modulate shippers' geographic decisions to push logistics clustering over a border. With the deregulation of US interstate trucking in 1980, state trucking rate regulations still held sway over intrastate shipments. The California Public Utility Commission set such high rates that a fifteen-mile state-regulated shipment from San Francisco to Oakland often cost more than a 200-mile deregulated interstate shipment from San Francisco to Reno, Nevada.[32] Needless to say, shippers moved across the border to locations such as Reno. Although California eventually partially deregulated intrastate trucking, other state government differences between California and Nevada continue to make the latter state more attractive for logistics. On business taxes, Nevada ranks nearly the best (#3 in the United States in 2012) and California is nearly the worst (#48).[33] Nevada logistics companies explicitly highlight the tax advantages of their state.[34] As a result, the Reno area has more than sixty-five major freight companies, intermodal yards for Union Pacific and BNSF, forty-eight million square feet of industrial space, and a 7,500-acre Free Trade Zone.[35] Companies such as Amazon.com, Barnes and Noble, Walmart, Petsmart, and Starbucks use Reno for cost-effective over-night access to fifty-three million consumers on the West Coast. Amazon.com and other Internet retailers, especially, use Reno to avoid California sales taxes that they would have to pay if they put a distribution center in California.

Conveyance Size Limits

Conveyance regulations affect carrier efficiency and how carriers structure their networks. One of the key factors for controlling transportation costs is the ability to utilize large conveyances, which have better efficiency both in terms of labor and fuel. But sometimes government regulations stand in the way of cluster development. Much of FedEx's early history was defined by its battle to deregulate the air transport industry. In particular, FedEx led two years of intense lobbying effort in the US Congress, which culminated in the 1977 Airline Deregulation Act. The law enabled FedEx (and all other cargo airlines) to use larger aircraft with no geographic restrictions on routes. FedEx promptly bought seven Boeing 727 aircraft with cargo capacity of 40,000 pounds each to augment its fleet of twenty Dassault Falcon converted executive jets. The cargo capacity of the 727 is almost seven times larger than that of the Falcon.

Ironically, the old US civil aviation laws were rooted in logistics: the US Postal Service's use of private carriers for air mail began in the 1920s. These laws (Air Mail Act of 1925, Air Mail Act of 1934, Civil Aeronautics Act of 1938, and Federal Aviation Act of 1958) were intended to maintain a viable, safe, non-monopolistic air transportation system. The laws heavily regulated the aircraft, routes, and pricing of air transport. Over time, the unintended consequence was the creation of an anticompetitive oligopolistic system.[36]

Had FedEx been prohibited from using larger aircraft, it would have been forced to rely on a large network of much smaller hubs, assuming the company would have been able to survive at all. Without using ever-larger aircraft, the Memphis Aerotropolis cluster would never have formed and no such air-freight cluster would have formed in the United States. The reason is that the total volume of airfreight at any one airport would have been strictly limited by aircraft size and the aircraft spacing limits for landings or take off. That limitation on volume, in turn, would have made it uneconomical to develop the kind of end-of-runway, time-sensitive, nation-spanning distribution operations seen in massive logistics cluster hubs like Memphis, Louisville, and dozens of others around the world.

The same holds true for other modes of transportation. Singapore, Rotterdam, or LA/LB would not have been able to become such important logistics clusters if only small ships were allowed to operate the high seas or if train length or truck sizes were limited. The resulting congestion—both seaside and stateside—would have prevented the positive feedback loop that led to the development of these clusters, keeping them from reaching their current potential.

Market-Oriented Infrastructure Operations

How governments manage critical pieces of public infrastructure makes a significant difference to the volumes of logistics business using that infrastructure. When the United States ran the Panama Canal, it viewed the canal as a strategic asset, rather than a commercial asset. Consequently, the United States managed the canal as a not-for-profit utility: tolls were set just to cover operating costs and little was done to promote the canal or optimize its operation to improve service. After the 1999 hand-over, in contrast, the Panamanian government pursued a market-oriented business model—one that focused on customer service and reliability.

Under Panamanian control, canal fees increased, but so did service levels, because the Panamanians reinvested the profits in maintenance and upgrades to the canal. The Panama Canal Authority (ACP—Autoridad del Canal de Panamá) instituted a sophisticated system of booking transit slots, including an auction mechanism that allowed time-pressed ships to pay for jumping the queue to enter the canal. This is just one example of the philosophical change from setting tolls based on cost under the American regime to setting tolls based on the value of the service provided, under the Panamanian regime.[37] Freight volume surged, and not just because Asia-US trade increased. The canal's market-share in handling northeast Asia to US East Coast shipments grew from 11 percent in 1999 to 40 percent in 2006, at the expense of West Coast ports and the US transcontinental intermodal system.[38] "We have demonstrated to the world that we are not only able to operate the canal, but we can do it efficiently and with big benefits for the country," the authority's head, Alberto Aleman Zubieta told me. "Today, we serve customers better," he added emphatically.

Free Trade Zones

In clusters like Rotterdam and Singapore, the vast majority of goods do not remain in the host nation but are re-exported to other countries. Paying import duties on all these re-exported items would damage the viability of these clusters. Governments can encourage transshipment activities in logistics clusters by creating special zones that are exempt from the usual litany of import duties, quotas, and export paperwork. These include Free Trade Zones (FTZ), also called Foreign Trade Zones, bonded warehouses, export processing zones, free ports, and special economic zones. The legal details of which taxes are deferred or eliminated, what paperwork is not required, or which licenses do not have to be obtained if operating within the confines of these zones, vary. Regardless of the name or details, they share the common characteristic of reduced or deferred government taxes and import/export regulations in exchange for private investment (often by foreign companies) and export-oriented economic activities.

Logistics park developers such as CenterPoint, Hillwood, and Watson tout the availability of FTZs in their parks. Although traditionally associated with ports and border crossings, FTZs can be found in inland dry-ports (e.g., Alliance and Joliet) and freight-handling airports (e.g., Memphis and Louisville). With an FTZ, goods can come through a seaport and travel by rail, truck, or airplane without "entering the country" in a legal sense. FTZs let companies perform value-added activities such as assembly of imported parts or the addition of local content and then re-export the finished goods, often at lower duty rates.[39]

FTZs also offer financial benefits even if the goods remain in country. Companies often hold inventory bound for domestic consumption in the FTZ to defer any import duties. This tactic is beneficial to matching the wide variations in seasonal goods demands to the limited supply of manufacturing and transportation capacity. For example, the limits of manufacturing operations in China and cross-Pacific maritime transportation capacity mean that consumer goods companies must begin stockpiling goods on American shores well in advance of the December holiday season. An FTZ or bonded warehouse lets a company hold these growing inventories and then do the legal formalities of importation, including the payment of customs and duties, only when the goods leave the facility and sent to retail outlets.

Unintended Consequences of Restricting Passenger Travel

Other, nonfreight-related laws and policies can impact logistics and the attractiveness of a region for logistics operations. For example, prior to 9/11, significant numbers of passengers transited the United States through the Los Angeles International Airport (LAX). LAX handled people changing planes and planes refueling for flights between Asia, South America, and Europe. After 9/11, new rules requiring visas even for transiting passengers induced a two-thirds drop in transiting passengers, leading to a reduction in the number of flights. This affected freight operations because many of these international flights carried belly freight, too. With lower frequency of flights resulting in less total capacity, LAX became less attractive for airfreight logistics.

Government Efficiency

In logistics, time really is money. Both speed (having items delivered quickly) and reliability (having items delivered consistently) affect operating costs. Both elements of service influence inventory carrying costs because inventory is required to cover long lead times and uncertain deliveries. Government policies affect delivery times and delivery time variability through management of public infrastructure, the provision of government services, and social stability. To the extent that governments regulate logistics operations directly and indirectly, the efficiency and timeliness of those government functions modulate the attractiveness of any logistics cluster.

A World Bank survey of global logistics indicators found that the government burden on logistics services varies markedly throughout the world and impacts trade.[40] Exporting a twenty-foot container of cotton apparel takes ninety-three days in Kazakhstan, sixty-seven days in Mali, and only six days in Sweden. A typical export transaction requires forty-two approval signatures in the Democratic Republic of Congo, forty in Azerbaijan, thirty-nine in Nigeria, and thirty-three in Mali—but only two in Australia, Austria, and Canada, and one in Germany. Customs-clearance times range from about one day for Hong Kong (China) and the Netherlands to twenty-one days for the Syrian Arab Republic and twenty-five days for Uzbekistan. Countries with high government "overhead" have significantly less trade.

Consider, for example, the ports of Jebel Ali in Dubai and Jeddah in Saudi Arabia. Jeddah is right on the trunk line between Asia and Europe in the Red Sea and has the potential to also handle the massive Saudi internal trade. This geographical and market advantages, however, are counterbalanced by Dubai's better policy and processes. "We would be happy to have services into Jeddah," said Biji Thomas, transport manager for Schneider Electric, a French maker of power equipment. "But Saudi Arabia has customs issues that Jebel Ali doesn't. It takes five days to clear a container in Jeddah where you get same-day clearance in Jebel Ali. Maybe in the future that will change."[41]

The relatively undifferentiated nature of distribution facilities makes it potentially easy for companies to shift distribution operations from locations with inefficient or non-accommodating governments to locations with logistics-friendly governments. For example, a company creating a pan-European distribution center might consider Antwerp, Rotterdam, or Hamburg. All three have large, efficient ports and hinterland access that can be used for distribution of items coming from Southeast Asia into Europe. But differences in import/export processes, VAT collection, and paperwork might influence which location wins the new distribution center. Of course, some countries make it easier to set up a warehouse than others do. Setting up a warehouse takes 528 days in Russia, 481 in Zimbabwe, 363 in China, but only 56–60 days in Finland and South Korea.[42] Ultimately, locations with efficient government processes, such as Singapore and Hong Kong, become magnets for regional and global distribution facilities and logistics clusters.

Faster Service: Time-Efficient Government

Singapore epitomizes the kind of government efficiency that promotes logistics cluster development. To eliminate the problems with paper, Singapore introduced TradeNet in 1989, creating a single-point portal for submitting trade declarations to twenty separate Singaporean government agencies. "We have a very healthy, very high-tech customs. In Singapore, no longer do you have to do a lot of pen and paper stuff. You don't have to sign big sheets of that declaration, or small sheets of receipts," said UPS's Yeo. Before TradeNet, companies had to prepare multiple application forms, employ dispatch clerks and couriers to rush documents to and from government offices, and could only transact with the government during normal business hours. The processing of paper-based declarations took on the order of two days for most shipments.

With TradeNet, companies submit a single electronic document directly to the online system anytime of the day or night and get the needed approvals in ten seconds to ten minutes.[43] Automated algorithms with more than 7,000 rules replace the labor of government functionaries and enable the system's high-speed 24×7 response to declarations. TradeNet has 12,000 users and handles about thirteen million trade declarations per year. "We actually can declare everything on-line, so less paperwork, everything is more efficient," Yeo added.

Singapore also developed PortNet, which was the first nationwide business-to-business portal and e-community to provide integrated services to shipping lines, hauliers, freight forwarders, shippers, and local government agencies.[44] Currently, PortNet has 8,000 users and handles 130 million transactions per year.[45] TradeNet and PortNet were part of a much broader government-initiated master plan to make Singapore an "intelligent island, where IT permeates every aspect of society."[46]

At other clusters, similar systems accelerate the customs inspection process. At UPS, US Customs and Border Protection agents work in the depths of the Louisville Worldport using classified computer algorithms, pattern search tools, and the agent's keystroke commands to direct UPS's conveyors to route selected packages directly to the customs agent for inspection. After inspection, if the agent finds nothing suspicious, the agent puts the package back on the conveyor and it resumes its journey to its destination. Smart systems mean that most packages clear customs instantly, and yet the system catches more contraband than the old manual inspection methods.

Supramunicipal Status for Clear Management of Super Projects

Prospective cluster members and developers also experience government efficiency, or lack thereof, in terms of jurisdictional issues. Logistics developments, with their sprawling size and impacts on regional public infrastructure, can become entangled in approvals processes of multiple jurisdictions. In Memphis, several local executives mentioned to me the complexity of government approvals in their area. Both the city of Memphis and Shelby County claim overlapping jurisdiction. Seeking approvals for large-scale private projects, getting public investments, or affecting changes in ordinances means gaining the endorsement of two mayors and seeking majority approvals from thirteen council members and thirteen county commissioners.

In contrast, the regional government of Aragón dealt with overlapping jurisdictional issues with a special law in 1999 for "supramunicipal" projects by which the regional government took priority for urban planning and could make fast-track land use decisions for projects such as PLAZA (see p. 21 in chapter 1). Although the City of Zaragoza retained some overall approval rights and got a 20 percent equity stake in PLAZA, the city government didn't have day-to-day oversight and couldn't become an obstacle to timely decision-making.

Sustainability

Transportation—especially trucking—can have detrimental impacts on the environment and on the people working in and living around logistics clusters. In addition to air pollution, transportation activities also bring congestion to public infrastructure and noise that might take place twenty-four hours a day.

Logistics clusters are cleaner than many industrial clusters because they don't have the smokestacks, heavy metal emitting smelters, industrial solvents, and exotic chemicals used in many manufacturing industries, including high-tech clusters. Some parts of Silicon Valley and other high-tech clusters suffered serious groundwater pollution from the heavy metals and solvents used to make chips, disk drives, and electronic circuits.[47] Nonetheless, logistics operations that use current transportation technologies do bring smog, particulates, and greenhouse gas emissions. Efforts are underway to implement cleaner diesel technologies in the United States through various federal and state initiatives, including the Environmental Protection Agency's SmartWay program.

No Easy Solution for Pollution

The diesel engines typically used on trucks, locomotives and ships are more fuel efficient than gasoline engines, but they tend to emit higher levels of dangerous particulates. The black soot that belches from an exhaust pipe contains a host of carcinogens and respiratory irritants.

This problem led Los Angeles mayor Antonio Villaraigosa and the port of LA to create the Clean Truck Program in 2008. "Los Angeles has said enough is enough. When 1,200 lives are cut short every year by toxic emissions coming from the Port, we have a moral mandate to act fast and effectively," said Mayor Villaraigosa. "That is why I am signing into law the cornerstone segment of the world's most comprehensive, sustainable plan to clean up a major port."[48]

The tough terms of the law[49] included: a ban on all older trucks as well as trucks not meeting some of the toughest environmental standards in the nation; a proof of off-street parking to prevent congested on-street parking in neighborhoods around the port; requirements for maintenance, safety, security, and driver training; and incentives and fees to accelerate replacement of old, heavy-polluting trucks.

Of Carbon and Clusters

In addition to local concerns about the impact of trucking on city streets, concerns about global climate change and greenhouse gases (GHG) accumulations mean a growing array of government regulations and taxes on fuel consumption and CO_2 emissions. These government interventions could have three main impacts on logistics clusters, affecting both the volume of freight in clusters and the locations of clusters.

First, higher fuel prices tend to favor manufacturing and distribution centers in local and "near-shored" locations rather than distantly produced goods. Thus, as fuel prices rise, Eastern Europe and Mexico may prove more attractive than Southeast Asia for manufacturing, assembly, and distribution into Europe and North America, respectively.

Second, higher fuel prices and pressure to reduce the carbon footprint of logistics operations may push shippers and carriers to use more fuel-efficient transportation modes, which generally involve larger and slower shipments (e.g., from LTL to TL, from TL to rail, and from rail to water, as well as less airfreight).

Fuel-efficiency-driven consolidation of freight means more freight flowing through logistics clusters because large shipments need to be handled in central locations.

Third, regional government GHG policies, mandates, and taxes have the potential to remake the map of logistics clusters. For example, starting on January 1, 2012, airlines have been introduced into the European Emissions Trading Scheme (ETS).[50] Consequently, all flights into, out of and within Europe will be subject to increasing cap-and-trade fees. Over time, this regulation may penalize global logistics clusters within Europe as airfreight (as well as passenger) airlines shift their operations to minimize the ETS burden by flying through hub airports in Dubai or North America instead of Europe, increasing the attractiveness of the former and fueling their development as logistics clusters.

Biofuel for the Road

Biofuels such as ethanol and biodiesel, when produced efficiently, provide a low- or zero-carbon footprint fuel source as one possible replacement for fossil fuels to power trucks, railroads, and even aircraft. Governments are mandating more biofuel use, such as the EU mandate for a 10 percent use of renewable transportation fuels by 2020.[51] Government carbon taxes and emissions trading schemes have the potential to create incentives for more biofuel production by lowering—and possibly inverting—the price difference between biofuels and fossil fuels.

Logistics clusters make ideal locations for biofuel production because of the ready availability of bulk shipping, bulk storage, and bulk-handling infrastructure for both agricultural feedstocks and produced liquid biofuels. In 2010, Neste Oil Corporation opened the world's largest biodiesel plant in Singapore, not far from Jurong Port, with a capacity of up to 800,000 metric tons per year. In 2011, the Singapore plant will be matched when Neste Oil completes construction of a similarly sized plant in Rotterdam.[52] With the new plant online, Rotterdam will have four biofuel producers with a combined production capacity of over two million metric tons per year.[53] In an elegant environmental feedback loop, one of Rotterdam's biofuel producers, Abengoa Bioenergy Netherlands

B.V., pipes CO_2 created by its biofuel production processes to greenhouses in the Dutch agricultural cluster of Westland, just north of the port. Enriching the air in the greenhouses with CO_2 spurs plant growth, directly absorbs the CO_2 waste byproducts of biofuel production, and eliminates the burning of natural gas that greenhouse operators formerly used to boost their greenhouses' CO_2 in the past.[54]

Old Cities and New Ideas

Distribution to urban retailers and end consumers creates congestion on urban roadways. This problem can be acute in crowded cities, especially older cities in which medieval cart routes or cow paths defined the original narrow, meandering road networks. In the late 1990s and early 2000s, with the rise of "Green" political parties, several city governments in Germany launched projects to reduce urban truck traffic.

For example, the ISOLDE project in Nuremberg consolidated urban deliveries of parcels and LTL freight into a single "freight village" ("Gueterverkehrszentrum" or "GVZ") located outside the core urban area. Partially filled trucks were prohibited from entering the city center, necessitating consolidation in this freight village. Similar projects started around the same time in Heidelberg, Freiburg, Berlin, Duisburg, Frankfurt, and other German cities. Each freight village consolidated a single city's distribution activities into one logistics park with good intermodal access.

Yet in the ten-year period after the initial euphoria, most projects were abandoned or stillborn for a variety of reasons, mostly because of the added costs and delays of filling the trucks in the freight village and making multiple stops. One novel idea for distributing retail goods via the city's mass transit system—wheeling goods-laden dollies onto subway cars during off-hours—proved to be too unwieldy, slow, and costly. Other projects became superfluous because retailing evolved from city-center small format stores to suburban "big-box" large format stores located outside the congested city center. At the same time, retailers themselves created their own efficient approaches to replenishing.

Some concepts did survive. The freight villages continue to operate, even if they do so to serve broader commercial needs rather than the originally intended government-envisioned urban logistics needs. As my colleague Professor Peter Klaus of Nuremberg University describes it, Nuremberg still uses its narrow battery-powered delivery trucks to navigate the old city's twisting streets and pedestrian shopping districts.[55]

GOVERNMENTS' MEDIATION OF CLUSTER RELATIONSHIPS

Governments play a major role in mediating relationships between clusters in different regions and within the cluster's region. Logistics in clusters thrives on trade, especially high-volume global trade. Governments play an inevitable role in promoting or inhibiting free trade through the quality of relationships with other countries, trade agreements, and the regulations that governments place on the free flow of goods, conveyances, and money across their borders.

Internal Cluster Governance and Jurisdiction

Within a region, governments mediate relationships among different constituent interest groups by balancing the competing interests and adjudicating local disputes. The priorities and ideologies of the government affect resource allocation, taxation, and regulations of the various constituents. Some governments use bottom-up consensus methods, while others use top-down economic leadership models. Either strategy can marshal a region's resources toward a development goal such as nurturing a logistics industry to support economic development. The constituents within a region might also organize into an industry group or chamber of commerce to pool the resources of the industry and represent its interests.

Consensus vs. Command

Different societies manage the cluster development process differently. In the case of PLAZA, the government creators conveyed a sense of the strategic importance and public correctness of the project for the region. Sitting in his office at the Aragón Ministry of Science, Technology, and University, Javier Velasco described the process leading to the establishment of PLAZA. "We were able to reach a consensus with civil society to do this [PLAZA] because, for some time, people had theorized about the geostrategic location of Aragón and, more specifically, of Zaragoza. When we conceived the project, we presented it with the firm belief that we would be able to deliver. We asked everyone to collaborate. Not long after that, business confederations, trade unions, the Chamber of Commerce, the city of Zaragoza and other institutions—all agreed to back the plan. At the time, both the Central Government and the city of Zaragoza were run by the center-right Partido Popular (PP) party, and we, the Partido Socialista Obrero Español (PSOE) party in the government of Aragón, were the political opposition there. Nonetheless, we succeeded in garnering support from all quarters."

Whereas the developers of PLAZA created consensus to gain support, the creators of Singapore's logistics cluster relied on top-down development and strong guidance of the economy by the central government.[56] When Singapore gained independence from Malaysia in 1965, it was a rough-and-tumble place with open sewers, opium dens, and high rates of tuberculosis. The first postindependence prime minister, Lee Kuan Yew, formed a government dedicated to cleaning up the island, attracting foreign investment, and driving economic development.

Singapore's Economic Development Board (EDB) is billed as "Singapore's lead government agency for planning and executing strategies towards shaping the future of Singapore's economy." EDB created Jurong Port in 1963 as part of the EDB's National Industrial Estate Infrastructure Development Program. When the government of Singapore decided the country should become an "intelligent island," the EDB drove development of leading-edge information technology applications to improve port operations and efficiencies.

By 1988, Singapore surpassed Rotterdam in total freight to become the largest container port in the world (it was surpassed, in turn, by Shanghai in 2010). While some lament the Singaporean government's heavy hand in some cases, it has created an extraordinarily trustworthy business culture virtually free of corruption.

The World Bank ranks Singapore number 2 in the world on its logistics performance index.[57]

Institutions for Collaboration

Organizations such as industry associations and chambers of commerce play a special public-private role in clusters. Porter calls these organizations "Institutions for Collaboration" (IFCs), which are intermediary entities that aren't commercial enterprises, government organizations, or educational institutions.[58] As collaborative groups, each IFC consists of interacting members who share some common purpose and who may be companies, individuals, governments, or even other IFCs. Activities of IFCs include: facilitating the exchange of information and technology, conducting joint campaigns (e.g., marketing, lobbying, shared investment, etc.), and fostering coordination among members. IFCs create formal mechanisms for collaboration that go beyond the asset sharing among cluster members described in chapter 4.

In the context of logistics clusters, the most salient IFCs are local chambers of commerce and logistics industry organizations. Clusters create critical mass for niche IFCs that can focus on specific issues in specific areas. For example, in addition to its Chamber of Commerce, Rotterdam sports the Association of Rotterdam Shipbrokers, Association of Rotterdam Bulk Cargo Stevedores, Terminal Operators Association of Rotterdam, and other niche IFCs. These IFCs can cross-coordinate, electing other IFCs as members. For example, the board of the Rotterdam Port Promotion Council includes representatives of Deltalinqs (a Rotterdam association of logistical and industrial companies), The Rotterdam Chamber of Commerce, the Netherlands Association for Forwarding and Logistics (FENEX) and the Association of Rotterdam Shipbrokers and Agents (VRC).[59]

The privately funded Greater Memphis Chamber includes a subgroup called the Regional Logistics Council,[60] which exemplifies the types of activities pursued by logistics cluster IFCs. The council consists of four committees pursuing a variety of projects chosen by the members. The first council committee oversees transportation infrastructure over a sixteen-county, four-state area. The strategic alliances committee works to build mutual cooperation agreements with other logistics-intensive regions such as: the port of Prince Rupert, British Columbia, Canada; Seattle, Washington; Mobile, Alabama; Rotterdam, the Netherlands; and Antwerp, Belgium. The marketing committee promotes Memphis through national and international advertising and by publishing *HUB* magazine, which goes to 1,500 site-selection consultants. The workforce development committee focuses on education and training, such as supporting the development of the Mid-American Transportation Technology Education Center.

Note that the four committees' efforts parallel common functions of governments. Governments also work on economic development, strategic alliances with other jurisdictions, infrastructure development, and education. IFCs often work with government by acting as collective representatives for their members in lobbying the formal government and in affecting policy.

External Alliances, Diplomacy, and Trade Relations

World trade underpins the largest logistics clusters like Rotterdam, Singapore, Panama, Hong Kong, Shanghai, Los Angeles and New York/New Jersey. Even inland clusters, such as Memphis, Zaragoza, Alliance, and Joliet, carry a high volume of international goods. Trade relations, especially free trade agreements, help foster a free flow of goods which, in turn, implies a growing need for logistics activities.

International Trade Relations

Preferential Trade Agreements (PTAs), such as the North American Free Trade Agreement (NAFTA), Common Southern Market (Mercosur), Asia-Pacific Trade Agreement (APTA), the Greater Arab Free Trade Area (GAFTA) and others, change trading patterns by reducing the cost, time, and variability associated with border crossings. NAFTA created a progressive lowering of trade barriers between Canada, the United States, and Mexico after 1994. Trade between the United States and its NAFTA partners—Canada and Mexico—had more than doubled in dollar value by 2010. Mexico's growing share of imports[61] and analysis of trade data[62] suggest that a significant fraction of the growth was due to the agreement. NAFTA also increased trade between Canada and Mexico. Between 1993 and 2009, trade between Canada and Mexico increased almost fivefold in dollar terms.[63]

Growing volume of traded NAFTA goods (including continent-spanning Mexico-Canada trade) moving across the United States[64] means increases in logistics activity. Texas, in particular, handles the entry of 56 percent of land-based Mexican freight, and almost two-thirds of NAFTA freight traverses Texas at some point in its journey.[65] AllianceTexas touts its favorable distance to Mexico and adjacency to Texas's main north–south interstate highway (I-35) as one of its connectivity advantages. That's one reason LEGO moved its central distribution center to Alliance. LEGO produces its toy blocks in Monterrey, Mexico just over the border. It ships the toys in large quantities to a warehouse in AllianceTexas and then distributes the toys as needed to North American retailers. A proposed second main NAFTA corridor, I-69, is slated to pass through the Memphis area and its rich logistics cluster.

Marketing to Companies and Foreign Governments

Governments can also help attract tenants to a cluster directly through marketing and recruitment efforts. Economic development agencies, trade delegations, support for trade expos, hosting of visiting company representatives, and government-funded marketing all help "sell" the cluster. Singapore's EDB and the Netherlands Foreign Investment Agency (NFIA) take the lead in actively recruiting companies who are looking to set up logistics and distribution facilities in those countries. NFIA, for example, maintains a network of twenty offices around the world, including in other logistics cluster cities such as Singapore, Dubai, and Chicago. As Marco Smit, the NFIA executive director in Boston explained to me, NFIA identifies companies looking for expansion in Europe, brings their representatives to the Netherlands, and works with them on all aspects of locating there. Likewise, Kelvin Wong, EDB's logistics executive director, told me, "The government has always believed that by bringing in global companies to Singapore, we will actually accelerate the growth of our industries, bring in technologies, bring in capabilities, and hopefully with these capabilities, then we residents in Singapore will do good for our local companies as well." Similar active efforts to attract logistics operations include Belgium's Flanders Investment and Trade Organization, Germany's Invest and Trade GMBH, the Hungarian Investment and Trade Agency, and many others.

Local, private boosters such as IFCs also help in marketing the cluster and in recruiting companies. Recruiting new companies requires intense effort on the part of the local government and the local economic development team. Key activities in recruiting a company include marketing and advertising to generate leads; visiting prospective recruits; answering requests for information from prospects (including dozens of pages of questions); hosting visits and tours by the prospects; matching the prospect to local land developers or real estate options; completing proposals; and negotiating government incentives.

"People don't understand how competitive recruiting is. They just think somebody ends up showing up at the door and they are asking for an incentive and that's it. They don't realize there might have been two or more years' worth of work to get them to that point," sighed Dexter Muller of the Great Memphis Chamber of Commerce.

On-site visits play a big role in fostering external relationships and recruiting companies. Delegations of government officials and local companies often travel to recruit companies or lobby governments for mutual benefit. Tom Schmitt, senior vice president of FedEx Solutions told me, "Our new city mayor is open for business. He goes with us to China and he went to New York and DC, because we had to close a deal with Sharp [Electronics Corporation] to expand here. We also had to convince Smith & Nephew [Plc] that the US headquarters should be here and not in North Carolina. And the mayor said, 'let's pack our suitcases and go.' And then we pitched and he's the main pitchman for our community saying, 'we're gonna make this work for you, Sharp or Smith & Nephew.'"

Cluster-Cluster Cooperation

Custer-to-cluster relationships help to coordinate growth, exchange knowledge, and enhance flows, as all logistics clusters are part of the global trade network. For example, the port of Charleston, South Carolina, is one of the logistics hubs hoping to cash in on the Panama Canal expansion. To this end, Panamanian officials visited various East Coast ports, including Charleston, while Charleston port officials and South Carolina lawmakers visited Panama to understand the expansion efforts better.

Governments play a key role in these cluster-to-cluster relationships. Politics may be local, but logistics is global; enlightened politicians know that collaborating with other global logistics clusters brings local economic benefits. For example, in 2009, Marcelino Iglesias, president of Aragón, went to Tangier, Morocco, for a two-day official visit for the signing of a joint cooperation between PLAZA and Tanger-Med seaport development. President Iglesias brought Aragónese entrepreneurs on the visit to meet with Moroccan government ministers and port officials over possible business opportunities. During his visit he stressed the need to "deepen relations between Aragón and Morocco."

The Aragón/Tanger-Med cooperation agreement requires improving infrastructure on both sides to connect the two hubs to each other and to broader population centers (e.g., from PLAZA up to Paris and the rest of Europe and from Tanger-Med down into Morocco and the rest of Africa). The cooperation agreements also include joint promotion of each other's logistics activities, sharing of platform design and operating knowledge, and ongoing meetings between the two clusters.

Gaining Greater Expo-sure

Governments help boost economic development of their region through high-profile fairs and expositions. "Zaragoza was the perfect location for many companies to place their logistics headquarters. The only problem was that the city wasn't nice enough for living or investing, and there wasn't enough promotion," said José Atarés, mayor of Zaragoza from 2000 to 2003. Along with contributing to the development of PLAZA, Zaragoza contributed to other transportation infrastructure improvements, including high-speed rail links, attracting discount airline flights, and expanding bus service. "Now that the infrastructure problem was solved, we had to promote ourselves," Atarés said. In 2004, Zaragoza won the right to host World Expo 2008. In total, World Expo 2008 attracted over 5.6 million visitors over three months. "Zaragoza's main long-term goal is to become the third most important city in Spain," said Alberto Belloch, mayor of Zaragoza since 2003.[66] Logistics industry conferences are often hosted in logistics clusters who are interested both in attracting a large audience and in giving conference goers a chance for site visits of local facilities (e.g., a tour of the port). Almost all large logistics clusters hold regular professional conferences and expositions.

POSITIVE FEEDBACK IN GOVERNMENT AND THE ECONOMY

Individually, no single government-provided factor (such as high infrastructure investment, low taxes, fast permitting processes, free trade, or low crime) alone suffices to attract outside logistics investment. But each factor increases the probability that logistics operators will consider a location favorably. Some of these factors aren't logistics-specific. Attractive corruption-free government, low crime rate, and good schools will be attractive to any business decision-maker. Attracting companies who can operate profitably will, in turn, provide the tax base and economic energy that gives governments their resources and mandates to continue investment in the region and in the cluster.

Although there are many cases where government incentives needlessly subsidize for-profit companies (and these cases grab headlines), most monies invested in promoting logistics clusters seem to be reasonably well invested. In most cases, logistics cluster developments convert low-value, under-utilized land into much higher-value property with a growing tax base.

For example, in addition to building much of PLAZA, the Aragón Government offered extremely favorable land and project-completion guarantees to Inditex's Zara in order to convince the well-respected clothing retailer to drop its prior plans to develop a site in neighboring Catalonia. In explaining the incentives, Velasco said, "They are only justifiable from an economic perspective. The logic here was that we could give away land to a company that would generate economic interest, prestige, and publicity for PLAZA." The government's strategy worked. With Zara's corporate parent, Inditex, as the anchor tenant, some 160 companies subsequently moved to the park, creating over 10,000 direct jobs. Chapter 9 delves into this issue of economic impacts—showing that governments can and do recoup their investments in logistics clusters.

Governments have to balance competing objectives and accommodate the different priorities of disparate groups of citizens. For example, the industry contacts and even government officials I interviewed in Los Angeles spoke of the legendary antibusiness climate of California. Tough environmental laws, bulky approvals processes, and lawsuits asserting environmental claims make logistics infrastructure development and operations more challenging. California ranks dead last of the fifty US states in ChiefExecutive.net's annual CEO survey of states' business climates.

Yet it was equally clear that companies continue to ship freight through Los Angeles and Long Beach, even though they could go to competing West Coast ports or ship via the Panama Canal to East Coast and Gulf Coast ports. These alternatives, however, are not dominant—for example, it takes longer to go from China to the US heartland (and even the East Coast) through the Panama Canal than to use the LA/LB plus rail option. In addition, other West Coast ports are not significantly friendlier to businesses than California. Furthermore, despite tough development policies, the governments around Los Angeles did provide significant support for the region's logistics cluster through projects such as the Alameda corridor, ongoing port expansion projects, and congestion-reducing improvements to road infrastructure. People at the companies I interviewed complained about California's regulatory burden, but most seemed committed to staying.

8

EDUCATION AND HUMAN CAPITAL

Logistics professions span a range of skill levels and specialties, including equipment operators and mechanics, inventory managers, supply chain managers, information systems professionals, and distribution executives. To supplement workforce recruitment and on-the-job training, many logistics clusters attract, develop, or partner with educational institutions for vocational, undergraduate, postgraduate, and professional education.

Leading logistics clusters also support research and development institutions, which are set either as independent organizations, or in conjunction with educational institutions. A cluster provides a rich environment for new knowledge creation because cluster companies can provide data, experience, and problem framing that anchor logistics research in real world issues. The research's outcomes can then give the participating companies a competitive edge by leading to better logistics equipment, processes, and services.

Both research and education contribute to the attractiveness of a cluster. In fact, almost all business plans to develop or invest in logistics activities highlight the availability of academic institutions and training facilities. For example, the Banner Center 2011 report on the logistics industry in Florida devotes over 20 percent of the document to educational issues;[1] the supply chain "pitch" of Lansing, Michigan, touts "the expertise of Michigan State University's internationally known supply chain management program"[2]; and Conexus, Indiana, states that "Indiana must do a better job preparing the next generation of manufacturing and logistics workers. Today's jobs aren't about standing at assembly lines—they're about running computerized equipment and robotic systems, about teamwork and problem-solving."[3]

VOCATIONAL EDUCATION

Although warehouse work seems like a low-skill vocation, modern-day logistics companies have little use for untrained labor. Safe and effective use of the automated equipment that handles goods requires professional workers. The increasing use of technology to track and manage all movements of goods requires even more skills. A large logistics park may need thousands or even tens of thousands of workers. In fact, creating a single large distribution center might call for hiring 1,000 workers. Logistics clusters need vocational education resources to supply all these workers. These vocational education skills include materials handling, conveyance operations, conveyance maintenance, and value-added activities performed on the goods passing through the logistics networks.

Getting Good Goods-Handlers
The AllianceTexas logistics park alone employs 31,000 people at more than 290 companies,[4] which does not include the companies and employment in the area surrounding the park. To help ensure a steady supply of logistics workers, the developer recruited a local community college to create a training center within the cluster. Tarrant County College Corporate Training Center trains people to become foundation-level certified logistics associates (CLA) and midlevel certified logistics technicians (CLT).[5] The comprehensive training program includes industry-defined standards, online and classroom courseware, textbooks, instructor training, assessments, and credentials. Certifications such as CLA and CLT provide a uniform skills base so that hiring companies know the capabilities of those they hire.[6] "This certification will increase the value of those who complete the training," said Kay Lee, senior manager of Tarrant County College Corporate Services. "Alliance companies will benefit by having highly trained logistics professionals, which will improve efficiency and quality control at their facilities."[7]

Training programs like Tarrant's seek to both raise the income potential of less-skilled workers in the local area and improve the labor supply for AllianceTexas. "This project has created a true career pipeline for dislocated workers who are changing professions, students looking for careers in an ever-expanding industry, and veterans who are transitioning from military to civilian life," said Sal Adamski, business services manager of Workforce Solutions of Tarrant County.[8]

On a visit to AllianceTexas on a hot July day, the discussion turned to the training of logistics operators. Sitting around the table in the Spartan office attached to the cavernous LEGO distribution center were Julie Bianchi, director of LEGO's Distribution America; Greg Kadesch, Exel's director of operations for Contract Logistics—Americas; and Steve Boecking, vice president of Hillwood Properties, the company that developed AllianceTexas Logistics Park. After discussing the human resources needs of several of the companies in the park, Steve Boecking pointed out that Alliance extended the training program to reach more people. "We're taking this into the high schools, so when the high school kids graduate, if they don't go to college they can go into the warehouses to work. This will give them exposure to the workplace and start to increase the size of the workforce," he explained.

The Alliance CLA/CLT training program also illustrates the multilateral partnership nature of concerted training activities in logistics clusters. Seven partners contributed to the development of the Alliance training program: the Manufacturing Skill Standards Council, the Texas Manufacturing Assistance Center, Workforce Solutions for North Central Texas, Workforce Solutions of Tarrant County, Tarrant County College, the North Texas Commission, and the Alliance Global Logistics Hub/Hillwood.[9] Companies in the Alliance cluster helped to define the program and agreed to guarantee job interviews for new certificate holders. Federal dollars from the US Department of Labor paid for the training. Thus business, industry bodies, local economic development agencies, educators, and the federal government all had a hand in creating the program.

The CLA and CLT programs at Alliance are part of a broader menu of courses designed to support the educational needs of the Alliance cluster. Tarrant County College offers other courses to the businesses in Alliance, such as technical skills, computer skills, management skills, and communication skills.[10] In fact, Tarrant County College will even train people to become CLA/CLT instructors themselves.[11] This train-the-trainer strategy helps spread the knowledge into the cluster and means that cluster companies can create in-house training programs for CLA/CLT.

Training can also go beyond general logistics skills to include specialized skills. Some products—such as foods, pharmaceuticals, medical devices, and hazardous materials—require special handling because of regulatory or cultural requirements. For example, to attract more business, Singapore's Coolport trained its workers to handle Halal-certified perishables (useful for serving the large Muslim populations in neighboring Malaysia and Indonesia) and to get certificates for Good Distribution Practice for Medical Devices and for Hazard Analysis and Critical Control Points.[12]

Drivers Wanted: Training for Equipment Operations

Many entry-level jobs in logistics require operating, servicing, loading/unloading and directing expensive, potentially dangerous conveyances and large materials-handling and transportation assets such as forklifts, trucks, cranes, ships, rail cars, and airplanes. Logistics clusters have the physical assets and depth of experienced operator-instructors to train the next generation of these equipment operators. The port of Singapore Authority's PSA Institute provides a wide range of vocational and professional training to logistics equipment operators. At any given time, the PSA Institute has some 11,000 students taking a wide range of courses on equipment operations, pilotage, port management, safety, and logistics. Since its founding in the 1970s, the institute has trained some 400,000 employees.[13] The PSA Institute uses a mentor system in which experienced operators sit with trainees to provide hands-on instruction, feedback, and monitoring of the novice operators.

In addition, Singapore built a SGD12 million (~$9.5 million) Integrated Simulation Centre (ISC) in 2002.[14] The ISC includes multiple simulators that are shared by the PSA Institute and Singapore Polytechnic. The crown jewel of the facility is a full mission ship-handling simulator that includes a 360-degree virtual view from the bridge of any of several types of large ships. Other simulators cover tugboat pilotage, engine room operations, crisis management, vessel traffic management, and electronic chart displays.[15]

Although the PSA Institute was set up by the port of Singapore Authority to serve the needs of the port, it also serves the entire country of Singapore, including the logistics, warehousing, transportation, and construction industries.[16] Moreover, trainees from fifty-five countries have come to Singapore for education. The PSA Institute has conducted customized training programs for ports in places such as Indonesia, Sri Lanka, and the Republic of China. For example, when Vietnam created its first deep-sea container terminal in 2009, it sent seventy staff members to Singapore for training to learn port operations and how to handle Vietnam's brand new large Post-Panamax cranes.[17]

In a similar fashion, the Dutch "Scheepvaart en Transport College" (STC) in Rotterdam offers basic professional certification in port operations such as basic stevedoring, radio operations, crane operations, container handling, forklift operations, bulldozer driving, tank storage, cargo surveying, tanker jetty operations, and hazardous material handling. In addition, it offers an array of shipping management and safety courses. STC is a public-private partnership with the Dutch Maritime Cluster (which is an industry association) supervising the quality of training.[18]

Conveyance Repair

Logistics clusters and transportation hubs create a nexus of conveyances and a natural location for conveyance maintenance and repair. But this requires sufficient specialized labor, especially for procedurally exacting and regulated mechanical tasks such as aircraft repair and maintenance. The growth of a cluster can create shortages of mechanics and motivate an expansion of education in the area. For example, when I visited AllianceTexas in July 2010, Russell Laughlin, senior vice president at Hillwood Properties mentioned that the North Texas region around the Alliance cluster has a shortage of 500 aviation mechanics. This has motivated Tarrant County College to buy thirty acres in the Alliance logistics park and expand its aviation-related training programs.

Training for Value-Added Services

Chapter 5 described how companies go beyond just storage and shipping of products to perform value-added services such as kitting, product repair, and packaging in logistics clusters. For the reasons described in that chapter, companies prefer to locate their time-sensitive warranty repair operations in logistics hub locations. Dense and frequent transportation options mean better service for the customer, but repairing or manipulating a product to add value requires more technical skills, such as those of electronic technicians. Value-added services also require highly specific knowledge of particular products and ongoing training to match constant new product introductions.

Some of the value-added services that UPS Supply Chain Solutions offers in its Louisville campus include test, repair, and refurbishment services to a range of electronics companies. Customers include makers of cell phones, laptops, and printers. UPS personnel test, troubleshoot, and repair the product as needed. But this implies that UPS SCS, like other hub-based repair operations, needs large numbers of trained technicians. For example, UPS's repair operations for Toshiba require a workforce of some 120 technicians. At UPS, this training takes two forms.

First, UPS provides education for general electronics-technician skills. When UPS faced technician shortages, the company partnered with Ivy Tech Community College to provide a training program for assistant electronics technicians. The program enabled warehouse workers to upgrade skills from plain logistics to entry-level assistant technician. These assistants could handle some of the more routine tasks (e.g., recharging devices and simple diagnostics) while the full-fledged technicians worked on more demanding, higher-skill tasks (e.g., disassembly and repair). The short program didn't earn a degree but it did give students a taste for the program and encouraged them to get the full two-year associate's degree.

Second, UPS also provides training for specific value-added activities (e.g., repair) on specific products. New employees get a four-to-six week training program that slowly introduces certain processes to them. Existing employees also receive ongoing product-related training. Each time Toshiba introduces a new laptop, UPS and Toshiba must train UPS technicians on the specific troubleshooting diagnostics and repair procedures of the new model.

Get' Em While They're Young

Other clusters have programs that target younger populations even beyond the outreach effort of AllianceTexas. Memphis has the highest percentage of warehouse and transportation workers among the top 100 US cities.[19] For that reason, workforce development is one of the top four priorities of the Regional Logistics Council of the Greater Memphis Regional Chamber of Commerce.[20] Financial support from the Department of Labor and the National Science Foundation is helping establish a high school curriculum for logistics, a certificate for logistics, and an associate's degree at a local community college. Dexter Muller, senior vice president at the Memphis Chamber of Commerce, explained, "What we're trying to do is to get the kids coming out of high school doing dual enrollment and actually taking some of these logistics classes when they're juniors and seniors. And then when they get out, in less than a year they could have a certificate in logistics. If they want to go another year, they'll have an associate's degree. If they want to go on, all of those courses transfer into a bachelor's degree." Furthermore, Dexter added that "most of the companies will reimburse their tuition when they get their associate's degree."

Local non-profit organizations in Memphis help with youth training in logistics, too. The Boys and Girls Club of Greater Memphis—which provides after-school programs for kids aged eight to eighteen—crafted a logistics vocational program at its Technical Training Center. "We want the kids that grow up in this community to have the skills to go out and make a decent living," said Joe Sing, executive director of the center.[21] The logistics course covers the basic skills of supply chain management, receiving procedures, safety procedures, and certification-related hands-on training on using forklifts and power jacks. "What this does is provide the kids an opportunity to have a real heads up [on the logistics field]," says Richard Goughnour, instructor in the logistics program.[22] "What I try to do is to steer them into an entry-level position that they can be successful in," Goughnour added. "We want to build life skills that apply not only to logistics, but also to what it's like in the real world."[23]

Cluster Support

Touring the port of LA, any visitor can see the wide scope of logistics-related education. Not far from the port's main building and sitting next to its main channel is the Maritime Law Enforcement Training Center (MLETC). Along with international trade comes the specter of international crime such as smuggling, piracy, human trafficking, and terrorism. "To keep the port of Los Angeles safe, we must invest in our personnel and provide them with the latest training tactics and procedures to be on alert for any signs of potential terrorism," said Los Angeles mayor Villaraigosa.[24] Thus, the port of Los Angeles, in partnership with the state of California Emergency Management Agency and the US Department of Homeland Security, created the MLETC and developed a Maritime Training Program specifically designed for state and local law enforcement personnel.[25]

The size of the cluster and concomitant numbers of maritime-knowledgeable law enforcement officers makes LA among the best locations in the United States for such a center. The center's instructors come from members of the Los Angeles Port Police, the Los Angeles County Sheriff's Office, the Long Beach Police Department, and the United States Coast Guard.[26] At MLETC, law enforcement professionals learn about topics ranging from boat handling to boarding procedures, water survival, navigation, rescues and counter-terrorism. A state of California port security grant paid for the multimillion-dollar facility and student tuitions cover the operating costs. The MLETC not only trains LA and California law enforcement officers, but it is also open to full-time officers and military personnel from around the United States and even abroad.

PROFESSIONAL EDUCATION

Although logistics may seem like a blue-collar activity of moving boxes and driving trucks, it encompasses significantly more. White-collar positions provide almost 25 percent of logistics jobs: office and administrative support (including stock clerks, dispatchers, and customer service representative, as well as office clerks) represent 17 percent of the workforce; first-line supervisors cover 3.4 percent; and positions in management, business, and finance are 4 percent of all jobs in the industry.[27] With rising global trade and competitive demands for efficiency come rising demand for professionals, managers, and executives with knowledge of supply chain management including advanced management and control processes for warehousing, transportation, procurement, distribution, supplier management, information technology, and a host of related disciplines.

College Degrees

"To support Singapore's growth as an international maritime center, a steady stream of high-quality maritime-ready graduates is required," said Maritime and Port Authority chief executive Brigadier General Tay Lim Heng.[28] To help increase the supply of graduates, Singapore established an SGD80 million Maritime Cluster Fund in 2002[29] and extended it in 2007 with another SGD80 million injection. The government applied the majority of the funds to creating new college education programs in Singapore and to sending Singaporean students to local and international programs.

The Singaporean government helped establish nine tertiary (college-level) programs in areas such as maritime business studies, maritime law, and economics, as well as naval architecture and offshore and marine engineering. This effort includes a deep partnership between the Maritime and Port Authority (MPA) and the National University of Singapore (NUS). "The partnership between MPA and NUS in developing the new programs is a step towards building that pool of graduates and also reflects our shared commitment to developing the right skills for the maritime industry," added Tay Lim Heng.[30] Other Singaporean educational institutes that conduct related courses and executive programs in Singapore include the Singapore Maritime Academy, PSA Institute, the local polytechnics (Nanyang Polytechnic, Temasek Polytechnic, and Singapore Polytechnic) and academic institutions, namely the National University of Singapore, Nanyang Technological University, and Singapore Management University. "Boosting the pipeline of maritime-ready graduates from our universities and polytechnics is a major part of our strategy," said Singapore's transport minister Raymond Lim.[31]

The Maritime Cluster Fund also supports a wide range of course fee subsidies and scholarships. These can defray the costs of seminars and courses as well as local and overseas post-graduate studies. As of early 2008, some 750 companies had used the Maritime Cluster Fund to send over 2,000 employees to a wide variety of maritime education and training programs.[32] Because the government wants to support local industry, "MPA is therefore continuously engaging employers in the maritime industry, so as to develop training programs, courses and scholarships that meet the industry's needs for seafarers, shore-based personnel and maritime engineers," said minister of state for finance and transport Lim Hwee Hua.[33]

Other clusters show a similar pattern of local universities supplying logistics-related graduates for the logistics cluster. The University of Memphis Fogelman College of Business and Economics offers a degree in logistics and supply chain management. The university works with local businesses to customize courses and programs to business needs. Hillwood and the companies in AllianceTexas interact with and support several of the institutions offering logistics education in the area. These include Texas Christian University, which offers an undergraduate major in supply and value chain management,[34]and the University of North Texas, which provides a bachelor of science degree in logistics. Beyond Alliance, however, the Dallas/Ft. Worth Metroplex area is one of the largest logistics clusters in the United States. Thus, in addition to TCU and UNT, local universities with significant logistics and supply chain educational programs include the Dallas County Community College District, Tarrant County College District, Texas A&M

University-Commerce, the University of Texas at Arlington, and the University of Texas at Dallas.

Specialized Degrees

As logistics clusters grow in size, they grow in sophistication, requiring professionals with more specialized degrees. For example, Singapore used some of the money from its ongoing Maritime Cluster Fund to create a Postgraduate Maritime Law Program at the National University of Singapore (NUS). This includes new degree programs such as a master's in Maritime Law (LL.M) and a graduate diploma in maritime law and arbitration. "Shipping and transport-related subjects have always been important offerings at our law school, with its diverse slate of subjects and courses," said Alan Tan, vice-dean and director of graduate programs at the NUS Faculty of Law.[35]

Universities in other clusters have similar specialized degree programs. For example, Erasmus University Rotterdam offers a master of science in maritime economics and logistics,[36] a master in economics and business specializing in urban, port, and transport economics,[37] as well as an LL.M. in business, corporate, and maritime law.[38] In response to the needs of AllianceTexas as well as other logistics parks and activities around the Dallas-Ft. Worth area, the University of North Texas (near Alliance) created a new four-year degree program, the bachelor of science in aviation logistics.[39] A logistics cluster's demand for graduates in a specific topic motivates cluster-affiliated institutions to create new degree programs in that specialization.

Singapore's effort in maritime law education also illustrates how logistics clusters give rise to ancillary clusters of economic (and educational) activity. "Our commitment is to work with Maritime and Port Authority (MPA) and other agencies, as well as shipping companies and law firms specializing in shipping law, to be the foremost maritime law training centre in the Asian region," said Prof Tan of NUS. The MPA believes the new degrees will "further push forth Singapore's aspiration to be the region's legal services hub and complement the suite of undergraduate maritime law modules at the NUS Law Faculty."[40] As pointed out in chapter 5 and further described on p. 254 in chapter 9, logistics clusters often spawn other industry clusters, creating the need for other types of educational offerings.

Post-Graduate Education

Designing, managing, and constantly renewing logistics and supply chain systems requires a great deal of sophistication and analytic knowledge. Logistics systems analysis makes heavy use of mathematics—especially operations research methods—to optimize the movement of goods, assets, and people under constraints of costs, time, capacity, and uncertainty. Although a worker using muscles can move a box, it takes intellectual muscle to know which thousands of boxes to put in which hundreds of trucks to move at each point so that thousands of store shelves will always have just the right amount of product. Tasks such as designing a network of distribution centers, planning conveyance movement patterns, and optimizing inventories in the face of an uncertain future require significant technical sophistication. Consequently, logistics-intensive companies need managers and engineers with university and postgraduate education. For example, UPS employs 4,700 engineers to design and optimize its operations as well as 4,342 information technology specialists. Every year, UPS spends over $1 billion on information and communications technology, which is almost twice its yearly outlay for vehicles (package cars, trailers, and tractors), raising the question of whether it is a transportation and logistics company or a technology company.

In response, universities offer master's and PhD programs that focus on logistics, supply chain management, and shipping-related disciplines. For example, the University of Southern California (in Los Angeles) offers a master of digital supply chain management program that includes a wide range of analytics-focused courses such as statistics, operations management, enterprise information systems, time series analysis, inventory systems, network flows, and project management.[41] In port city clusters like Rotterdam and Singapore, some universities offer even more specialized logistics master's degrees that focus on maritime issues, such as Nanyang Technological University's master of science program in maritime studies offered in conjunction with the Norwegian School of Management.[42]

Research and Education

For the most part, vocational and professional education programs are knowledge dissemination processes seeking to teach large numbers of students the accumulated knowledge of the logistics profession. Yet this raises the question of where logistics knowledge is created. To this end, leading academic institutions go beyond knowledge dissemination to the creation of new knowledge.

Master's degree programs—such as the MIT-Zaragoza master of engineering in logistics and supply chain management (ZLOG) Program,[43] the Netherlands Maritime University-Rotterdam's master shipping and transport program,[44] and the University of North Texas's MBA program in logistics and supply chain management[45]—share a common structure. They all combine a series of lecture-based classes with some kind of culminating research project or internship. Many of these thesis projects or internships arise from the companies in the cluster with which the university program is associated. Students apply their newly acquired analytical tools to create new knowledge while performing research for the cluster's companies. Thus, the program becomes a knowledge-creating resource to the cluster as it trains the next generation of cluster professionals.

PhD programs and university research go a step further, explicitly seeking to expand the warehouse of human knowledge about logistics. Doctoral candidates in logistics embark on a three-to-five year research effort to create new scientific or engineering knowledge about supply chains and logistics. For example, in 2011, ongoing PhD projects at the Center for Maritime Economics and Logistics at Erasmus University Rotterdam included: the role of logistics costs in international trade, the economics of specialized bulk shipping markets, ship finance techniques, maritime logistics, and competition-and-cooperation in liners and terminals.[46] This doctoral research often includes data collection, mathematical modeling, software development, and simulated or real-world testing of hypotheses with the cooperation of companies in the cluster.

Cluster companies often help logistics doctoral research by providing operational statistics, survey data, and case studies as well as sometimes acting as guinea pigs for students' experiments. Forty-eight prominent logistic organizations cooperate with Erasmus University Rotterdam, including Maersk, APM Terminals, APL, port of Rotterdam, ECT (Europe Container Terminals), and BIMCO (an international shipping association).[47] The relationship between these logistics cluster companies and the logistics cluster universities creates a feedback loop of new logistics-related knowledge that is directly relevant to the cluster's logistics companies. In addition to doctoral student research, the faculty, postdoctoral researchers, and staff of logistics cluster universities also perform research, sometimes as part of government or company-sponsored projects.

The Zaragoza Logistics Center (ZLC), located in the midst of the PLAZA Logistics Park, offers various graduate degrees, including a PhD in logistics and supply chain management. Since the summer of 2008, it has offered a PhD Summer Academy, inviting leading logistics scholars and PhD candidates from around the world for a six-week intensive program covering advanced topics in supply chain management. Topics covered in 2011 included: contracts and negotiations; design of service operations; healthcare operations management; inventory management; environmental concerns; and queuing theory.[48] In 2011, some of the ZLC PhD students' research interests included: green logistics; behavioral operations; closed loop supply chains; supply chain coordination; humanitarian logistics; supply chain strategy; inventory and warehousing management; finance and logistics; collaborative strategies; econometric analysis of healthcare operations; and reverse logistics.

The Nature of Academia in Logistics Clusters

In knowledge-intensive clusters, academic research strongly supports the local activities. The strength of computer science at Stanford and Berkeley, and biotechnology and engineering at MIT and Harvard, mean that companies located in Silicon Valley and Bio-Cambridge have access to state-of-the-art research and have a steady supply of highly educated employees, while faculty and students have access to cutting-edge real-world problems using the latest data. Such symbiotic relationships between university and industry are not limited to the information technology or biotechnology clusters; they also feed logistics clusters. The role of academic research in logistic clusters follows a somewhat similar pattern to those found in knowledge-intensive clusters such as Silicon Valley and Bio-Cambridge, with one possible difference: what came first. Whereas with traditional high-tech knowledge-intensive clusters, strong academic institutions played a founding role in sowing the seeds of the nascent technology industry, many logistics clusters began with industrial developments that then motivated the creation of specialized academic resources.

In many logistics clusters, the academic institutions supported the further development of the cluster, after the initial rise of the core of the industry. The reason may be due to the commodity-like nature of basic logistics operations. In the early phase of a cluster's development, the cluster's first entrants use industry-standard conveyances, equipment, and processes. Only when the cluster reaches scale does it become more differentiated and look for new growth through knowledge-intensive research and innovation. At this stage, the recognition of the role of knowledge creation drives the development of post-graduate programs and the development of avenues for research funding. Such "demand pull" is not unique to logistics clusters. For example, as described in chapter 2, California university programs on viticulture and enology followed the development of the Sonoma Valley wine-making cluster, rather than preceding it.

The distinction is important in the economic development process because it means that national and local government should not start with building educational institutions. Instead, the right location, physical infrastructure, regulatory framework, and tax regime create the main early building blocks of logistics clusters. The supply of labor, supported by general and vocational education, is the next priority, while creating postgraduate logistics institutions is important after the cluster is operational.

INFRASTRUCTURE FOR EDUCATION

Many logistics clusters have educational institutions created specifically to meet the needs and schedules of logistics operations, including deep integration of education with cluster operations. Coordinating the timing of educational programs with companies' operations can benefit both functions: companies gain higher-skilled workers (and managers), and educational institutions gain greater student populations as well as benefactors in the community. In addition, some of the leading logistics clusters have invested in specialized university facilities to support their logistics mission, upgrading their capabilities through partnerships with international centers of excellence.

College + Job = Education + Retention

When UPS was planning a massive expansion of Worldport, its Louisville hub, in 1997, it knew it would need several thousand part-time workers willing to work the night-shift sortation. The challenge was to find enough part-time night-owls. "Business, education and government must work together as equal partners to find solutions to our workforce development challenges and we must do it now!" said Dave Adkisson, president and CEO of Kentucky Chamber of Commerce.[49]

The state of Kentucky, UPS, and three local colleges found a solution: offer a free college education as a benefit to part-time night-shift workers. The partnership created Metropolitan College, housed in a 14,000-square foot classroom complex inside the UPS Worldport. Students work part-time at UPS and get paid standard wages and benefits. They can also go to school at Metropolitan College classrooms right at Worldport or take classes at the participating local colleges, getting reimbursements for tuition and a stipend for textbooks as long as they pass their classes.

UPS also created a school-to-work program for Louisville-area high school students. These younger students work a part-time day-sort afternoon shift at UPS, take college courses through Metropolitan College at UPS, and gain valuable educational and work experience. After they graduate high school, many of these students go on to work the UPS night shift and attend Metropolitan College.[50]

The results benefit all parties. The state of Kentucky got thousands of new jobs and thousands of new college graduates. Students got a free education and work experience. UPS solved its workforce supply issues. What was once an 80 to 90 percent employee turnover rate for UPS in some areas is now an 80 to 90 percent retention rate.[51] Moreover, UPS gets to cherry-pick the students—offering full-time post-graduation jobs to the best students/workers. This strategy fits well with UPS's start-at-the-bottom and promote-from-within human resources strategy, described on p. 242 in chapter 9.

Embedded Education and Research

Whereas many educational institutions in logistics clusters focus on vocational and lower-level professional education, the Zaragoza Logistics Center in PLAZA targets more advanced postgraduate education degrees and academic research. The ZLC offers international master's and PhD degrees as well as master de logística (MdL), a degree in Spanish aimed at upgrading capabilities of the local workforce. More than 80 percent of MdL students at the ZLC come from Aragón and more that 85 percent of MdL alumni work in Aragón companies.

As with Metro College and UPS, the ZLC sits inside the logistics park campus, which makes the institution convenient for park members. The proximity also brings an opportunity for creating new cutting-edge logistics knowledge. Master's and PhD students can do research projects tied to the park's 160+ companies. In essence, the companies of PLAZA are a living laboratory for ZLC's students and researchers. Engaging these advanced students in projects both expands the student's knowledge of logistics and helps the companies solve tough problems, innovate, and become more competitive.

ZLC's research creates new logistics knowledge for use within (and outside) the park. That's one reason the Spanish Ministry of Education and Science designated ZLC as an official Knowledge Transfer Office (KTO). This KTO creates "the link between the ZLC and the community in terms of the exchange of knowledge, know-how, skills and expertise, for both commercial and non-commercial applications."[52] The Spanish government also designated the ZLC as the headquarters and leader of Spain's network of technology science stakeholders in the field of integrated logistics, called the National Integrated Logistics Competence Center (CNC-LOGISTICA).[53]

ZLC's structure and background reflect the global nature of logistics and logistics knowledge. ZLC is a partnership between Zaragoza University, the MIT Center for Transportation and Logistics, PLAZA, and the government of Aragón. Javier Velasco, the former government official who helped create and run PLAZA, declared, "If we want to be players in this industry, it is only natural that we want to also be in a privileged position in logistics research. So we created the Zaragoza Logistics Center, and we did it in collaboration with the Massachusetts Institute of Technology, an institution of proven quality... our goal was that anybody who wants to be a first class logistician will have to study in Zaragoza."[54]

The ZLC-MIT partnership is not unique. The success of PLAZA and ZLC spurred MIT's Center for Transportation and Logistics to create two other similar partnerships in Malaysia and Colombia as part of its global Supply Chain and Logistics Excellence (SCALE) Network.[55] Other logistics clusters and academic institutions have partnerships, too. For example, the government of Singapore funded the Logistics Institute Asia-Pacific, a partnership between Georgia Tech's Supply Chain and Logistics Institute and the National University of Singapore,[56] as well as the MIT-Singapore transportation initiative, which is part of the Singapore-MIT Alliance for Research and Technology (SMART). Other foreign universities with logistics-focused Singapore programs include the France-based École Supérieure des Sciences Économiques et Commerciales and a partnership between the India-based School of Business Logistics in Chennai and the Singapore Institute of Purchasing and Material Management.

Recruiting Nexus: Alliance Opportunity Center

Other initiatives go beyond education to provide workforce recruitment and job access functions. Alliance Opportunity Center in

Texas merges education, job placement, and recruitment. The Opportunity Center, established in 1998, is a nonprofit collaboration of five local organizations, including Hillwood, developer of Alliance Logistics Park; Tarrant County College; Fort Worth Chamber of Commerce; Tarrant County Workforce Solutions, and Texas Workforce Commission.[57]

In addition to offering various educational opportunities, Alliance Opportunity Center created a nexus to serve employers, workers, and the community in centralized job-matching functions. Job seekers can find openings at all of the employers at Alliance by applying at the Alliance Opportunity Center rather than applying for each specific job at each specific potential employer. The center tests and prescreens the applicants and stores their application profiles in a massive database, available to potential employers. In total, 125,000 applicants have gone to the Alliance Opportunity Center, creating a central repository of available labor—a warehouse for human resources.

The service is especially useful for new members of AllianceTexas or tenants going through large expansions calling for large numbers of new employees. For example, an incoming company might say, "we need 500 employees and here are our requirements. We need ten managers, twenty fork-lift operators." As Russell Laughlin recounted to me, "that company can come in one day and go through pre-screen, identify qualified candidates, interview, hire, and they're done."

Knowledge Creation Nexus: Dinalog

In 2010, the Dutch Government created the Dutch Institute for Advanced Logistics (Dinalog) with a mission to coordinate the Dutch Research and Development Program for Logistics and Supply Chain Management. Dinalog is envisioned as the (physical and virtual) place where the private sector will cooperate with universities on tackling logistics challenges and developing technology and processes to enhance the country's efficiency (see p. 160 in chapter 6 for Dinalog's expected contributions to information technology for logistics). Dinalog is an explicit fusion of private, public, and academic sector activities under the auspices of a de novo institution. Its three-person supervisory board has one representative each from government, academia, and private enterprise. As of the beginning of 2011, Dinalog had ten partner knowledge institutes and 100 partner companies.

Dinalog addresses crucial education-related issues on several fronts. First, Dinalog supports workforce development under its "Human Capital" initiatives. These efforts include events such as a breakfast lecture series, multiday master classes for supply chain professionals,[58] and a planned winter school for PhD students in logistics modeled after the ZLC's summer PhD Academy.[59] During Dinalog's first year, 5,000 visitors attended various Dinalog-supported events.[60]

Second, Dinalog directly supports knowledge dissemination to the nation's small and medium enterprises with a €4 million multifaceted effort. Dinalog is creating six regional Knowledge Distribution Centers (KDCs) with representatives from partners, education institutes, line organizations, and development corporations.[61] "The knowledge that we develop together at Dinalog and the knowledge present in the Dutch knowledge infrastructure has to be used as widely as possible within the industry, so that companies can renew their business," explained Wim Bens, managing director of Dinalog.[62]

Third, the bulk of Dinalog's budget supports academic and applied research at Dutch universities. "Dinalog is the initiator of large applied research projects in which knowledge from universities and universities of applied science are used to realize practical innovations with Dutch industry," said Professor Henk Zijm, scientific director of Dinalog.[63] By mid-2011, Dinalog had started eight multiyear R&D projects to which it has committed €13 million. Dutch universities involved in the research include: Delft University of Technology, Eindhoven University of Technology, Erasmus University Rotterdam, Fontys University of Applied Science, University of Amsterdam, University of Tilburg, University of Twente, and VU University Amsterdam. An international scientific advisory committee, drawn from leading non-Dutch academic institutions, independently assesses Dinalog's R&D projects for innovative strength and expected economic impact.

This research then feeds back into Dinalog's education and knowledge dissemination activities. As Professor Zijm said, "If, under the coordination of these applied universities, we can feed those networks with the knowledge that is developed within Dinalog, businesses in all the regions in the Netherlands will eventually profit from it, and the knowledge can contribute to the education at the intermediate vocational level."[64]

Last, Dinalog supports development of the country's logistics education infrastructure. It goes further than the other cluster-related education institutions mentioned in this chapter because it seeks to systematically advance the nation's education system as a whole. Dinalog supports these universities in curriculum development, marketing, and research. For example, it takes stock of all the courses available across the Netherlands to look for gaps in the nation's logistics education system. Dinalog itself does not fill these gaps, but facilitates and finances the development and promotion of logistics courses. "Together with our partners, we finance and subsidize the development of programs in higher education," Bens said.[65]

Dinalog is a cornerstone in the Dutch ambition to propel Holland, by 2020, to a leadership position in controlling the flows of goods throughout Europe.

OTHER KNOWLEDGE DISSEMINATION PROCESSES

Formal education and training programs aren't the only processes for distributing knowledge in a cluster. Several phenomena that are more prevalent inside clusters than outside them help increase the flow of knowledge. As with other types of clusters, many of these phenomena arise from the movements and interactions of people who bring knowledge to the cluster or move knowledge around the cluster.

Tacit Knowledge Exchange

In addition to being a center for formal, explicit knowledge creation and dissemination, logistics clusters also foster the creation and flow of tacit logistics and supply chain management knowledge. As logistics systems and services become more intricate and global, much of the planning and operations knowledge becomes embedded in people and in their informal work routines rather than encoded in formal documents and specifications. That is, as complexity increases, more and more of the operational knowledge becomes tacit.

The exchange of implicit knowledge through chance meetings among employees of companies in the cluster, as well as visits to each other's facilities, is one of the benefits of any industrial cluster mentioned by many economists. For example, Rodríguez-Posea and Crescenzi argue that "the process of knowledge accumulation gives rise to spillovers that could benefit a whole set of potential (intended or unintended) beneficiaries."[66]

As part of the research for this book, I visited dozens of logistics facilities in clusters all over the world. When you tour places like ports, railroad yards, and warehouses, you cannot help seeing how the physical space is organized, where goods are stacked, where people are most busy, and how people spend their time. The ebb and flow of people, goods, and conveyances is on display everywhere. My casual observations and casual conversations at these locations always revealed a host of small innovations in each location, such as a clever way of staging shipments, a visual indicator to help coordinate packing, a physical layout that improved flow, an information technology application used in a different way, or a trick to reduce damage to pallets. Although almost anyone can see these innovations, only those people living and working in the cluster are likely to notice them and, more important, understand their significance.

In a logistics campus environment, job rotations, exposing workers to varied operations, are constant. When UPS SCS in Louisville gets a new customer, they don't staff the new activity with inexperienced people. Instead, they carefully pick skilled, knowledgeable people from inside UPS without harming any of the existing functions or customers. By picking one person from one team, another from a different team, and so on, UPS can create an experienced new team and back-fill the minor vacancies in the existing teams. These lateral job rotations bring knowledge and experience together in new combinations, helping spread sound processes.

These job movements are easy to manage within the context of a campus like UPS's Worldport because it has a sufficient number of large-scale operations; each large-scale operation can contribute one or a few experienced people without harming the existing operation while creating a large-enough core team for the new operation. Some of what UPS does within its campus, other logistics parks, such as AllianceTexas, foster within their borders, too, by providing information and contacts. And while logistics campuses and parks manage labor pools actively, the phenomenon takes place in other logistics clusters through chambers of commerce, staffing companies and local Internet sites dedicated to logistics labor requirements.[67]

Importing Foreign Skilled Labor

Countries can directly import knowledge and education by encouraging immigration of skilled workers and managers. Both Singapore and Panama encourage immigration by offering incentives for companies to locate regional or global headquarters in their countries. Panama uses personal income tax breaks to attract executive-level foreigners to work in Panama with the expectation that the incoming executives, managers, and companies will hire and train local workers. "They bring their employees for three years, train Panamanians, and then those Panamanians will grow into those jobs," explained Henry Kardonski, managing director of Panama Pacifico, the developing logistics park situated on the site of the former Howard Air Force Base.

Singapore also directly supports immigration of workers with a more targeted approach that includes both skilled and unskilled labor. "Where local talent is difficult to find, the government policy on foreign manpower facilitates the sourcing of talent from overseas," said Singapore's transport minister Raymond Lim.[68] Singapore's foreign manpower regulations include both restrictions on foreign-to-local worker ratios and price mechanisms to permit, but regulate, the number of foreign workers in specific industries and skill levels.[69]

In addition to recruiting workers and managers, Singapore's Maritime Cluster Fund includes SGD16 million to endow four visiting professors or distinguished visitor positions at local universities.[70] These four positions are all related to ocean shipping. The visitors bring their knowledge and experience to Singapore and transfer that knowledge through undergraduate and postgraduate courses as well as seminars, specialist workshops and conferences for the maritime community in Singapore.[71]

Cosmopolitan Culture: Jet-Setters and Air-Freight

Along with the issue of human capital comes the issue of human cultures. The prevailing attitudes and behaviors of people in a location affect how they live and work. Companies, executives, and skilled workers can choose where they live, especially in the context of global logistics. Cultural issues influence those decisions and influence a location's proclivities in participating in global trade and logistics.

Chapter 3 touched on the cosmopolitan cultures of places like Singapore and Rotterdam. Companies, traders, and workers from foreign lands flock to port cities to seek their fortunes and, in turn, these foreigners help make these cities into vibrant, cosmopolitan places. Kelvin Wong, logistics program director at the Singapore Economic Development Board, mused about the topic in his EDB office on the twenty-eighth floor of the Raffles City Tower. "Companies will need a good place in Asia to grow their business that is Asian-centric, and grow new businesses for Asia, and we believe that Singapore is the best place to do that. Because we have a very international population, we have a very international outlook." Xenophobia isn't compatible with global trade and logistics.

Few places can match the entrepreneurial spirit of logistics companies in Miami. The so-called capital of Latin America attracts a constant flow of immigrants who come to the United States to build a new life. Those immigrants have connections to their homelands, which they can use to start coordinating logistics activities as brokers, forwarders, customs brokers, and other trade facilitators (see the discussion of new business creation on pp. 245–252 in chapter 9).

A cluster location's culture ranks high in the site selection decisions of global companies. Angélica Bertoli, legal director of

Panama Pacifico, relayed to me the story of her negotiations with Procter & Gamble: "I sat with P&G when they were trying to establish themselves in Panama-Pacifico, and they said the number one reason is, of course, the tax breaks but the number two reason is the social aspect. Panama is very cosmopolitan. You have immigrants here from all over the world. Nobody feels like a foreigner. This was more of a social thing." If the executives of a company are going to establish operations in a foreign logistics cluster, those executives will want to feel comfortable visiting or relocating to that cluster. "Their expats wanted to come to Panama to live. And that was very important," Bertoli added.

Collaboration and Trust

Yet there's more to the culture of logistics clusters than just interesting restaurants and a babble of foreign tongues on the sidewalks. Lean and efficient supply chains require collaboration of buyers, sellers, carriers, warehouse operators, and a host of ancillary service providers that broker and support logistics flows. Collaboration requires trust between logistics partners—knowing that each partner will handle its part of the process of storing and moving the goods, the information, and the cash. "Because of our reliability, because of our trust, because of our connectivity, because of our capabilities, we believe that we have actually attracted the many sophisticated global distribution centers and global supply chain projects that you have seen in ALPS [Air Logistics Park Singapore], and people like Dell having global decision makers here," said EDB's Wong.

AnnaLee Saxenian, author of *Regional Advantage: Culture and Competition in Silicon Valley and Route 128*,[72] credits free knowledge exchange among potential competitors as one reason for the ascendancy of the upstart Silicon Valley high-tech cluster over the more established high-tech cluster of Route 128 in Massachusetts. Logistics has an analog of this cultural combination of collaborating and competing because logistics is a service; logistics workers know that the goods need to get to the customer on time and on budget. If that means facilitating a smooth hand-off with a competing carrier, then they'll do it because the customer comes first, naturally (see also the discussion on cooperative behavior on p. 117 in chapter 4). Otherwise, everybody loses.

Workshops as Knowledge Distributors

Many clusters use education and knowledge-transfer activities like workshops, seminars, and conferences to inform potential trading partners and boost trade volume through the cluster. For example, the port of Los Angeles created free workshops called Trade Connect to help small and medium-sized enterprises in the LA area to export goods. Each half-day workshop provides information on the financial, marketing, documentation, and logistical issues that will help these businesses export more, and export more successfully. The workshops include experts from places such as the port of Los Angeles, Los Angeles World Airports, US Department of Commerce, US Small Business Administration Export Assistance, LA Customs Brokers and Freight Forwarders Association, and the Center for International Trade Development.[73]

With the success of the workshops, the port expanded Trade Connect efforts along three dimensions. First, it expanded the program to cosponsor more targeted conferences and seminars on doing business in particular regional markets such as India, China, Japan, and Korea. Second, it held more focused workshops for particular industries, such as providing a program to members of the California Fashion Association aimed at promoting exports of fashion, apparel and accessories. Finally, it took the workshops to the US Midwest. Trade Connect is part of the National Export Initiative, which is a federal government program to boost the US economy by increasing US exports and improving the balance of trade. As one port official put it, "We are tired of exporting air."

FROM EDUCATION TO IMPACT

Education underpins many of the beneficial economic impacts of logistics clusters discussed in the next chapter. Education creates a growing workforce with rising skills that leads to higher wages in the region. Professional and graduate degree programs lift some cluster workers into the upper echelons of white-collar employment. Educational institutions produce a growing educated workforce that provides one more incentive for companies to relocate to a cluster. Knowledge creation in cluster-affiliated universities and think tanks also helps spur the development of new companies that create innovative services.

9

REGIONAL IMPACT

Many regional and state governments solicit investments by specific industries because they recognize the synergistic value of industrial clusters in creating competitive advantage. "Trade and Invest" organizations in most European countries as well as similar local and national organizations compete for foreign direct investment. In trying to attract tomorrow's industry and not yesterday's, these governments often focus on recruiting "sexy" industries employing highly paid knowledge workers (and in many cases, industries with a perceived lower carbon footprint). Yet replicating Silicon Valley appears to be difficult. Moreover, creating a high-tech cluster may fail to address pressing social problems like unemployment among less-skilled citizens.

While visiting numerous logistics clusters throughout the world and interviewing local executives, government officials, logistics park operators, consultants, legal experts, economists, and other parties, it became clear that logistics clusters generate significant economic and social benefits. Beyond the obvious economic growth and jobs impacts, logistics clusters offer diversified economic bases and even an element of economic justice. While they require infrastructure investment, in many cases these investments offer positive economic returns to the government.

CREATING NEW AND BETTER JOBS

Many of the knowledge-based clusters pursued by governments around the world favor highly educated employees. For instance, information technology clusters favor those with college and postgraduate education in computer science while offering comparatively meager opportunities for unskilled labor. In contrast, logistics clusters offer a broad spectrum of employment opportunities: blue-collar, white-collar, and no-collar jobs. Moreover, these clusters provide social mobility because the logistics profession and the industry value deep operational experience "on the floor" even among its executives. Thus, many logistics firms promote from within the company and within the industry, while providing educational opportunities to their employees who wish to improve their skills, certifications, and degrees.

Large Labor Forces in Logistics Clusters

To see the job impact of logistics clusters, consider the following examples:

- The port of Rotterdam employs 55,000 people directly and 90,000 more indirectly.[1]
- Louisville International Airport (primarily UPS Worldport) provides 55,000 jobs and a $2 billion payroll, generating $277 million in annual state and local taxes.[2]
- The Memphis International Airport is responsible for 220,000 jobs in the local economy, 95 percent of which are tied to cargo operations. The airport is responsible for more than one out of three jobs in the metro Memphis area.[3]
- AllianceTexas attracted over 265 companies employing 30,000 people to the logistics park, in addition to creating over 63,000 indirect jobs by 2011.[4]

Ricardo García-Becerril, the manager of the PLAZA Park in Zaragoza, told me in 2010 that "the original goal of creating 14,000 jobs at PLAZA by 2014–2015 is still [in force]; currently there [are] more than 10,000 people working here."

When the Union Pacific Railroad added a $370 million intermodal terminal in Joliet to support growing rail volumes in the Chicago cluster, "the building of this facility created nearly 6,000 construction jobs," said Jim Young, Union Pacific chairman and chief executive officer. "If we look at CenterPoint Properties' entire development, we can also expect up to 1,300 permanent intermodal facility jobs, 4,500 industrial park jobs and more than 3,000 new truck driver positions," he added.[5]

Range of Logistics Employment

Chapter 2 noted that many communities aspire to become another Silicon Valley. That dream, however, may fail to create balanced job growth across the spectrum of education levels. Marco Smit, the Boston representative of the Netherlands Foreign Investment Agency, shared some of his triumphs and frustrations when we talked in his office on the fifth floor of the Park Plaza building in Boston. He expressed frustration at politicians' fixation with high tech and gave an example of trying to recruit a major biotech company to put their research and development center in the Netherlands. The company said they required 250 PhD microbiologists, which, Smit sighed, "is more than we have in the entire country." Rather than employing Dutch citizens, landing this company would require hiring foreign technologists. Moreover, highly educated workers are the least in need of jobs—in the United States the unemployment rate for college graduates is about half that of the general population.[6] Although there's no doubt that high-tech clusters such as semiconductors, software, or biotechnology can create "good jobs," these aren't the ones most needed; high-tech clusters may fail to create jobs for those who have no jobs.

In contrast to high-tech clusters, logistics taps labor pools across a very wide range of skill levels. At the low-end of the spectrum, jobs such as truck driver, forklift operator, or warehouse worker require little formal education and modest levels of training or work experience. Yet logistics isn't all manual labor because the industry now makes such heavy use of information and communications technology to interact with suppliers and customers around the globe, control product flows, cope with global risks, satisfy exacting customer service requirements, and cut costs at the same time.

The profile of skills employed in a logistics clusters expands further in three directions beyond those required to perform logistics and supply chain management activities. First, companies hire people to perform value-added services that can most efficiently and effectively occur in a logistics cluster. Chapter 5 provided numerous examples of value-added services in logistics clusters that require more skilled nonlogistics labor such as electronics technicians, assembly workers, florists, photographers, and pharmacists.

Second, as mentioned in chapter 8, many clusters actively recruit companies to relocate their headquarters, not just their logistics, to the cluster. The need to be in the "center of the action" can motivate companies to locate their global, regional, or divisional headquarters to the same location handling distribution of products to customers. In Singapore, Kelvin Wong, the logistics program director of Singapore's EDB, told me "when we say 'home,' we believe that Singapore can be the home for business, home for innovation, home for talent." Headquarters brings additional nonlogistics jobs across a wide range of white-collar corporate functions such as marketing, IT, strategy, and executive management.

Third, logistics clusters also provide jobs for the creative class, because many design-intensive consumer goods companies (such as clothing, toys, and housewares) choose to colocate headquarters and design centers near their major global distribution hubs. For example, designers for Tabletops Unlimited in Los Angeles work next to and even in the warehouse, ensuring a tight coupling between the designer's vision for houseware products and the supplier's delivery of goods coming in and going out of the distribution center. Mattel's Los Angeles headquarters combines both the imagination and the distribution of the toy maker in a fashion similar to Imaginarium, almost 6,000 miles away, where designers and warehouse workers share the same facility in the PLAZA logistics cluster in Zaragoza.

A later section of this chapter (see p. 257) describes the move of manufacturing and other companies for which logistics is an important component into logistics clusters. Naturally, these companies bring with them even more jobs.

Paying High Wages

Not only do logistics clusters bring jobs, they also bring increased wages and productivity improvements relative to noncluster regions. Based on quantitative analysis of all German clusters, the Wiesbaden Center for Cluster Competitiveness estimates that a 1 percent increase in cluster presence in a region was associated with a €302 per employee increase in the average wages and a 44 euro-cents per person per hour increase in regional productivity.[7]

The result is that logistics clusters offer a decent average wage. Dr. John Husing studies the impact of the logistics industry in Southern California. During breakfast at the Blu Restaurant in San Pedro, he shared with me data about jobs in Southern California. In the LA Basin, three sectors offer median or average wages above $20/hour for non-college-educated workers: logistics, manufacturing, and construction. In the economic environment of 2011 and looking ahead, only logistics promises long-term growth. Other growing, low-skill sectors such as retail, hotels, entertainment, and Indian gaming pay an average of under $15/hour. Of the four sectors that added jobs in Southern California between 1990 and 2004, Husing found that logistics offers the highest average annual wages ($45,987). These wages rivaled those of the manufacturing sector. A study by the Chicago Metropolitan Agency for Planning echoes these findings: transportation and logistics salaries in Northern Illinois were close to and in some cases higher than those in the so-called Chicago manufacturing "super cluster."[8]

While the number of employees in US manufacturing jobs has been almost stable over the last sixty years, the share of nonfarm workers employed in manufacturing has been steadily declining from nearly 34 percent in 1950[9] to 9 percent in 2009.[10] For example, the abovementioned CMAP study notes that while the transportation and logistics sector added jobs in Northern Illinois between 2000 and 2007, the manufacturing super cluster lost 27% of the jobs by 2007. And this was before the deep recession that started in 2008.

Creating Upward Mobility: Opportunities for All

Logistics clusters do more than just hire low-skill workers; they provide a conduit for social mobility. All of the investment in work-force development, training, education, and research described in chapter 8 means that logistics clusters create opportunities for a broad population, including unskilled, entry-level workers. Part of this opportunity arises from fluctuating work levels (e.g., a holiday surge, new product launch, or reconfiguration of a distribution operation) found in many logistics operations. Surges in the volumes of flowing packages mean that many companies hire temporary and part-time workers.

Surges have two beneficial effects on upward mobility for unskilled labor. First, the surge brings fresh temporary workers into the workplace who might then be hired fulltime if they prove themselves. Temporary and low-skill work let the employer see the employee's intangibles (e.g., work ethic and ability to handle the coordination complexities of logistics) prior to committing to fulltime hiring and training investments. Consequently, near-minimum wage and temporary jobs in logistics provide an entry point for better-paying permanent jobs for unskilled labor.

Second, surges in volume mean that when a company hires temporary workers, the existing staff shifts upward into de facto higher-skill positions and frontline management positions. For example, a company's existing low-skill freight handlers might help oversee new temporary freight handlers or might help plan workgroup activities. This allows managers to have insight into which workers might be management material.

Most logistics service providers value operational experience and thus hire from within the industry and promote from within the company, fueling social mobility. For example, one of the basic values of UPS is a commitment to long-term employment relationships, which often starts with students working at UPS part time. UPS has a "promote-from-within" culture that includes multiple opportunities at every junction, as well as training and career development, starting at entry level.[11]

The numbers from UPS bear this out: an Accenture 2006 report mentions that "54 percent of UPS's current full-time drivers were once part-time employees; 68 percent of its full-time management employees rose from non-management positions; and 78 percent of its vice presidents started in non-management positions."[12] This culture of internal promotion was more common than not in most of the logistics service providers I visited. With immersive on-the-job training plus occasional continuing education classes, an employee's lack of a formal education need not prevent him or her from rising into white-collar and even executive levels.

This upward mobility brings higher wages to formerly low-skill, low-wage workers. Although wages vary from cluster to cluster and even among companies within a cluster, my interviews with Dr. Husing and Steve Arthur, director of operations at CEVA Logistics Inc. in Los Angeles provided a picture of the upward mobility of logistics work for noncollege-educated workers in that cluster. Some smaller companies may pay only $7 or $8 an hour in wages for unskilled entry-level workers, basically minimum wage. Larger logistics firms might have starting wages in the $10 to $12 an hour range. As logistics workers gain experience and skill, their wages can climb to $24 to $30 an hour. Some workers, even those with no college degree, go on to fill executive positions or start their own companies, leading to significantly higher incomes.

The same wage-improvement pattern is evident around the world. When Manzanillo International Terminals came to Panama in 1993 to create a port terminal for inexpensive imported Russian cars, they picked a location near the impoverished area of Colón. I met Juan Carlos Croston, vice president of marketing at the Manzanillo Panama offices, after driving along the modern highway leading from Panama City, on the Pacific Ocean, to the port of Colón, on the Atlantic. "At the beginning when we came here, Colón had a 40 percent unemployment rate," said Croston. The company had eighteen months to produce the blueprints, secure financing, train people, commission the equipment, sign up customers, and get the terminal running. "We took out some ads asking for people to interview for jobs, we got 10,000 applications," he added.

"I think one of the key decisions the company made was to hire people with no port experience whatsoever," Croston explained. "We joke that they (new employees) were first driving these $4,000 cars and then they were promoted to truck drivers so they were driving a $40,000 vehicle and then they were promoted to forklift drivers—a $400,000 piece of equipment. And they were promoted to crane operators—and they're [operating a] $4 million piece of equipment." People in Colón found out that they could start out in an entry-level position and end up driving a $4 million piece of equipment and earning six to seven times the prevailing wage in the area. As of 2010, the terminal had 850 employees, 93 percent of whom come from Colón and about half have eight or more years with the company. "Basically, we gave them the opportunity to be promoted," Croston said proudly.

CREATING NEW LOGISTICS BUSINESSES

Logistics clusters, like other types of industry clusters, spawn new and growing businesses in the cluster that add additional capacity, offer new services, and provide suppliers to the growing cluster. When one sees the scale of FedEx and UPS hubs; BNSF and UP intermodal yards; Walmart and ZARA distribution centers; the ports of Singapore and Hong Kong; PLAZA in Aragón; and the Inland Empire area in South California, or any of the other large logistics clusters, it may seem like logistics is a big-company's game, but that's not the case. Underneath and all around the mega-entities of the logistics industry lie a multitude of small companies. Although logistics, in general, does require a significant base of physical assets, that doesn't mean that small logistics providers cannot arise and thrive.

New logistics companies typically form in and around two types of clusters. The first is a logistics cluster, which houses multiple distribution and supply chain management activities. The other is an economic cluster that requires logistics services, such as a manufacturing cluster (e.g., the Detroit area) or a trading hub (such as Chicago in its early days). Naturally, both types of new company formation phenomena go hand in hand. As discussed on p. 132 in chapter 5, the services offered in logistics clusters attract manufacturing, trading, and other companies requiring logistics services, to logistics clusters. And logistics clusters also develop to serve industrial clusters. Both types of clusters, regardless of their origin, may be a fertile ground for spawning new logistics enterprises.

Opportunities for Small Logistics Firms

Although big transportation carriers may haul the bulk of all cargo on many trade lanes, no single carrier provides end-to-end service among all origin-destination pairs on all modes of transportation.

Moreover, a given shipment may require multiple modes and multiple carriers in moving from road to ocean to rail to road. This creates an opportunity for small asset-less (or "asset-light") firms that broker, synchronize and manage logistics activities between carriers, suppliers, customers, service providers, and government agencies.

For instance, freight forwarding entails helping shippers move goods internationally from a shipper's loading dock to the origin port, across the ocean, through customs, and from the destination port to the consignee's dock. The work requires many phone calls, fax and email communications, arranging and coordinating space and loading/unloading to/from several transportation carriers, and preparation of paperwork to comply with export/import regulations and customs regimes. Personal relationships are important to get through customs or inspection stations quickly in faraway lands, making sure that each shipment gets to its destination on time and damage-free. But the job doesn't require any expensive physical assets. Anyone with a foot in two countries, logistics knowledge, and personal contacts can start a freight forwarding business. Consequently, many small forwarding companies are started by employees of established freight forwarders who split off to form their own companies.

The logistics business in Miami still retains some of its early "Wild West" business mentality, which was evident when I visited the area in 2011. The Miami Super Pages listed no less than 946 freight forwarding companies in the area,[13] with new ones appearing seemingly every week. Most of these are, naturally, small operators founded by an entrepreneur who left one of the larger forwarders. The new entrepreneur, typically, trades on existing relationships and a strong connection to a particular region in South America. The Miami area brims with entrepreneurial activity of logistics service providers dealing with imports and exports through the Miami International Airport and the port of Miami. An October 2011 article in the *Miami Herald* makes the point that "hundreds of small trade logistics companies give South Florida a competitive edge in international commerce as a 'one-stop-shop' for companies moving products and improving their supply chain."[14]

Even the asset side of the industry spawns large numbers of small enterprises. Anyone who is willing and able to drive a truck in the United States can finance the equipment and then obtain loads from many trucking brokers. These brokers, such as C. H. Robinson, Hub Group, Landstar, Pacer, and Total Quality Logistics,[15] help independent truckers find loads, arrange for payments, create a buyer's association for discount fuel purchases, and so forth. In addition, the low cost of information technology and widespread use of wireless systems mean that more and more independent truckers can find loads on their own. In 2010, over 100,000 new motor carriers applied to initiate operations in interstate commerce or the intrastate transportation of hazardous materials in the United States.[16] About 256,000 truck drivers in the United States are self-employed[17] and out of the 500,000 US trucking companies, 82 percent operate fewer than six trucks.[18]

Finding a Pack of Professionals for Coyote Logistics

Deep pools of high-skill logistics professionals make a logistics cluster attractive to logistics entrepreneurs. Jeff Silver was working for American Backhaulers in Chicago when the company was acquired by C. H. Robinson Inc. in 2001. Silver spent the next two years going back to school and contemplating his next move. In 2003, Jeff planned his start-up during the second semester of his nine-month master's program in supply chain management at MIT's Center for Transportation and Logistics.

After getting two master's degrees, Silver returned to Chicago and, when his noncompete agreement with C. H. Robinson expired, launched his company, Coyote Logistics. Coyote brokers truck services. This means that Coyote quotes certain rates to customers (shippers who have to move loads) and then searches for an independent trucker, among the millions roaming the US highways, who would agree to carry this load, preferably for a lower rate than what Coyote quoted to its customers. The company uses sophisticated home-grown software to match truckers and loads. The company also re-engineers customer shipping patterns in order to reduce the customers' costs.

Coyote became a huge success. In 2010, *Inc.* magazine named Coyote as number 6 on the list of the ten fastest-growing companies in North America, and the fastest-growing logistics company, reporting a three-year growth rate of 13,846 percent.[19] As of 2011, Coyote had over 600 employees. In January 2012, Chicago mayor Rahm Emanuel announced during a visit to the company that Coyote will hire 400 additional people for "cutting edge" jobs in the Chicago area in 2012.[20]

Sitting in my MIT office with two of his lieutenants, Bill Driegert and Chris Pickett (both graduates of MIT's logistics program—the same one from which Silver graduated), Silver explained why he chose Chicago. He focused first on professional logistics labor. As the largest Midwestern city, Chicago attracts a large number of young university graduates from Wisconsin, Iowa, Illinois, Michigan, Ohio, and Pennsylvania. Moreover, unlike other hotspots for young professionals (such as the San Francisco Bay Area, Boston, or New York), these graduates know about logistics. In fact, many of Coyote's competitors reside in the Chicago area, including American Transport Group, AFN Logistics, Strive Logistics, Circle 8 Logistics, Trek Freight, Echo Global, and Command Transportation. In addition, there are many full-service logistics companies located in the area. Other companies, such as C. H. Robinson (based in Minneapolis) and Total Quality Logistics (in Cincinnati), recruit from the same labor pool. Just as important, the very large number of logistics service providers in Chicago makes the profession a recognized and visible career opportunity.

Finally, Silver mentioned that his first two customers were in the Chicago area. Both of them decided to work with Silver's new company based on social relationships with Silver that predated the founding of Coyote Logistics. In talking about his first customer, Silver added, "I've known him very well over the course [of several years] and it would have been hard to have that same type of relationship with somebody in a different city."

Morphing of a Company: YCH

A logistics cluster creates opportunities for local companies to grow in both size and sophistication with the cluster. In the early

1970s, the transportation company founded by Mr. Yap Chwee Hock in Singapore suffered a crisis. Its largest customer, the Public Utilities Board, canceled its contract to transport workers in its trucks. As the eldest son of Yap Chwee Hock, Dr. Robert Yap, who just graduated from the University of Singapore, stepped in to help.

The young Dr. Yap turned out to be a shrewd, smart, and energetic entrepreneur. In 1977, he abandoned the passenger transportation business and redirected the company to cargo transportation, becoming a major contractor to the Singapore Port Authority. In the early 1980s, the company diversified into warehousing and forwarding and then expanded to offer complete third-party logistics services including distribution, inventory management, and freight management. In the early 1990s YCH, as the company was called by then, developed a logistics park ("Distripark') to serve the logistics needs of sophisticated multinational corporations. Throughout this period, it grew from a local Singaporean player to a regional logistics services provider serving the regional distribution needs of companies such as DuPont, Roche, and HP.

YCH took another important step in the late 1990s with the release of the first of a suite of proprietary information technology applications providing comprehensive supply chain solutions, including manufacturing and inventory management, consumer goods order fulfillment, and service and returns logistics management. These information technology solutions were adopted by several leading multinationals worldwide, expanding the range of services offered by YCH.

Hosting me in YCH offices in the Distripark on Tuas Road in Singapore, Robert and his team, including James Loo, chief information officer, and Lilian Tan, director of supply chain solutions, described YCH's various supply chain software applications. The software is based on internally developed algorithms and capabilities stemming from YCH's experience as a logistics service provider and supply chain management consultancy. At the time of the interview, the company had over 3,000 associates operating in twelve countries throughout Asia Pacific.

The growth and development of YCH from a company ferrying local workers on trucks to a sophisticated regional supply chain management powerhouse demonstrates the potential for new companies and new innovative services anchored in a local logistics clusters.

From Serving a Local Industry to Global Logistics: Armellini Industries

In 1945, Jules and Sarah Armellini began transporting flowers from Vineland, New Jersey, into Philadelphia and New York. The business started with a single truck and a barn for storage. After the company began hauling flowers out of Florida in 1953, it moved its headquarters to southern Florida to the heart of the flower-growing region in 1963 and offered logistics services to the local growers. But when increasing globalization and air cargo availability enabled the growth of the South and Central American flower industry, new competition drove the company to make a strategic decision. In 1977, Armellini created a subsidiary, J. A. Flower Services (JAFS) to clear fresh flowers through customs and USDA inspection. Today, JAFS is the largest customs broker for clearing perishables out of Miami International Airport, which is the fourth busiest US airport by cargo traffic. Furthermore, another subsidiary, Fresco Service, founded in 1983, is today one of the largest refrigerated bonded warehouses serving perishables brought by air from South America.[21]

Armellini, however, is not the only player in the logistics cluster importing fresh flowers and other perishables through the Miami International Airport and the port of Miami. As the global trade in flowers intensified, Miami became a cluster of logistics companies specializing in flower importation and distribution. The Association of Floral Importers of Florida cites seventy-five fresh-cut flower importing companies located near Miami International Airport in 2011.[22] Every day, 40,000 boxes of flowers arrive at the airport, accounting for over 80 percent of flower imports into the United States.

Armellini's refocusing of its business—from hauling flowers by truck within the United States to importing flowers from international locations—required new expertise, which was easily found in the Miami cluster. Furthermore, once the company established itself as a flower importer, it could branch out to be an importer of other time-sensitive, cold-chain-requiring items such as food products. Armellini, and companies like it, increased the demand for air cargo services, bolstering the Miami cluster and leading more logistics companies to start operating there.

A Fertile Ground for a New Type of Logistics Service Company: LogiCorp

In the mid-1980s, a few years after the deregulation of the transportation industry in the United States, some logistics professionals saw the still-unfulfilled potential of deregulation. Although trucking companies no longer needed government approval to offer new services, shippers (such as manufacturers, retailers, and distributors) were not enjoying many of the potential benefits. With this in mind, my friend Lorne Darnell (who was at the time director of logistics at the automotive division of Rockwell International) and I cofounded LogiCorp Inc. in 1988. The company may have been the first nonasset-based third-party logistics provider in the United States. LogiCorp's customers outsourced their transportation management function to LogiCorp, which ran reverse auctions among carriers, chose the winning ones, negotiated the transportation contracts, managed the payment to the carriers, and monitored their performance on behalf of its customers (the shippers). It also worked with its customers to improve their logistics processes and re-engineer their logistics networks.

The company was based in the Detroit metropolitan area because of our experience in automotive logistics and the professional contacts Darnell had in the area. The concentration of automobile manufacturers and their suppliers in the area meant a significant amount of transportation activity and a vast cluster of distribution centers dealing with automotive parts, subassemblies, and machinery. Indeed, all the initial customers of LogiCorp were automotive companies and automotive suppliers concentrated around southeast Michigan. These early customers collaborated with LogiCorp to help it refine the idea of outsourcing the transportation management function. These included developing unique software solutions as well as new (at the time) processes for reverse auctions for contracting transportation services.[23]

The idea of consolidating volumes and offering carriers large amounts of freight worked well because the carriers could take advantage of economies of scope (see the conveyance cycle discussion on p. 97 in chapter 4) when bidding on the various movements, allowing them to bid aggressively, thus reducing shippers' costs. The company grew quickly, and at the end of 2004 it managed more than $600 million worth of freight business. That year, LogiCorp was acquired by Ryder System Inc.,[24] which renamed the new division Supply Chain Solutions, added many more services, and grew the unit to several billion dollars of freight under management.

Incubating and Testing Innovation

Some clusters explicitly incubate innovation by building a crèche for innovative start-ups. For example, PortTechLA is a clean technology transfer, incubation, and commercialization organization sponsored by the port of Los Angeles, the San Pedro Chamber of Commerce and the Wilmington Chamber of Commerce. Its mission is to "attract and mentor companies with technologies that will enable the port of Los Angeles—and ports world-wide—to meet environmental, energy, security, and logistics goals."[25] PortTechLA's chairman, Herb Zimmer, added, "We're looking to attract to our port the type of innovators who are developing new standards-setting technologies."

"We can accelerate companies with sales, and incubate those that need more time to develop their business model," said PortTechLA executive director Jeff Milanette.[26] "And just as importantly, we want to help connect them with investors and users who share their vision and want to reap the benefits—financially, operationally and environmentally—from what gets developed here."[27]

Los Angeles is not the only logistics cluster with an incubator or assistance program for logistics-related startups. The Dinalog Incubator in the Netherlands has eight fledging logistics businesses.[28] Just as important, Dinalog has an ambitious research and development agenda, including some far-reaching goals (see also the discussion of Information Infrastructure on p. 160 in chapter 6 and the review of Dinalog on p. 227 in chapter 8). Likewise, Singapore's Government's "SPRING Singapore" program runs the Logistics Capabilities Development Program (see also the discussion of government efficiency on p. 194 in chapter 7). The program aims to develop new logistics capabilities, information technology tools, data interchange mechanisms, and strategic alliances among logistics operators. It offers funding and services to support entrepreneurs, small businesses, and local companies in the logistics sector.[29]

The Business of Creating Businesses: WTDC

Business incubators can also be private and quite informal. Consider, for example, WTDC in Miami. In 2002 Gary Goldfarb, fresh from selling his own forwarding business, Golden Eagle, ran into Ralph Gazitua, who was rebuilding his own family business in Miami, WTDC, after 9/11. When Ralph asked Gary what he is doing, Gary answered "nothing," to which Ralph came back with "so why don't you do 'nothing' here?"

WTDC developed a full set of supply chain management services. It takes advantage, for example, of flow imbalances—there is more cargo flowing from Miami to the east coast of Latin America than northbound (about 70/30 split in 2011). Consequently, the rate for hauling a standard twenty-foot container from Miami to Santos in Brazil, in January 2012, was $1,600, while the northbound rate was $850 for the same container. Similarly, there are many more truck shipments coming into Miami than going out of Miami to the US hinterland. Thus, the rate for a 53 foot truckload from New Jersey to Miami was $2,900 in January 2012 vs. a northbound rate of $1,850. Maritime container flows between Europe and Miami are even more out of balance but an equalization system diminishes Miami's advantage.[30] Taking advantage of these imbalances, one of the WTDC businesses books cargo from Latin America to Europe and to the US Northeast and Midwest, through Miami, at competitive rates.

Like many other logistics service providers in South Florida, WTDC grows by providing whatever customers need and then building a business around it. It moves furniture from Spain and China for Concepts & Design Studios LLC; manages cold storage for perishables; runs bonded warehouses for importers, and manages inventories in Brazil for its customers shipping into that country. It even obtained a license as an automobile dealer so it can locate, purchase, and ship automobiles all over the world.

Aside from its active foray into new businesses and its agility in serving its customers, WTDC is also in the business of providing infrastructure for budding entrepreneurs who are trying to build logistics business and businesses dependent on logistics. WTDC provides such companies with warehouse space, equipment, systems, marketing, and help with the regulations governing international supply chain management. In December 2011, there were thirty-two start-up tenants in the WTDC facility. Goldfarb described four of these companies: two recent startups, including a forwarder and a customs broker; one later stage forwarding enterprise; and a small food company, building on logistics capability. In his words:

Swift Custom House Brokerage and Logistics
Rolando Ayala was known to us because he was the regional director for FedEx Trade Networks. He left FedEx for an opportunity with OHL,[31] building their business in Latin America. Eventually he said, "I'm going to start my own business." At the same time, he was going out with a girl who was a customs broker at Expeditors. So, they got together, created a company called Swift Custom House Brokers. They started a company and a family at the same time. We gave them a little office, and I'm talking little. Two people fit in that office. They're generating container load business, and they're working so hard. Rolando told me the other day he hadn't gone to sleep earlier than 3:00 am in the last two weeks. But, you know what, only in Miami can you all of a sudden just cobble a company together and two weeks later you have a business. So, they're doing business and growing.

CEP Brokers
You have the mother, Carmen Puga and her daughter; a beautiful story because it's a mother and daughter that work as customs brokers. They started very small, now the third generation was born and they come in and the baby crying while they're taking care of the phone. You go there, it's like you cannot but respect these people's effort and work.

Tran Logistics
Lily Tran was an executive at Oriental Logistics, which is the big freight forwarder out of Asia, and had an opportunity to start her own business by renting an office from us and having the instant access to all the tools you need to be competitive against anybody else. So, she opened up an office, it's done fantastic, she's got like 10 people working for her.

Nueva Cocina

I met with a lady called Celeste De Armas. Celeste De Armas has a young company called Nueva Cocina. Nueva Cocina is new kitchen, new cooking. They sell prepared Latin foods that are preserved in pouches and whatnot. But, a very nice brand. And they want to penetrate the Latin American market. They started two years ago; it was an idea. Two ladies that cook well. Today these people are in Publix, Winn Dixie, in many of the local markets and they're entering big time distribution into Latin American with Price Mart and Costco and Walmart and all of those guys. It's incredible.

DIVERSIFYING THE LOCAL ECONOMY

The story of Zara and Caladero in chapter 1 illustrates one of the special qualities of logistics clusters: the cluster's tendency to diversify the economy of the region. Every major logistics cluster supports activities in a wide variety of industries. For example, Louisville is a distribution hub for aircraft spare parts, cell phones, repair parts for office equipment, industrial products, digital cameras, shoes, pharmaceuticals, and many other products. Logistics clusters even support companies that have no physical products at all—UPS in Louisville provides laptop repair, refurbishment, and delivery to Ernst & Young's peripatetic global workforce of accountants and business consultants. Thus, logistics clusters diversify the local economy as they attract companies from a wide variety of industries that rely on efficient logistics services.

Resisting Recessions

This diversification effect is the biggest qualitative difference between logistics clusters and other types of economic clusters. While any given industry cluster has the potential to boost the local economy, it is also vulnerable to downturns in that one industry. The dot-com boom brought great riches to Silicon Valley, and the dot-com crash brought a significant downturn. Detroit rises and falls with the American auto industry. In contrast, a logistics cluster includes a diversity of shippers, distribution centers, and value-added activities, each subject to its own industry business cycle. Aragón's investment in a logistics cluster has helped the area mitigate the effects of the 2008–2009 recession; during that time, Aragón had half the unemployment rate of the rest of Spain.[32]

Moreover, some value-added services in logistics clusters provide countercyclical economic activities. Repair, refurbishment, and field service distribution centers in clusters such as Panama, Louisville, AllianceTexas, and Memphis suffer less during recessions because many people choose to repair items or buy second-hand refurbished items instead of purchasing new goods. When the global 2008–2009 recession hit, Neptune Lines in Panama enjoyed a massive surge in refurbishment revenues from trade-in second-hand, earth-moving and construction equipment.

The effects of scale on transportation costs and service levels—some of the same factors that make clusters grow (see chapter 4)—mean that larger clusters are more robust than smaller ones. Between 2008 and 2009, total freight volume to Europe fell 16 percent.[33] But the decline was concentrated in the smaller container ports. The largest European port, Rotterdam, lost only 9.6 percent of its traffic while Antwerp, the second busiest port by tonnage lost 15.6 percent and Hamburg, the third busiest by tonnage, plunged 28 percent.[34] By 2010, Rotterdam rebounded to above prerecession levels while Antwerp and Hamburg, as well as many others, still lagged.

Similarly, Russell Laughlin in AllianceTexas told me that they, too, saw drops in airfreight as FedEx consolidated activity from peripheral hubs such as AllianceTexas to the Memphis core. Airfreight data confirm this observation. Between 2008 and 2009, air cargo volumes did not drop at all in Memphis and only dropped marginally in Louisville (–1.3 percent) while dropping significantly more in peripheral hubs such as Anchorage (–15 percent), Miami (–13.8 percent), Los Angeles (–7.4 percent), New York's JFK (–21.2 percent) and Chicago's O'Hare (–17.1 percent).[35] During a recession, the same mechanism that helps fuel the growth of logistics clusters works to preserve the largest logistics clusters at the expense of smaller ones. As total freight volumes drop, service to and from most locations deteriorates, and both shippers and carriers relocate inventory and distribution activities to the largest hubs from which they can still maintain good service. Furthermore, as volumes drop, some shippers change from large shipments using direct operations (such as TL moves) to small shipments using consolidated operations (LTL moves). Thus, the largest consolidation hubs see relative increases in freight as carriers eliminate direct point-to-point service between smaller hubs and ocean carriers skip smaller ports. All these phenomena generate a negative feedback mechanism for all but the largest clusters, where relocation of activities from small clusters compensates for the general reduction in volumes.

Transcending Industry Obsolescence

The logistics cluster that triggered the writing of this book, PLAZA in Zaragoza, arose because government officials feared over-reliance on a single industry. When Juan Antonio Ros first conceived the idea in 1993, he told then-president Emilio Eiroa, "Mr. President, Aragón needs to look for something new; we cannot rely on the GM factory forever." Later officials agreed. "When we took up office," Consejero Velasco warily chose his words, "entering the government of Aragón in 1999, we performed a careful analysis of the region's situation. We determined that Aragón was excessively dependent on the automobile industry."

At the time of the decision to launch PLAZA, GM was a local powerhouse. Zaragoza had hosted General Motors' largest European production plant since 1982. A quarter of a century of car-making saw GM's Opel plant build ten million cars and play a pivotal role in the Aragónese economy. GM and its top suppliers spent close to €400 million per year on salaries and employed 7,000 workers directly and another 13,000 indirectly in the region. By some accounts, GM generated as much as 50 percent of the exports of Aragón. Despite GM's might, Velasco summed up the situation: "We decided our best bet was to add new features to increase the scope of activity in the regional economy."

Aragón's fears about its dependency on auto making proved prescient. When the financial crisis hit in 2008, Detroit imploded. Europeans feared the carmaker's bankruptcy and stopped buying Opels. By the end of 2008, the government of Aragón had to rescue GM-Opel, offering a €200 million line of credit.[36]

Economic robustness is one of the key differences between an industry-specific cluster and a logistics cluster. Whereas Detroit and the old Aragón tracked the ebb and flow of the automobile industry, Memphis and Louisville float on a succession of logistics-intensive industries. Where Western producers of consumer electronics suffer from the globalization and the off-shoring of manufacturing, logistics clusters thrive on the added trade flows. Whereas high-tech factories and their skilled workers represent extremely specialized assets that can become obsolete, logistics infrastructure and logistics workers offer flexibility in handling a range of products and services.

New Clusters of Logistics-Intensive Industries

The broad and deep service portfolios of a logistics cluster can become the scaffolding for other types of industrial and high-technology clusters. Chapter 5 described the rise of value-added services and the clustering of companies that require high-performance logistics such as the biomedical device cluster in Memphis or the fresh produce cluster in Rotterdam. Chapter 6 noted how logistics firms serve as infrastructure, attracting other companies to the area. For example, some 140 companies have moved to Louisville because of the UPS Worldport. These logistics-dependent industries help diversify and grow the local economy.

Logistics' role as industrial infrastructure, where logistics clusters spur industrial development and the formation of industrial clusters, means that economic data tend to undercount logistics' contribution to jobs and wages. For example, when Rolls Royce Jet Engines puts its assembly and test facility, as well as its joint ventures of engine repair and overhaul in Singapore, the country counts Rolls Royce's employment there as "aerospace." When Medtronic manufactures artificial joints in Memphis, it's counted as biomedical manufacturing.[37] When Caterpillar or Komatsu refurbish construction equipment in Panama, it's counted as part of the heavy equipment industry. But none of these companies would likely be in their respective locations if those locations weren't logistics clusters.

Promoting Trade and Exporting Expertise

Many economic studies have demonstrated that reducing the cost and improving the quality of logistics and transport systems improves international market access and leads directly to increased trade. For example, a 2002 World Bank study[38] showed that the differences in logistics prowess among Asian countries—including ports infrastructure, customs clearance procedures, regulatory administration, and e-business use—are significantly related to differences in trade performance. Trade has been shown to be linked directly to improved standards of living and, most important, to alleviation of poverty. A 1999 paper in the *American Economic Review* argues that each one percent rise in the trade to GDP ratio increases income per person by at least 0.5 percent.[39]

By improving the performance of global supply chains, logistics clusters facilitate trade, with its resulting economic benefits. Logistics clusters also create exports of logistics technologies, services, and products through the expertise of home-grown logistics firms that grow into global players. Singapore offers several examples that illustrate the various types of logistics-derived exports. YCH grew from a local transportation company to a global service and technology provider; CrimsonLogic is a worldwide software and service company created by the spin-off of the technology behind TradeNet (described on p. 194 in chapter 7)[40]; and Singapore's PSA now operates in twenty-eight ports in sixteen countries around the world.[41] These examples illustrate the growth of exports through progressive expansion of services based on locally developed logistics technology and know-how.

DELIVERING THE GOODS—ECONOMIC IMPACTS

As mentioned above, logistics is a critical enabling service for other economic activities. These include both value-added services performed by logistics service providers, and manufacturing, which is attracted to a place that offers a superior global trading infrastructure.

Economic Growth

Growing employment, high wages, and the robust volume of goods flowing through a cluster mean that a logistics cluster can boost the region's GDP. Approximately 10 percent of the Netherlands' GDP is generated by logistics activities[42]; the port of Rotterdam, alone, adds about €22 billion annually to the Dutch economy.[43] Similarly, Memphis Airport's cluster creates $28.6 billion in annual economic impact, 95 percent of which arises from airfreight.

When I visited Breda in the Netherlands, where the Dinalog campus is located, Stephan Satijn, vice president logistics of the Holland International Distribution Council, took me through an estimate of the economic impacts of bringing one additional full-time logistics job to the Netherlands.[44] Various factors—such as labor cost mark-ups, the percentage of labor out of third-party logistics providers' revenues, and shippers' expenditure on 3PL services—create a series of multipliers for the total economic activity attached to that one added job. Accounting for the customs and VAT paid by the shipper, the contribution of the 3PL in terms of corporate taxes, VAT and labor benefits, and taking into account a modest economic multiplier effect, the study concludes that each additional full-time equivalent worker in the 3PL industry adds €81,851 per year in contribution to the Dutch society.

Individual companies in clusters also conduct their own impact studies to justify incentives and show the key role they play in the local economy. During my visit to DHL in Singapore, Stephan Muench, head of DHL in-house consulting Asia Pacific, described how DHL carefully analyzed the economic, social development, and technological innovations DHL brings to Singapore. The company enlisted the aid of Singapore's Economic Development Board and other government agencies to ensure the soundness of the methodology and data. DHL found that the company's three divisions in Singapore provided 4,000 direct jobs and contributed SGD 2.2 billion to the economy through wages and business with local subcontractors.

Similarly, BNSF has an internal analytical group that works with local government officials to estimate the economic impact of its facilities. John Lanigan, BNSF's executive vice president sales, marketing, and business development, explained that BNSF uses these analyses to counter the antidevelopment groups that invariably protest each project. The protesters and even the local development officials often lack the information to estimate the economic benefits of a new facility, like an intermodal yard, for the local economy. BNSF's analytics group and the company's deep experience can develop well-grounded projections based on actual data and historical experience.

Tragedy of the Commons

When trying to attract new business investments, local and central governments have to be aware of the "Tragedy of the Commons." This phenomenon (which has been hotly debated in the economics literature) can take place as local governments compete with each other in order to attract business and investments through incentives such as lower taxes and loan guarantees. The tragedy of the commons was articulated first by William Lloyd in 1833.[45] Lloyd described a pasture open for grazing to several separate cattle herds. Each herd owner has the incentive to add more and more heads to his herd because each extra head adds to the owner's welfare, while the marginal cost associated with each extra head of cattle (less available grass as a result of the incremental grazing) is everybody's problem. The herds keep growing since all the herd owners behave in the same way. At some point, however, the pasture is depleted and everybody loses. Thus, while each individual entity acts in its own best interest, the common ecosystem in which they operate can fail, to the detriment of all the operating entities.

One can imagine regional governments each offering better and better terms (no tax, expensive government support, etc.) for attracting companies. All the while the country as a whole experiences a lower and lower tax base. This argument is particularly acute when the central government does not have its own taxing authority, as is the case in the European Union. There, countries can compete with each other while the EU cannot tax businesses directly. (In 2012 business taxes ranged from 12.5 percent in Ireland to 34 percent in Belgium.) Consequently, this issue is at the heart of the efforts by the European Union to address the "tax competition" between member countries.[46]

The tragedy of the commons, to the extent that it exists, is an issue affecting not only business investments but many aspects of economic activities and markets. All solutions to the tragedy of the commons involve some type of restriction. These restrictions—just like most laws—work for the betterment of the whole society at the expense of the short term benefit of the individual (company or person). Solutions can also be developed through voluntary restrictions based on education—changing mindsets so individuals understand their impact on the system and self-regulate their behavior, as is the case with individuals' and companies' efforts toward environmental sustainability.[47]

Return on Government Investment

Government's economic goals typically include job creation, increased standards of living, business development, and general economic growth. While a cluster strategy may provide many of these benefits, the benefits must be offset against the government's costs of providing education, infrastructure, amenities, and development incentives as described in chapters 6, 7, and 8. To be sustainable, a logistics cluster must create a tax base that at least defrays or repays all these government expenditures and debts incurred in creating the cluster.

Governments subsidize businesses for strategic, economic, and political reasons. These subsidies can generate healthy or unhealthy consequences, the very quality of which may not be apparent for many years and may not even be measureable. The US Government, for example, subsidizes sectors such as energy, agriculture, transportation, and defense, to name a few. And, as mentioned above, local governments offer subsidies, incentives, and tax abatements to attract companies of all kinds to their state or region. While in many cases such subsidies of strategic industries do contribute to national or regional prosperity, they also distort the market and involve potentially corrupting political influences. Subsidized companies also fail occasionally, as was the case with the 2011 bankruptcies of Solyndra, following the receipt of $535

million in federal loan guarantees, and Evergreen Solar, which received $58 million from Massachusetts tax payers.[48]

The logistics clusters I visited, however, seem to offer a more
positive story and data. Ricardo García-Becerril, the manager of
the PLAZA Park in Zaragoza, told me in 2009 that "for the government of Aragón, there has already been a return on the investment. It has created an economic base by attracting businesses to
the area, and it has generated employment." Similarly, the Memphis Chamber of Commerce tracked the incentives issue for more
than a decade and found that government inducements to businesses did work out well for the region. The chamber determined
that most companies delivered on their promised levels of hiring
and stayed in the region beyond the term of the incentives.

Of all the logistics clusters studied, the AllianceTexas Logistics
Park has been the most meticulous in accounting for every contribution (public and private) to the development of the cluster and
for the cluster's return on the government's investment. When Ross
Perot created the concept in the 1980s, his team developed an economic impact analysis to attract both public and private investors
to the project. And in order to stay true to their promises and prove
that this was a good use of public resources, they kept account of
every dollar invested and returned over the years.

After an exhilarating aerial tour of the AllianceTexas Logistics
Park in a fast helicopter, I sat down with the Hillwood team, led by
L. Russell Laughlin, senior vice president of Hillwood Properties.
"If I told you that you could invest one dollar and over ten years
I could give you 20 in return, on a multiplying effect, you'd say,
"That's a good deal," and I'd say, "Yes. All right, here's what we
need to do,'" Laughlin explained.

To create AllianceTexas back in 1987, local, state, and federal
governments invested a combined $135 million to pave roads, pro-
vide public utilities, build the airport, and extend Fort Worth city
services to encompass the development. Governments also donated
2,500 of the 17,000 acres of the development. That land and $387
million in total public investment ultimately attracted $6.8 billion
in private investment and produced a $36 billion economic im-
pact. Incremental taxes paid to local governments totaled more

than $1.2 billion through 2008, representing a more than 11 per-
cent annual direct return on the government's investment. All these
benefits, and the taxes paid, keep growing every year as the park
continues to grow and attract new companies. "Nobody believed
the economic impact numbers that we generated, but we thought
they were conservative. And of course, we turned out to be right,"
Laughlin added.

10

LOGISTICS CLUSTERS EVOLUTION

As a reflection of the world's dynamic economies, logistics clusters continue to evolve, with new clusters arising, existing ones changing, and some potentially declining. Rising standards of living in emerging market countries, changing infrastructure, environmental concerns, and new technologies combine to influence both the volume and the routing of trade flows, leading to new and changing logistics clusters. Overall, logistics seems to be growing in both importance and concentration. The long term growth rate of the logistics industry in Europe (through 2007) was 2.5 times the average GDP growth.[1] Furthermore, the logistics property market in 2010 accounted for around 10 percent of the European property investment market compared with only 6 percent in 2006.[2] Labor figures for the United States show that logistics employment rose from 17 percent of the workforce in 1998 to 20 percent in 2008. Moreover, the number of logistics clusters grew in the United States between 1998 and 2008, as did the degree of labor concentration in those clusters.[3]

CREATING AND PROFITING FROM A "FLAT" WORLD

Thomas Friedman's book, *The World Is Flat*, highlighted a growing array of forces leading to a "flattening" of the competitive playing field around the world and a surge in global trade. In the United States, exports grew from 6 percent of GDP in 1970 to 11 percent of GDP in 2009 while imports grew from 5 percent of GDP to 14 percent of GDP in the same timeframe.[4] On one hand, globalization provided an ever-wider array of consumer goods at lower prices to people around the world. On the other hand, the flat-world phenomenon led to job losses and factory closures in many developed countries.

Logistics and supply chain management have a special relationship to this flat-world phenomenon in that logistics businesses both benefit from and cause "flattening." Logistics clusters in the developed world, even inland ones such as Indianapolis, Kansas City, Chicago, Duisburg, or Zaragoza, thrive on trade and enjoy more flows as manufacturing moves overseas. The increases in US foreign trade imply that import/export logistics more than doubled from handling 11 percent of GDP in 1970 to handling 25 percent of GDP in 2009. Yet the more efficient global supply chains become—including the logistics clusters underpinning these chains—the more manufacturing can move overseas. At the same time, logistics clusters in the developing world—in Shanghai, Chongqing, Saõ Paulo, or Cartagena—allow manufacturers there to distribute their products around the world.

The realization of logistics' role in globalization changed the perception of the industry. Dexter Muller of the Greater Memphis Chamber remarked to me that years ago, "there weren't that many cities that were interested in it [logistics]. Then Tom Freidman wrote his book and was talking about how you can outsource everything, but you can't outsource distribution. It's interesting; now everybody wants it."

Logistics Is Local and Global

Whether locally made or imported, all goods require local distribution, which implies on-shore warehouses, local deliveries, and local value-added services. Thus, logistics is one industry that is relatively immune to off-shoring.

Intensifying globalization increases the importance of supply chain management in general and logistics clusters in particular. First, rising imports and exports of raw material, parts, and consumer goods lead to growing freight volumes at key waypoint clusters, such as the international ocean shipping centers in Singapore, Hong Kong, Shanghai, Dubai, Rotterdam, and Antwerp. The same holds true for airports that are distribution hubs for high-value and time-sensitive products such as computer chips, pharmaceuticals, fashion goods, and repair parts. For example, "to ensure that the company's new, translucent blue iMacs would be widely available at Christmas … [Steve] Jobs paid $50 million to buy up all the available holiday airfreight space," said John Martin, a logistics executive who worked with Jobs to arrange the flights.[5] The largest airfreight waypoints include Hong Kong, Memphis, Shanghai, Seoul, Anchorage, Paris, Frankfurt, Dubai, Tokyo, Louisville, and Singapore.

A similar sentiment and a testament to the role and growth of logistics activities and logistics clusters was voiced by Ricardo García, PLAZA's general manager: "The original concept involved not just logistics, but a combination of logistics activity and light industry," García told me. "At that time, we believed that logistics was not a sector that, on its own, would suffice to guarantee the viability of the project. The project would be guaranteed by an industrial sector, which would enable us to develop logistics activities which we would be able to subsidize with what we obtain from the industrial sector. We had the wrong idea; it's funny how it has evolved over time."

Logistics as the Flattener

Ultimately, efficient supply chain management and the logistics clusters that anchor supply networks have a "flattening influence" because they enable efficient globalization and global competition. Part of the remaining "hilliness" of the world's playing field is in the transportation costs, delays, cross-border complexities, and various risks, all of which increase when using distant suppliers. Efficient logistics, such as that fostered by logistics clusters—with their frequent service, low costs, and far-reaching distribution capabilities—make the flow of products and parts from distant lands efficient and simple, intensifying the competition between local and global suppliers.

As discussed throughout this book, large logistics clusters generate sufficient freight volume to justify the use of more economical larger vessels, higher-capacity cargo planes, and longer trains over long distances. In addition, the volume of freight in a large cluster creates higher service frequencies, reducing inventory carrying costs and improving customer service. Both low cost and good service make the economics of logistics hubs compelling, resulting in efficient global supply chains and leading, in turn, to more trade and even more logistics clustering. From a study published by the *World Bank Economic Review*, one can infer that a 10 percent decrease in trading costs can create a 20 percent increase in trading volume.[6] That increase in volume then feeds back to further improvements in delivery time, service options, and costs.

TOWARD SUSTAINABLE CLUSTERS

Increasing pressure—locally and globally—to green all economic activities affects both shippers and carriers. Rising concerns over fossil fuel consumption and environmental sustainability have three effects on supply chains and logistics clusters. First, environmental concerns about the effects of greenhouse gases on global warming, as well as concerns about the health effects of air pollution and diesel fumes around logistics clusters, mean increased government and public demand for reduced emissions (see p. 196 in chapter 7). Second, economic concerns about the high cost of oil motivate carriers to improve efficiencies and reduce fuel consumption through innovative conveyance designs and vehicle operating procedures. Third, rising awareness of the limited supplies of natural resources also implies increased recycling and a growing need for reverse logistics and services that convert the waste stream into usable materials. The scale and density of logistics clusters makes them a natural location for developing, testing, and deploying innovations in green logistics.

Forthcoming Low Emissions Conveyances

The high carbon footprint of freight transportation, as a result of its conspicuous use of fossil fuels, make logistics clusters a focus for environmental regulations and an early-adopter of green technologies. For example, the Rotterdam Climate Initiative seeks a 50 percent reduction in CO2 emissions from the city as well as the port of Rotterdam by 2025 from the 1990 level.[7] In southern

California, the landmark 2006 Clean Air Action Plan (CAAP) imposed stringent requirements and deadlines on the ports of Los Angeles and Long Beach to reduce emissions and mitigate health risks around the ports. A 2012 deadline in CAAP motivated the ports of Los Angeles and Long Beach to pursue a multiprong effort at both replacing old trucks and developing new vehicle technologies (see the discussion of sustainability on p. 196 in chapter 7 and the innovation discussion on p. 251 in chapter 9).

Environmental mandates spur technology development in the affected clusters. CAAP, for example, pushed the LA/LB ports to create the Technology Advancement Program (TAP). TAP seeks innovations that reduce emissions from on-road trucks, cargo handling equipment, harbor craft, and locomotives.[8] Projects include port-generated ideas, solicited proposals for specific innovations, and unsolicited proposals for novel advanced technologies. TAP works with the ports, carriers, and technology providers. Many of the technology providers are start-up companies in the Los Angeles area pursuing green technology innovation for logistics, transportation, and other applications.

The ports have funded demonstration projects on several different hybrid vehicles.[9] Hybrid technology combines a traditional fossil-fuel engine with an electric drivetrain powered by a battery or other energy-storage technology. This combination can significantly reduce fuel consumption and emissions in three ways. First, hybrids can run off the batteries and turn off the fuel engine when the conveyance is stationary or moving slowly, thereby eliminating fuel consumption and emissions from idling and low speeds. Second, hybrids can use regenerative systems that convert braking power into battery energy. Third, the battery can provide a boost to the traditional engine so that the conveyance can be designed around a smaller, more efficient diesel or gasoline engine without sacrificing peak performance. The fuel engine needs to operate only when the battery needs charging or when the conveyance requires peak power.

TAP prototypes and studies utilize the ports of Los Angeles and Long Beach and the surrounding logistics cluster to test competing designs for performance and user acceptability. For example, as of

2011, TAP included four competing drayage truck projects: two zero-emissions drayage trucks (battery and hydrogen fuel cell), a hybrid drayage truck, and a compressed natural gas drayage truck. These different projects reflect the fundamental uncertainties that come with true innovation. Until someone in the logistics industry tries these new technologies in real-world use, it is difficult to ascertain the actual fuel economies, emitted pollution, performance peculiarities, and reliabilities of the different approaches. Before replacing the 11,000 heavy-duty drayage trucks used at the ports of Los Angeles and Long Beach, the ports need to understand which innovations in conveyance design provide the most cost-effective improvements on a variety of emissions metrics.

A few miles from the port of LA, start-up VYCON Inc. developed a new flywheel energy storage system for regenerative braking and hybrid drivetrains on dockyard cranes. The duty cycles and energy consumption patterns of these cranes make them ideal for regenerative braking and storing the energy recovered from putting one container down to help lift the next container up. The system enables cranes with smaller diesel engines to offer the same speed and load performance as standard technology cranes but with 32–38 percent less fuel consumption[10] and a certified 30 percent reduction in NOx emissions.[11] VYCON's system is currently in use in the port of Los Angeles, port of Long Beach, and several Asian ports. VYCON also sells the technology for use in large ship-to-shore cranes, uninterruptible power supplies, electric railroad applications, and wind power applications.[12] In 2010 and 2011, VYCON was named one of the 500 fastest-growing private companies in America by *Inc.* magazine, increasing revenues from $737,000 in 2007 to $6.6 million in 2010.[13]

Alternative Fuel Conveyances

Alternative fuels can offer lower emissions and reduced environmental impact. FedEx, for example, has tested and is already using nearly a dozen different combinations of alternative fuel and vehicle combinations such a biodiesel, CNG (compressed natural gas), LNG (liquefied natural gas), LPG (liquefied petroleum gas), and all-electric vehicles. The company partners with numerous vehicle and engine makers to develop, test, and deploy green technologies that work in high-volume logistics applications. Applications include ground-support vehicles in hubs, large trucks, delivery trucks, and small electric vehicles for couriers in dense cities like Paris and New York. In turn, FedEx saves fuel and cuts pollution. The company found that its 330 hybrid trucks improve fuel economy by 42 percent, reduce greenhouse gas emissions by 25 percent and cut particulate pollution by 96 percent.[14]

The ports of Los Angeles and Long Beach are testing numerous alternative fuel vehicles, including an LNG yard hostler, CNG port drayage truck, and an LNG locomotive. As of 2012, the port of Los Angeles has some 900 alternative fuel vehicles in use. The result of this and other programs helped slash emissions from container-hauling trucks by 89 percent. The ports, however, seek even more radical innovations that offer zero vehicle emissions, such as entirely new battery-powered, zero-emission heavy-duty trucks invented by a local company, Balqon Corporation.[15] The port funded the development of the technology, a multiphase testing process in port drayage applications, and an initial purchase of five units.[16] The results are three innovative commercial products—the Nautilus E20, Nautilus E30, and Mule M150—for medium- and heavy-duty hauling for ports, logistics clusters, and inner city applications. Not only do these trucks produce zero tailpipe emissions, but their total energy consumption is 70 percent less than that of a normal diesel-powered vehicle.[17]

Balqon's innovations in electric drive technology help improve the performance of battery-powered vehicles on three crucial dimensions: power output, operating range, and battery lifespan. These improvements in drive technology and the overall design of the device led to a Class 8 battery-powered tractor capable of pulling legal and even overweight loads of up to 100,000 pounds. The company designed battery packs that can last one or two workshifts and that will provide five years of service. In addition to funding the Balqon truck, the port of LA is also funding work on a hydrogen-powered fuel-cell vehicle created by Vision Industries.[18] The port is pursuing a development and testing plan similar to what it used for the Balqon battery-electric vehicle. Real-world testing helps establish the load-pulling performance, reliabilities, and operational requirements of these alternatively powered vehicles.

Investments in new green technologies around the port of Los Angeles also include more speculative innovations, such as algae-based biofuels. Advanced Algae, Inc., is a start-up developing a new biofuel production system at the PortTechLA, the Los Angeles port area incubator described in chapter 9. The company grows a special breed of algae in a specially designed transparent chamber. The algae convert sunlight into oil that can be harvested and refined into diesel fuel or jet fuel. As a side benefit, the algae absorb air pollutants, including CO_2, NO_x, and SO_x, to create a negative-emission footprint. Other algae byproducts can also provide animal feed and fertilizers for soil.[19] The company won the Most Innovative Technology Award at the 2010 PortTechExpo and Venture Conference.[20]

Innovations that depend on alternative fuels, especially biofuels, raise the issue of the logistics for these fuels. Logistics clusters, such as the LA Basin or Chicago, make ideal locations to test and deploy alternative fuels because they have the needed concentration of vehicles operating over short ranges. A single refueling/charging depot can serve as a prototype for initial deployments of vehicles in a hub, logistics park, port, or airport. But the transition to a green economy will require large-scale production and distribution of green fuels. To the extent that logistics clusters are early adopters of alternative fuels or have the infrastructure for distribution of bulk liquids or gases (e.g., tanker ports, storage farms, and pipelines), then these clusters will become centers for the storage and distribution of alternative fuels. Major logistics clusters, which are also often petrochemical clusters (see chapter 6), can become biofuel production clusters. As mentioned in chapter 7, the two largest biofuel-producing centers on the planet are Singapore and Rotterdam.

Reducing Other Environmental Impacts of Logistics

Some innovations help counter other noxious side-effects of logistics in clusters. When one or two jets operate from an airport late at night, the noise might be merely irritating. But when 50 or 100 jets operate from an airport late at night, the noise can be excruciating and illegal. Airfreight clusters, with their late-night air hub operations, are especially likely to create an intolerable noise nuisance under the flight paths of the planes. When the US Federal Aviation Administration tightened regulations on the average noise around airports, FedEx engineered a "hushkit" to reduce the noise created by its older, noisier Boeing 727 freighters.[21] The kits were far cheaper than replacing the planes or their engines, and they didn't affect the aircraft's fuel efficiency or cargo capacity. Not only did this innovation help FedEx avoid excessive replacement costs, but the invention became a profit center for the company. FedEx sold 740 of these hushkits to more than sixty owners and operators of 727s.

Some innovations target reduction in waste by carriers. Marine Oil Technology Inc. (MOT) is a startup manufacturer that recently opened its doors at PortTechLA. MOT's innovative oil filter reduces the need for oil changes by 90 percent. Not only does the invention reduce the volume of waste oil, but it also reduces maintenance labor. Truckers who need to change their oil monthly might go almost a year between oil changes. "We could save millions of gallons of oil per year," said Alex Weil, president and majority owner of the company. The invention beats conventional oil filters by filtering out extremely small particles (as small as one micron) and removing liquid impurities that degrade the lubricating oils in truck and marine diesel engines. "One of our missions is to help start-up companies like Marine Oil Technology develop, test and market products that are environmentally beneficial to the maritime industry," said Jeff Milanette, executive director of PortTechLA.[22]

Fixed logistics assets, such as warehouses and office parks, can use alternative sources of electricity like solar energy and wind power. In 2011, UPS installed a rooftop solar array on its Lakewood, New Jersey, facility. The 250-kilowatt solar power system is expected to provide 30 percent of the building's energy needs. The facility harnesses light from the sun during the day, feeding the power into the public energy grid. "At night, when we are sorting packages, we will draw from the grid the energy needed to power the facility," said Scott Wicker, UPS chief sustainability officer. UPS took advantage of New Jersey's net metering rules, which offer compensation for generating excess power during the day for sale by the utility to its other customers.[23] UPS also uses solar energy in one of its California facilities and in its European hub in Cologne-Bonn, Germany.

At the Joliet Intermodal Terminal, Union Pacific installed 273 solar panels.[24] "Union Pacific built the Joliet Intermodal Terminal with an eye toward the environment. We installed solar panels to harness the sun's energy to provide electricity to our office at the entrance to the terminal, and we purchased air compressors equipped with 'soft start' technology, which requires less energy when starting, in our effort to make this facility the 'greenest' terminal on our system," said Jim Young, Union Pacific chairman and CEO.[25]

In November 2010, Walmart opened a fresh and frozen food distribution center in Balzac, Alberta, Canada, to serve 100 retail outlets in Western Canada. Andy Ellis, senior vice president of supply chain and logistics for Walmart Canada, described the facility in a presentation during a supply chain conference in Dallas in December 2011. The warehouse generates electricity from both on-site wind turbine generators and roof solar panels. The refrigerated building uses LED lights that not only consume less energy but also burn cooler than traditional incandescent lighting, reducing refrigeration costs even further. "Custom-designed dock doors minimize the loss of cool air from the refrigerated warehouse and electronic monitoring ensures that dock doors are not opened unnecessarily," he said. The facility is also using hydrogen fuel cells to power its fleet of lift trucks and material handling equipment. Walmart expects to save well over $2 million in energy costs annually in its Balzac operation.[26]

Some energy-saving innovations require minimal upfront investment—only clever changes in operating processes. Bob Stoffel, former senior vice president of UPS talked about a simple yet innovative way UPS saved money, time, and energy. In an interview with *Fortune* magazine in 2011,[27] he said that UPS re-engineered its vehicle delivery routes to include right-turns only. As a result,

UPS routing software shaved 20.4 million miles from the routes in 2010 while delivering 350,000 more packages than the previous year. It also diminished annual CO_2 emissions by 20,000 metric tons.[28]

Logistics Clusters and Sustainability

Most air quality standards define a threshold concentration of pollutants.[29] For that reason, a concentrated source of pollution (e.g., large numbers of trucks or ships in a logistics cluster) faces a higher likelihood of violating air pollution safety thresholds than would an area with more dispersed logistics facilities. Furthermore, the clustering of transportation terminals and distribution centers implies more circuitous transportation routing and more miles traveled as compared to traveling directly from origin to destination. At first glance, logistics clusters seem like major polluters and that less clustered freight transportation operations would be environmentally beneficial. A more systematic analysis, however, leads to the opposite conclusion.

The correct metric for energy consumption is not the fuel consumed per conveyance movement or the number of miles traveled, but the fuel consumed per shipment moved. Logistics activities gravitate to clusters in order to improve efficiencies and reduce costs, as described in chapter 4. Vehicle operating costs, especially fuel, dominate the cost-calculus of transportation decisions—the act of determining how to move the greatest total volume of goods at the least cost can be seen as the same as minimizing the carbon-footprint of trade. Minimizing fuel per shipment requires consolidation to larger conveyances, and this means clustering. Moreover, clustering creates higher freight volumes on hub-to-hub lanes, which enables using more fuel-efficient modes such as rail, barge, short sea, and pipelines. Accordingly, a nonclustered logistics network would actually create higher total fuel consumption because of poor utilization of conveyances and the use of more, smaller, and less efficient (in terms of fuel per ton-mile hauled) conveyances.

Thus, while logistics clustering leads to less total pollution, it leads to concentration of pollutants, increasing health hazards around such clusters. The result is a tradeoff between local and global benefits of logistics clustering. In the long term, however, many of the green innovations mentioned in the previous sections are likely to be deployed first in and around logistics clusters, mitigating the local environmental impacts.

THE EMERGING AND EVOLVING GEOGRAPHY OF CLUSTERS

Supply chain and distribution patterns continue to evolve, and logistics clusters evolve with them. In the long term, rising affluence in large swathes of the globe creates new patterns of consumption and production. New infrastructure changes the connectivity, velocity, and capacity of global supply networks. Steadily improving logistics technologies increase the performance of logistics clusters.

Moreover, the flow through logistics clusters also changes on a shorter time scale. Many global companies, such as Cargill, constantly rebalance their global portfolio of production sites according to a complex trade-off between costs of raw materials, manufacturing efficiencies, inventory carrying costs, and transportation costs. Jon Thompson, the international business development manager of the Cargill corn sweetener plant in Memphis told me, "what's happening with natural gas out of Russia to feed the Netherlands actually affects whether we ship out of this plant [Memphis], Europe, China or Brazil." These decisions change product flows and therefore logistics activities around the world. "Every three to six months, it's a different game," Thompson concluded.

A case in point is the growth of the port of Tanjung Pelepas (PTP) in Malaysia. It received its first maiden vessel on October 10, 1999, and then set the world record for the fastest growing port in the world, mostly attracting business that used to be conducted in Singapore. On August 18, 2000, Maersk, the largest container shipping carrier in the world, moved its transshipment operations from Singapore to PTP, followed by Evergreen, the fourth largest carrier, on April 2002.[30] (Maresk's move alone caused a 10 percent reduction in Singapore's traffic.) Several other carriers signaled their intent to follow suit. Despite the sophistication and good services offered by the Singapore Port Authority in Singapore, these carriers have shifted to PTP, which is also a sophisticated operator, because it offers lower costs. And as the ocean carriers call on PTP, the port has developed a set of maritime services and a logistics cluster, established to take advantage of the new sailing schedules.

Emerging Clusters in Emerging Market Countries

Currently, some two billion people are enjoying rapidly increasing standards of living as they join the middle class in what have come to be known as the BRIC countries (Brazil, Russia, India, and China) or the newly emerging CIVETS countries (Colombia, Indonesia, Vietnam, Egypt, Turkey, and South Africa). The combination of rapid economic development and large populations is fertile turf for creating massive new logistics clusters. In China, these clusters are developing along the coasts in Beijing, Tianjin, Shanghai (where DHL located its North Asian hub), Dalian, Guangzhou (where FedEx opened its Asia-Pacific hub), and Shenzhen (where UPS located its Asia-Pacific hub), as well as next to hinterland cities such as Chongqing, Wuhan, and Changsha.[31] In January 2012, Shenzhen announced its plan to create one of the world's biggest logistics centers in Qianhai, with an investment of 285 billion yuan.[32]

In central India, the Development Authority of Naya Raipur, the upcoming capital of Chhattisgarh (approximately halfway between Mumbai and Kolkata), asked for proposals in 2011 to develop a new logistics hub, as part of developing the economic base for the new city. About 500 miles to the southwest, the city of Hyderabad also requested proposals for a public-private partnership aimed at developing a trucking hub and logistics cluster in that city. Such developments are taking place all over the world.

In Brazil, some of the largest clusters can be found around the state of São Paulo. During a breakfast meeting in the historic Octavio Cafe in the heart of the bustling city of São Paulo, a dozen Brazilian logistics executives helped me identify the leading and upcoming logistics clusters around São Paulo. In addition to the large port of Santos, these clusters seem to be situated along the (still incomplete) ring road around São Paulo in Campinas, Jundiai, Barueri, and the São Paulo International Airport.

Logistics clusters are also being developed in the CIVETS countries. For example, in a meeting at the Sheraton Hotel in Bogota,

Carmenza Isaza Suárez, the executive director of ZAL (Zona de Actividad Logística de Cartagena de Indias), a new logistics park in the Colombian port city of Cartagena, described the region's ambitions and efforts to develop a leading cluster. Cartagena's aim is to rival and even overtake Santos in Brazil, which is the leading Latin American port measured by container traffic.

As mentioned several times in this book, many companies follow their customers in deciding where to locate facilities. In a telephone conversation with several supply chain executives arranged by the Supply Chain 50 organization, Randy Eck, director of global transportation and global outsourcing at Intel said, "The first thing we actually look at in terms of locations for a distribution center is basically manufacturing clusters where our large customers are." Given that almost all PC manufacturing has moved to China, he added, "We spend a lot of time working on putting distribution centers in Southern China, down in the Shenzhen region, in Shanghai, and now we're actually spending a lot of time investigating what's happening in the Central Western part of China, with a bunch of our customers moving towards the Chengdu-Chongqing region. We also continuously look into other areas around the world where, again, our customers' manufacturing clusters are."

These emerging market economies will continue to affect existing logistics clusters by influencing the flows of raw materials into these economies and the outbound flows of manufactured goods. China's economic ascent directly caused several developments in the United States. These include the growth of the Pacific ports; the expansions of the BNSF, UP, and CN railroads that move goods from the Pacific ports inland; and the growth of inland logistics clusters in Chicago, Kansas City, Memphis, and Dallas. But more changes are in store as the emerging economies integrate into the world trading system. The growth of the megacities of the world, such as Chongqing (China), with a metro population of 32 million inhabitants, Jakarta (24 million), Shanghai (23 million), Mumbai (21 million), Mexico City (21 million), and Saõ Paulo (20 million),[33] is already spurring the rise of new logistics clusters aimed at serving these sprawling complexes.

New Routes: Bypassing the Old, Creating the New

Various proposed or anticipated changes in trade routes could bypass current clusters and create new logistics clusters. For example, the long-fabled Northwest Passage might appear if global warming melts enough Arctic sea ice. If it does, then freight from Asia to northern Europe and to the northeastern United States could bypass the Suez and Panama canals, respectively. The proposed Kra Canal across Thailand could bypass Singapore. Both Nicaragua and Colombia propose maritime and rail routes competing with the Panama Canal. And in the southern part of Latin America, both Chile and Argentina have already passed legislation to enable the Bioceánico Aconcagua Corridor project. The project will end up connecting Buenos Aires on the Atlantic with Santiago and the ports of Valpariso and San Antonio in Chile on the Pacific with an integrated road/rail system that includes a fifty-two kilometer tunnel through the Andes. These changes will lead to increasing volumes at seaport clusters at both ends of the new ocean routes, new rail routes, and new inland logistics clusters.

As routes change or emerge, other clusters prepare for the changing trade flows. As mentioned in chapter 6 (see p. 167), almost every port along the US East Coast is preparing for the opening of the enlarged Panama Canal and hoping to seize a large portion of the increased traffic. For East Coast ports to realize these higher trade flows, they have to be able to handle the larger ships that will soon traverse the Panama Canal. That means billions of dollars in investments in dredging deeper channels, enlarging quays, and installing larger cranes. The Panama Canal expansion is also spurring portside and inland development as real estate developers buy land, warehouse operators develop distribution centers, railroads design intermodal yards, and trucking companies plan larger transloading and consolidation hubs.

Evolving Government Support for Clustering

As governments in both emerging and mature markets learn of the contribution of logistics clusters to economic growth, they begin supporting the development of logistics clusters more aggressively. Some national governments have an explicit economic clustering strategy and have chosen logistics as one of the types of clusters to create. For example, visiting the Fraunhofer Logistics Institute in Dortmund, I discussed Germany's plans to promote logistics excellence with Thorsten Hülsmann, CEO of the German public-private partnership EffizienzCluster Management GmbH, and several other executives and academics participating in the logistics cluster initiative there. The German Government is promoting what it calls Spitzenclusters (excellence clusters) in ten different industries to create a set of economic powerhouses.

Germany chose logistics as one such industry to invest in. Based on an internal competition, the German Government chose to develop EffizienzCluster LogistikRuhr in the country's industrial heartland. The five-year, €100 million initiative includes thirty collaborative projects involving more than 120 companies and eleven research institutes. Hülsmann shared with me the project's goals for 2015, which include creating 100 new software and hardware-based logistics products with a combined market potential of €2 billion, 4,000 new jobs, and a 25 percent reduction in costs and resource consumption. Similarly, the Walloon region of Belgium chose logistics as one of its fifteen economic clusters.[34]

Some local governments are looking to emulate successful logistics clusters: weighing the costs of improving infrastructure, offering tax inducements and incurring other costs, versus the benefits of new local employment opportunities that cannot be outsourced. In 2011, the St. Louis Regional Chamber and Growth Association presented a plan to position St. Louis as a global center for commerce and transportation. The association proposed developing Lambert-St. Louis International Airport with the intent to replicate the significant economic growth enjoyed by aerotropolis clusters like Memphis, Louisville, and Indianapolis.[35] In Michigan, Wayne County, Detroit Renaissance, Detroit Regional Chamber, and several local communities plan to develop the area between Detroit Metro Airport and Willow Run Airport as an aerotropolis logistics hub.[36]

Elsewhere, governments with well-established clusters are planning for more growth. As of 2010, Dubai had the ninth busiest container port in the world,[37] the eighth largest airfreight volume,[38] and 6,400 companies operating in an expansive free trade zone.[39] But the emirate is looking to grow the contribution of trade and logistics to its GDP even further. It embarked on developing its "Logistics City" as a 2,150-hectare logistics hub for the Middle East and beyond. The hub is envisioned as an integrated logistics platform with all transportation modes, an array of logistics services, and a range of value-added operations. It is adjacent to what the kingdom plans to be the largest airport in the world.

Other governments with well-established clusters are tackling specific issues to improve logistics performance. In the Netherlands, government-supported Dinalog is developing the Cross Chain Control Center mentioned in chapter 6. The result would be a system of software, sensors, processes, and control systems to monitor and direct the entire flow of physical shipments and the associated financial flows and information flows in and out of Holland. A similar system is envisioned for Rotterdam with the objective of controlling all transportation movements around the port and into the European hinterland, focusing on the efficient use of infrastructure.

Evolving Risks to Clusters

Although logistics clusters generally improve a region's economic robustness, they aren't entirely immune to economic downturns and geopolitical risks because they do depend on trade, especially global trade. Economic, political, and social phenomena that inhibit production, consumption, or the movement of goods can all reduce the volume of global trade and diminish the amount of logistics activities handled by logistics clusters. Consequently, these clusters are vulnerable to overall downturns in the economy as well as to rising energy prices and protectionist trade policies.

High energy prices reduce the price advantages of distant low-cost producers such as China. Higher prices are likely to motivate a shift from long-distance transportation of imported and exported goods toward domestic production and consumption. Such local production and consumption reduce the need for large clusters because each region can develop small distribution hubs that funnel modest volumes of local production for local consumption. High energy prices also blunt total demand because they can lead to decline in consumption and recessions, thereby lowering trade volumes and shipment flows worldwide. FedEx almost went bankrupt during the 1970s surge in oil prices, which likely would have stalled the development of Memphis as a logistics cluster.

The other risk factor is protectionist, antitrade regulations such as quotas, import duties, and local content laws that create obstacles to global trade. Protectionism by the country hosting a logistics cluster means reduced imports flowing through the cluster. Protectionism by major trading partners means reduced exports flowing through the cluster. The threat of a tit-for-tat trade war would be doubly damaging. Restrictive trade regulations might hurt or help other kinds of industries (and industrial clusters) through curtailed exports or curtailed competitors' imports, respectively. Trade restrictions, however, are likely only to impair most logistics clusters.

New Technologies

New technologies change cost structures and performance envelopes, affecting the competitiveness of various logistics clusters. For example, the port of Singapore and other ports are investing in new cranes that lift four containers at the same time. Similarly, new so-called "easy loading" bulk carriers can cut loading times by half to reduce dwell times and port congestion.[40] Anything that increases the rate of goods flow, reduces the transportation cost per ton-mile, decreases the dwell time of assets, or improves the productivity of logistics workers will enhance the competitive attractiveness of a logistics cluster.

Larger conveyances create new economies of scale and greater consolidation of freight flows. In February 2011, Denmark's Maersk Line, the largest container shipping carrier in the world, contracted Korea's Daewoo Shipbuilding and Marine Engineering Company to build ten new 18,000 TEU container ships, with options to build twenty more. In June 2011, Maersk exercised an option for ten more of the gargantuan vessels. Called the "Triple-E" class (for Economy of scale, Energy efficient and Environmentally improved), these vessels will provide greater economies of scale—being 16 percent larger than the largest container ships now in existence.[41] In addition, advanced engine and energy recovery systems will create an industry record for fuel efficiency and reduced CO_2 emissions per container moved.

Larger, more efficient vessels encourage further consolidation of freight to the largest ports. At 400 meters long, 59 meters wide, and 14.5 meters draft, the Triple-E class will be the largest container ships on the water. The ships' size makes them too large for current American ports or the Panama Canal (even after the canal's expansion), so the ships will be deployed on Asia-Europe trade lanes. The use of such ships will increase the attractiveness of the largest ports in the same way that the new Boeing 747-8 freighters (with maximum take-off weight of almost a million pounds) will serve the largest airport-based logistics clusters. Ports that want to remain competitive in the face of larger vessels must invest in dredging, longer quays, and larger cranes—or they run the risk of becoming marginalized.

Cluster Mortality: Failures and Fading

Not all new clusters grow as expected, and not all thriving clusters survive over the long term. Inadequacies, misjudgments, and change can all contribute to the demise of logistics clusters, young or old.

In some cases, locations that seem ideal for cluster development never achieve the promise of their geography. For example, Port Said at the northern mouth of the Suez Canal would seem to offer a perfect location for a major transshipment cluster. The canal funnels massive volumes of ocean traffic from ports in China, East Asia, South Asia, and the Middle East to ports in Europe, northern Africa, western Africa, and the eastern side of the Americas. Some 18,000 large vessels transit the Suez Canal every year, more vessels than pass through the Panama Canal.[42]

Port Said had a promising start. By the end of the nineteenth century, it was the largest coal bunkering port in the world.[43] But it failed to maintain its role in global trade. In 2010, of the 6,852 container vessels crossing the Suez Canal, only 499 called on Port Said, and the port handled less than 3 percent of the containers passing through the canal.[44,45] The reasons Port Said has not developed into the "Singapore on the Mediterranean" probably have to do with local shortcomings in areas such as government accountability and efficiency, where Singapore excels. Singapore ranks number 1 on the World Bank's "ease of doing business" index; Egypt ranks number 110.[46]

Another lagging would-be cluster is Global TransPark near Kinston, North Carolina. Starting in 1991, the state of North Carolina invested heavily in developing a 2,400-acre industrial and logistics park. The location seems geographically well positioned midway between two deep-water ports and within one day's trucking of New York, Miami, and the Midwest. More important, the project had strong state support, a favorable tax structure, a long runway for the heaviest aircrafts, a foreign trade zone authority, a highly trained workforce, attractive utility rates, and a low cost of living. Initial studies projected that the park would generate 55,000 jobs by 1998.[47]

Despite all these advantages and generous state subsidies, the park failed to attract viable tenants. Boeing passed on the opportunity to assemble the 787 Dreamliner there in 2003. The first companies lured by the state to the park arrived only in 2008. As of 2011, the park's fourteen tenants support only a few hundred jobs. Three factors may have contributed to Global TransPark's failure to fulfill the original vision. First, Kinston is too small a city (population of just over 22,000 in 2008), so there was no base of local distribution activities.[48] Second, the park has poor highway connections, with no nearby interstate freeways and no easy rail connections to the park. Third, the park suffers from long dray distances to the port of Norfolk, Virginia (150 miles), and the much smaller port of Wilmington (90 miles).

In another example, the Lower Mississippi Port Cluster (LMPC) runs from the mouth of the Mississippi river 243 miles to Baton Rouge and handled 18 percent of the throughput of all US ports in 1990. But LMPC lost market share, especially to the port of Houston, as a result of a lack of collective investment in infrastructure, education, marketing, and innovation.[49] Governments, local port authorities, and the business community didn't work together to improve hinterland access, create education infrastructure for

port-related jobs, or sufficiently participate in trade missions promoting LMPC in Latin America. LMPC's Gulf-region market share
in container traffic dropped from 48 percent in 1985 to 15 percent
in 2001.

The story of the Erie Canal demonstrates the decline of a major
logistics artery resulting from the lack of logistics cluster development. While the story is almost two centuries old, it offers lessons
for today. Proposed in 1808[50] and completed 1825, the Erie Canal
had a huge impact on opening up trade to the Midwest. The canal
connected the port of New York to the inland resources of New
York State, and to the Great Lakes with the lakes' connections to
the vast agricultural resources of the US Midwest. It made New
York City the preeminent commercial center of the United States in
the nineteenth century, spurred the first great westward movement
of settlers, and spawned multiple new cities such as Troy, Syracuse,
Rochester, and Buffalo all along the route and on the shores of
the Great Lakes. Over the next century, this canal system would
be enlarged multiple times to accommodate ever-larger ships and
trading volumes.[51]

The Erie Canal declined as an artery of commerce because of
the lack of development of terminal facilities along the canal,
which would have spurred the development of logistics clusters
around such terminals. Logistics facilities along the canal (terminals, cranes, warehouses) were an afterthought, and the lack of
these facilities at each end and along the route of the canal se-
verely limited the flow of goods. The few existing terminals were
mostly owned by the railroads, which did everything they could
to prevent more terminals from being constructed so they could
continue to charge monopolistic rates (which also depressed traffic
all along the route). The canal's flow declined with the rise of the
railroads and the highway system in the United States, as well as
with the construction of the St. Lawrence Seaway in 1959 (which
let Midwest cargo bypass New York). Major canal-side cities, such
as Rochester and Buffalo in New York, lost more than one-third of
their population during the second half of the twentieth century.[52]
Although the ports of New York and New Jersey remain important
to this day, they no longer serve a major transshipment function

between the world and the broader US economy. Some 80 percent of the freight arriving in the ports of New York and New Jersey stays within one day's drayage of the ports.[53]

Technological change also drives the decline of some clusters. The port of Amsterdam was the largest port in the Netherlands in the seventeenth century. But Amsterdam lost its preeminence as ships grew larger than Amsterdam's canal-based connections to the sea could support. In contrast, Rotterdam's location on the Maas River and investments in dredging large, deep channels let Rotterdam surpass Amsterdam in the late nineteenth century. Today, the port of Rotterdam is about five times larger than the port of Amsterdam in terms of developed area, total tonnage, and vessel arrivals.[54]

As mentioned earlier, ongoing increases in ship size motivated the current expansion of the Panama Canal. They also motivated several expansions of the Suez Canal in 1956, 1962, 1980, 1994, 1996, 2001, and 2010.[55]

In some cases, logistics clusters develop in ways not initially foreseen or intended. AllianceTexas was intended to be an airfreight hub. The original crown jewel of the development was a brand-new, privately financed airport built specifically for air cargo. Although some airfreight does come to Alliance, nearby Dallas/Fort Worth International Airport (DFW) handles nearly seven times more air cargo than does Alliance.[56]

Russell Laughlin of AllianceTexas opined to me that DFW has two important advantages over Alliance for air cargo. First, DFW has a lower cost of capital because it is financed by tax-exempt municipal bonds from the cities of Dallas and Fort Worth. "But the other thing is, when you talk to these air freight forwarders, they're going to colocate with the passenger airlines as much as possible, because they can get that freight on a passenger airline, get it out today, or at worst case, the next day," Laughlin added. Instead of an aerotropolis, the park became an intermodal hub and an inland port with many logistics service providers performing value added activities, with the majority of the freight coming via rail and distributed by truck rather than by air.

Regional Competition in Transshipment and Global Distribution

The rise of new markets, new routes, and new technologies raises the issue of cluster-to-cluster competition both between routes and between terminals at the ends of new routes. The synergies between logistics and global trade don't mean that every logistics cluster will win. Tan Puay Hin, CEO of PSA International for Southeast Asia, pointed out that "Transshipment competition is actually worldwide." For example, the expansion of the Panama Canal creates three loci of competition.

First, the expansion creates new competition between Panama and nearby ports in the Caribbean for transshipment, warehousing, and value-added activities. Juan Carlos Croston of Manzanillo International Terminals in Panama hypothesizes that Panama's biggest future competitors are likely to be a range of Caribbean ports such as Kingston (Jamaica), Punta Caucedo (Dominican Republic), Cartagena (Colombia) and Freeport (Bahamas). In the long term, Cuba, with its educated work force, low wage rates, and advantageous geographical position vis-à-vis the United States, might develop to be a powerful logistics cluster.

Interestingly, the cautionary tales of the Erie Canal and Amsterdam are well understood by the Panamanian authorities who are investing in both the canal expansion, port facilities along the canal, the Transisthmian Railway, and in logistics parks in various locations along the canal such as Colón Free Trade Zone and Panama Pacifico. As mentioned on p. 73 in chapter 3, the Panamanians understand that the canal can be leveraged to be more than just a "toll road." It can bring to Panama transshipment activities and many value added operations that can be performed in these logistics clusters. These activities, in turn, can provide further employment, create a robust tax base, lead to knowledge creation, and raise living standards.

Second, the enlarged canal is creating a new round of competition among the ports that are the potential destinations of the larger ships that will start passing through the canal in 2014. In the United States, many East Coast and Gulf ports are competing for post-expansion trade by investing heavily in larger, deeper port facilities in hopes of attracting larger numbers of larger ships (see

chapter 6 and the discussion of new routes earlier in this chapter).
Each port markets itself as the best link between ocean freight and
ground modes that serve US population centers. Yet the total volume of added port capacity may exceed what's needed; some East
Coast ports will likely fail to provide a return on investment on
their expanded infrastructure.

Third, the enlarged canal increases the competition between
Panama and other noncanal routes. For the Asia-North America
trade, West Coast ports plus rail or truck will remain faster than
transiting the Panama Canal, but the enlarged canal may provide
lower costs resulting from better economies of scale with larger
vessels. Some of the cluster denizens I interviewed in the LA Basin
worried about the ongoing competitiveness of their cluster once
the expanded Panama Canal opens. Their concerns were focused
on the possible loss of traffic and distribution activities as a result of the troubled labor relationships in the ports, environmental restrictions, decaying infrastructure, short-sighted politicians,
and traffic congestion. The 2008–2009 recession demonstrated to
Southern California's business, unions, and governmental leaders
that a drop in traffic was both possible and painful.

For better or worse, logistics is a mobile industry: carriers can
change routes and redeploy conveyances to different locations;
shippers can switch warehouse locations merely by changing a
shipping label; and global third-party logistics providers and warehouse operators can support a company's network redesign from
uncompetitive locations to more cost-competitive ones. I interviewed several senior logistics executives in the Los Angeles area
who mentioned that their companies review their network design
annually. These companies, which import much of their parts and
merchandise from the Far East, compare the costs of shipping
through the ports of Las Angeles and Long Beach to other alternatives such as Prince Rupert, British Columbia; Lazaro Cardenas,
Mexico; and Savannah and Norfolk on the US East Coast. In addition, these companies carefully plan and monitor container stowage positions, vessel arrival days, container diversion opportunities
and inland transportation options, in moving their freight to the
US hinterland. Although they remain in Los Angeles, all options

remain open every year. And if one of the leading importers finds a reason to relocate, chances are that other companies will come to a similar conclusion, and the volume in the LA cluster will drop, reducing its viability.

Recall from chapter 2 that geography plays a major role in the locations of logistics clusters, but it is not enough to ensure the success of a specific location. Singapore seems like the ideal geographic location for a transshipment port, but numerous neighboring ports in Malaysia and Indonesia compete with Singapore by offering nearly the same geographic advantages. In fact, Singapore's island geography would seem to put it at a geographic disadvantage to its larger neighbors. The scarcity of land in Singapore means that warehouse space can cost more than twice as much as in neighboring Malaysia.[57] Higher land costs would also affect the costs of port quays, container yards, and all the land-intensive shared infrastructure such as roads, highways, and ramps. Singapore faces an analogous challenge on wages, which are six times higher than those in Malaysia and thirty-three times higher than those of Indonesia. Singapore's only recourse is innovation that improves asset productivity, accelerates logistical activities, or provides some form of added value. To the extent that Singapore can execute more logistics activities per square meter or provide more value per square meter, it can offset the country's higher cost. Singapore's leading education system (chapter 8), advanced infrastructure (chapter 6), and effective government (chapter 7) make it competitive. But the competition is relentless.

ATTRIBUTES OF SUCCESSFUL LOGISTICS CLUSTERS

In a European Commission study of "freight villages" throughout Europe,[58] the authors concluded that the average productivity (in 1997) of companies located within freight villages was about 25 percent higher than companies located outside such freight villages. The productivity was measured as tons per square meter (weight of freight handled divided by the area of the total distribution center space). Furthermore, companies within villages were 65 percent more productive in terms of intermodal freight flows. In addition, the study found a productivity increase of about 40 percent from 1997 to 2002 for companies located within integrated freight villages (where intermodal transportation was readily available) as compared with approximately 10 percent reduction for companies located outside. The study concluded that freight villages are important in furthering the EU goal of encouraging intermodal freight transportation. Even a cursory analysis of the role of intermodal yards in the United States would support such a conclusion. For example, as mentioned above, AllianceTexas thrives on its BNSF intermodal yard, rather than its airport.

The dynamics of the world economy offer plenty of opportunities for existing and new logistics clusters to develop and thrive. While developing economies are in the process of building hundreds of small and large logistics clusters in order to encourage exports and make intracountry commerce more efficient, regional governments in developed countries recognize that many distribution jobs cannot be outsourced and are therefore also developing and enlarging logistics clusters. China is continuing to develop logistics parks throughout the country. In fact, researchers at Beijing's Jiaotong University found that "large and medium cities of the coastal developed provinces carried on the plan of Logistics Park one after another.[59]

There are many on-going efforts in the United States and Europe. For example, chapter 7 mentioned the 2011 efforts to build a logistics cluster in Michigan, following on the efforts of the Detroit Regional Chamber;[60] the Montreal Port Authority issued a press release in February 2011 titled "Towards a Logistics and Transportation Industrial Cluster in Montreal";[61] and, as mentioned earlier, the state of Missouri has been working on developing an airport-based cluster (an aerotropolis) in St. Louis's Lambert International Airport.

While each chapter of this book described different attributes of logistics clusters, this section summarizes six factors found in successful logistics clusters. Some of them are natural attributes; others have to do with existing conditions in the region and the stage of development of the society involved. Yet several attributes can be described as success factors, requiring either initial investment or planning for the spontaneous development which governments and developers hope to ignite.

Favorable Geography

Because of the technology and economics of transportation, geography matters more for logistics clusters than for many other types of industrial or knowledge clusters. The origins and destinations of goods follow geographic patterns tied to population centers, industrial clusters, and natural resources concentrations, as described in chapter 3. The physical necessity or economic advantages of mode changes (such as ship-to-rail, rail-to-truck, and air-to-truck) drive the development of clusters at seaports, airports, and intermodal complexes. Operational issues, described in chapter 4, drive the consolidation of shipments and distribution of goods to central cluster locations. Thus, clusters often form at land-ocean edges (Shanghai, Rotterdam, Los Angeles, Saõ Paulo) or midpoints near or between population centers (Singapore, Chongqing, PLAZA, Chicago, AllianceTexas, Kansas City).

Logistics clusters also require large expanses of inexpensive land and a climate that rarely disrupts operations. In situations where land near a port is scarce or expensive, some clusters displace logistics activities to inland ports or use land reclamation projects to create new land.

Supporting Infrastructure

Chapter 6 argued that a logistics cluster is only as good as its transportation infrastructure. This includes not only the local infrastructure within the cluster, but, just as crucially, the network that connects the cluster to other clusters and to industry and population centers. Wide roads, deep ports, long runways, and spacious rail yards all support efficient cluster operations. Much of the investment in building and maintaining logistics clusters has to do with building the physical infrastructure. Moreover, this is an ongoing investment since the infrastructure requires maintenance and upgrading. As logistics clusters grow they also need robust supply of fuel for transportation conveyances.

Logistics clusters also require access to sophisticated financial services and information technology services in addition to physical infrastructure. These "soft" infrastructure elements are examples of factors required only at some basic level in order to start the cluster's organic growth process, but they have to be planned for and supported as the cluster starts growing.

Supportive, Efficient Government

More than many other types of economic clusters, logistics clusters depend on supportive governments for reasons enumerated in chapter 7. Governments are the main providers of public infrastructure, often paying for, maintaining, and regulating the use of key infrastructure assets such as roads, canals, ports, and airports. Logistics also depends on accommodative regulations on land use, infrastructure use, conveyance operations, and trade. Furthermore, the competition between logistics clusters for attracting tenants and distribution activities means that tax regimes have to be favorable for logistics activities, including taxes on inventories and international trade.

Just as important are general government characteristics. For example, the Singapore Government is renowned for both high efficiency and low corruption, an ill affecting many other governments and logistics agencies. In addition, the social and political stability of the island adds to its attractiveness.

While those general government characteristics may be difficult to change in the short term, direct government support is crucial. Furthermore, world ranking of cargo ports, airports, and countries' logistics capabilities (see, for example, the World Bank's Logistics Performance Index[62]) can create competitive pressures[63] that may lead to improvements in government characteristics.

Education, Research, and Innovation

All economic clusters depend on people to do the work efficiently and effectively. In fact, governments support economic clusters because they expect the cluster to create jobs. More than many other types of clusters, logistics clusters provide a full skills-range of job functions from warehouse picking and packing, to operating expensive equipment, to using sophisticated software tools, to managerial and executive positions. To create an adequate workforce, successful logistics clusters develop local training programs and supporting academic institutions to educate and upgrade the capabilities of the local workforce, as described in chapter 8. As mentioned in that chapter, however, educational institutions usually follow the development of logistics clusters and support further growth. In most cases, such educational institutions were developed through partnerships between industry and local governments.

Tied to such educational institutions are research and innovation centers, such as Dinalog in the Netherlands and the Zaragoza Logistics Center in Spain, as well as independent research and innovation centers such as PortTechLA in San Pedro, California. Such institutions are not prerequisites to cluster development but rather a later-stage investment that helps propel existing clusters further. Higher education and research centers are the engines of innovation for new software applications, advanced logistics processes and clever supply chain concepts. New ideas then flow back into the local cluster through research reports, consulting projects, student internships, entrepreneurial graduates, and commercialization activities.

Accordingly, governments contemplating the development of logistics clusters should plan for such institutions rather than developing them first. Naturally, if such institutions exist already, it is an advantage.

Collaboration

One crosscutting factor, found in nascent successful clusters and clusters undergoing significant new investment, is a spirit of collaboration and a unity of purpose across all stakeholders. While collaboration is important for any large-scale project, the scale and regional impact of significant transportation infrastructure development requires cooperation between local, regional, and national transportation authorities in conjunction with urban planning authorities, chambers of commerce, and real estate developers.

Education development depends on government funding but, when discussing business logistics, it also requires collaboration between the educational institutions and private companies. These companies need training and cutting-edge ideas, but they can help to define relevant curricula and provide living-laboratory sites for cutting-edge research.

Locations like Fort Worth, Singapore, the Netherlands, and many others have an effective partnership between the governments at all levels, the business community, academia, and other institutions. For example, the Kansas City SmartPort organization is dedicated to promoting Kansas City as America's main logistics hub. Its board of directors includes representatives of the BNSF Railroad, the Greater Kansas City Foreign Trade Zone, Johnson County Airport, the area's Development Council, the Kansas and Missouri departments of transportation, and other organizations.

Chapter 1, and the original impetus of this book, began with the development of PLAZA—the huge logistics park in Zaragoza, which exemplifies these multifaceted collaborations. Not only did the government and its bitter opposition parties join forces to bring the vision of Zaragoza as a logistics hub to fruition, but virtually all local businesses—including several institutions for collaboration, such as Aragón Exterior[64]—came together to support the project. Notably, while the government of Aragón funded the partnership with MIT to create the Zaragoza Logistics Center, two local banks (Ibercaja and CAI) were instrumental in cofunding and supporting this research and graduate education institution.

Value-Added Services

Many of the most prominent clusters go beyond moving and storage activities to include value-added services that transform, modify, augment, tag, sequence, or repair goods. Success in attracting value-added services raises the competitive stance of a cluster, making it more difficult for companies to change locations. Many value-added services involve relatively sophisticated, higher-paying jobs than those taking place on the warehouse floor.

Ultimately, a logistics cluster can provide the core infrastructure and services that support many industries, leading to other types of economic clusters. In fact, many manufacturing clusters started with a base of superior transportation and distribution services anchored in a logistics cluster. For example, starting with an aerotropolis concept around Memphis airport, the region developed as a logistics cluster and then attracted life science companies, advanced manufacturing, clean-tech energy, and information technology enterprises.

Both the provision of value-added services and attracting new industries are elements that governments should be planning for but not acting on (in terms of recruiting companies) before the basic logistics cluster is operational. The attraction of manufacturers and other industrial companies is part of the process that feeds the positive growth of a cluster in later stages.

A FINAL WORD

Niels Bohr, the famous Danish physicist, once quipped, "Prediction is very difficult, especially about the future." Indeed, given the innumerable variables affecting our future, most of which cannot be measured or even identified, any efforts to make long term predictions are questionable. Nonetheless, some trends are already evident and seem likely to accelerate. One such ongoing trend is the increasing trade of goods and services around the globe over the next several decades. Businesses continue to move away from vertical integration; information technology keeps connecting more people and businesses; and, most important, the world is barely halfway through a transformation that will raise several billion people up from poverty to the middle class. As a result, one can paint with some confidence the details of the logistics landscape, even if we cannot yet envision the entire sweep of it.

Rising standards of living in Brazil, China, India, and elsewhere around the world—made possible, in large part, by the efficiency of the world's supply chain management and logistics systems—will create massive increases in demand for natural resources and manufactured goods, from cars and refrigerators to microprocessors and lipstick. And increasing demand will inevitably increase trade flows across the globe. Growth may happen in fits and starts but, surely, it will happen.

Yet this global growth has its challenges. The rising quality of life for the planet's billions of people has to balanced against the strained natural resources needed to feed their growing appetites. Few industries play a greater role in sustaining this balance than those that create an efficient chain of resource cultivation, processing, and distribution. Global supply chains can facilitate the world's migration from majority-poor to majority-middle-class, thus affecting public well-being broadly and deeply. Logistics, therefore, is an essential element in efficiently delivering more necessities and goods to more people in more places at low cost and at minimal environmental impact per unit.

The *why, where, when,* and *how* of successful logistics clusters affect the efficiency and effectiveness of global supply chains. This book parsed some of the challenges and opportunities of logistics clusters, describing the economic and business imperatives that motivate clustering; the elements that contributed to some of the more successful clusters; the challenges of developing clusters; and the mistakes of those that have not succeeded as well as planned. I am hopeful that some of these findings—made richer by the works of others—will lead to a public-private consensus that a well-executed logistics cluster creates a quintuple win: good jobs for workers, low-cost necessities for all people, robust growth for jurisdictions that support clusters, profits for participating companies, and sustainability for the Earth on which we live.

NOTES

CHAPTER 1

1. "The future of fast fashion; Inditex," *Economist* (June 18, 2005).

2. Pankaj Ghemawat and Luis Nueno, "Zara: Fast Fashion," *Harvard Business Review*, Case Study no. 703497 (April 2003).

3. Kerry Capell, "Zara Thrives by Breaking All the Rules," *Business Week* (October 9, 2008).

4. InditexAnnualReport2010,Availableat:http://www.inditex.es/en/shareholders_and_investors/investor_relations/annual_reports.

5. Mark Arend, "Something Old, Something New," *Site Selection Magazine* (September 2007) Available at: http://www.siteselection.com/features/2007/sep/Aragon/

6. As of 2011 Zara had more than 1,500 stores worldwide and the parent company, Inditex, had more than 5,000, including all of its brands.

7. Zara does not have its own truck fleet. According to Raul Estradera Vazquez, Zara's director of communications, it uses common carriers, some of which dedicate assets to Zara's business.

8. Available at: http://www.inditex.es/en/who_we_are/stores.

9. Fabón García played basketball from 1991 to 2000 in four teams: Cai Zaragoza, Granada, Valencia, and Canarias.

10. In September 2010 Mercadona SA acquired the remaining interest in Caladero that it did not already own.

11. A. M. Spence, "Entry, Capacity, Investment and Oligopolistic Pricing," *Bell Journal of Economics* 8, no. 2 (Autumn 1977): 534–544.

12. German economist Heinrich Freiherr von Stackelberg described the game model in his 1934 monograph, *Market Structure and Equilibrium*.

CHAPTER 2

1. François Perroux, "Economic Space: Theory and Applications," *Quarterly Journal of Economics* 64, no.1 (1950): 89–104.

2. Albert Hirschman, *The Strategy of Economic Development* (Westview Press, Boulder, 1988).

3. Available at: http://www.paintmaking.com/historic_pigments.htm

4. Cristina Acidini Luchinat et al., *The Medici, Michelangelo, and the Art of Late Renaissance Florence* (Yale University Press, November 2002).

5. There is actually little evidence that Watson ever made this statement. *The Economist* referred to the story as a myth in 1973 in volume 368, issues 8322–8326, p. 201.

6. Christophe Lécuyer, *Making Silicon Valley: Innovation and the Growth of High Tech, 1930–1970* (MIT Press, 2006).

7. Dario Borghino, "Intel Unveils the World's First Working 22nm Chips," Gizmag (September 24, 2009). Also available at: http://www.tomshardware.com/news/Intel-22nm-CPU-core-2011,8710.html

8. Available at: http://www.visual-arts-cork.com/history-of-art/renaissance-in-florence.htm; see also http://www.visual-arts-cork.com/painting/linear-perspective.htm

9. Available at: http://www.visual-arts-cork.com/old-masters/lorenzo-ghiberti.htm

10. Available at: http://en.wikipedia.org/wiki/Renaissance

11. Available at: http://www.mmi.unimaas.nl/people/veltman/articles/leonardo/Lenardo%20da%20Vinci%20Studies%20of%20the%20Human%20Nody%20and%20Prinicples%20of%20Anatomy.html

12. A. Zucchiatti, A. Bouquitton, I. Katona, and A. D'Alessandro, "The Della Robbia Blue: A Case Study for the Use of Cobalt Pigments in Ceramics During the Italian Renaissance," *Archaeomentry* 48, no. 1 (2006): 131–153.

13. Available at: http://www.italianpottery.com/italian_ceramics.html

14. Available at: http://www.visual-arts-cork.com/sculpture/luca-della-robbia.htm

15. G. A. Lee, "The Coming of Age of Double Entry: The Giovanni Farolfi Ledger of 1299–1300," *Accounting Historians Journal* 42, no. 2 (1977): 79–95.

16. Available at: http://en.wikipedia.org/wiki/History_of_banking

17. Raymond A. de Roover, *The Rise and Decline of the Medici Bank, 1397–1494* (Beard Books, 1999).

18. Ibid.

19. Richard A. Goldwaite, *Banks, Palaces and Entrepreneurs in Renaissance Florence* (Collected Studies) (Variorum, UK, August 1995).

20. Available at: http://www.nga.gov/collection/gallery/gg7/gg7-main1.html

21. Evelyn S. Welch, *Art in Renaissance Italy, 1350–1500* (Oxford University Press, May 2001).

22. Emma Barker, Nick Webb, and Kim Woods, *The Changing Status of the Artist* (Yale University Press, 1999).

23. Available at: http://www.artexpertswebsite.com/pages/artists/bartolomeo.php

24. Michael Wayne Cole, *Sixteenth-Century Italian Art* (Wiley-Blackwell, August 2006).

25. Fred S. Kleiner, *Gardner's Art through the Ages: A Global History*, 13th edition (Wadsworth, January 2010).

26. AnnaLee Saxenian, *Regional Advantage: Culture and Competition in Silicon Valley and Route 128* (Harvard University Press, March 1996).

27. Available at: http://en.wikipedia.org/wiki/Raphael or: http://www.visitflorence.com/florence-history-and-culture/raphael.html

28. Available at: http://www.keytoumbria.com/Perugia/Perugino.html

29. Alfred Marshall, *Principles of Economics* (Macmillan, 1920).

30. See also M. Peneder, "Creating a coherent design for cluster analysis and related policies," paper presented at the OECD Workshop on Cluster Analysis and Cluster Based Policies (Amsterdam, October 10–11, 1997).

31. W. Isard and T. Vietorisz, "Industrial Complex Analysis and Regional Development," *Papers and Proceedings of the Regional Science Association* 1, no. 1 (1955): 227–247.

32. W. Isard and E Schooler, "Industrial Complex Analysis, Agglomeration Economics and Regional Development," *Journal of Regional Science* 1, no. 2 (1959): 19–33.

33. M. Porter, "Clusters and the New Economics of Competition," *Harvard Business Review* (Nov.–Dec. 1998): 77–90.

34. A. Shain, "Boeing Jobs: Suppliers Likely to Relocate," *Post and Courier* (November 1, 2009).

35. Tom Friedman, "Doing Our Homework," *New York Times* (June 24, 2004).

36. Yossi Sheffi, Yui Dai, and Xiaowen Yang, "Supply Chain Principles in the Shanghai Knock-off Retail Clusters" (MIT CTL Research Paper 3-C-10, 2010).

37. Tom Friedman, *The World Is Flat: A Brief History of the Twenty-First Century* (Farrar, Straus, and Giroux, 2005).

38. R. O'Brien, *Global Financial Integration: The End of Geography* (Royal Institute of International Affairs, 1992).

39. R. Cairncross, *The Death of Distance* (Harvard Business School Press, 1997).

40. United Nations Population Fund, *State of the World's Population, 2007*. Available at: http://www.unfpa.org/swp/2007/english/introduction.html

41. S. Sassen, *The Global City* (Princeton University Press, September 2001).

42. A. Rodríguez-Posea and R. Crescenzi, "Mountains in a Flat World: Why Proximity Still Matters for the Location of Economic Activity," *Cambridge Journal of Regions, Economy and Society* 1, no 3 (2008): 371–388.

43. Michael E. Porter and Willis M. Emmons III, "Institutions for Collaboration: Overview," *Harvard Business Review Note School Note* (January 29, 2003).

44. Vivek Wadhwa, "Top Down Tech Clusters Often Lack Key Ingredients," *Bloomberg Business Week* (May 4, 2010).

45. Ann Markusen, "Sticky Places in Slippery Space: A Typology of Industrial Districts," *Economic Geography* 72, no. 3 (1996): 293–314.

46. Klaus Schwab, *The Global Competitiveness Report 2011–2012* (World Economic Forum, 2012). Available at: http:// www3.weforum.org/docs/WEF_GCR_Report_2011-12.pdf

47. Available at: http://www.doingbusiness.org/economyrankings/

48. J. Zhang and N. Patel, *The Dynamics of California's Biotechnology Industry* (Public Policy Institute of California, San Francisco, 2005).

49. Edward B. Roberts and Charles Eesley, *Entrepreneurial Impact: The Role of MIT* (Kauffman Foundation, February 2009). Available from: http://entrepreneurship.mit.edu/sites/default/files/files/Entrepreneurial_Impact_The_Role_of_MIT.pdf

50. AnnaLee Saxenian, *Regional Advantage: Culture and Competition in Silicon Valley and Route 128,* (Harvard University Press, March 1996) .

51. M. P. Feldman, J. Francis, and J. Bercovitz, "Creating a Cluster While Building a Firm: Entrepreneurs and the Formation of Industrial Clusters," *Regional Studies* 39, no.1 (2005):129–141.

52. Roberts and Eesley, *Entrepreneurial Impact.* These numbers are even more impressive when considering that the study excluded companies that were not successful or were acquired by others.

53. Ronald H. Coase, "The Nature of the Firm," *Economica* 4, no 16 (1937): 386–405. Reprinted in G. J. Stigler and K. E. Boulding, eds., *Readings in Price Theory,* (Richard D. Irwin, 1988).

54. Porter, "Clusters and the New Economics," *Harvard Business Review* (Nov.–Dec. 1998).

55. Stuart Rosenfeld, "Creating Smart Systems: A Guide to Cluster Strategies in Less Favored nations, " paper presented at the *European Union Regional Innovations Strategies Conference,* Carrboro, NC, April 2002. Available at: http://www.rtsinc.org/publications/pdf/less_favoured.pdf

56. W. Lazonick, "Industrial Organization and Technological Change: The Decline of the British Cotton Industry," *Business History Review* 57, no. 2 (1983): 195–236.

57. E. Newell, "'Copperopolis': The Rise and Fall of the Copper Industry in the Swansea District, 1826–1921," *Business History* 32, no. 3 (1990): 75–97.

58. Donald Sull, "From Community of Innovation to Community of Inertia: The Rise and Fall of the Akron Tire Cluster," *The Academy of Management Best Paper Proceedings* (2001). Available at: http://www.donsull.com/downloads/cluster_inertia.pdf

59. R. Pouder, and C. H. St. John, "Hot Spots and Blind Spots: Geographical Clusters of Firms and Innovations," *Academy of Management Review* 21, no. 4 (1996): 1192–1212.

60. L. G. Zucker, "The Role of Institutionalization in Cultural Persistence," *American Sociological Review* 42 (October 1977): 726–743.

61. Bryce Hoffman, *American Icon: Alan Mulally and the Fight to Save Ford Motor Company.* Crown Business (March 2013).

62. Emily Maltby, "So Much Promise, but Sometimes So Few Results," *Wall Street Journal* (August 22, 2011).

63. David Barkley and Mar Henry, "Targeting Industry Clusters for Regional Economic Development: An Overview of REDRL Approach," Clemson University Research Report 01-2005-03 (2005).

CHAPTER 3

1. Adam Smith, *An Inquiry into the Nature and Causes of the Wealth of Nations* 3 vols. (Dublin: Whitestone, 1776).

2. David Ricardo, *On the Principles of Political Economy and Taxation* (London: John Murray, 1817). A fully searchable text is available at http://www.econlib.org/library/Ricardo/ricP.html

3. Paul Krugman, "A Globalization Puzzle," *New York Times* (February 21, 2010).

4. Paul Krugman, "Increasing Returns and Economic Geography," *Journal of Political Economy* 99, no. 3 (June 1991): 483–499. The point is also mentioned in Krugman's *New York Times* article (ibid.).

5. D P S Peacock, "The Rhine and the problem of Gaulish wine in Roman Britain" in *Roman Shipping and Trade: Britain and the Rhine Provinces*, J. du Plat Taylor and h. Cleere, eds. (The Council for British Archaeology Research Report no. 24, 1978): 49–51.

6. Tacitus, *Annales Book 2*, Section 6. Available at:. http://www.sacred-texts.com/cla/tac/a02000.htm

7. Available at: http://www.livius.org/ga-gh/germania/lugdunum.html

8. Strabo, *The Geography*, Book IV, 5, Par. 2. Available at: http://penelope.uchicago.edu/Thayer/E/Roman/Texts/Strabo/4E*.html

9. Jan De Vries and Ad van der Woude, *The First Modern Economy: Success, Failure, and Perseverance of the Dutch Economy, 1500–1815* (Cambridge University Press, May 1997).

10. R. Parthesius, *Dutch Ships in Tropical Waters: The Development of the Dutch East India Company (VOC), Shipping Network in Asia 1595–1660* (Amsterdam University Press, July 2007).

11. Jean Sutton, *The East India Company's Maritime Service, 1746–1834: Masters of the Eastern Seas* (Boydell Press, November 2010).

12. http://www.slideshare.net/sclgme/sclg-corporate-presentation

13. Airport Council International, Cargo Traffic 2009 Final. Available at: http://www.airports.org/cda/aci_common/display/main/aci_content07_c.jsp?zn=aci&cp=1-5-54-4819_666_2

14. See, for example, 2008 statistics in American Association of Port Authorities, World Port Rankings. Available at: http://aapa.files.cms-plus.com/Statistics/WORLD%20PORT%20RANKINGS%2020081.pdf

15. Port of Rotterdam, *Port Statistics*. Available at: http://www.portofrotterdam.com/en/Port/port-statistics/Documents/Port_Statistics_2009_tcm26–64785.pdf.

16. Ibid.

17. Estimates given by Professor Peter de Langen of Eindhoven University.

18. Daniel Defoe, *A Plan of the English Commerce*, 1728, p. 192 (reprint, Kelley Publishers, 1967).

19. Singapore Port Authority Web site. Available at: http://www.singaporepsa.com/

20. Choy, K.M., *Trade cycles in the re-export economy: The Case of Singapore (Report WP 2009/05 Economic Growth Center, Division of Economics*, Nanyan Technological University, Singapore, 2009).

21. Available at: http://www.singstat.gov.sg/stats/keyind.html#popnarea

22. Alberto Vallarino Clement, *Strategic Plan of the Government 2010–2014, Republic of Panama* (Ministry of Economy and Finance, Panama, January 2010).

23. G. J. Medina, "Exploraciones entre Chagras a Panamá: cartografía de la ciudad," *Revista Loteria* 50 (1991): 5–45.

24. Susan Harp, "History of the Las Cruces Trail and Adjacent Canal Area," (Albrook, Panama, June 2001) Available at: http://trail2.com/graphics/panama.pdf

25. David McCullough, *The Path between the Seas: The Creation of the Panama Canal 1870–1914* (Simon and Schuster, October 1978).

26. Panama Railroad, History of the Panama Railroad. Available at: http://www.panamarailroad.org/history1.html

27. McCullough, *The Path*, p. 34.

28. Ibid., p. 35.

29. Ibid..

30. Available at: http://historical.whatitcosts.com/facts-panama-canal-pg2.htm

31. Isthmian Canal Commission, *Panama Canal Record,* Volume 1 (The Canal, 1908). Original from the University of Michigan.

32. Available from: http://historical.whatitcosts.com/facts-panama-canal-pg2.htm

33. In April 2012 the consortium building the new locks, Frupo Unidos por el Canal, notified the ACP of a delay until April 2015.

34. Both the 2004 and the 2007 statutes are known as "Law 41." This is only a coincidence as these laws happened to be the 41st laws enacted in the two respective years.

35. Available from: http://www.memphislibrary.org/history/memphis2.htm#mfac

36. Available from: http://www.memphisflyer.com/backissues/issue419/cvr419.htm

37. *Tennessee Encyclopedia of History and Culture* (University of Tennessee Press, 2002). Online edition available at: http://tennesseeencyclopedia.net/entry.php?rec=1104

38. Railroad class is determined based on revenue, with "Class I" implying the largest revenue (at least ~$400 million annually in 2010). The five US Class I freight railroads include the BNSF, CSX, NS, KCS and the UP. The two Canadian Class I Railroads, CN and CP, operate both in the United States and Canada.

39. "Memphis: North America Logistics Center," *Inbound Logistics*, Oct. 2009 (special advertisement supplement).

40. Vance Trimble, *Overnight Success: Federal Express and Fred Smith, Its Renegade Creator* (Crown, January 1993).

41. Available at: http://news.van.fedex.com/files/FedEx%20Express%20Super%20Hub%20in%20Memphis.pdf

42. "Memphis: North America Logistics Center, *Inbound Logistics,* 2009.

43. The term was coined originally by John Kasarda, "Logistics & the Rise of the Aerotropolis," *Real Estate Issues* 25 (Winter 2000/2001): 43–48.

44. See, for example, the list of the world's busiest cargo airports published by the Airport Council International, available at: http://www.airports.org/cda/aci_common/display/main/aci_content07_c.jsp?zn=aci&cp=1-5-54-4819_666_2__

45. Greater Memphis Chamber Bragging Rights (January 2012). Available at: http://www.memphischamber.com/Articles/Community/MemphisBraggingRights.aspx

46. Peter de Langen, "Transport, Logistics and the Region," Inaugural Lecture presented January 22, 2010, at the Eindhoven University of Technology, Holland.

47. Liliana Rivera and Yossi Sheffi, *Logistics Clusters in the US: An Empirical Study* (MIT CTL Research Paper CTL/1-A-12, January 2012).

48. Bernard Fingleton, Danilo Igliori, and Barry Moore, "Employment Growth of Small High-Technology Firms and the Role of Horizontal Clustering: Evidence from Computing Services and R&D in Great Britain, 1991–2000," *Urban Studies* 41, no. 4 (2004): 773–799.

49. In fact, Singapore has been losing business to the Port of Tanjung Pelepas in Malaysia in the first decade of the twenty-first century—see the section *Emerging Cluster in Emerging Market Countries* in chapter 10.

CHAPTER 4

1. Location optimization models require minimizing the concave transportation cost functions as well as complex decompositions to deal with the integrality of the locations. As a result, their solutions are rarely real mathematical optima, let alone business optima. Simulation models require prespecification of the prospective distribution location. Thus, they should be understood as cost and performance calculators for trial network configurations. Both types of models require a relatively accurate forecast of the expected flows and transportation costs over

the life of the distribution network, a difficult and possibly unattainable goal. While most operations research professionals typically understand these limitations, many managers take the face value of the results with more confidence than the nature of the analysis can reasonably justify.

2. This is why, in many cases, optimization models are used in order to choose the optimal locations from among a small set of locations identified previously as "sensible" ones.

3. A somewhat different version of this quote appeared in the September 29, 1980, issue of *Time* magazine in an article titled "Business: Airport 1980: Atlanta's Hartsfield"

4. Figures are correct for the US for February 2011. Available at: http://wwwhst.com/freightrateindex/index_files/page0012.htm

5. Antoine Delorme, Dominik Karbowski, and Phil Sharer, *Evaluation of Fuel Consumption Potential of Medium and Heavy Duty Vehicles through Modeling and Simulation*, Report to the National Academy of Sciences (Argon National Laboratory, October 23, 2009).

6. Available at: http://en.wikipedia.org/wiki/Road_train

7. Available at: http://www.globalsecurity.org/military/systems/ship/container.htm

8. Available at: http://www.apl.com/history/html/timeline_c10story.html

9. Allyson Bird, "Panama Canal to Shape Future," *Post and Courier* (August 30, 2010).

10. Enrico Paglia, "Container Shipping Outlook," Presentation at the *4th Mare Forum & Euromed Management* (Marseille, France, September 14, 2010). Available at: http://www.mareforum.com/EUROMED_PRESENTATIONS_2010/PAGLIA_Containers.pdf

11. Available at: http://www.marinelog.com/index.php?option=com_content&view=article&id=532%3A2011feb0002100&Itemid=107

12. Available at: http://gcaptain.com/vale-brasil-worlds-largest-carrier?26044

13. Vale has announced in May 2011 that it will invest $2.9B to expand Ponta de Madeira so it will be able to load two vessels simultaneously.

14. Einat Paz-Frankel, "Containers Moving on Inland Waterways," *Memphis Business Journal* (August 6, 2006).

15. On March 19, 2012, UPS announced it entered into an agreement to buy TNT express. In a subsequent announcement UPS said that they have no plans to shut down the cargo facility at Liège Airport.

16. Werner Enterprises Inc., *Annual Report Form 10-K* (March 1, 2011).

17. Swift Holding Corp, *Annual Report Form 10-K* (March 29, 2011).

18. *NPTC 2011 Annual Benchmarking Survey*, National Private Truck Council (August, 2011), 20.

19. See, for example, Julie Urlaub, "Sustainable Transportation: Extracting Value from an Empty Truck," Taiga Company Blog (February 2011).

20. Based on the costs of a new 747 of between $225 and $325 Million (estimate provided by my colleague, Professor John Hansman).

21. Lisa Graham, "Transport Collaboration in Europe," *Prologis Research Insights Report* (Winter 2011).

22. Available at: http://www.hero.nl/

23. Available at: http://www.freshparkvenlo.nl/en/fresh-park-venlo/facts-figures/

24. J. George Stalk and Thomas M. Hout, *Competing Against Time: How Time-Based Competition is Reshaping Global Markets*, (Free Press, March 1990).

25. Exel employs approximately 40,000 associates in the Americas. It is part of the supply chain division of Deutsche Post DHL.

26. Available at: http://www.dhlsupplychainmatters.com/innovation/recalls

27. David Grant, "Maclaren Stroller Recall: What to Do if You Have One," *Christian Science Monitor* (November 9, 2009).

28. Chris Malone, "The Surprising News About Product Recall," *Bloomberg Businessweek* (October 19, 2010).

29. Available at: http://www.supplychainbrain.com/content/technology-solutions/sc-finance-revenue-mgmt/single-article-page/article/at-advanced-biohealing-a-critical-product-requires-critical-care/

30. Available at: http://www.utsandiego.com/news/2011/sep/08/widespread-power-outages-across-san-diego-county/

31. *An Innovation That Heals*, UPS Case Study available from UPS.

32. Eddie Baeb, "Warehouse Dreams Derailed," *ChicagoBusiness* (November 2, 2009).

33. Available at: http://www.hillwood.com/story.aspx?ID=3080

CHAPTER 5

1. As the expected value of the demand for a certain product or product variant decreases, the ratio of the standard deviation to the expected value of demand—known as the *coefficient of variation*—increases. This is the same phenomenon which is at the heart of the liquidity argument outlined on p.107 in chapter 4 and the "risk pooling" effect mentioned there and on p. 109 of the same chapter. In this case the argument is reversed; while high volume generally leads to stability, low volume is inherently irregular.

2. Available at: http://www.ups-scs.com/solutions/case_studies/cs_nikon.pdf

3. Telephone interview with Jim O'Brien conducted by Susan Reitze, MIT 2005.

4. The case study is titled: "Consumer Goods Secondary Packaging: Co-locating Customization and Distribution Activities Reduces Costs, Improves Service and Quality for Consumer Packaged Goods Giant." Available at: http://www.dhl.com/content/dam/downloads/g0/logistics/case_studies/consumer_americas_secondary%20packaging_2012.pdf

5. The phrase was coined in 1958 by Bert Bell, the then commissioner of the NFL, after the Pittsburgh Steelers upset the Chicago Bears, 24-10 for the Steelers' first win over the Bears in 14 games spanning more than 24 years. It is the league's most prominent axiom to this day. See Tom Callahan, *Johnny U: The Life and Times of John Unitas* (Crown, September 2007).

6. In 2005 Reebok was acquired by Adidas AG.

7. John C. W. Parsons, *Using a Newsvendor Model for Demand Planning for NFL Replica Jerseys*, master's thesis, MIT (June 2004).

8. "The Indianapolis Region: A New Logistics Leader Has Emerged," *Inbound Logistics* (January 2007).

9. Susan M. Rietze, *Case Studies of Postponement in the Supply Chain*, master's thesis, MIT (June 2005).

10. Hau L. Lee, Corey Billington, and Brent Carter, "Hewlett-Packard gains control of inventory and service through design for localization," *Interfaces* 23 (July/August 1993): 1–11.

11. Corey Billington, Blake Johnson, and Alex Triantis, "A Real Options Perspective on Supply Chain Management in High Technology," *Journal of Applied Corporate Finance* 15, no. 2 (Summer 2002): 32–43.

12. UPS Case Study available at: http://healthcare.ups.com/resources/case-study-dr-reddy.html

13. Ibid.

14. Available at: http://www.fda.gov/Food/GuidanceComplianceRegulatory Information/CurrentGoodManufacturingPracticesCGMPs/default.htm

15. Available at: http://www.fda.gov/RegulatoryInformation/Guidances/ucm125067.htm

16. Available at: http://www.freedomcorp.com/Solutions/QAD/Success_stories/ARD.pdf

17. Andreas Kruse, Director DHL Solutions and Innovations, "Case Study Automotive Industry," presentation in the conference *Meeting the Challenge of Europe 2020*, Confindustria Headquarters (Rome, February 17, 2011).

18. *Big Trouble with "No Trouble Found" Returns*, Accenture Report (2008). Available at: http://www.accenture.com/SiteCollectionDocuments/PDF/Accenture_Returns_Repairs.pdf

19. For medical devices.

20. Available at: http://www.azpharmacy.gov/pdfs/guidelines%20(rph%20-%20 reciprocity).pdf

21. Available at: http://www.payscale.com/research/US/Job=Pharmacist/Salary

22. Available at: http://www.payscale.com/research/US/Job=Warehouse_Worker/Hourly_Rate

23. List available at: http://www.shipserv.com/search/results/index/searchWhat/ Ship+Repair+Services/searchWhere/SG/searchText/Singapore/searchType/produc t?searchStart=10&searchRows=10

24. Available at: http://www.zappos.com/

25. Available at: http://blogs.zappos.com/fiftythousand

26. Available at: http://www.portofrotterdam.com/nl/actueel/Nieuwsbrieven/ breakbulk/Breabulk%20nieuwsbrieven/Breakbulk%20Juni%202008%20Eng. pdf

27. Available at: http://www.worldportsource.com/ports/NLD_Port_of_Rotter- dam_106.php

28. Available at: http://www.portofrotterdam.com/en/Brochures/Breakbulk-Eng. pdf

29. Available at: http://www.be-logic.info/files/BE-LOGIC_Report_WP3_Task_3- 2__11-6-09_.pdf

30. Michael Sheffield, "Implant Device Spinoffs Thriving," *Memphis Business Journal* (August 10, 2010). Available at: http://www.bizjournals.com/memphis/ stories/2010/04/19/story2.html

31. Available at: http://www.indypartnership.com/Business_Clusters-Life_Sciences. aspx

32. Sheffield, "Implant Device Spinoffs."

33. Ibid.

34. Ibid.

CHAPTER 6

1. UPS United Parcel Service Inc. Annual Report Form 10K for 2010, Files 2/28/2011.

2. Available at: http://www.ups.com/content/us/en/about/facts/worldwide.html

3. F. P. van den Heuvel, L. Rivera, K. H. van Donselaar, Y. Sheffi, P. W. de Langen, and J. C. Fransoo, "Accessibility of US Counties and Location of Logistics Com- panies," paper presented in Dinalog Winterschool (January 30, 2012).

4. Available at: http://www.alliancetexas.com

5. Available at: http://www.hillwood.com/story.aspx?ID=3816

6. Available at: http://acresinc.com/Alliance/AllianceGlobalLogistics.pdf

7. Available at: http://www.worldtradewt100.com/articles/print/840208. Avail- able at: https://www.bnsf.com/media/news/articles/2004/11/2004_11_18a.html

9. Available at: http://www.alliancetexas.com/Portals/0/PDF/Alliance_Air_Trade_ Center_Brochure.pdf

10. Available at: http://www.scribd.com/doc/55989808/What-is-the-TEU

11. Available at: http://www.csav.com/pages/weight

12. Or, in more typical cases, two ocean containers to three over-the-road con- tainers.

13. Available at: http://www.centerpoint-intermodal.com/pdfs/CICJ_brochure.pdf

14. Available at: http://www.progressiverailroading.com/freightnews/article.asp? id=20028

15. Available at: http://www.rotterdam.nl/tekst:some_facts_and_figures

16. Available at: http://www.deltawerken.com/The-functioning/463.html

17. Available at: http://www.deltawerken.com/Indispensable-/464.html

18. Available at: http://www.eib.org/attachments/pipeline/20070125_nts1_en.pdf

19. Available at: http://www.worldportsource.com/ports/NLD_Port_of_Rotterdam_106.php

20. Available at: http://www.portofrotterdam.com/en/Brochures/Dry-Bulk-Eng.pdf

21. Available at: http://www.worldportsource.com/ports/NLD_Port_of_Rotterdam_106.php

22. Peter de Langen, *The Performance of Seaports Clusters*, PhD Thesis, Erasmus University of Rotterdam (January 2004).

23. Available at: http://www.bts.gov/publications/freight_in_america/pdf/entire.pdf

24. Available at: http://epp.eurostat.ec.europa.eu/statistics_explained/index.php/Freight_transport_statistics

25. Available at: http://rta.org/Portals/0/Documents/Crossties%20Magazine/Jan%20Feb%2011/AAR.pdf

26. BNSF Railway Company, Annual Report Form 10K, 2010.

27. Bill Mongelluzzo, "BNSF Building Intermodal Business," *Journal of Commerce* (February 10, 2010).

28. Available at: http://ec.europa.eu/transport/inland/index_en.htm

29. Available at: http://www.hkv.nl/documenten/Tension_between_navigation_maintenance_and_safety_verkortvoorWEBSITE.pdf

30. Association of American Railroads, *US Freight Railroad Statistics*, based on Bureau of Transportation Statistics data, April 2010.

31. The directions of runways, which can generally be used for take-offs and landings in both directions, are stated in degrees magnetic north, divided by ten. So, if a runway direction is stated as 36/18, then that the runway can be used (for take-off or landing) either from a heading of 360° magnetic north or 180° magnetic north.

32. Available at: http://www.siteselection.com/ssinsider/pwatch/pw060601.htm

33. Warren Hausman, Hau Lee, Graham Napier, and Alex Thompson, *How Enterprises and Trading Partners Gain from Global Trade Management*, Stanford University Research Report (October 21, 2009).

34. Triennial Central Bank Survey: Foreign Exchange and Derivative Market Activity in April 2010, Bank for International Settlements Preliminary Report (September 2010).

35. Available at: http://www.pressroom.ups.com/Fact+Sheets/UPS+Worldport+Facts

36. Available at: http://news.van.fedex.com/taxonomy/term/381

37. Available at: http://www.ida.gov.sg/Infrastructure/20060411230420.aspx

38. Available at: http://www.dinalog.nl/institute/news/start-5-research-and-development-projects/262

39. Available at: http://www.dinalog.nl/media/Factsheet_Planning_Services.pdf

40. Available at:

http://www.dinalog.nl/institute/projects/research-development-projects/cross-chain-order-fulfillment-coordination-for-internet-sales/269

41. Available at: http://www.dinalog.nl/media/Factsheet_Value_creation_by_closing_the_loop.pdf

42. Available at: http://www.dinalog.nl/institute/projects/research-development-projects/4c4d-city-distribution/590

43. Available at: http://www.dinalog.nl/files/publications/ultimate-factsheet-project.pdf

44. Available at: http://www.dinalog.nl/media/Factsheet_4C_LF%20(1).pdf

45. John Moavenzadeh, Maria Torres-Montoya, and Timothy Gange, eds., *Repowering Transport*, Project White Paper, World Economic Forum (April 2011).

46. Jean-Paul Rodrigue, Claude Comtols, and Brian Slack, *The Geography of Transportation Systems* (Routledge, May 18, 2009), chapter 8.

47. http://www.platts.com/RSSFeedDetailedNews/RSSFeed/Shipping/8404275

48. William Logue, Congressional Testimony, Committee on Energy and Natural Resources, US Senate, January 30, 2007.

49. Rodrigue, Comtols, and Slack, *The Geography of Transportation*, chapter 5.

50. Available at: http://www.multicorerotterdam.com/mmfiles/factsheet_multicore_rotterdam_tcm141-26888.pdf

51. Available at: http://www.portofrotterdam.com/en/News/pressreleases-news/Pages/vtti-builds-rotterdam-antwerp-pipeline.aspx

52. Available at: http://www.portofrotterdam.com/en/Brochures/Facts-Figures-Rotterdam-Energy-Port-and-Petrochemical-Cluster-Eng.pdf

53. Available at: http://www.worldbunkering.com/news/summer-2011/0637-south-east-asia---still-expanding.html

54. Bob Violino, "What Can Logistics Do for You?" *Global Services* (May 25, 2006).

Available at: http://www.globalservicesmedia.com/IT-Outsourcing/Enterprise-Applications/What-Can-Logistics-Do-for-You/22/3/0/general200705211326

55. Ibid.

56. Available at: http://www.panynj.gov/bayonnebridge/

57. Available at: http://www.nj.com/bayonne/index.ssf/2010/12/port_authority_announces_plans.html

58. Brian Wingfield, "The World's Most Delayed Airports," *Forbes* (January 14, 2008).

59. Available at: http://www.dredgingtoday.com/2010/08/30/panama-canal-expansion-is-a-game-changer/

60. Available at: http://www.dredgingtoday.com/2010/10/05/usa-port-of-miami-up-to-the-challenge-in-2014/

61. Russ Bynum, "US Ports Race to Keep Up with the Bigger Panama Canal," Bloomberg Businessweek (February 7, 2011).

62. Available at: http://www.acta.org/gen/faq.asp#

63. Available at: http://www.tsacarriers.org/fs_alameda.html

64. Available at: http://www.acta.org/gen/faq.asp#

65. Available at: http://www.tsacarriers.org/fs_alameda.html

66. Hnah Dam Le-Griffin and Melisa Murphy, "Container Terminal Productivity: Experiences at the Ports of Los Angeles and Long Beach," paper presented at the *National Urban freight Conference*, Long Beach, CA (February 1, 2006): 8. Available at: http://www.metrans.org/nuf/documents/Le-Murphy.pdf

67. Peter van Baalen, Rob Zuidwijk, and Jo van Nunen, "Port Inter-Organizational Information Systems: Capabilities to Service Global Supply Chains," *Foundations and Trends in Technology, Information and Operations Management* 2, nos. 2–3 (2008): 81–241.

68. Available at: http://www.spacedaily.com/reports/Union_Pacific_Railroad_Celebrates_Opening_Of_Joliet_Intermodal_Terminal_999.html

69. Available at: http://info.jctrans.com/jcnet/news/osn/20071224575766.shtml

70. Available at: http://www.maasvlakte2.com/en/home/

71. Johan Swinnen, Pavel Ciaian, and d'Artis Kancs, *Study on the Functioning of Land Markets in the EU Member State under the Influence of Measures Applied under the Common Agricultural Policy*, Final Report, Center for European Policy Studies (September 3, 2009), p. 220. Available at: http://ec.europa.eu/agriculture/analysis/external/landmarkets/report_en.pdf

72. Hans Koster and Jan Rouwendal, "The Impact of Mixed Land Use on Residential Property," *Tinbergen Institute Discussion Paper* TI 2010-105/3 (October 15, 2010). Available at: http://www.tinbergen.nl/discussionpapers/10105.pdf

73. Available at: http://www.harahanbridge.com/Main/HomePage

CHAPTER 7

1. See, for example, Vivek Wadhwa, "Top Down Tech Clusters Often Lack Key Ingredients," *Bloomberg Businessweek* (May 4, 2010).

2. Gert-Jan Hospers, Frederic Sautet, and Pierre Desrochers, "Silicon Somewhere: Is There a Need for Cluster Policy?" *Handbook of Research on Innovation and Clusters*, vol. 2, ed. Charlie Karlsson (Edward Elgar Publishing, 2008). Available at SSRN: http://papers.ssrn.com/sol3/papers.cfm?abstract_id=1321496

3. Michael. E. Porter, *On Competition* (Harvard Business School Press, January 1998).

4. South Dakota Department of Transportation, *SDOT Briefing: Truck Weights and Highways* (2002).

5. David Cole et al., *Freight Mobility and Intermodal Connectivity in China*, US Federal Highway Administration Report FHWA-PL-08-020 (May 2008).

6. Available at: http://www.railway-technology.com/projects/betuweroute/

7. Richard Wronski, "Monster Trains Coming Down the Track?" *Chicago Tribune* (August 12, 2008).

8. Available at: http://www.createprogram.org/about.htm

9. Available at: http://www.createprogram.org/about.htm#facts

10. Available at: http://www.shanghai-daily.com/news/shanghai-daily-news/a-silk-road-for-the.htm

11. Available at: http://www.zlc.edu.es/

12. Available at: http://www.dinalog.nl/

13. Available at: http://www.tliap.nus.edu.sg/

14. Available at: http://www.misi.edu.my/

15. Available at: http://www.maasvlakte2.com/en/index/show/id/694/Sustainable+dialogue

16. Available at: http://www.panamapacifico.com/Explore-Ease_Of_Business.aspx

17. Available at: http://www.jada.org/pdf/brochure25-sml.pdf

18. *Strategic Plan for the Development of the Joliet Arsenal Development Authority Property*, report by the University of Illinois at Springfield and Crawford, Murphy & Tilly, Inc. (December 1999).

19. Available at: http://www.envisionfreight.com/issues/pdf/Joliet_Austell.pdf

20. Available at: http://www.prologis.com/docs/ProLogis+Byline+Final.pdf

21. Available at: http://njzoningwatch.com/2007/03/08/portsfield-initiative-touts-17-brownfields-sites-as-solution-to-rising-cargo-demand/

22. "And Worse to Come," *Economist* (January 22, 2009).

23. Unfortunately, Aragón and Zaragoza were hit hard during the 2010–2011 Spanish (and European) crisis. Aragón's unemployment rate climbed to over 17 percent during the second part of 2011. At the same time Spanish unemployment hit 23 percent.

24. Available at: http://www.dot.gov/documents/finaltigergrantinfo.pdf

25. Vance Trimble, *Overnight Success: Federal Express and Fred Smith, Its Renegade Creator* (Crown, 1993) 143–144.

26. Available at: http://ops.fhwa.dot.gov/freight/publications/freightfinancing/sect3.htm

27. Ben Krizner, "Making the Grade," *World Trade Magazine* (May 1, 2010).

28. Available at: http://www.lowtax.net/lowtax/html/panama_international_law.html

29. "Shades of Grey," *Economist* (October 29, 2009).

30. Available at: http://www.treasury.gov/press-center/press-releases/Pages/tg1144.aspx

31. Michigan State University and Detroit Regional Chamber of Commerce, *Economic Development Stimulation for Southeast Michigan, Northwest Ohio, and Southwest Ontario via Emerging Global Supply Chain Management Solutions: Opportunity Assessment for a Regional Supply Chain Hub*, report submitted to the New Economy Initiative for Southeast Michigan (May 31, 2010).

32. Cassandra Crones Moore, *Intrastate Trucking: Stronghold of the Regulators*, Cato Institute Policy Analysis no. 204 (February 16, 1994).

33. Available at: http://www.taxfoundation.org/research/show/22658.html

34. Available at: http://www.its4logistics.com/why-choose-its/why-nevada/nevada-vs-california-tax-analysis

35. Available at: http://www.crossroadscommercecenter.com/location/

36. Available at: http://www.centennialofflight.gov/essay/Government_Role/Econ_Reg/POL16.htm

37. Jon Tarjei Kråkenes, *The Panama Canal, the Gateway between the Atlantic and the Pacific Ocean: A Case Study*, Norwegian School of Economics and Business Administration (Bergen, Spring 2008).

38. Reece Shaw, "A Primer on the Effect of the Panama Canal Expansion on World Commerce," Presentation at the AAPA Facilities Engineering Seminar, (San Diego, Calif., November 7, 2007).

39. Available at: http://www.medey.com/pdf/Bonded%20Warehousing.pdf. Also see http://ia.ita.doc.gov/ftzpage/tic.html

40. Warren Hausman, Hau Lee, and Uma Subramanian, *Global Logistics Indicators, Supply Chain Metrics and Bilateral Trade Patterns*, World Bank Policy Research Working Paper 3773 (November 2005).

41. http://www.aviainform.org/index.php?option=com_content&task=view&id=533&Itemid=41

42. Government of India, Planning Commission, Transport Division, *Report of the Working Group on Logistics* (New Delhi, 2010).

43. A. de Meyer and T. Shimada, *CrimsonLogic: The Evolution of the Trading Community via a B2B e-Commerce Hub*, INSEAD case 604-066-1 (Fontainebleau, 2004).

44. Peter van Baalen, Rob Zuidwijk, and Jo van Nunen, "Port Inter-Organizational Information Systems: Capabilities to Service Global Supply Chains," *Foundations and Trends in Technology, Information and Operations Management* 2, nos. 2–3 (2008): 81–241.

45. Available at: http://www.singaporepsa.com/portnet.php

46. G. Choo, "IT 2000: Singapore's Vision of an Intelligent Island," in P. Droege, ed., *Intelligent Environments: Spatial Aspects of the Information Revolution* (Elsevier, 1997): 49–65,.

47. Conrad de Aenlle, "Silicon Valley Seeks New Ways to Attack High Tech Pollution," *New York Times* (December 19, 1991).

48. Available at: http://www.ens-newswire.com/ens/jun2008/2008-06-26-093.html

49. Available at: http://www.portoflosangeles.org/ctp/idx_ctp.asp

50. European Federation for Transport and Environment, *Including Aviation in the EU's Emissions Trading Scheme (EU ETS)*, Background Briefing (June 2008).

51. Available at: http://www.biodieselmagazine.com/articles/3103/eu-adopts-10-percent-biofuels-mandate/

52. Ariel Schwartz, "World's Largest Biodiesel Plant Opens in Singapore," *Inhabitat* (November 18, 2010). Available at: http://inhabitat.com/singapore-scores-worlds-largest-biodiesel-plant/

53. Available at: http://www.portofrotterdam.com/en/Brochures/Facts-Figures-Rotterdam-Energy-Port-and-Petrochemical-Cluster-Eng.pdf

54. Available at: http://www.e-energymarket.com/news/single-news/article/abengoa-deal-in-the-pipeline.html

55. Available at: http://www.bestufs.net/download/Workshops/BESTUFS_II/London_Jan05/BESTUFS_London_Jan05_Klaus_UoN.pdf

56. Baalen, Zuidwijk, and Nunen, "Port Inter-Organizational Information Systems."

57. Available at: http://info.worldbank.org/etools/tradesurvey/mode1b.asp

58. Michael Porter and Willis Emmons, "Institutions for Collaboration: Overview," *Harvard Business Review Background Note* (January 2003).

59. Available at: http://www.rppc.nl/en/index.php

60. Available at: http://www.memphischamber.com/The-Chamber/Councils/Regional-Logistics.aspx

61. John Romalis, "NAFTA and CUSFTA's Impact on International Trade," *Review of Economics and Statistics* 89, no.3 (August 2007): 416–435.

62. Howard Wall, *NAFTA and the Geography of North American Trade*, Federal Reserve Bank of St. Louis (2003).

63. Available at: http://www.parl.gc.ca/Content/LOP/ResearchPublications/2010-50-M-e.htm. Naturally, most of the increase is due to the expanding economies, but a nontrivial amount is also due to NAFTA.

64. Steven Beningo and Fahim Mohamad, *North American Trade Growth Continued in 2007*, Bureau of Transportation Statistics Special Report SR-011 (2009).

65. Cambridge Systematics, Inc., *Texas NAFTA Study Update*, Final Report prepared for the Texas DOT (2007).

66. Available at: http://www.schoolvoorjournalistiek.com/europe/?p=2199

CHAPTER 8

1. *Comprehensive Industry Analysis, Logistics Industry, State of Florida*, The Banner Center report (February 2011).

2. Available at: http://www.leapinc.biz/supply_chain_mgt_logistics.php

3. *Indiana Scores "A"s on 2011 Manufacturing & Logistics Report Card, but Poor Showing on Workforce Threatens Future Growth*, Conexus Report (Indianapolis, Ind., June 2011).

4. Available at: http://www.alliancetexas.com/

5. Available at: http://www.hillwood.com/story.aspx?ID=36

6. Available at: http://www.msscusa.org/?page_id=109

7. Available at: http://www.msscusa.org/?page_id=317

8. Ibid.

9. Ibid.

10. Available at: http://www.ntscc.org/documents/TCC_072109.swf11. Available at: http://www.msscusa.org/?page_id=192

12. Available at: http://www.sedb.com/edb/sg/en_uk/index/news/articles/asia_s_newest_perishable.html

13. Available at: http://psa-institute.com/about-us.aspx

14. Available at: http://www.mpa.gov.sg/sites/global_navigation/news_center/mpa_news/mpa_news_detail.page?filename=020702.xml

15. Available at: http://www.mpa.gov.sg/sites/education_and_careers/maritime_education/isc.page

16. Available at: http://psa-institute.com/about-us.aspx

17. Available at: http://www.sp-psa.com.vn/index.php?c=news&m=newsDetail&category_id=1&id=49

18. Available at: http://www.stc-r.nl/

19. Available at: http://www.memphischamber.com/Newsroom/Access/May-2011/Getting-a-head-start-in-the-logistics-industry.aspx

20. Available at: http://www.memphischamber.com/The-Chamber/Councils/Regional-Logistics.aspx

21. Available at: http://www.commercialappeal.com/news/2011/jun/08/2-brothers-another-man-arrested-burglarizing-boys/?print=1

22. Available at: http://www.memphischamber.com/Newsroom/Access/May-2011/Getting-a-head-start-in-the-logistics-industry.aspx

23. Available at: http://www.memphischamber.com/getattachment/The-Chamber/Newsroom/Memphis-Crossroads-Magazine/Crossroads--summer-2011_FINAL-low-res.pdf.aspx

24. Available at: http://abclocal.go.com/kabc/story?section=news/local/los_angeles&id=8092396

25. Available at: http://socalscanner.com/2011/08/18/maritime-law-enforcement-training-center-holds-first-classes/

26. Available at: http://www.portoflosangeles.org/newsroom/2011_releases/MLETC_info.pdf

27. US Bureau of Labor Statistics, *Career Guide to Industries 2010–2011*. Available at: http://bls.gov/oco/cg/cgs021.htm

28. Available at: http://www.sgmaritime.com/Singlenews.aspx?DirID=72&rec_code=42237

29. Available at: http://www.marinelink.com/news/article/mpa-to-set-up-mcf/320939.aspx

30. Available at: http://www.sgmaritime.com/Singlenews.aspx?DirID=72&rec_code=42237

31. Available at: http://www.sgmaritime.com/Singlenews.aspx?DirID=103&rec_code=103566

32. http://www.mpa.gov.sg/sites/pdf/singapore_nautilus_issue2.pdf

33. Available at: http://www.sgmaritime.com/Singlenews.aspx?DirID=72&rec_code=42237

34. Available at: http://www.admissions.tcu.edu/academics/new_mm.asp?id=76

35. Available at: http://www.sgmaritime.com/Singlenews.aspx?DirID=72&rec_code=42237

36. Available at: http://www.eur.nl/english/post_experience/master/maritime_economics_logistics/

37. Available at: http://www.eur.nl/english/prospective/master/programmes/economics_business/urban_port_transport_economics/

38. Available at:
http://www.esl.eur.nl/home/education/llm_business_corporate_and_maritime_law/. Please verify the URL.

39. Available at: http://www.unt.edu/pais/insert/ulgav.htm

40. Available at: http://www.sgmaritime.com/Singlenews.aspx?DirID=72&rec_code=42237

41. Available at: http://www.usc.edu/dept/publications/cat2010/schools/business/masters/mm.html

42. Available at: http://global.ntu.edu.sg/joint/Pages/Norwegianschoolof Management.aspx

43. Available at: http://www.zlc.edu.es/

44. Available at: http://www.stc-nmu.eu/masterST/index.htm

45. Available at: http://www.cob.unt.edu/programs/masters/mba-logistics.php

46. Available at: http://www.erim.eur.nl/ERIM/Doctoral_Programme/PhD_in_Management/current_phd_projects

47. Available at: http://www.maritimeeconomics.com/corporate_network_members.htm

48. Available at: http://www.zlc.edu.es/content/files/brochure_phd.pdf

49. Available at: http://www.metro-college.com/partners/default.aspx

50. Available at: http://www.metro-college.com/aboutus/history.aspx

51. Available at: http://blog.ups.com/2010/05/26/ups-honors-2010-school-to-work-graduates/

52. Available at: http://www.zlc.edu.es/about-us/kto/

53. http://www.cnc-logistica.org

54. Translated from: http://www.epiprensa.com/logistica-transporte/logistica-servicios/plataforma.html

55. Available at: http://ctl.mit.edu/about_us/global_scale_network

56. Available at: http://www.tliap.nus.edu.sg/

57. Available at: http://www.alliancetexas.com/OverviewMaps/JobsTraining/AllianceOpportunityCenter.aspx

58. Available at: http://www.dinalog.nl/institute/education-training/master-classes/750

59. Available at: http://www.dinalog.nl/institute/education-training/winterschool/751

60. Available at: http://www.dinalog.nl/media/Djv_grid182x297_ENG.pdf

61. Available at: http://www.dinalog.nl/institute/education-training/knowledge-dcs/783

62. Available at: http://www.dinalog.nl/media/Djv_grid182x297_ENG.pdf

63. Ibid.

64. Ibid.

65. Ibid.

66. Andrés Rodríguez-Posea and Riccardo Crescenzi, "Mountains in a Flat World: Why Proximity Still Matters for the Location of Economic Activity," *Cambridge Journal of Regions, Economy and Society* 1, no.3 (November 2008): 371–388.

67. See, for example: http://www.JobsInLogistics.com

68. Available at: http://www.sgmaritime.com/Singlenews.aspx?DirID=103&rec_code=103566

69. Available at: http://www.mom.gov.sg/foreign-manpower/foreign-worker-levies/Pages/levies-quotas-for-hiring-foreign-workers.aspx

70. Available at: http://www.mpa.gov.sg/sites/business_and_enterprise/expanding_your_business_operations/developing_manpower/mpa_professorships.page

71. Available at: http://www.mpa.gov.sg/sites/pdf/030605b.pdf

72. AnnaLee Saxenian, *Regional Advantage: Culture and Competition in Silicon Valley and Route 128* (Harvard University Press, March 1, 1996).

73. Available at: http://www.portoflosangeles.org/pdf/Trade_Connect_Flyer_CD6.pdf

CHAPTER 9

1. Van Den Bosch, F., R. Hollen, H. W. Volberda, and M. G. Baaij, *The Strategic Value of the Port of Rotterdam for the International Competitiveness of the Netherlands,* report prepared for the port of Rotterdam Authority by the Rotterdam School of Management (Erasmus University, 2011).

2. Available at: http://www.wdrb.com/story/11354883/louisville-airports-generate-over-55000-jobs?redirected=true

3. Available at: http://www.mscaa.com/news/study_shows_economic_impact

4. Available at: http://www.hillwood.com/story.aspx?ID=3843

5. Available at: http://www.rejournals.com/2010/10/19/union-pacific-opens-370m-intermodal-terminal-in-joliet/.

6. Tara Kalwarski, "The Benefits and Costs of College," *Bloomberg Business-Week.com.* Available at: http://images.businessweek.com/mz/10/12/20100322_numbers.pdf

7. Falk W. Raschke, "Identification, Analysis and Management of Clusters: Testing the Theory of Regional Competitive Advantage," presentation at the Supply Chain Management Institute, European Business School (April 2009).

8. Chicago Metropolitan Agency for Planning, Industry Clusters: CMAP Regional Snapshot.. Report available at: http://www.worldbusinesschicago.com/files/data/Industry%20Cluster%20Snapshot_lowres.pdf

9. William Strauss, "Is US Manufacturing Disappearing?" Federal Reserve Bank of Chicago (August, 2010) Available at: http://midwest.chicagofedblogs.org/archives/2010/08/bill_strauss_mf.html

10. James Hagerty, "US Factories Buck Decline," *Wall Street Journal* (January 19th, 2011).

11. Available at: https://ups.managehr.com/workingatupsfaq.htm

12. Robert J. Thomas, Jane C. Linder, and Ana Dutra, "Inside the Value-driven Culture at UPS," *Accenture Outlook Journal* (September 2006).

13. Available at: http://yellowpages.superpages.com/listings.jsp?C=forwarders&CS=L&MCBP=true&search=Find+It&SRC=&STYPE=S&SCS=&channelId=&sessionId=.

14. Joseph Mann Jr., "Trade Logistics Firms Vital for South Florida's International Commerce," *Miami Herald*, (October 17, 2011).

15. Available at: http://www.3plogistics.com/Top_DTMs.htm

16. Available at: http://www.fmcsa.dot.gov/documents/facts-research/CMV-Facts.pdf

17. Available at: http://www.bls.gov/oco/ocos246.htm

18. Available at: http://www.truckinfo.net/trucking/stats.htm#Size%20Stats

19. "America Fastest Growing Logistics Company," *Inc. Magazine* (September 2010). Available at: http://www.inc.com/magazine/20100901/americas-fastest-growing-logistics-company.html

20. Available at: http://www.nbcchicago.com/blogs/ward-room/Coyote-Logistics-Adding-400-Jobs-in-Chicago-137007683.html

21. Available at: http://www.armellinistorage.com/armellini_history.htm

22. http://www.afifnet.org/south_floridia_stats.html

23. At the time that LogiCorp was founded, the 3PL industry did not exist in the United States and early investors insisted on LogiCorp getting a broker license, even though it conducted no brokerage business. Still having the "prederegulation" mentality, they were sure that one needs some kind of license to operate a business tied to transportation.

24. "Company News: Ryder Systems Acquires Logicorp Inc.," New York Times, Business Day Section (April 12, 1994).

25. Available at: http://www.portoflosangeles.org/latitude/content/articlePDFs/March%202011/a_port_and_a_partner_003.pdf

26. Available at: http://www.californiagreensolutions.com/cgi-bin/gt/tpl.h,content=3892

27. Available at: http://www.portoflosangeles.org/latitude/content/articlePDFs/March%202011/a_port_and_a_partner_003.pdf

28. Available at: http://www.dinalog.nl/institute/projects/sme-and-knowledge-dissemination/dinalog-incubator/781

29. Available at: http://www.spring.gov.sg/EnterpriseIndustry/LOG/Pages/logistics-capability-development-programme.aspx

30. Since little ocean freight comes from Miami to Europe (or Asia), vessels tend to visit other ports in the Eastern Seaboard to pick up European destined cargo. The shipping lines equalize the rate, quoting, typically, the same single rate from any US East Coast port to Europe regardless of the actual port visited. Owing to the blended rate, Miami does not have such an advantage on the Miami-Europe routes.

31. The full name of the company is Obrascón Huarte Lain S.A., one of the largest 3PLs in the world.

32. As mentioned in chapter 7, Aragón has not been immune to the 2011 economic collapse of the Euro zone and the austerity measures taken by the Spanish Government. While it is still doing better than the Spanish average, unemployment shot to ~17 percent at the end of 2011 vs. ~23 percent in Spain as a whole.

33. Available at: http://www.globalporttracker.com/PDF_download/2010/Europe_Port_Tracker_November_2010.pdf

34. Theo Notteboom and Jean-Paul Rodrigu, "The Ramifications of the Crisis: Revising Future Expectations," presentation at the Terminal Operators Conference—Europe (Valencia, June 2010).

35. Data available at: http://www.airports.org/cda/aci_common/display/main/aci_content07_c.jsp?zn=aci&cp=1-5-54-4819_666_2__

36. Nelson Schwartz, "Global Car Industry Fearful for Detroit," New York Times (December 15, 2008).

37. Medtronic also has its Asian regional headquarters in Singapore, its Latin American center in Miami and a service center in Amsterdam's Schiphol Airport, as well as a manufacturing facility in Kerkrade, The Netherlands—all important logistics clusters.

38. John S. Wilson, Catherine Mann, Yuen Pau Woo, Nizar Assanie, and Inbom Choie, *Trade Facilitation: A Development Perspective in the Asia Pacific Region* (World Bank, October, 2002).

39. Jeffrey Frankel and David Romer, "Does Trade Cause Growth?" *American Economic Review* 89 no. 3 (June 1999): 379–399.

40. Available at: http://www.crimsonlogic.us/corporate/overview/

41. Available at: http://www.internationalpsa.com/about/investorsrelation.html

42. Available at: http://www.ndl.nl/files_content/publicaties/Logistics_gateway_to_Europe.pdf

43. Frans van den Bosch, Rock Hollen, Henk Volberda, and Marc Baaij, *The Strategic Value of the Port of Rotterdam to the International Competitiveness of the Netherlands*, Erasmus University Research Report, ISBN: 978-90-817220-2-5 (May 2011).

44. The estimate was developed by McKinsey and Co.

45. William Forster Lloyd, *Two Lectures on the Checks for Populations,* (Oxford University Press, 1833). Reprinted (in part) in *Population, Evolution, and Birth Control,* ed. G. Hardin (Freeman, 1964): 37.

46. See, for example, the EU report, *Code of Conduct (Business Taxation)*, by ECOFIN (Economic and Financial Affairs Council of the European Union). See also Wolfgang Schön, *Tax Competition in Europe,* Genera Report (Max Planck Institute, 2003).

47. The problem, in the context of overpopulation, was described in a well-known article by Garrett Hardin, "The Tragedy of the Commons," *Science* 162, no. 3859 (December 13, 1968): 1243–1248. The article generated significant controversy and disagreements. See, for example, George Appell, "Hardin's Myth of the Commons: The Tragedy of Conceptual Conclusions," Working Paper 8 (Social Transformation and Adaptation Research Institute, 1993). See also Partha Dasqupta, *Human Well-Being and the Natural Environment* (Oxford University Press, May 2004).

48. "A Third Solar Company Files for Bankruptcy," *New York Times*, Business Day Section (September 6, 2011).

CHAPTER 10

1. Dieter Webitzer, "The European Logistics Market," in M. Dijkman, *Europe Real Estate Yearbook 2007* (Real Estate Publishers BV, 2007), 113.

2. Available at: http://www.cbre.eu/emea_en/news_events/news_detail?p_id=4993

3. Liliana Rivera and Yossi Sheffi, *Logistics Clusters in the US: An Empirical Study* (MIT CTL Research Paper CTL/1-A-12, January 2012).

4. Presentation by Chris Caplice, *MIT CTL Roundtable on Managing Global Supply Chains*, Cambridge, MA, October 18, 2011. The data were combined from the US Census Bureau, Foreign Trade Division. Available at: http://www.census.gov/foreign-trade/statistics/historical/gands.txt and from the US Bureau of Economic Analysis, available at: http://www.bea.gov/national/xls/gdplev.xls

5. Adam Satariano and Peter Burrows, "Apple's Supply Chain Secrets: Hoard Lasers," *Newsweek* (November 3, 2011).

6. Nuno Limão and Anthony J. Venables, "Infrastructure, Geographical Disadvantage, Transport Costs and Trade," *World Bank Economic Review* 15, no. 3 (2001): 451–479. The article states that a 10 percent increase in transportation costs can lead to a 20 percent decrease in trade.

7. Available at: http://www.rotterdamclimateinitiative.nl/documents/021ProgRCIEngherdr.pdf

8. Available at: http://www.cleanairactionplan.org/programs/tap/techdemos.asp

9. Ibid.

10. Available at: http://www.vyconenergy.com/pages/pdfs/REGEN_White_Paper_4_8_08.pdf

11. Available at: http://www.arb.ca.gov/diesel/verdev/level1/eode07006.pdf

12. Available at: http://www.prnewswire.com/news-releases/vycon-announces-admission-to-the-alternative-investment-market-on-the-london-stock-exchange-52176547.html

13. Available at: http://www.inc.com/inc5000/profile/vycon

14. Available at: http://about.van.fedex.com/corporate_responsibility/the_environment/alternative_energy/cleaner_vehicles

15. Available at: http://www.balqon.com/history.php

16. Available at: http://www.cleanairactionplan.org/

17. Available at: http://www.balqon.com/product_details.php?pid=1

18. Available at: http://www.cleanairactionplan.org/

19. Available at: http://www.advancedalgae.com/technology.php

20. Available at: http://www.porttechla.org/media/news.asp?id=9

21. Roger Mola, "Hush Kits," *Air and Space Magazine* 2 (Smithsonian, January 2005).

22. Available at: http://www.porttechla.org/media/news.asp?id=5

23. Available at: http://www.pressroom.ups.com/Press+Releases/Archive/2011/Q2/UPS+to+Harness+Solar+Power+at+New+Jersey+Facility

24. Available at: http://www.uprr.com/customers/intermodal/attachments/featured/joliet/joliet_brochure.pdf

25. Available at: http://www.uprr.com/newsinfo/releases/capital_investment/2010/1018_jitopening.shtml

26. "A Peek Inside Wal-Mart Canada's 'Green' Distribution Center," *Supply Chain Quarterly* (CSCMP, December 21, 2011).

27. Geof Colvin, "Bob Stoffel's UPS Green Dream," *Fortune Magazine* (April 27, 2011). A video of the interview is available at: http://money.cnn.com/video/news/2010/12/13/n_cs_ups_no_left_turn.fortune/?iid=EL.

28. Available at: http://articles.businessinsider.com/2011-03-24/strategy/30081749._1_routes-engineers-map-ups#ixzz1gGl5niKg.

29. Available at: http://www.epa.gov/air/criteria.html

30. Anton Kleywegt, Mee Leng Goh, Guangyan Wu, and Huiwen Zhang, "Competition between the Ports of Singapore and Malaysia" (The Logistics Institute Asia-Pacific, April 4, 2002).

31. For a list and classification of Chinese logistics clusters, see Wenjin Yu, Ding Weidong, and Kai Liu, "The Planning, Building and Developing of Logistics Parks in China: Review of Theory and Practice," *China–USA Business Review* 4, no.3 (2005): 73–78.

32. Fiona Tam and Colleen Lee, "HK Urged to Partner in Logistics Hub," *South China Morning Post* (January 10, 2012).

33. Available at: http://www.citymayors.com/statistics/largest-cities-mayors-1.html

34. Available at: http://clusters.wallonie.be/federateur/en/clustering-policy/the-walloon-clusters/index.html

35. Available at: http://www.stlrcga.org/Documents/library/Institute_St._Onge_Report.pdf

36. Available at: http://blog.mlive.com/oak_business_review/2008/05/supporters_say_aerotropolis_ga.html

37. Available at: http://www.mardep.gov.hk/en/publication/pdf/portstat_2_y_b5.pdf

38. Available at: http://www.airports.org/cda/aci_common/display/main/aci_content07_c.jsp?zn=aci&cp=1-5-54-4819_666_2__

39. Available at: http://www.dwc.ae/project-details/logistics-district/

40. Available at: http://www.dnv.com/industry/maritime/publicationsanddownloads/publications/updates/bulk/2008/2_2008/EasyLoading.asp

41. Available at: http://www.marinelog.com/index.php?option=com_content&view=article&id=532%3A2011feb0002100&Itemid=107

42. Available at: http://www.bloomberg.com/news/2011-02-25/suez-canal-annual-shipping-volume-and-toll-revenue-table-.html

43. Available at: http://www.worldportsource.com/ports/EGY_Port_Said_135.php

44. Available at: http://www.pscchc.com/press.aspx

45. Available at: http://www.suezcanal.gov.eg/TRstat.aspx?reportId=8

46. Available at: http://www.doingbusiness.org/rankings

47. Emily Maltby, "So Much Promise, but Sometimes So Few Results," *Wall Street Journal* (August 22, 2011).

48. Available at: http://en.wikipedia.org/wiki/Kinston,_North_Carolina

49. Peter de Langen and Evert-Jan Visser, "Collective Action Regimes in Seaport Clusters: The Case of the Lower Mississippi Port Cluster," *Journal of Transport Geography* 13 (2005): 173–186.

50. Early ideas of such a canal date back to 1768.

51. Available at: http://www.canals.ny.gov/cculture/history/

52. Available at: http://247wallst.com/2010/12/27/american-cities-that-are-running-out-of-people/

53. Jean-Paul Rodrigue, Claude Comtols, and Brian Slack, *The Geography of Transportation Systems* (Routledge, May 18, 2009), chapter 8.

54. Available at: http://en.wikipedia.org/wiki/Port_of_Amsterdam and at: http://en.wikipedia.org/wiki/Port_of_Rotterdam

55. Available at: http://www.suezcanal.gov.eg/sc.aspx?show=12

56. Available at: http://www.bizjournals.com/dallas/print-edition/2011/04/22/alliance.html

57. Kleywegt, Goh, Wu, and Zhang, "Competition between the Ports of Singapore and Malaysia."

58. Available at: http://www.transport-research.info/Upload/Documents/200310/fv2000.pdf

59. Yu, Ding, and Liu, "Logistics Park in China."

60. Available at: http://www.detroitchamber.com/uploads/DRC%20Tranlinked%20Presentation.pdf

61. "Towards a Logistics and Transportation Industrial Cluster in Montreal," Port of Montreal Press Release (February 15, 2011).

62. Available at: http://info.worldbank.org/etools/tradesurvey/mode1b.asp

63. Available at: http://supplychain-africa.org/blog/?p=89#respond

64. Available at: http://www.aragonexterior.es/

THANKS

As mentioned in the prologue, this book, which is based mostly on primary research, benefited from the contribution of numerous people. I hope I did not forget too many of them, because their hospitality, openness, and helpfulness not only made the research possible, but also made it fun.

COMPANY	NAME	TITLE	CITY	COUNTRY
Accenture Singapore	Jonathan Wright	Managing Director, Supply Chain	Singapore	Singapore
Agility Logistics	Charbel Abou-Jaoude	Managing Director, Global Operations	Kuwait City	Kuwait
Agility Logistics	Russ Krueger	Senior Vice President, Distribution Services	Atlanta, GA	United States
Agility Logistics	Tarek Sultan	Chairman and Managing Director	Kuwait City	Kuwait
AMB Property Corporation	David Twist	Director of Research	San Franciso, CA	United States
Associação Brasileira de Empresas e Profissionais de Logística	Anderson Moreira	President	São Paulo	Brazil
ATC Logistics and Electronics	Art Smuck	Vice President/ General Manager, Operations	Fort Worth, Texas	United States
ATC Logistics and Electronics	Dave Lyon	Director of Operations	Fort Worth, Texas	United States

COMPANY	NAME	TITLE	CITY	COUNTRY
ATC Logistics and Electronics	Ed Grigalis	Director of Operations	Fort Worth, Texas	United States
Atlas Transportes & Logística	André A. de Almeida Prado	General Director, Logistics Division	São Paulo	Brazil
B. Braun Medical Industries	Yenni Lim	Vice President, Operations/Supply Chain, Asia Pacific	Penang	Malaysia
Bank Negara Central Bank of Malaysia	Marzunisham bin Omar	Assistant Governor	Kuala Lumpur	Malaysia
BASF SE	Thomas Franck	Senior Vice President, Logistics Services	Ludwigshafen	Germany
BASF SE	Ulrich Eberhard	Director, Supply Chain Strategy	Ludwigshafen	Germany
BASF SE	Robert Blackburn	Senior Vice President, Global Supply Chain Operations	Ludwigshafen	Germany
BNSF Railway Company	J. Vann Cunningham	Assistant Vice President, Economic Development	Fort Worth, Texas	United States
BNSF Railway Company	John Lanigan	Executive Vice President Sales, Marketing and Business Development	Fort Worth, Texas	United States
BOM Foreign Investments Brabant	Bodo de Witt	Senior Project Manager	Brabant	The Netherlands
Braslog	José Adair Prestes	Owner	São Paulo	Brazil
Breda University of Applied Sciences	Jan Willem Proper	Professor	Breda	The Netherlands
Buck Consultants International	Patrick W. Haex	Managing Partner	Nijmegen	The Netherlands
Buck Consultants International	René J. Buck	President	Nijmegen	The Netherlands
Caladero Seafood	Alfredo Fabón García	Commercial Director	Zaragoza	Spain

COMPANY	NAME	TITLE	CITY	COUNTRY
Caladero Seafood	Angel Sanchez de Toro	Director of Logistics Planning	Zaragoza	Spain
Caladero Seafood	Javier Pascual Betrán	Industrial Director	Zaragoza	Spain
Camara de Comercio de Cartagena	Analucia LeCompte Cabarcas	Director of Regional Development and Competitiveness	Cartagena	Colombia
Cargill	Jeffrey P. Rott	Facility Commercial Operations Manager	Memphis, TN	United States
Cargill	Jon M. Thompson	International Business Development Manager, Memphis Corn Plant	Memphis, TN	United States
Caterpillar Logistics Services	Daniel Stanton	Senior Logistics Consultant	Morton, Ill	United States
CenterPoint Properties	Matthew J. Mullarkey	Senior Vice President, Special Projects	Oak Brooks, Illinois	United States
CenterPoint Properties	Neil P. Doyle	Executive Vice President, Infrastructure and Transportation Development	Oak Brooks, Illinois	United States
CenterPoint Properties	Scott C. Zimmerman	Chief Information Officer	Oak Brooks, Illinois	United States
Century Logistics Holdings	Mohamed Amin Kassim	Deputy Managing Director	Port Klang	Malaysia
Century Resources	Bobby Rao	Country Director	Port Klang	Thailand
CEVA Logistics	Steve Arthur	Director of Customer Service and Operations	Los Angeles, CA	United States
China Council for the Promotion of Investment	Zou Xaopinig	Chairman	Chongqing	China
City of Knowledge Foundation	Isabel C. Donato Miranda	Project Manager, Academic Area	Panama City	Panama

COMPANY	NAME	TITLE	CITY	COUNTRY
City of Knowledge Foundation	Ricardo Endara	Director, International Technopark of Panama	Panama City	Panama
City of Knowledge Foundation	Rodrigo Tarte	President of the Board of Directors	Panama City	Panama
Cold Chain Holdings	Ariffin Buranudeen	Managing Director	Selagor	Malaysia
Consulate-General of the Kingdom of the Netherlands	Marco Smit	Executive Director, Netherlands Foreign Investment Agency, Gulf Region	Dubai	Dubai
Coyote Logistics	Bill Driegert	Systems Design Engineer	Chicago	United States
Coyote Logistics	Chris Pickett	Engineer	Chicago	United States
Coyote Logistics	Jeff Silver	Founder and CEO	Chicago	United States
Cromo Steel	Mario Schioppa Neto	Director	São Paulo	Brazil
Damco Distribution Services Inc.	Brett Bennett	Vice President	New Jersey	United States
Deltalinqs—Port and Industries' Association	Niels (N.A.) Dekker	Secretary	Rotterdam	The Netherlands
DHL	Stephan Muench	Head of In-house Consulting, Asia Pacific	Singapore	Singapore
Economics & Politics Inc.	John Husing	Consultant	Redlands, CA	United States
EDLP Investments	Fernando Sanches	Consultant	São Paulo	Brazil
EffizienzCluster Management GmbH, Mulheim on the Ruhr	Thorsten Hülsmann	CEO	Darmstadt	Germany
Erasmus School of Economics	Michiel Nijdam	Port and Transport Economist	Rotterdam	The Netherlands
Erasmus University	Klaas Wassens	Business Director, Executive Education and Development	Rotterdam	The Netherlands

COMPANY	NAME	TITLE	CITY	COUNTRY
European Container Terminals	Wando P.G.H. Boevé	Director, Marketing and Sales, Member of the Management Board	Rotterdam	The Netherlands
eyefortransport	McKinley Muir	Head of Research and Market Insight	London	United Kingdom
FedEx	Lee Roberts	Senior Manager, AFW SW Regional Hub Operations	Fort Worth, Texas	United States
FedEx Solutions	Becky Babineaux	Executive Project Advisor	Memphis, TN	United States
FedEx Solutions	Tom Schmitt	Senior Vice President	Memphis, TN	United States
Flagler Real Estate Development	Eric D. Swanson	Executive Vice President	Coral Gables, FL	United States
Flagler Real Estate Development	Jose M. Gonzales	Vice President	Coral Gables, FL	United States
Flagler Real Estate Development	Rafael Rodon	Executive Vice President	Coral Gables, FL	United States
Flanders Investment and Trade	Marc Struyvelt	Investment and Trade Commissioner	Anwerp	Belgium
Flextronics Global Services	Denise Jack	Director, Operations	Memphis, TN	United States
Florida East Coast Railway	Jim Hertwig	President	Miami Springs, FL	United States
Forschungszentrum GmbH	Dieter Labruier	Project Management Jülich	Darmstadt	Germany
Frankfurt House of Logistics and Mobility, Frankfurt Airport	Jack Thoms	Senior Manager	Frankfurt	Germany
Frankfurt House of Logistics and Mobility, Frankfurt Airport	Stefan Walter	Geschäftsführer	Frankfurt	Germany

COMPANY	NAME	TITLE	CITY	COUNTRY
Fraunhofer Institute of Material Flow and Logistics	Uwe Clausen	Professor	Dortmund	Germany
Friedrich-Alexander-Universitat Erlangen	Peter Klaus	Professor	Nuremberg	Germany
FUJIFILM da Amazônia Ltda.	Carlos A.S. Calogeras	Integrated Supply Chain Manager	São Paulo	Brazil
GE Healthcare	Charles Phoon	Logistics Operations Manager	Singapore	Singapore
Germany Trade and Invest	Kenneth Bremer	Representative	Chicago	United States
Government of Aragón	Alberto Larraz Vileta	Minister of Economic Affairs and Employment	Zaragoza	Spain
Government of Aragón	Fernando Beltran	Vice Minister for Science and Technology	Zaragoza	Spain
Government of Aragón	Javier Velasco Rodriguez	Minister of Science, Technology and University	Zaragoza	Spain
Government of Aragón	José Moliner	Foreign Investment Manager, Aragon Exterior	Zaragoza	Spain
Greater Miami Chamber of Commerce	Alice Ancona	Senior Vice President, Governmental Affairs	Miami, FL	United States
Greater Miami Chamber of Commerce	Barry E. Johnson	President and CEO	Miami, FL	United States
Greater Miami Chamber of Commerce	Cornelia Pereira	Senior Vice President, Domestic Business Development Communications and External Affairs	Miami, FL	United States

COMPANY	NAME	TITLE	CITY	COUNTRY
Greater Memphis Chamber of Commerce	Dexter Muller	Senior Vice President, Community Development	Memphis, TN	United States
Hapag-Lloyd Rotterdam Branch	Albert Thissen	Managing Director, Benelux Area	Rotterdam	The Netherlands
Hellmann Worldwide Logistics	Christian Finnern	Regional Vice President	Miami, FL	United States
Hillwood Properties	L. Russell Laughlin	Senior Vice President	Fort Worth, Texas	United States
Hillwood Properties	Reid Goetz	Marketing Manager	Fort Worth, Texas	United States
Hillwood Properties	Steve Boecking	Vice President, Foreign Trade Zone 196	Fort Worth, Texas	United States
Holland International Distribution Council	Dirk't Hooft	President	Amsterdam	The Netherlands
Holland International Distribution Council	Stephan Satijn	Vice President, Logistics	Amsterdam	The Netherlands
Home Depot	Colby Chiles	Director, Transportation Fullfilment	Atlanta, GA	United States
Hong Kong Ministry of Information and Communications	Horace Jao	Section Chief, Department of Navigation and Aviation	Taipei	Taiwan R.O.C
iCognitive	John Paul	Managing Director	Singapore	Singapore
Imaginarium	Félix Tena	President	Zaragoza	Spain
Industrial Development International, Inc.	Matt O'Sullivan	Executive Vice President and Chief Development Officer	Atlanta, GA	United States
Industrial Development International, Inc.	Rita Skaggs	Vice President, Marketing and Communications	Atlanta, GA	United States
Industrial Development International, Inc.	Tim Gunter	Chief Executive Officer and President	Atlanta, GA	United States

COMPANY	NAME	TITLE	CITY	COUNTRY
Intel Corporation	Quah Hosk Soon	Manager, Regional Logistics Customer Service	Penang	Malaysia
Intel Corporation	Randy Eck	Director, Global Distribution and Logistics	Portland, OR	United States
Intel Corporation	Sukdarshen Singh	Logistics Manager, SEA/ South Asia	Penang	Malaysia
Jabil	LC Chin	Operations Director	Penang	Malaysia
Jurong Port	Lek Yuan Leng	Vice President, Corporate Development	Singapore	Singapore
Keppel Logistics	Gui Eng Hwee	CEO, Far East Organizations	Singapore	Singapore
Los Angeles County Economic Development Corporation	Christine Cooper	Director, Economic Policy Analysis Group	Los Angeles, CA	United States
Los Angeles County Economic Development Corporation	Ferdinando (Nando) Guerra	Economist	Los Angeles, CA	United States
Los Angeles Mayor Office	David Reich	Liaison to the Port of Los Angeles	Los Angeles, CA	United States
Los Angeles World Airports	Erroll Southers	Assistant Chief Airport Police, Intelligence and Counter-Terrorism	Los Angeles, CA	United States
Los Angeles World Airports	Mark Thorpe	Director of Air Service Development	Los Angeles, CA	United States
Maersk Malaysia	Bjarne Foldager	Managing Director Malaysia, Singapore and Brunei	Shah Alam	Malaysia
Malaysia Airlines Cargo	Shahari Sulaiman	Managing Director	Selagor	Malaysia
Malaysian American Electronics Industry	Wong Siew Hai	Chairman and CEO	Kuala Lumpur	Malaysia

COMPANY	NAME	TITLE	CITY	COUNTRY
Malaysian Industry-Government Group for High Technology	Mohd Yusoff Sulaiman	President and CEO	Penang	Malaysia
Mallory Alexander International Logistics	Neely Mallory	President	Memphis, TN	United States
Manzanillo International Terminal	Enrique Clement	Customer Service Manager	Colón	Panama
Manzanillo International Terminal	Juan Carlos Croston	Vice President Marketing	Colón	Panama
Maritime and Port Authority of Singapore	Manjit Singh Randhawa	Deputy Director, Policy Division	Singapore	Singapore
Mars, Incorporated	Les Woch	Director, Global Logistics	Leicester	United Kingdom
Mattel	Selwyn Moore	Senior Director, Global Ocean Operations and Supply Chain Optimization	El Segundo, CA	United States
McKinsey	Santiago Kraiselburd	Operations Expert	São Paulo	Brazil
Medtronic	Rob Varner	Senior Director, US Distribution Operations	Memphis, TN	United States
Miami International Airport	Ken Pyatt	Deputy Aviation Director	Miami, FL	United States
Miami International Airport	Sunil Harman	Division Director, Aviation Planning Division	Miami, FL	United States
Michaels	Eric Bice	General Manager, Alliance Distribution Center	Fort Worth, Texas	United States
Michaels	Jeff Martin	Assistant General Manager, Alliance Distribution Center	Fort Worth, Texas	United States
Massacusetts Institute of Technology	Bruce Arntzen	Director, Supply Chain Management Master Program	Cambridge, MA	United States

COMPANY	NAME	TITLE	CITY	COUNTRY
Nestlé	Patrick Hartless	Executive Director, Supply Chain Malaysia and Singapore	Selagor	Malaysia
Nucor Steel	Thad Solomon	General Manager, Nucor Bar Mill Group	Memphis, TN	United States
OKI Data do Brasil	Cleverson Dilmar Casteluci	Operations Manager	São Paulo	Brazil
Panama Canal Authority	Alberto Alemán Zubieta	Administrator	Panama City	Panama
Panama Ministry of Commerce and Industry National Office of Investment Promotion	Michele M. Sellhorn Vallarino	Director General of Marketing and Investment	Panama City	Panama
Panama Pacifico	Angélica Bertoli	Legal Director	Panama City	Panama
Panama Pacifico	Henry Kardonski	Managing Director	Panama City	Panama
Pantos Logistics Company, Ltd.	Jay Q. Park	Executive Operation Group/ Senior Vice President	Seoul	Korea
Penang Seagate Industries	KG Thanabalan	Senior Director, Materials	Penang	Malaysia
PLAZA	Ricardo García Becerril	Managing Director	Zaragoza	Spain
Port of LA	David Libatique	Senior Director of Government Affairs	Los Angeles, CA	United States
Port of LA	Kraig Jondle	Director of Business and Trade Development	Los Angeles, CA	United States
Port of LA	Mike Christensen	Deputy Executive Director of Development	Los Angeles, CA	United States
Port of Rotterdam	Hans Smits	President and CEO	Rotterdam	The Netherlands

COMPANY	NAME	TITLE	CITY	COUNTRY
PSA Corporation Ltd	Eugene Tay	Manager, Corporate Communications Department	Singapore	Singapore
PSA Corporation Ltd	Oh Bee Lock	Head of Operations, Singapore Terminals	Singapore	Singapore
PSA International Pte Ltd	Tan Puay Hin	CEO Southeast Asia	Singapore	Singapore
Ralph Lauren Corporation	Howard Smith	Senior Vice President, Global Supply Chain Operations	New York, NY	United States
Ralph Lauren Corporation	Russ LoCurto	Senior Vice President, Logistics and Operations	New York, NY	United States
RRC Desenbras	Gino Romanelli	Owner	São Paulo	Brazil
Ryder	Cindy Haas	Director, Corporate Communications	Miami, FL	United States
Ryder	Jill Schmieg	Marketing Manager	Miami, FL	United States
Ryder	Marcia Narine	Vice President, Global Compliance and Business Standards Deputy General Counsel	Miami, FL	United States
Sany Heavy Industry	He Xi	Director, Purchasing	Changsha	China
Sany Heavy Industry	Tan Bo	Vice President, Purchasing	Changsha	China
SC Johnson Company	Michael Murphy	Director, Customer Supply Chain	Racine, WI	United States
Schiphol Area Development Company	Michel van Wijk	Project Leader	Amsterdam	The Netherlands

COMPANY	NAME	TITLE	CITY	COUNTRY
Schiphol Area Development Company	Paul van den Brink	International Marketing Director	Amsterdam	The Netherlands
Schiphol Area Development Company	Peter Joustra	Engineer	Amsterdam	The Netherlands
Schiphol Area Development Company	Ruud Bergh	Director	Amsterdam	The Netherlands
Sime Darby	Mohd Salem Kailany	Senior Vice President, Strategic Master Development	Shah Alam	Malaysia
Singapore Armed Forces	Col Lam Sheau Kai	Chief Supply Officer, HQ Supply	Singapore	Singapore
Singapore Economic Development Board	Jane Chen	Assistant Head, Logistics	Singapore	Singapore
Singapore Economic Development Board	Kelvin Wong	Logistics Program Director	Singapore	Singapore
Singapore Economic Development Board	Xian Ying	Senior Officer, Logistics	Singapore	Singapore
Singapore Ministry of Defense	BG (NS) Tsoi Mun Heng	Director, Industry and Systems Office	Singapore	Singapore
Singapore Ministry of Trade and Industry	Lim Hng Kiang	Minister for Trade and Industry	Singapore	Singapore
Skechers	Daniel Passos	Operations Director, Brazil	São Paulo	Brazil
Sodexo, Inc.	Mike Heil	Senior Director of Distribution	Washington DC	United States
Staples	David Rocco	Director of Logistics Strategy	Framingham, MA	United States
Sustainable Supply Chain Consulting	Kevin Smith	President and CEO	Orlando, FL	United States
Tabletops Unlimited	Fred Rabizadeh	Chief Operations Officer	Carson, CA	United States

COMPANY	NAME	TITLE	CITY	COUNTRY
Target Corporation	Steve Carter	Director of Transportation Planning and Strategy	Minneapolis, MN	United States
Technische Universität Darmstadt	Herbert Meyr	Professor	Darmstadt	Germany
Technische Universiteit Eindhoven	Jan Fransoo	Professor	Eindhoven	The Netherlands
Technische Universiteit Eindhoven	Peter de Langen	Professor	Eindhoven	The Netherlands
Technische Universiteit Eindhoven	Frank van der Heuvel	PhD student	Eindhoven	The Netherlands
The Allen Group	Richard Allen	Founder and Chief Executive Officer	Dallas, TX	United States
The Home Depot	Colby Chiles	Senior Manager, Supply Chain Development	Atlanta, GA	United States
The Logistics Institute—Asia Pacific	Robert de Souza	Executive Director	Singapore	Singapore
The Metro Chamber of Commerce	Daryl W. Snyder	Vice President, Economic Development, Greater Louisville Inc.	Louisville, KY	United States
Universität Duisburg—Essen Centre for Logistics and Traffic	Klaus Krumme	Managing Director, Coordinator, Urban Systems	Duisburg	Germany
University of Saõ Paulo	Hugo Yoshizaki	Professor	Saõ Paulo	Brazil
University of Wuerzburg	Richard Pibenik	Professor	Wuerzburg	Germany
UPS Foundation	Ken Sternad	President	Atlanta, GA	United States
UPS International	Dan Bruto	President	Atlanta, GA	United States
UPS Supply Chain Solutions	Bob Stoffel	President (Ex)	Atlanta, GA	United States

COMPANY	NAME	TITLE	CITY	COUNTRY
UPS Supply Chain Solutions	Emily McDonald	Sales Operations Specialist	Louisville, KY	United States
UPS Supply Chain Solutions	Lai Sing Kiew	Solutions Manager	Singapore	Singapore
UPS Supply Chain Solutions	Mary Yao	Vice President, Supply Chain Operations South Asia Pacific	Singapore	Singapore
UPS Supply Chain Solutions	Richard Shaver	Division Manager, UPS Global Logistics and Distribution, Healthcare Operations	Louisville, KY	United States
UPS Supply Chain Solutions	Stephen Hydrick	Vice President, Operations, North America	Louisville, KY	United States
Vanzoline Business School	Fabiano Stringher	Professor	São Paulo	Brazil
Vopak Asia	Eelco Hoekstra	President	Singapore	Singapore
Walt Disney Parks and Resorts	John Lund	Senior Vice President, Supply Chain Management	Los Angeles, CA	United States
Watson Land Company	Kirk Johnson	Executive Vice President	Carson, CA	United States
Watson Land Company	Lance P. Ryan	Vice President, Marketing and Leasing	Carson, CA	United States
Westports Malaysia	Ruben Emir Gnanalingam	Executive Director	Selangor	Malaysia
World 50	Bill Marrin	Managing Director	Atlanta, GA	United States
World Class Logistics Consulting	Jon DeCesare	President and CEO	Long Beach, CA	United States
WTDC	Gary M. Goldfarb	Executive Vice President	Miami, FL	United States

COMPANY	NAME	TITLE	CITY	COUNTRY
Y.Y. Lin International	Joseph M. Yesbeck	Associate Vice President Planning, Transit and Rail Director South Region	Miami, FL	United States
YCH Group	James Loo	Chief Information Officer	Singapore	Singapore
YCH Group	Leonard Jayamohan	Vice President, Electronics and Strategic Businees Unit	Singapore	Singapore
YCH Group	Lilian Tan	Director, Supply Chain Solutions	Singapore	Singapore
YCH Group	Philip Tan	Vice President, Strategic Business	Singapore	Singapore
YCH Group	Robert Yap	Chairman and CEO	Singapore	Singapore
Zaragoza Logistics Center	Cristina Tabuenca Bielsa	Marketing Director	Zaragoza	Spain

INDEX